# Quality
## IN
# HIGHER
# EDUCATION

# *Quality* IN HIGHER EDUCATION

BRENT D. RUBEN

EDITOR

WITH A PREFACE BY
FRANCIS L. LAWRENCE

Transaction Publishers
New Brunswick (U.S.A.) and London (U.K.)

Copyright © 1995 by Transaction Publishers, New Brunswick, New Jersey 08903

Library of Congress Catalog Number: 94-38240
ISBN: 1-56000-190-9 (cloth); 1-56000-795-8 (paper)
Printed in the United States of America

Library of Congress Cataloging-in-Publication Data

Quality in higher education / edited by Brent D. Ruben; with a preface by Francis L. Lawrence.
   p.  cm.
   Includes bibliographical references (p.      ).
   ISBN 1-56000-190-9 (alk. paper).—ISBN 1-56000-795-8 (pbk. : alk. paper)
   1. Education, Higher—United States—Aims and objectives.  2. Universities and colleges—United States—Administration.  3. Total quality management—United States.  I. Ruben, Brent D.
LA227.4.Q35   1995
378.73—dc20                                                             94-38240
                                                                              CIP

# Contents

# Part III

## APPLYING THE QUALITY APPROACH IN HIGHER EDUCATION

## SUGGESTED RESEARCH, READINGS AND RESOURCES

# Preface
# Quality in Higher Education

*Francis L. Lawrence*

### The Fall from Grace

A college or a university is an institution where financial incentives to excellence are absent; where the product line is not a unit or an object but rather a value-laden and life-long process; where the goal of the enterprise is not growth or market share but intellectual excellence; not profit or proprietary rights but the free good of knowledge; not efficiency of operation but equity of treatment; not increased productivity in economic terms but increased intensity of thinking about who we are and how we live and about the world around us (A. Bartlett Giamatti, *A Free and Ordered Space*, W. W. Norton, 1988).

Few in academe would disagree with this eloquent formulation by Bart Giamatti of the fundamental values that define the differences between our for-profit businesses and our institutions of higher education. This definition of colleges and universities by antithesis with business is embedded in a speech in which, following his stint as president of Yale, Giamatti addressed the academic mission of a university largely through decrying the creeping encroachment of a corporate managerial style on the campus. He believed that the graft of a corporate management structure on what is essentially an ecclesiastical-style institution splits apart the faculty, with their traditional antipathy to the corporate, from the administration and that, when this corporate model is completed, we will, like corporations, be committed to "long-range planning for short-term goals." Instead of an ethical center where ideas are examined and debated, truth is pursued, thinking is independent, and culture is studied, a university will be just another tightly regulated, hierarchically structured corporate workplace rigidly separated into management and labor.

The ideal university community (which Giamatti elegized in the best humanistic tradition as a golden age now slipping from our grasp) exists in the earnest aspirations and continuing efforts of most faculty members of good will who are, indeed, the great majority. Learning in this community goes on through a constant dialogue of free inquiry, mingling the voices of professors and students in open exchange as they strive toward intellectual excellence in a collaborative effort that supports and increases the human dignity of the participants. The title of my university's plan for a revised undergraduate curriculum, "Rutgers Dialogues; A Curriculum for Critical Awareness," explicitly acknowledges and reconfirms this understanding of the nature and purpose of a university.

Could any purpose, any structure, any strategy be a more perfect, more dynamic model of the quality approach than this classic academic process of teaching, learning, and research? The small, independent creative groups, the lively exchange of ideas, the complete freedom to challenge accepted concepts, the ceaseless striving for new and higher levels of excellence are all intrinsic to traditional academic values and methods. Traditional corporate structures and values, in contrast, have been rigidly hierarchical, dominated by top-down management strategies, and motivated by economic gain as their primary goal, to which the pursuit of excellence was secondary.

If we grant this premise of the contrasting values of the traditional corporate and academic worlds, then how is it that corporate quality improvement experts are coming to academe in order—if I may use a pithy old country saying—to teach your grandmother how to suck eggs? Primarily because, I am sorry to say, when Giamatti issued his warning in 1987, most of what he feared had already come to pass. In large state institutions like Rutgers, the collegial spirit, the confidence in shared faculty and administrative effort in the process of learning, had withered. The University Senate was not attended by administrators, who regarded it as a forum for union oratory. The establishment of research centers and institutes separate from the academic departments institutionalized the separation between research and teaching. Union leaders and activist students supported one another in militant demands for higher wages and lower tuition that gave added meaning to Clark Kerr's assessment of the multiversity as "a mechanism held together by administrative rules and powered by money."

The corporatization of university management was only one element in the alienation of faculty from involvement in the institution as a learning community.

The other, much more widely recognized and popularly blamed factor, was given an erudite, philosophical exposition by a Rutgers professor, Bruce Wilshire, in 1990 with his book *The Moral Collapse of the University: Professionalism, Purity, and Alienation* (State University of New York Press). In his view, the disunification of the university stemmed not only from its bureaucratic structure but from the transformation of the faculty into an elite cadre of professional specialists, isolated from one another and from undergraduate students, singlemindedly pursuing professional status through publication. Stripped of the philosophical underpinning and filled out with specific, anecdotal criticism of teaching, research, and academic disciplines, *Profscam* (St. Martin's Press 1990) by Charles Sykes, a journalist and the son of a professor, brought down to the popular level the criticism of professors as the self-centered culprits who have destroyed academic community. The same accusation forms the basis of Martin Anderson's *Impostors in the Temple* (Simon and Schuster 1992). Anderson adds charges of plagiarism, fraud, and "political corruption," that is, liberal bias, to the list of professorial sins.

## The Ascent of Research

As exaggerated and sometimes mean spirited as the more sweeping, popularly marketed attacks on academic research are, there is a grain of truth at their base. The glamour and excitement of scholarly communication through meetings and publications and the professional camaraderie of scholars in their associations, usually supported and enhanced by recognition at one's home institution and flattering offers of advancement from other universities, transformed even the most cloistered of humanists into members of international sets of specialists, citizens of their disciplines more than of their campuses. Scientists, who needed more elaborate equipment and staff than their institutions could afford in order to pursue their research, became private contractors, in effect. They sold their projects to government agencies, private foundations, and corporate sponsors in order to pay their way. Faculty members naturally and instinctively used continuous quality improvement techniques of the highest order to produce a tremendous outpouring in basic and applied research. Faculty scholars assiduously put to work every element of a continuous improvement process: creativity, zeal for doing the very best work possible, drive to exceed one's own mark and to surpass all competitors, greatly increased output, and constant, close attention to the demands of "customers" (peer reviewers).

While American business and industry have just in the past few years fully awakened to the opportunities and imperatives of the commercial global market, the global exchange of ideas has been for generations a fiercely defended article of faith vigorously pursued by university and college faculty in their scholarly work. Often even in defiance of government pressure and misplaced public censure, scholars have persisted in their beliefs and their practice of the free exchange of the results of research and discovery. The power of ideas and dissemination of information have proven to be beyond the ability of even the most repressive of governments to contain. Scholars have carried on the busiest and most effective free market on the globe: no trade barrier has succeeded in blocking it. International exchange of students and teachers has also been an important part of the show-and-tell spread of ideas that inspired worldwide aspirations for higher standards of living under freer, more open and democratic governments.

Back at the local campuses of colleges and universities, the effects of this furious upward trajectory of continuous quality improvement in research were not unambiguously beneficial. Granted that it added to the reputation of the institution that employed the faculty member (who might then university-hop to reach the highest bidder in terms of money and/or prestige). Certainly, university research benefited society, but even projects financed by external grants barely covered the costs to the institution. The most enlightening philosophical debates and the most inspired scientific hypotheses had absolutely no monetary value. Or, if by chance some profit eventually came from research discoveries, universities had very small or no share in them. Although an extraordinary gesture of generosity on the part of Selman Waksman did give Rutgers royalties from streptomycin, $E = mc^2$ made not a dime for Einstein or for Princeton.

Even the applied work of the land-grant institutions was disseminated free or at cost to the citizens of their states. It is wonderful indeed to improve and expand knowledge continuously to ever higher levels of quality for the benefit of mankind but, like any other associations providing free services, universities became, increasingly, mendicant orders, begging resources for the means to accomplish their mission of contributing to the advancement of knowledge.

Thus, as successful as this gargantuan, many-splendored enterprise of quality improvement in research undoubtedly is, it began to be felt that, as learning communities in their purely parochial incarnation, universities and even colleges may leave something to be desired. The pursuit of knowledge on a global scale is a utopian goal: it takes a great deal of time; it requires substantial (largely unreimbursed) resources; and it has unintended consequences upon cooperation, communication, and good will inside the institution. The scientific and technological fields with the greatest potential for practical financial pay-off attracted from industry and government the funding for new facilities, higher salaries, expensive research equipment, technical staff, and graduate student training. C. P. Snow's two cultures confined in the limits of each institution spawned corrosive mistrust on a hitherto undreamed-of scale. Much of the bitterest and most damaging criticism of the increased importance of research and the time devoted to it came from within the academy as nonscientists saw a growing salary and working conditions differential. Universities could not meet external employment opportunities for scientists, but they were forced to make gestures in that direction that surpassed anything the institutions offered most faculty in the humanities and social sciences.

Students, including undergraduate students, were part of the new order and the conflicts associated with it. The students in scientific and technological fields worked in the new laboratories alongside their professors, learning by doing and often taking a role in research projects. For example, Randal Pinkett, one of Rutgers' two 1994 Rhodes scholars, worked with his teacher in designing a computer program to detect explosives in luggage. According to a 1992 survey of all Rutgers seniors, 43 percent have had the opportunity to participate in research with a professor. Such experiences engage students in active learning and discovery more challenging and effective than traditional lectures or conventional by-the-book laboratory exercises. At the same time, political science students and others in nonscience majors at Rutgers protested and demonstrated against the construction of science facilities on the university's Busch Campus, alleging that money that should be spent on instruction was being spent on research.

Corollary issues further muddying these troubled waters were the facts that facilities were built with specially designated state bond funding and that state-inspired and state-seeded cooperative university-industry advanced technology centers were housed in them. These centers were founded in the mid-1980s to support the competitiveness of existing New Jersey industry, spawn new enterprises, and attract additional corporations to the state. They have been very successful in achieving all of these goals as well as in offering research internships to undergraduates and outreach activities to the schools, like the newsletter on the use of discrete mathematics in the classroom that goes to 12,000 teachers across the nation. But the conspicuous success of research made it a large, easy target for all those (and there were many) dissatisfied with the teaching in colleges and universities across the nation.

### The Teaching Mission Changes

At Rutgers and across the nation, on the campus and in the public eye, the international success of American university research driven by tireless zeal for excellence and constant competitive improvement became, in the minds of many, a subject of reproach rather than congratulation. The least sophisticated, most direct young critics went straight for the jugular of science and technology. The clever, older critics kept their diatribes about faculty who teach a reduced number of hours and do a great deal of research just as vague and general as they could. Well aware that the lightest per-contact-hour teaching loads were in the sciences but wary of the obvious silliness of excoriating scientific research, these public critics targeted only those ideological movements and interdisciplinary fields that a conservative, nonacademic public would find strange, inexplicable, not worthy of investigation, and emphatically not what students ought to learn. The reason for the storm of criticism was not simply that the balance between research and teaching had been overweighted on one side and needed to be corrected, though that was part of the problem. The other and perhaps larger factor was that the size and aspirations of both the research and the teaching missions of higher education had ballooned to gigantic dimensions and corresponding difficulty.

In their instructional mission, universities and colleges threw themselves with great enthusiasm and dedication into the high, praiseworthy, and quality-centered enterprise of affording ever-broader access to young Americans of increasingly widely assorted educational preparation, academic talent, cultural diversity, and financial resources. While industries can specify their materials and change suppliers if necessary, institutions of higher education do not have that kind of control. Certainly, they can and do work with primary and secondary schools to improve the preparation of their students, but students are products not only of their schools but of their families, their peer pressures, their entertainment choices, their communities, the pervasive media influence, and a thousand other factors, as well as their own drive, their hard work or idleness, and their goals. Character and culture are at least as important as schooling in the making of a student.

What the colleges and universities could control as they took on this ambitious mission was their own contribution. We must remember that, at the beginning, in the late 1960s and early 1970s, the idea of access was not as all-encompassing as it later became. The original concept was to deepen and broaden the demographic profile of each institution and to offer the opportunity for higher education to students who, in a phrase that now seems quaint, were "college material." Among the many factors that have transformed the educational mission of colleges and universities into an ideal of universal access, the major driving forces were, first, the sobering realization of the economic fact that the shrinkage of the manufacturing sector made access to good jobs and middle-class prosperity impossible without a college education and, second, the moral conviction that the environmental forces that created so many who were not "college material" must be remedied by the educational system, not only for the sake of groups and individuals but for the sake of the nation.

## The Learning Community Returns—Transformed

The educational mission of higher education in America has changed for all of the right reasons: reasons of equity, reasons of humanity, reasons of justice, reasons of economics, reasons of domestic tranquillity, reasons of international competitiveness, all excellent, all necessary—in fact, all indispensable—no matter how difficult they may be to accomplish. But it must be acknowledged that the teaching mission of colleges and universities has changed out of recognition and multiplied in its difficulty by an exponential factor, especially during the past few years. Teaching is no longer a matter of a gentlemanly group of old boys gracefully offering to carry on a polite, learned conversation with a small, homogeneous group of young people. Our teaching task has been transformed, and we must transform ourselves to meet it.

In my inaugural address at Rutgers in 1991, I proposed a new model of the land-grant university that recognizes the challenges of our society by a serious effort to transform itself through responding to the pervasive, continuing need for advanced knowledge with a comprehensive statewide network of outreach; educating a broader, more inclusive spectrum of our society; strengthening the learning community with additional support for teaching and learning; focusing our attention on undergraduate education with an examination of baccalaureate requirements; taking the scholar/mentor as our model in the learning community; and building strength through diversity by the acceptance of personal responsibility for the achievement of individual ambitions and community goals. Since then, inaugural addresses across the country, from Columbia to Duke, have announced similar aims of restoring the balance between research and teaching.

Having begun early, Rutgers is probably a bit further along the way in our efforts to improve quality by renewing commitment to the learning community. Budget reductions forced the university even before I arrived to direct resources to instruction as its highest priority and to take the largest reductions in its administrative and service areas. On my arrival, we launched a series of internal efficiency and effectiveness studies, along with external reviews of administrative structure and management policy, in order to focus our efforts on ways that we could accomplish more with less. We eliminated some vice presidencies, added others in undergraduate education, and this year began a Quality and Communication Improvement Program already at work on several projects throughout the university. In our administrative and service units, we are undertaking the same reconceptualization and movement toward involving all workers in quality improvement teamwork that business and industry are putting into practice.

In the academic core of the university, as I have observed, what we did was to renew the tradition of the learning community. To increase the emphasis, the rewards, and the value placed upon teaching, we now require that all recommendations for hiring, tenure, and promotion present substantive evidence of the candidate's qualifications and accomplishments in teaching. Our external reviews of academic programs now include an evaluation of the undergraduate program. Teaching Excellence Centers are in operation on every campus, conducting university-wide teaching evaluations, offering lectures and workshops in teaching, and awarding grants to faculty for teaching improvement projects. Learning Resource Centers now offer thousands of undergraduates a rich variety of learning assistance keyed to helping every student, from a floundering first-year novice to a nervous pre-med junior aiming for a 4.0. Supplemental instruction supports difficult courses, computer-assisted learning allows students to progress at their own pace, and peer tutoring is carried on one-to-one or in groups. The undergraduate curriculum revision project, Rutgers Dialogues, is now in its pilot implementation stage throughout the university. Computing for undergraduates is the object of a massive effort of improvement financed by a student fee, the university operating budget, and a state bond issue for instructional equipment. Planning for realization of our ambition to offer a broader outreach network of advanced knowledge throughout the state is also underway with a review of our continuing education operations and consideration of the options for distance learning. These measures, along with renewed commitment to participation in the University

Senate and departmental affiliation for research institute faculty, have allowed us to make progress in restoring academic community.

Between a rock and a hard place, between two equally necessary visions of quality, the drive for world-class excellence in research and the imperative for educating all of America's children, higher education must accomplish both because America must have both in order to survive and prosper. In order to do this, we need to return to the concept of the university as a community working together toward its goals. A true university learning community is by definition a community of constant improvement. As I described it earlier, in the ideal university community learning goes on through a constant dialogue of free inquiry, mingling the voices of professors and students in open exchange as they strive toward intellectual excellence in a collaborative effort that supports and increases the human dignity of the participants. This is certainly as valid and effective a model of the learning community today as it has always been, but the participants are more diverse, the means more varied, the issues more complex, the sensitivities more tender, the barriers more numerous, and the needs both more acute and more difficult to satisfy. We have made at least a credible start.

Francis L. Lawrence
President
Rutgers, The State University of New Jersey
27 June 1994

# Acknowledgments

The goal of this volume is to introduce college and university administrators, faculty, and staff to quality philosophies and concepts as they relate to higher education. Toward this end, the book provides a collection of readings that includes reprints of a number of classic articles along with chapters published for the first time.

The book is designed for higher education personnel seeking a better understanding of quality for their own purposes, and also for quality administrators, consultants, trainers, or classroom instructors who need a publication on quality to recommend to colleagues and students within their institutions.

Most basically, this book represents an answer to the question, What does the quality approach have to do with higher education? I am indebted to a great many colleagues at Rutgers who have posed this question in one form or another, those who have been engaged with me in the pursuit of an answer, and others who have urged a sharing of our insights through the preparation of this volume.

I particularly want to thank Francis L. Lawrence, President of Rutgers and the author of the preface to this book, whose insight, enthusiasm, and support have been essential in the development of the approach reflected in this volume. Special thanks also to members of the University Quality and Communication Improvement coordinating committee: Vice-Presidents Christine Haska and Richard Norman; Associate Personnel Director, David Waldman; and University Data Administrator, Sherrie Tromp.

I also want to acknowledge the contributions of members of the President's Cabinet, and the growing Rutgers Quality and Communication Improvement network, many members of which read and provided suggestions on preliminary drafts of several chapters.

Gratitude is also expressed to Johnson & Johnson and AT&T—both international leaders in corporate quality—for their encouragement and support. Special thanks to Jeff Nugent, Bob Bury, Denis Hamilton, and their colleagues in the Quality Institute at Johnson & Johnson, and to Phil Scanlan, Andy Kemeny, and Barry Schimmel of AT&T.

A particular note of acknowledgment to Jennifer Lehr for invaluable assistance in the preparation of the manuscript. Thanks also to Ann Volpe for her ongoing contributions. The professional guidance of Scott Bramson,

Irving Louis Horowitz, and Mary Curtis of Transaction Books is also much appreciated.

Finally, thanks to my wife Jann, my daughter Robbi, and my son Marc for their interest, suggestions, and encouragement.

# 1

# The Quality Approach in Higher Education: Context and Concepts for Change

*Brent D. Ruben*

## Introduction

There is certainly nothing new about a concern for quality in higher education. By one definition or another, colleges and universities have always held the pursuit of excellence as the primary goal, and by most accounts they have been relatively successful over the years. Higher education in the United States is generally regarded as the international standard of excellence and the policies and practices that led to this distinction continue in place today at most institutions. Why, then, is the quality approach, developed and popularized in industry and increasingly applied in health care and government, receiving so much attention in higher education? What does the perspective add to the approaches to excellence which we have long embraced?

Essentially, these are the two questions that this book seeks to address. It is the goal of this introductory chapter to provide the blueprint for this effort and a foundation for the chapters that follow.

## The Context for Quality in Higher Education

The public spotlight is shining more brightly on higher education these days than it has in many years. At center stage are a number of issues that are apparent from even a cursory review of the content of popular media and public discourse:

- Dismay over rising tuition costs
- Frustration about the tight job market for graduates
- Calls for increased faculty productivity and accountability
- Accusations of inefficiency, duplication, and waste
- Industry critique regarding the poor preparation of graduates
- Charges of an imbalance between teaching and research

1

- Uneasiness about "political correctness," campus safety, academic integrity, and "hate speech"
- Questions regarding the use of graduate teaching assistants
- Criticism of a lack of service and assistance with problems facing local communities, the state, the nation, and the world community

While none of these individual issues is particularly new, their collective significance, their prominent role on the public agenda, and the vigor of the dialogue which they are spawning may be.

The critique is not limited to the general public. Substantial criticism of higher education is originating from within the field, in books such as *ProfScam* (Sykes 1988), *The Moral Collapse of the University* (Anderson 1992), *Impostors in the Temple* (Wilshire 1990), *Killing the Spirit* (Smith 1990), and *Moving a Battleship with Your Bare Hands* (Weinstein 1993). These same issues permeate the text of the 1993 Report of the Wingspread Group on Higher Education, prepared by a group that included a number of noted educational leaders. Entitled *An American Imperative: Higher Expectations for Higher Education,* the report endeavors to issue what it describes as a "wake-up call":

> A disturbing and dangerous mismatch exists between what American society needs of higher education and what it is receiving.... The American imperative for the 21st century is that society must hold higher education to much higher expectations or risk national decline.... Education is in trouble, and with it our nation's hopes for the future. (1993, 1)

What should be done? The report continues:

> Our wake-up call places a heavy burden on the shoulders of the men and women in higher education. It will require rethinking the assumptions of the education enterprise and reinventing many of its ways of doing business. Educators, particularly faculty members, must demonstrate that they have noted the warning signs, understand the potential for institutional and national decline, and are ready to act.

> Solutions for the problems...will require vigorous, creative, and persistent leadership on campus, in the community, in state capitols, and in Washington. (1993, 23)

Together, the public and professional dialogue on higher education raise fundamental questions about the purpose, value, competitiveness, effectiveness, efficiency, and confidence in the future of higher education that are difficult—and probably very dangerous—to ignore. Consideration of these discussions and the issues involved leads to three rather obvious conclusions: (1) Higher education is a topic of extensive public attention, debate, and scrutiny; (2) the image being projected is predominantly critical and, as a consequence; (3) higher education faces an increasingly skeptical, questioning, and demanding student population and public, and in turn a greater challenge in the period ahead for all who care about and work in colleges and universities.

## Higher Education's Challenges are Not Unique

The challenges we face in higher education are not wholly unique. The issues are common among a variety of organizations and so too are some of the underlying dynamics giving rise to these circumstances. Colleges and universities, like other organizations, create products or services to meet a particular set of needs. To the extent that an organization achieves success and stability, the structures, systems, policies, work practices, and leadership styles associated with those accomplishments become accepted and institutionalized. The same can be said of the organizational culture that supports and nourishes these patterns. In the short run, this set of relationships is often a prescription for continued success and vitality. In the longer term, patterns that once led to success can lead to rigidity, insulation, lack of innovation, and gradual distancing from the needs of the marketplace and expectations of consumers. Over time, changes may also occur in the needs of key consumers or sponsors. Competition, technology, economics, regulatory factors, and other marketplace conditions also evolve, sometimes in dramatic ways, and organizations or industries that are unable to accommodate or shape these changes are at risk as they become increasingly closed systems. Unless new ways of thinking and working—and new cultures to support these changes—are developed, the prognosis for vitality is poor. Whether one considers the rise and fall of an educational institution, a local video store, a community group, U.S. electronics manufacturers, or the Swiss watch industry, the underlying dynamics are remarkably similar.

## Higher Education as a Service Industry

Generically speaking, higher education is a "service industry." The core of our service is generating, integrating, and communicating knowledge for a variety of audiences—academic, professional, student, and public. In the words of a Carnegie Foundation report, "Scholarship Reconsidered," the work of higher education is the discovery, integration, communication, and application of knowledge (Boyer 1994, A48).

In addition to being in the teaching/learning, scholarship/research and service/outreach business, most colleges and universities also manage a complex array of subsidiary service businesses. These include dining and housing facilities, transportation services, health care centers, maintenance and security operations, personnel and procurement services, and sports and recreational enterprises. At Rutgers, for instance, our primary business involves approximately 2,600 faculty and 48,000 students enrolled in 16,000 course sections, pursuing majors in some 100 areas on one of our three major campuses in New Brunswick/Piscataway, Newark, and Camden, New Jersey. Annually, faculty members publish some 350 books, author 4,000 book chapters and journal articles, and provide roughly 400 artistic performances or exhibits. Each year, faculty work on some 1,500 externally funded research and/or training projects that generate more than $130 million. In addition, faculty members serve as editors of 450 scholarly journals and as members of editorial boards of 2,100 journals.

Our support and subsidiary services enterprises include a library and research support system that circulates some 1 million books annually, a chain of 41 hotels (dormitories), 6 restaurants that serve 3.7 million meals per year, a transportation company with 6.14 million riders per year, a health care system that provides 80 thousand patient visits per year at 5 centers, a facilities service that maintains 800 buildings on 5000 acres, a procurement unit that oversees the purchase of $278 million in goods and services per year, and many others.

*Opportunities for Service Gaps Abound in Higher Education*

Despite the best efforts of bright, well-educated, and well-intended faculty and staff, there are innumerable opportunities for breakdowns in the excellence of primary and subsidiary services in any higher education institution. Consider the following typical examples:

- A student waits in a long line for assistance at a student services office. When her turn finally arrives, the staff person is brusque and impersonal, and informs her that she will need to complete a form and then wait in line again.
- A student writes and submits a five-page essay as a part of a class assignment. The paper is returned with a grade but no comments. The student goes to the faculty member's office on several occasions during the scheduled office hours to discuss the paper, but the faculty member is never there.
- During holiday vacation a student complains to parents and relatives that he has two teaching assistants whose English is so poor that they can't be understood at all.
- A student calls State University in an effort to get a message through to a faculty member before an evening class and gets a taped message that the college switchboard is closed for the evening.
- An instructor opens the first day of class by remarking: "I just learned yesterday that I would be teaching this course. It's not my area of expertise, and I'm not pleased about the situation, but we'll all just have to make the best of it."

Events such as these result in dissatisfaction, through the creation of what can be termed *service gaps*—gaps between the performance of the institution on the one hand, and the needs and expectations of our those for whom services are being provided on the other.[1]

With any organization, some gaps are attributable to problems in *perfor-mance,* and point to the need to improve work processes within organizations. Many other gaps result from problems in *communication,* and suggest a need to evaluate and refine the ways in which the organization relates to its constituencies.

In higher education, satisfaction gaps may be present in academic, support service, and operational services and may involve administrators, faculty, and/or staff, as suggested by the vignettes above. In some cases, these gaps result from outdated or inappropriate work practices, policies, or systems. Often however, in higher education gaps develop because the value of our institutions, or the work of their faculty and staff, are not well understood or fully appreciated. These represent *communication gaps,* and indicate a need to tell our story more effectively, to improve the way we interact with those we serve, and to more effectively educate our consumers.

*Images of Higher Education Institutions and their Impact*

Regardless of their origin, service gaps lead to stories that are often told and retold many times by the persons affected, often resulting in substantial damage to the reputation of the institution among various constituents within the college or university community, and beyond.[2]

Like other organizations, the long-term health of a higher education institution depends on providing excellence and value in its services and being recognized as doing so. Judgments by constituents about the quality of services—or the lack thereof—translate directly into institutional reputation, which forms the basis for individual decisions—and patterns of decision-making—as to whether to *attend or not, support or not, recommend or not, hire or not, contribute or not,* and so on, as depicted in figure 1.1. These decisions, in turn, have direct consequences for what an institution is, and can become.

### The Quality Approach: A Comprehensive Framework for Organizational Excellence

*Quality: A Popular Term and a Pervasive Trend*

What we term *the quality approach* has achieved a high level of visibility as a philosophy and method for addressing the challenges, dynamics, and service gaps that confront many contemporary organizations. The term *quality* has become one of the most familiar terms of our age. From Ford's early use of the slogan "Quality is Job 1," to language on inspection tags in pockets of new garments purchased from discount stores, the preoccupation with *quality* is pervasive. Books about quality and quality-related topics fill the shelves of

**FIGURE 1.1**
**Higher Education Images and Impact**

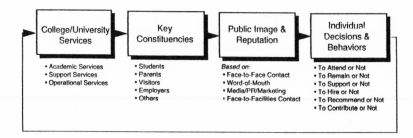

the business section of bookstores and several titles have enjoyed long-standing runs on the nonfiction best-selling list.[3]

The popularity and investment in the quality approach within the business community—where it is most often termed *TQM* (Total Quality Management)—has been remarkable. Studies indicate that more than three-fourths of the corporations in the United States have active quality programs aimed at enhancing competitiveness, operational efficiency, productivity, cost effectiveness, customer responsiveness, employee involvement, and ultimately market and financial position (Hiam 1993). Many organizations have had active programs for at least five years, and some for much longer. The number of staff involved with these programs varies substantially, depending upon the approach being taken. One company noted for its leadership in corporate quality, AT&T, has more than 1,500 full-time quality staff worldwide. Other corporations with major quality initiatives are: Xerox, Motorola, Procter & Gamble, IBM, Ford, Disney, Federal Express, General Motors, Milliken, and Johnson & Johnson.

Another significant development in corporate quality has been the Malcolm Baldrige National Quality Award program, initiated by the Department of Commerce, National Institute of Standards and Technology (NIST) in 1987. Between 1988 and 1993, 475 companies have applied for the awards, and any number of companies have introduced their own customized version of the awards.[4]

In health care, quality initiatives—often referred to as *CQI* (Continuous Quality Improvement)—are also increasingly popular following the lead of business. Health care quality programs are designed to track and improve clinical outcomes, increase cost effectiveness, refine treatment protocols, improve patient services, shorten turnaround time for laboratory and other procedures, provide better continuity of care (Al-Assaf and Schmele 1993; Merwick, Godfrey, and Roessner 1990; Lathrop 1993; Marszalek-Gaucher and Coffey 1990). NIST is now developing a Baldrige-based system for health care, with a 1995 pilot test planned.

Quality concepts are also being introduced in local and state government. The establishment of the Federal Quality Institute and the publication of *The Gore Report on Reinventing Government* (Federal Quality Institute 1994; Gore 1993) are examples of the prominence being given to the approach at the national level.

### Quality Initiatives in Higher Education

In education, quality initiatives are also underway at all levels, and quality programs are being implemented at a growing number of colleges and universities, using the labels CQI, TQM, TQ (total quality), CI (continuous improvement), and QCI (quality and communication improvement).[5]

Generally, these programs apply the models of corporate quality programs. Within higher education, an emphasis on quality in academics, management, and interpersonal relationships accompanies corporate concerns with competitiveness, operational efficiency, productivity, service orientation, and cost effectiveness. As indicated in figure 1.2, *academic quality* refers to discipline-based and technical services and products associated with instruction, scholarship, and service/outreach. *Management quality* relates to administrative services including organizational processes, systems, procedures, and information flows within a college or university. *Relationship quality* refers to the interpersonal relations among administrators, faculty, staff, and between these individuals and the publics being served.

A recent survey indicates that 92 percent of the colleges and universities are integrating quality concepts, practices, and tools into the curriculum; 75 percent are applying quality to the administration of the institution; 92 percent have implemented plans to survey the various publics they serve; and 83 percent will institute faculty development efforts relative to quality (Total

**FIGURE 1.2**
Dimensions of Quality in Higher Education

## ◆Academic Quality

- – Instruction
- – Research
- – Service/Outreach

## ◆Administrative Quality

- – Processes
- – Systems
- – Procedures
- – Information Flows

## ◆Relationship Quality

- – Relations with our publics/consumers and one another
- – Interpersonal sensitivity and skill
- – Cooperation and collaboration
- – Service orientation

Quality Forum V 1993). Examples include improvement projects focused on registration, information systems, recruitment, purchasing and financial aid, teaching-learning process evaluation, teaching large classes, retention, advising, curriculum review, department governance, and faculty/staff recognition systems. A number of business schools and engineering programs teach courses that introduce students to quality principles, tools, and practice. Several programs in education and communication have also incorporated quality courses into their curricula.

Encouragement and guidance from industry has been a significant influence in many higher education quality initiatives.[6] Corporate support reflects the view that the well-being of U.S. corporations is tied directly to their capacity to develop and market world-class products and services, and the sense that international competitiveness requires a level of excellence that substantially exceeds our contemporary standards in industry and higher education. The implication for colleges and universities from the corporate perspective: As the suppliers of leaders of tomorrow, higher education must broaden its horizons and raise its sights.

For many years, U.S. colleges and universities have been the international standard of excellence in higher education. In fact, we have come to enjoy a quasimonopolistic role—a role which corporate leaders suggest that we could mistakenly take for granted. They remind us that this was the error made by the U.S. automobile and electronics industries. Lessons from those industries: With changes in the marketplace, expectations of customers, and the vision of competitors, complacent industries become extremely vulnerable. If U.S. higher education is not perceived as addressing—or being committed to address-ing—the needs and realities of a changing world marketplace/community, our enviable position as the educational standard of excellence for the world may become increasingly tenuous (Total Quality Forum V 1993).

Many leading colleges and universities are undertaking quality initiatives in partnership with private industry. For example, IBM developed and funded partnership arrangements with nine higher education institutions in 1992. Five-year funding consisted of $1 million in cash, $3 million in IBM equipment, or a combination thereof. IBM indicates that 2000 copies of the competition guide-lines were distributed, and more than 200 proposals were received (Seymour 1993). The selected schools were Clark Atlanta University/Southern College of Technology, Georgia Institute of Technology, Oregon State University, Penn-sylvania State University, Rochester Institute of Technology, University of Houston-Clear Lake, University of Maryland-College Park, and University of Wisconsin-Madison.

In 1993, the Total Quality Forum reported that thirty-one universities and eighteen corporations have developed—or would soon develop—formalized cooperative arrangements for addressing quality improvement (Total Quality Forum V 1993, 1.1).

In addition to these formalized arrangements, many informal relationships exist. Additionally, some other colleges and universities are undertaking pro-grams with the assistance of consultants. The colleges and universities in-volved in the Total Quality Forum, were unanimous in recommending the partnership concept to other institutions (p. 1.3).

Lending additional impetus to the application of quality concepts in higher education is the announcement that the Department of Commerce/NIST has developed Baldrige-based educational criteria to be pilot tested in 1995. Sev-eral institutions of higher education have already used the Baldrige assess-ment in its "generic" form, and others are developing versions specific to the needs of their institutions.[7]

Another significant development is the initiation of funding for research in the area of quality. In the spring of 1994, the National Science Foundation announced that it has initiated a three-year program of research in the area of quality. The support will be for

multidisciplinary research on quality in organizations based on partnerships be-tween researchers and firms or organizations. The objective is to support research

FIGURE 1.3
University-Business Quality Partnerships

| | |
|---|---|
| Babson College-The New England | North Carolina State University-Milliken & Co. |
| Carnegie Mellon University-Xerox | |
| Cornell University-Procter & Gamble | Pennsylvania State University-DuPont |
| Duke University-Northern Telecom | Purdue University-Motorola, Inc. |
| Duquesne University-Westinghouse | Rider College-Johnson & Johnson |
| East Texas State University-Texas Instruments | Rochester Institute of Technology-IBM |
| Florida Agricultural & Mechanical University-3M | Rutgers University-AT&T, Johnson & Johnson |
| Georgia Institute of Technology-Milliken & Co. | Syracuse University-Corning, Inc. |
| | Texas A&M University-3M |
| Illinois Institute of Technology-Nalco Chemical | Tuskegee University-Procter & Gamble |
| | University of Arizona-Intel |
| Iowa State University-Texas Instruments | University of Maryland at College Park-Westinghouse |
| Lehigh University-Aluminum Company of America (Alcoa) | University of Michigan-General Motors |
| | University of North Carolina-Chapel Hill-Northern Telecom |
| Massachusetts Institute of Technology-IBM | University of Pittsburgh-Westinghouse |
| Michigan Technological University-3M | University of Tennessee-Knoxville-Eastman Chemical Company |
| North Carolina Agricultural & Technological State University-Northern Telecom | University of Wisconsin-Madison-Procter & Gamble |
| | Virginia Polytechnic Institute and State University-Westinghouse |

to develop or improve concepts, tools, and methods for better managing transformations to quality organizations. (Total Quality Forum V 1993)

Reports indicate that more than 500 proposals were submitted.

## Quality: Core Concepts

The focal point of the flurry of activity in industry, health care, government, and education is the word *quality*. *Quality* is certainly a familiar term, but what exactly does it mean in an organizational context, and what are the core concepts associated with the quality approach? Though the terminology varies somewhat from setting to setting, author to author, and program to program, six values that transcend the various approaches are:

1. Service Orientation
2. Leadership

3. Information
4. Collaboration
5. Communication
6. Continuous Improvement

*Service Orientation*

A service orientation directs attention to the needs, expectations, and satisfaction levels of the groups served by an organization. Within the quality framework, these groups are variously termed "customers," "constituencies," "stakeholders," "consumers," "publics," "clients," "audiences," "beneficiaries," or "users." The focus on service to consumers is based on a recognition that it is ultimately their judgments of the quality of a product, service, or institution—translated into marketplace behaviors—that are necessary to the continuing viability of the organization.

Traditionally, the word *quality* was associated with inherent features, characteristics, or attributes of a product, service, or process. The contemporary quality approach adds the stipulation that in order to possess quality, the needs and expectations of consumers must be satisfied. Conventionally then, the quality of a product such as an automobile would be determined by a technical evaluation of the inherent attributes of the product. In current perspective, quality determinations focus on the consumer: What does the customer want, expect, and value in a car? Reliability? Speed? Economy? Size? Service? A courteous dealer? How do these factors rank relative to one another? Does a particular product meet these requirements and expectations? If so, it has quality; if not, it doesn't. After-the-fact judgments of quality focus on consumer satisfaction and loyalty: How satisfied is a customer with a particular auto? Would he or she buy another? How likely is he or she to recommend the car to a friend?

Similarly, the quality of a legal document prepared by an attorney would have traditionally been judged solely by examining the document in terms of its technical and legal characteristics. In the contemporary perspective, judgments of quality would emphasize the expectations of clients. What did the client need and expect? Does the document meet these needs and expectations? Can the client understand the language of the document? Would the individual return to the attorney for future legal dealings?

As noted earlier, organizations of all types often become *internally* focused over time. That is, they become directed by internal concepts of quality, force of habit, and past practice. The quality approach maintains that survival and competitiveness require an *external* focus, one which directs attention to the needs and expectations of external constituencies.

The quality perspective suggests that practically—as well as theoretically— speaking, the definition of quality is dictated by the behaviors of consumers in a competitive marketplace for goods and services. No matter how organizational "insiders" assess the value of a particular product or service as producers/creators, these judgments are made in a vacuum, limited, and inevitably incomplete, if they don't take account of the perceptions of consumers for whom the products and/or services are intended.

The concept of service orientation also applies to services provided by support and operational units *within* an organization for other groups that are internal to the organization. Most basically, the concept of service orientation suggests that it is essential to:

1. Identify constituencies for which the organization provides products or services.
2. Determine and anticipate their needs and expectations.
3. Satisfy—ideally exceed—those needs and expectations.

How does the service orientation, with its emphasis on customers, relate to higher education? A service orientation directs a college or university's attention to individuals, groups, or organizations for whom the institution provides instructional, research, service/outreach, and administrative or support services, and to those external constituencies upon whose assessment of the quality of these activities and the support and reputation of the college/university or unit depends.

Thinking in terms of the marketplace and revenue streams that are central in corporate quality thinking, the most obvious customers of higher education are students, employers, and parents—individuals and groups who are viewed as paying for the services higher education institutions provide.

Faculty, especially, are often uneasy with the term *customer* and with the implication of "student as customer" or the "employer as customer," particularly if this way of talking is seen as suggesting that the "customer is always right." This same issue has been of concern in the health care industry, where the image of the "patient as customer" is often troublesome to health care professionals. Quality advocates are apt to dismiss such arguments as a matter of semantics and reflective of misunderstanding or defensiveness. Though these conclusions may have some validity, these are important issues that should be addressed rather than simply dismissed.[8] Many of these concerns are allayed when it is acknowledged that a service orientation implies consumer *awareness* and *responsiveness,* not necessarily consumer *control.* Additional reservations are addressed by a recognition that a service orientation refers not only to a focus on consumers of our instructional activities, but also to consumers of scholarly/creative and service/outreach activities within a university.

Given the perspective presented above, the list of individuals, groups, and organizations fitting the definition of consumer is quite long. Depending upon the institution involved, the list of key constituent groups may include: present and potential students, alumni, faculty members, staff, parents, academic and professional organizations, colleagues at other institutions, business and industry, governmental agencies, private foundations and donors, graduate and professional schools, citizens of the state, and others. Compared to most other service organizations, higher education institutions have a great many external consumers with which to be concerned. Often these key constituencies have differing—sometimes even contradictory—needs and expectations, a reality which stands as one of the major challenges facing higher education. As a consequence, a fundamental activity for any college/university or unit engaged in a quality initiative is to identify, prioritize, and ultimately appropriately balance the agendas of these multiple stakeholders.

Suppliers are another important external constituency. Suppliers provide resources, materials, and expertise that are inputs to the products or services created by an organization. In higher education, the *supplier* concept can be taken to refer to all groups, organizations, or agencies from which the university/unit purchases, leases, or contracts goods or services. The term should also be seen as including "academic suppliers"—high schools, community and junior colleges, organizations whose employees take courses, and other groups or institutions that serve as suppliers of students.

*Leadership*

A fundamental tenet of the quality approach is that leaders are most effective when they are personally involved in creating, communicating, explaining, reinforcing, and exemplifying the university/unit mission, vision, values, and a service orientation. These directions must be clear, visible, and well integrated into management systems. At the same time, university/unit leaders should serve as role models through their active leadership in public and professional activities.

Ideally, senior leaders' involvement will include a visible commitment to employees' growth, development, and satisfaction, and should encourage participation and collaboration among all personnel. Through ongoing personal involvement in activities such as planning, communication, reviews of performance, and recognition of individual and unit achievements, senior leaders serve as role models, reinforcing the organization's mission, vision, and values, and encouraging improved leadership at all levels.

*Information*

A third value of the quality approach is information utilization. The basic concept underlying this value is that organizational well-being, and a service orientation, are possible only with effective systems for information acquisi-

**FIGURE 1.4**
**Higher Education Suppliers, Services, and Constituencies**

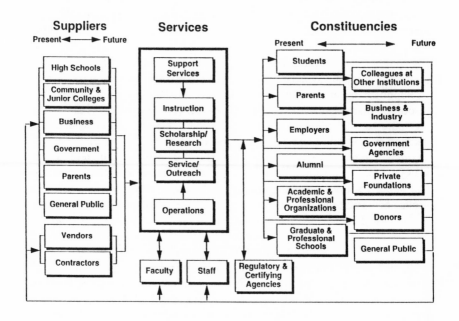

tion, analysis, and use. This includes identifying, studying, and comparing one's own activities to those of "benchmark" organizations—organizations that represent a standard of excellence, and a focal point for performance comparison and improvement.

Data may be gathered from external sources—key constituent groups, other organizations, and suppliers—or internally, from employees and through organizational self-study. Specific kinds of information to be collected and used would include:

- How do key external consumer groups evaluate products and/or services?
- What criteria consumers use in assessing products/services?
- What is the relative importance of these criteria?

- Who are the key competitors?
- How do products, services, management approaches, and operational performance compare to those of competitors?
- How do employees evaluate the organization, its performance, management, quality of work life, products/services, and/or processes?
- How do suppliers and gatekeepers in key stakeholder groups evaluate the organization and its products/services?

For colleges and universities, information sources include external constituencies; peer, competitor, and benchmark institutions; vendors; and high schools, junior colleges, and other "student-sending units." Internal information sources include administration, faculty and staff, and self-studies of academic, support, and operational units and processes. Accreditation reviews, external reviews, and strategic planning activities also serve as sources of useful information on internal performance.

As indicated above, a primary use of information is to determine what key constituent groups expect from the institution in the areas of instructional, scholarly and/or service/outreach, how satisfied they are with services in each of these areas, what criteria they use in making these judgments, and how these services compare to those of peer or competitive institutions. For instance, with regard to instruction and instructional support activities, basic information might be sought as to how students, parents, employers, and alumni assess quality. How satisfied are these constituent groups with instruction and instructional services provided by the institution? To what extent are these judgments based on the quality of the faculty and courses? To what degree are they tied to the quality of the physical facilities in which instructional activities occur? What role do libraries, dormitories, athletics, faculty availability, and support services play in expectation and satisfaction equations? Do faculty and staff interpersonal skills play an important role?

Other internal information sources might include measures of student recruitment, retention, achievement, and placement. How does the institution compare to peer, competitor, and benchmark institutions on such measures? Comparable information can be collected relative to consumers and processes associated with scholarship/research and service/outreach.

For suppliers, the objective is to identify and assess consumer and supplier perceptions and expectations. In the case of higher education, suppliers are also consumers in that they may be employers, alumni, parents, donors, and/or taxpayers.

Information relative to support, subsidiary, and operational processes is gathered through self-study and benchmarking.[9] Comparisons may be made with other units or processes within the institution, with other institutions, or with other industries where similar processes are involved. Thus, for example, an academic department could compare its faculty recruitment and orientation program or its research and teaching support services, with those of other

**FIGURE 1.5**
Types of Benchmarking in Higher Education

| | Within the College/ University | Within Higher Education | Outside Higher Education |
|---|---|---|---|
| **Outcomes** | Comparisons of outcomes with other units within the institution | Comparisons of outcomes with peers, competitors, and leading institutions | Comparisons of outcomes with leading institutions outside higher education |
| **Resources** | Comparisons of resources within the institution | Comparisons of resources with peers, competitors, and leading institutions | Comparisons of resources with leading institutions outside higher education |
| **Processes** | Comparisons of processes within the institution | Comparisons of processes with peers, competitors, and leading institutions | Comparisons of processes with leading institutions outside higher education |

departments within the institution, departments at peer or leading colleges or universities, or other types of institutions involved in recruitment, research, and/or instruction.

*Collaboration*

The fourth value emphasized by the quality approach is collaboration. Organizations are viewed as complex systems with numerous internal and external constituencies that interact with and depend upon one another. These interactions may take the form of exchanges of goods, services, capital, and information. The viability of organizations as systems and their ability to meet expectations of external constituencies depends largely on whether and how these internal interactions take place.

Traditionally, organizations have been structured around essential functions. Thus, a typical manufacturing company has divisions or departments of production, sales, operations, marketing, finance, research and development,

**FIGURE 1.6**
**Cross-Functional Approach to Basic Business Processes**

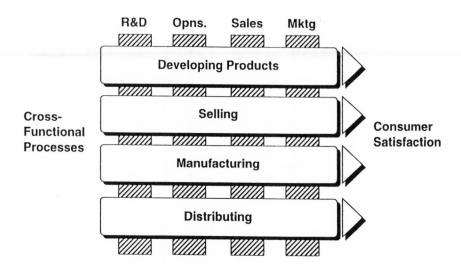

and so on. Each division is organized hierarchically, with the staff in that area reporting to supervisors who report to managers, who in turn report to directors, who report to vice presidents, who ultimately report to a president and/or chief executive officer. The result: elaborate vertical structures and reporting relationships within each functional area of the organization.

Vertical structures, sometimes termed *silos,* facilitate interaction *within* functional divisions. At the same time, they set up obstacles to interaction and coordination *between* units. Individuals and departments often become detached from the overall mission of the organization and, as a result, work process fragmentation, compartmentalization, and an "it's not my job" mentality tends to evolve. Thus, for example, the research and development division may design a product without the benefit of full collaboration with manufacturing, operations, and marketing, leading ultimately to any of a number of unfortunate outcomes, such as a wonderful design for a product that the company can not easily manufacture and for which there is no longer a viable market.

**FIGURE 1.7**
Traditional Structure in Higher Education

# Academic Departments    Service Units    Operations    Athletics

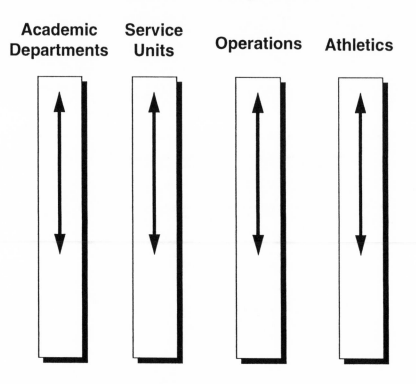

Simpler, "flatter," better integrated organizations, which facilitate cross-functional and cross-divisional collaboration, coordination, and teamwork are seen as means for addressing the consumer expectations, aligning individuals and functional units with the organization's mission, and improving organizational quality overall. In the case of manufacturing, the quality approach promotes structures and work process patterns that integrate functions—for instance, research and development, purchasing, marketing, sales, and perhaps even suppliers and customers, as shown in figure 1.6.

How do the themes of collaboration, teamwork, and cross-functionality apply in higher education? In some limited respects, higher education has traditionally been organized in a crossfunctional manner. Academic departments, for example, are organized crossfunctionally, to the extent that instructional, research, and service/outreach activities are performed by each faculty member.

When one thinks about higher education more broadly, however, it is apparent that many of the barriers of concern in other industries are also present in higher education. Many examples of hierarchical structures that are not

**FIGURE 1.8**
**Cross-Functional Approach to Higher Education**

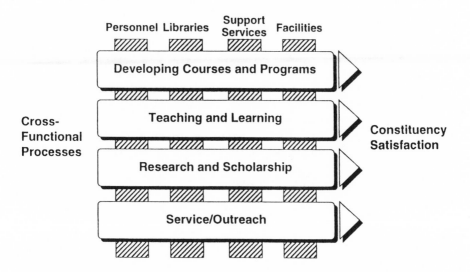

particularly well coordinated with one another, and which often foster fragmentation, can be identified. For instance, individual academic units often operate in relative isolation of one another. In some instances the relationships are even adversarial, as units perceive themselves to be in competition for students, faculty/staff lines, operating funds, physical facilities, and visibility and prestige within the institution. A lack of functional integration and/or coordination is also often present between faculty and staff groups. In the area of undergraduate education, for example, most faculty have little formal, direct involvement in areas such as recruitment, admissions, housing, student life, facilities, staff personnel, training, athletics, and so on, as suggested in figure 1.7.

From the consumer perspective, however, functions performed by individual academic departments, by faculty and staff, and by various service departments are all interrelated. Moreover, the quality of instructional processes and outcomes requires a coordinated effort in recruiting (students and faculty), admissions, advising, teaching, scheduling, housing, dining, student services, the library, classroom and study facilities, and many other areas, as illustrated in figure 1.8. In this instance, and in examples one might select relative to research/scholarship and service/outreach, most of the critical challenges we face, and the processes we must improve, are crossfunctional in nature. Few service gaps are solely academic or administrative, or exclusively the responsibility of faculty or staff groups. Few gaps can be eliminated by one department alone; rather they typically require more "seamless" integration, coordination, cooperation, and teamwork across functional units.

## Communication

Communication is the means through which information is gathered and disseminated to and from consumers, and the mechanism through which work process collaboration occurs. It is also the process through which relationships are formed and developed—relationships that are essential to the creation of a culture and spirit of teamwork that is necessary to support and maintain a service orientation, collaboration, and overall organizational quality.

Particularly in terms of higher education, the concept of communication is one of the most fundamental of the quality approach. Each of the mission components of most colleges and universities—instruction, scholarship, and service—fundamentally involves communication, whether with students, colleagues, or the public.

In the area of instruction, for example, a course outline, handouts, lectures, labs, discussions, reading assignments, and exams are examples of the formalized communication mechanisms through which teaching and learning take place. Teaching and learning also occur in less formalized, often unintentional communication events, such as through the tone of comments written on students' papers, or the manner in which a teacher responds to a student's question.[10]

Instructional communication within higher education is not the province of the faculty alone. By definition, all college and university employees function as teachers and contributors to the learning environment. Like faculty, administrators and staff teach by what they do, by what they say, and by the way they relate to one another, students, and other external constituency groups. In so doing, each teaches a number of practical and highly visible lessons in psychology, communication, economics, sociology, and management. These lessons poignantly address issues of diversity, interpersonal relations, ethics, dealing with conflict, handling complaints, and the way people can and should relate to one another in an organization, a community, and a society.

Whether the context is instruction, research, service, support services, or other areas within colleges or universities, communication functions play a central role in efforts to create and sustain organizational excellence and consumer satisfaction.

*Continuous Improvement*

The sixth quality value is continuous improvement. Quality is not seen as occurring naturally. Rather, it requires a substantial commitment of time and resources to a process of continuous improvement and ongoing change—what many writing in the quality area have called, a "journey." Whether the desired changes are being addressed incrementally, through more radical change, or reengineering, the same theme applies.[11]

Continuous improvement implies a commitment by everyone within the organization to a recursive process consisting of planning and testing improvements, evaluating outcomes, learning from failures, implementing and sustaining successes, planning and testing improvements, and so on.

## The Quality Approach: An Organizational Theory

In addition to a pervasive movement and a set of values and concepts, the quality approach represents a theory of organizational behavior and management practice. Viewed in this context, the Quality School of thought, as it might well be termed, takes on a level of significance comparable to that afforded to the Scientific Management School, the Human Relations School, and the Systems School, to which many of the roots of the quality approach can be traced.[12] Viewed in a historical and theoretical perspective, the Quality School can be seen as addressing significant and enduring issues of organizational theory from an interdisciplinary perspective utilizing concepts that are evolutionary rather than revolutionary.

*The Scientific School*

The Scientific Management approach to organizational behavior represented a collection of theories developed by business practitioners and academics. The most visible figure in the field was Frederick W. Taylor, whose 1911 book *Scientific Management* embodied the philosophy and theory of the approach.

Essentially, the Scientific School views the organization as a *machine*. Like a machine, an organization is seen as being effective to the extent that it runs efficiently. Workers are cogs in the organizational machine and are understood to be motivated primarily by financial considerations. The task of management is to engineer work and the workplace environment in order to achieve maximum productivity and profitability through the use of formal authority and formal, downward channels of communication.

*The Human Relations School*

What has come to be referred to as the Human Relations School of organizational behavior set forth a more social view of work life. Chester Barnard's

1938 book *The Functions of the Executive* was a major impetus for this perspective as were the well-known Western Electric, Hawthorne Plant studies, which focused on working conditions, morale, and productivity. Researchers F. J. Roethlisberger and William J. Dickson (1939) set up experimental work rooms and groups to study the impact of such factors as the length of the work day, the length of the work week, and the introduction of breaks during the day. Much to their surprise, the researchers found that regardless of what specific changes they introduced into the experimental environment—whether they shortened or lengthened working hours, days, and weeks, for instance—worker productivity improved. Every change they made in the subjects' environment seemed to increase productivity. By the end of the two-year study, efforts to explain the increased productivity had led to an examination of every imaginable explanation, including environmental factors, worker fatigue and monotony, wage incentives, method of supervision, even temperature, humidity, and seasonal variation.

Ultimately, the researchers concluded that differences in productivity were not due to specific changes. Rather, greater productivity resulted from the positive interpersonal relationships and unusual level of supervisor attention present in the experimental group at every phase of the research. The experiment had fostered closer working relations and had established greater worker confidence and trust in supervisors than were present in the normal working group situation.

If the *machine* is the dominant metaphor for the Scientific School, the *family* serves a comparable function for the Human Relations approach. Organizations are seen as effective when they address workers' needs. In this perspective, workers are thought to be motivated primarily by the desire for job satisfaction, recognition, attention, and participation in decision making. Management, accordingly, should strive to create a supportive, open, and trusting workplace climate where employees collaborate, are appreciated, and feel valued.[13]

*The Systems School*

General Systems Theory sought to provide an integrating approach to knowledge developed in fields as seemingly diverse as biology, sociology, communication, and engineering. Central to this framework was an emphasis on living systems and the way in which they maintain themselves through ongoing interactions between their parts and their environments (von Bertalanffy 1968; Miller 1965; Ruben and Kim 1975; Ruben 1992; and Thayer 1968).

Organizations are viewed as *complex systems*. Management is seen as creating and guiding organizations such that they are open and responsive to the needs and opportunities of the environment. Workers and the units of which they are a part are viewed as components of the organizational system, and information flow and feedback within and among these subsystems is understood to be necessary to the adaptability of the individuals, their units, and the organizations as a whole in their marketplace environment.[14]

## The Quality School

The contemporary approach to quality is very much descendent from the traditions of the three views of organizations and organizational behavior summarized above. Following the traditions of the Scientific Management School, the control of variability in products and services, and continual improvement, are basic concepts of contemporary quality thinking. Reflecting the perspectives of the Systems School, the quality approach regards organizations as effective when they are responsive to the demands and opportunities of the environment—specifically to external constituencies. Consistent with the views of the Human Relations School, the quality approach sees workers as seeking empowerment, trust, and the opportunity to do quality work. Rather than viewing the organization as a *machine,* a *family,* or a *system,* the dominant image in the programs and writings of quality is of the organization as a *team,* as shown in figure 1.9. Drawing together elements of the concepts of each of the other schools, managers are viewed as *coaches* who coordinate worker expertise and marketplace information to assess, meet, and exceed the product and/or service expectations of customers.

Among the most noted contributors to the development and popularization of the quality approach are Walter Shewhart, W. Edwards Deming, Joseph Juran, and Phillip Crosby.[15] Walter Shewhart, often referred to as the father of the quality approach, developed theories and techniques for preventing variability in manufacturing processes through statistical process control techniques (Lewis and Smith 1994; Shewhart 1931). W. Edwards Deming, a colleague of Shewhart, extended, popularized, and applied the quality control perspective. Deming is perhaps best known for his contributions to Japanese industry for which he served as an advisor as a part of the post-war reconstruction effort. His impact was substantial, and the Japanese named their most prestigious quality award, the Deming Prize, in his honor. Another name associated with the quality school is Joseph Juran, who emphasized the importance of continuous improvement and attention to consumers, describing quality as "fitness for use as perceived by the customer" (Lewis and Smith 1994, 54). Phillip Crosby has also played an important role in popularizing the quality approach. He developed what was named the Quality College in 1980, where an estimated five million people have attended courses (Lewis and Smith 1994).

The quality field today is interestingly interdisciplinary, with contributors to theory and practice from management, marketing, engineering, systems theory, communication, organizational development, statistics, sociology, and other fields.

FIGURE 1.9
Images of Organization

| School of Thought | Organizational Image |
|---|---|
| Scientific School | *Machine* |
| Human Relations School | *Family* |
| Systems School | *System* |
| Quality School | *Team* |

As stated at the outset of this section, the concepts of the quality approach are not revolutionary. Viewed in a theoretical and historical context, the Quality School can best be understood as an evolutionary approach to significant and enduring issues of organizational theory and management from an interdisciplinary perspective.

## Quality Strategies and Processes

What is the process by which the core quality values are implemented within an organization? Broadly speaking, the quality process has two phases, assessment and improvement.

### Quality Assessment

Fundamentally, *assessment* is a strategy for evaluating the performance of an organization in relation to the expectations of its constituencies, and the organization's mission and vision. The comparison leads to the identification of service quality gaps, which become priorities for improvement.[16] In the context of higher education, this suggests that assessment might proceed by:

1. Developing or reviewing the mission and vision of the college/university or unit.
2. Identifying key constituencies and assessing their service expectations and satisfaction levels.
3. Assessing college/university or unit performance levels.
4. Identifying and prioritizing gaps between college/university or unit performance, constituency expectations, and/or the college/university mission or vision.

A number of strategies, resources, and tools are available to assist with these steps. In the case of higher education, for instance, tools for assessment of constituency expectations and satisfaction levels include: interviews, focus groups, and surveys of students, alumni, faculty, staff, parents, and other key groups. A systematic analysis of comments and complaints is another tool, as are formalized service satisfaction feedback systems.

Assessment may also draw upon college/unit or unit performance self-studies, strategic planning, management audits, accreditation reports, external discipline reviews, communication audits, and benchmarking studies.[17] Many of these same approaches are useful for identifying and prioritizing gaps.

Another interesting assessment tool for higher education is the "Self-Assessment Checklist," published as a part of *An American Imperative: Higher Expectations for Higher Education* (The Wingspread Group 1993, appendix A). The "checklist" includes a number of provocative institutional self-examination questions relative to mission and values clarification, planning, management, integration with K–12 schools, responsiveness to student needs and those of potential employers, and others.

*The Malcolm Baldrige Award.* One of the most widely used assessment tools is the Malcolm Baldrige National Quality Award. The Baldrige Award, signed into law on 2 August 1987, was initiated with the intent of improving quality and workmanship in the United States. The National Institute of Standards and Technology (NIST) directs the award program.

Companies interested in being considered for the award must complete a comprehensive self-study and application process. Awards are given in three categories: manufacturing, service, and small business, with no more than two awards per category per year.

The development of the criteria for 1988 resulted in seven categories, which have changed slightly over the years. The 1994 criteria (National Institute of Standards and Technology), with brief descriptions of each, are as follows.

1. *Leadership:* Creating, clarifying, and conveying a sense of mission, vision, and values; promoting a customer focus and service orientation;

fostering a positive organizational culture; understanding the concepts of quality improvement and possessing necessary skills; organizing, leading, setting priorities and goals; serving as a role model ("walking the talk," rather than merely "talking the talk").

2. *Information and Analysis:* Gathering, analyzing, and using information from external and internal customers, suppliers, competitors, benchmark organizations, and self-study of day-to-day operations and overall performance.

3. *Strategic Quality Planning:* Short- and long-term planning to promote customer satisfaction, operational performance, and to support the organization's mission, vision, and values.

4. *Human Resource Development and Management:* Managing human resource planning, employee involvement, training, development, recognition, and rewards to facilitate consumer and employee satisfaction, and to support the organizational mission, vision, and values.

5. *Management of Process Quality:* Managing research, production, service, operational, and quality assessment processes to facilitate customer satisfaction, operational performance, and overall quality.

6. *Quality and Operational Results:* Achievement levels and improvement trends in quality, operational performance, and supplier relations, in comparison to other organizations.

7. *Customer Focus and Satisfaction:* Knowing who the customers are; measuring their needs, perceptions, expectations, and satisfaction levels; having processes and systems to meet and exceed consumer expectations; creating and maintaining relationships with consumers.

Over the years a number of corporations have developed their own Baldrige-based award systems, tailored especially to their needs. Among these are the Johnson & Johnson's "Signature of Quality Award" and AT&T's "Chairman's Quality Award."

As indicated previously, education and health care sector adaptations are being developed by NIST; the first trial round of applications and judging will take place in 1995. Several colleges and universities have utilized the Baldrige award in its general form to assess their institutions. General versions have also been developed for elementary through graduate school educational institutions, one of the best-known being the New York State's "Governor's Excelsior Awards." Specialized higher education versions will also likely become available. Rutgers University, for example, has developed its own customized criteria and self-assessment system, called the "Tradition of Excellence," based on the Baldrige system, but tailored to higher education institutions.[18] (See figure 1.10.)

*Quality Improvement*

Quality improvement involves developing plans and strategies, working to *reduce* gaps, and institutionalizing changes into the normal work processes of the organization. In a higher education setting, these two steps involve:

**FIGURE 1.10**
**Tradition of Excellence Assessment**

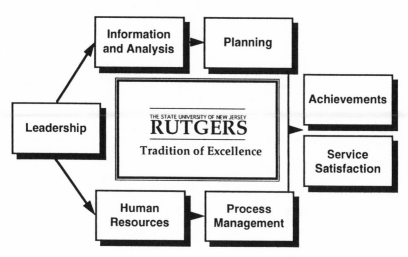

## Goals:

•Providing baseline measures

•Involving faculty and staff in the assessment process

•Highlighting strengths and areas for improvement

•Encouraging cross-functional and cross-unit information sharing and collaboration

•Aligning with Malcolm Baldrige/NIST initiatives

1. Identifying, planning and implementing improvement options for the college/university or unit.
2. Integrating improvements.

Basic to the improvement process are groups, or *teams*—often referred to as quality, or process improvement teams ("QITs" or "PITs"). A team simply is a group composed of individuals representing various facets and levels of a unit or process earmarked for study and improvement. The team includes individuals with a broad base of knowledge and experience with the processes being addressed, and typically includes workers and supervisors; often consumers and suppliers also participate. The team works together, with the guidance of a group facilitator, to clarify and eliminate gaps, and to develop an approach for ongoing monitoring and improvement.

Team activities typically consist of the following:[19]

• Meetings
• Planning improvements
• Understanding the process to be improved

- Understanding the problem
- Collecting information
- Using tools and techniques to analyze and interpret the information
- Identifying solutions
- Implementing and managing changes

Other improvement tools include strategic planning, advisory groups, work process design or redesign groups, quality and service skills instruction/training, partnerships with corporations experienced with quality programs, and external consultation.

## Implementation Issues

A discussion of the quality approach to higher education is incomplete without giving some attention to the practical challenges associated with applying quality concepts and practices.

### Facilitators

In some respects, the quality approach meshes well with traditional approaches to assessment and striving for excellence in higher education. First, the concepts of self-assessment and analysis—both of which are basic to the quality approach—are familiar within the higher education community. Disciplinary, unit, campus, and college/university self-studies and external reviews are customary forms of evaluation.

There is also considerable expertise available within most higher education institutions to assist with the assessment and improvement activities. On most campuses, expertise is available in areas such as quality control, organizational behavior and change, management, training, marketing, customer behavior, communication, information studies, and survey and interview methods, all of which are important components in any quality initiative.

A number of private- and public-sector organizations and a plethora of resources are available to support and assist quality initiatives in higher education, some of which are listed in the "Suggested Readings and Resources" chapter of this book. Many corporations are also willing to form quality partnerships to assist with these efforts.

Ironically, the many problems facing higher education are also factors that serve as catalysts for assessment and change. These include pressures for greater accountability and productivity, increased attention to measuring educational outcomes, greater operational efficiency, improved undergraduate instruction, enhanced student services, expanded continuing education and outreach activities, more programming for adult students, and more informed and aggressive competition for students and funding.

*Barriers*

Obviously, there are numerous barriers and impediments as well. First, the quality approach was developed in business, which creates terminological, conceptual, emotional, and sometimes financial issues when trying to translate the framework to higher education.

The widespread popularity of the quality approach and terminology is also at least as much an impediment as it is a facilitator. Terms such as "TQM," "BPR," "teams," "CQI," "guru," "SPC," "quality tools," "champions," "empowerment," "journey," "Baldrige," "process owner," and "empowerment," are linguistic markers of an incredibly pervasive approach to organizational assessment and change, artifacts of the quality culture, and tools for institutional change. The language of quality fills the pages of hundreds of books and the boardrooms of thousands of organizations worldwide.

On the one hand, the terms and tools are vehicles for communication and unity among those striving to develop and share a common vision and framework. These same terms and tools, however, serve to exclude those who are unfamiliar, unmotivated, uncommitted, confused, or cynical—often, ironically, the very people the quality approach must reach to be successful. At an extreme, too much "talking the talk" can marginalize the advocates of the quality approach, and diminish their opportunities to influence the organization or industry they seek to change. If the threat of exclusion and marginalization is a concern in business, it is a critical consideration in health, government, and education—especially higher education where critique is the coinage of the realm.

Beyond the usual academic cautions associated with adopting that which is popular are predictable reactions to the evangelical fervor of some quality advocates. Quality may also be dismissed by some as simply another management fad. Moreover, popularity of the term and concept has also led to substantial diversity, ambiguity, and confusion, which are impediments even for the serious student of the Quality School of organizational behavior.

The complexity of university structures and governance issues represents another significant challenge. In contrast to corporate environments, where the quality approaches may be mandated by management, the success of quality initiatives in higher education depends wholly on insight and skill in planning, informing, educating, promoting, and consensus building. This is a particularly critical issue if the quality approach is to have an impact on the primary services processes of the institution—instruction, scholarship, and outreach—and not solely on support services and operations.

There are also a number of cultural factors that may stand as barriers. Most colleges and universities have cultures that nurture, recognize, and reward individual accomplishments far more successfully than they do group, organizational, and community achievements. The culture of higher education is the source of many of the strengths and a number of the problems facing colleges and universities today.

Fundamentally, the cultural challenge for higher education is to achieve a better balance between cooperativeness and competitiveness, group orientation and individualism, commitment to one's institution and commitment to one's discipline or area, and finally, attention to public and consumer standards of excellence along with attention to academic standards.

## Conclusions

It has been the goal of this chapter to provide a broad overview of the quality approach and its relevance for higher education, and to present an agenda of concepts and issues to serve as a blueprint for the remainder of the book.

The following summary is offered as a guide for further reading and study:

- *The quality perspective is best viewed as an interdisciplinary school of thought regarding organizations, organizational behavior, and leadership.* Quality is a way of thinking about—and an approach to managing—organizations. It integrates organizational concepts and methods from various disciplines and traditions to provide a coherent and accessible framework for thought and action.
- *The quality approach addresses vital and enduring workplace issues.* While discussions of quality frequently focus on tools and techniques— teams, charts and diagrams, statistical process control, and the like—the core concepts have far more to do with fundamental issues such as leadership, service orientation, collaboration, decision making, communication, participation, and cultural change.
- *Higher education is usefully viewed as a service industry.* This perspective enables one to learn from the experiences of other industries, heightens sensitivity to the points of view of external constituencies, and increases awareness of areas where improvements are possible or necessary.
- *The quality approach has relevance and value for higher education.* The quality framework provides a generic analytical and operational approach for organizations of all types. This perspective can be extremely valuable for colleges and universities in their efforts to assess and improve academic service and operational processes.
- *The quality framework implies change.* Quality initiatives are generally both a response to a need—and a call—for change. Often the most obvious changes that accompany quality programs are terminological. Beyond changes to quality-oriented terminology—"talking the talk"—are more fundamental needs for changes that ensure that quality concepts are implemented behaviorally—how one, as they say, "walks the talk." An increase in "quality talk" in an organization can be mistaken for improved quality. "Quality talk" may be a mechanism to unify proponents of change,

but ultimately the changes that matter are not terminological, but behavioral, structural, managerial, and cultural.

*To be accepted and influential in colleges and universities, corporate quality models and methods must be adapted for higher education.* The mission, governance, tradition, and culture of higher education distinguish colleges and universities in a number of subtle and not-so-subtle respects from other institutions. These differences need to be identified and carefully considered in designing and implementing quality initiatives in higher education. The challenge is to adapt, not simply to adopt.

The adapt versus adopt issue comes clearly into play with regard to terminology and strategies for change. An insistence on the use of corporate quality terms like "customer" or "team" may create unnecessary resistance to the core concepts of quality within the education community. It is not necessary, for example, to use the terms "team" or "customer" to refer to a task force formed to collaborate to develop new methods for assessing and responding to the needs of students, parents, or alumni. No value is more fundamental to the corporate quality approach than responsiveness to the needs and expectations of those being served. The principle of "customer" focus suggests that linguistic and cultural sensitivity should also be a fundamental value in developing and implementing quality initiatives.

*The quality approach should not be seen as a quick-fix panacea.* In popular literature and discourse, the quality approach is variously envisioned as the solution to problems of downsizing, productivity, morale, inefficiency, diversity, accountability, communication, funding, competitiveness, student satisfaction, empowerment, and cultural change. While the quality approach represents a means for assessing and addressing such issues, no approach—regardless of its theoretical soundness, popularity, or pervasiveness—should be expected to quickly or easily resolve the many challenges facing higher education, or any other industry.

The gap between the macro-level quality visions espoused by senior administrators and the integration of that vision into the micro-behaviors of workers can be wide, indeed. It is one thing for senior management to affirm their dedication to a new level of responsiveness to their external groups and organizations and quite another to find the corresponding behaviors consistently displayed in the hundreds of situations in which workers interact with external constituents each day. Here, more obviously than in many contexts, it is clear that "information does not equal communication." Top administration articulation and support of the quality philosophy—through talk and behavior—does not simply, quickly, or automatically cascade down to permeate and transform the culture of an organization. While corporate cultures may encourage *overt* compliance with "top down" mandates, the cultures of most colleges and universities do not. In fact, the reverse is often the case. Quality culture change in higher education is a complex, long-term, interactive process requiring dedicated leadership, role modeling, supportive management systems, dialogue, and consensus building at every stage.

## Notes

1. The concept of higher education service gaps is discussed more extensively in chapter 12, this book.
2. Studies of consumer behavior demonstrate that dissatisfied customers are far more vocal about their experience than those who are satisfied, creating a multiplier effect. Research by Marriott, Inc., determined that on average, people who have unpleasant experiences will tell their stories to nine or ten people; in some instances consumers—approximately 13 percent—will tell as many as twenty people about their experience.
3. For example, Michael Hammer and James Champy, *Reengineering the Corporation* (New York: Harper Collins, 1993).
4. Source: National Institute of Standards and Technology, U.S. Department of Commerce.
5. "CI"—continuous improvement—is the designation used to refer to the quality initiative at the University of Wisconsin-Madison; "QCI"—quality and communication improvement—is the terminology used at Rutgers.
6. The Total Quality Forum, sponsored by American Express, Baxter, Ford, General Motors, IBM, Milliken, Motorola, Procter & Gamble, 3M, and Xerox, has been a particularly vocal and constructive force in fostering a dialogue between business and higher education. Beginning in 1989, the Forum has hosted an annual invitational conference bringing together leaders from corporations and higher education to explore issues related to quality and competitiveness, and to encourage the development of dialogue and formalized resource- and idea-sharing partnerships between businesses and institutions of higher education. More recently, other organizations at the state and local levels have been initiated to serve similar objectives.
7. Higher education institutions that have conducted assessments using the corporate Baldrige criteria include the University of Minnesota-Duluth and Belmont University. Rutgers University has developed and is pilot testing a Baldrige-based assessment system tailored to higher education, entitled *The Tradition of Excellence: Higher Education Quality Assessment Program* (Kendall-Hunt: Dubuque, IA, 1995). For further information, contact Dr. Brent D. Ruben, Executive Director, Rutgers QCI, University Program for Quality and Communication Improvement, 4 Huntington Street, New Brunswick, New Jersey 08903.
8. These issues are discussed more extensively in chapter 12, this book.
9. One example is The NACUBO (National Association of College and University Business Officers) Benchmarking Project, focusing on administrative and operational activities within colleges and universities. For further information, contact NACUBO, One Dupont Circle, Suite 500, Washington, D.C. 20036-1178.
10. These issues are discussed more extensively in chapter 14, this book.
11. The quality approach as presented here includes improvement goals that range from small- to large-scale in magnitude. Small-scale changes often referred to as *incremental* improvements, while large-scale change is typically referred to by the terms *reengineering, reinventing, redesigning, or remaking.*
12. For an extensive discussion of the three schools of thought, see Everett M. Rogers and Rekha Agarwala-Rogers, *Communication in Organizations* (New York: Free Press, 1976.)

13. Other significant contributors to the human relations school of organizational thought were Elton Mayo, Rensis Likert, George Homans, Frederick Herzberg, Warren Bennis, and Chris Argyris.

14. Key figures in the systems approach to organizational behavior were James G. Miller, Norbert Wiener, Lee Thayer, Herbert Simon, Paul Lawrence, Jay Lorsch, Daniel Katz, and Robert Kahn.

15. An excellent overview of the history of quality theory and practice summarized here is provided by Ralph G. Lewis and Douglas H. Smith, *Total Quality in Higher Education* (Delray Beach, Fla.: St. Lucie Press, 1994, 38–63).

16. These issues discussed more extensively in chapter 12, this book.

17. The NACUBO (National Association of College and University Business Officers) Benchmarking Project. For further information, contact NACUBO, One Dupont Circle, Suite 500, Washington, D.C. 20036-1178.

18. *Tradition of Excellence: Higher Education Quality Assessment Program* (Dubuque, IA: Kendall-Hunt, 1995). For further information, contact Dr. Brent D. Ruben, Executive Director, Rutgers QCI, University Program for Quality and Communication Improvement, 4 Huntington Street, New Brunswick, New Jersey 08903.

   Another special-purpose, higher education assessment approach has been developed by NACUBO. Named the Innovative Management Achievement Awards Program, it focuses specifically on business operations. For further information, contact NACUBO, One Dupont Circle, Suite 500, Washington, D.C. 20036-1178.

19. Adapted from *Quality Improvement Team Helper* (Holmdel, N.J.: AT&T Quality Technology Center, 1990, 17). Available from: AT&T Customer Information Center, PO Box 19901, Indianapolis, IN 46219. See also Peter R. Scholtes, *The Team Handbook* (Madison, Wis.: Joiner Associates, 1988).

## References

Al-Asaaf, A. F., and Schmele, J. A., *Textbook of Total Quality in Health Care* (Delray Beach, Fla.: St. Lucie Press, 1993).

Anderson, M., *Impostors in the Temple: American Intellectuals are Destroying our Universities and Cheating our Children of their Future* (New York: Simon and Schuster, 1992).

Barnard, C. I., *The Functions of the Executive* (Cambridge, Mass.: Harvard University Press, 1938).

Boyer, E. L., "Creating the New American College," *The Chronicle of Higher Education* (March 1994): A48.

Federal Quality Institute, "Lessons Learned from High-Performing Organizations in the Federal Government," *Federal Quality Management Handbook* (Washington, D.C.: Federal Quality Institute, 1994).

Gore, A., *Creating a Government that Works Better and Costs Less* (New York: Time Books/Random House, 1993).

Hiam, A., *Does Quality Work? A Review of Relevant Studies* (New York: The Conference Board, 1993).

Lathrop, J. P., *Restructuring Health Care* (San Francisco: Jossey-Bass, 1993).

Lewis, R. G., and Smith, D. H., *Total Quality in Higher Education* (Delray Beach, Fla.: St. Lucie Press, 1994).

Marszalek-Gaucher, E., and Coffey, R. J., *Transforming Health Care Organizations* (San Francisco: Jossey-Bass, 1990).

Merwick, D. M., Godfrey, A. B., and Roessner, J., *Curing Health Care* (San Francisco: Jossey-Bass, 1990).

Miller, J. G., "Living Systems," *Behavioral Science* 10 (1965): 193–237.

National Institute of Standards and Technology, *The 1994 Malcolm Baldrige National Quality Award Criteria* (Washington, D.C.: U.S. Department of Commerce, 1994).

Roethlisberger, F., and Dickson, W., *Management and the Worker* (Cambridge, Mass.: Harvard University Press, 1939).

Ruben, B. D., *Communication and Human Behavior,* 3rd ed. (Englewood Cliffs, N.J.: Prentice-Hall, 1992).

Ruben, B. D., and Kim, J. Y., *General System Theory and Human Communication* (Rochele Park, N.J.: Hayden Books, 1975).

Seymour, D. T., *The IBM-TQM Partnership with Colleges and Universities: A Report* (Washington, D.C.: American Association of Higher Education, 1993).

Smith, P., *Killing the Spirit* (New York: Penguin Books, 1990).

Sykes, C. J., *ProfScam* (Washington, D.C.: Regnery Gateway, 1988).

Taylor, F. W., *Scientific Management* (New York: Harper & Row, 1911).

Thayer, L., *Communication and Communication Systems* (Homewood, Ill.: Richard Irwin, 1968).

Total Quality Forum V, *A Report of Proceedings of the Total Quality Forum V: Rise to the Challenge: Best Practices and Leadership* (Schaumberg, Ill.: Motorola University, 1993).

von Bertalanffy, L., *General System Theory* (New York: Braziller, 1968).

Weinstein, L. A., *Moving a Battleship with Your Bare Hands: Governing a University System* (Madison, Wis.: Magna Publications, 1993).

Wilshire, B., *The Moral Collapse of the University: Professionalism, Purity, and Alienation* (Albany, N.Y.: State University of New York Press, 1990).

Wingspread Group on Higher Education, *An American Imperative* (Racine, Wis.: The Johnson Foundation, 1993).

# I

# The Context for Change in Business and Industry

# 2

# The New Productivity Challenge

*Peter F. Drucker*

The single greatest challenge facing managers in the developed countries of the world is to raise the productivity of knowledge and service workers. This challenge, which will dominate the management agenda for the next several decades, will ultimately determine the competitive performance of companies. Even more important, it will determine the very fabric of society and the quality of life in every industrialized nation.

For the last 120 years, productivity in making and moving things—in manufacturing, farming, mining, construction, and transportation—has risen in developed countries at an annual rate of 3 percent to 4 percent, a 45-fold expansion overall. On this explosive growth rest all the gains these nations and their citizens have enjoyed: vast increases in disposable income and purchasing power; ever-widening access to education and health care; and the availability of leisure time, something known only to aristocrats and the "idle rich" before 1914, when everyone else worked at least 3,000 hours a year. (Today even the Japanese work no more than about 2,000 hours each year, while Americans average 1,800 hours and West Germans 1,650.)

Now these gains are unraveling, but not because productivity in making and moving things has fallen. Contrary to popular belief, productivity in these activities is still going up at much the same rate. It is rising fully as much in the United States as it is in Japan or West Germany. Indeed, the increase in U.S. manufacturing productivity during the 1980s—some 3.9 percent a year—was actually larger in absolute terms than the corresponding annual increases in Japan and Germany, while the 4 percent to 5 percent annual rise in U.S. agricultural productivity is far and away the largest recorded anywhere at any time.

The productivity revolution is over because there are too few people employed in making and moving things for their productivity to be decisive. All told, they account for no more than one-fifth of the work force in developed economies. Only thirty years ago, they were still a near majority. Even Japan, which is still manufacturing intensive, can no longer expect increased productivity in that sector to sustain its economic growth. Indeed, the great majority of working people in Japan are knowledge and service workers with productivities as low as those in any other developed country. When farmers make up only 3 percent of the employed population, as they do in the United States, Japan, and most of Western Europe, even record increases in their output add virtually nothing to their country's overall productivity and wealth.

The chief *economic* priority for developed countries, therefore, must be to raise the productivity of knowledge and service work. The country that does this first will dominate the twenty-first century economically. The most pressing *social* challenge developed countries face, however, will be to raise the productivity of service work. Unless this challenge is met, the developed world will face increasing social tensions, increasing polarization, increasing radicalization, and possibly even class war.

In developed economies, opportunities for careers and promotion are more and more limited to people with advanced schooling; people qualified for knowledge work. But these men and women will always be a minority. They will always be outnumbered by people who lack the qualifications for anything but low-skilled service jobs—people who, in their social position, are comparable to the "proletarians" of 100 years ago, the poorly educated, unskilled masses who thronged the exploding industrial cities and streamed into their factories.

In the early 1880s, intelligent observers of every political persuasion were obsessed with the specter of class war between the industrial proletariat and the bourgeoisie. Karl Marx was hardly alone in predicting that the "immiserization" of the proletariat would lead inevitably to revolution. Benjamin Disraeli, perhaps the greatest of the nineteenth-century conservatives, was equally persuaded of the inevitability of class war. Henry James, the chronicler of American wealth and European aristocracy, was so frightened by the prospect that he made it the central theme of *The Princess Casamassima,* one of his most haunting novels.

What defeated these prophecies, which seemed eminently reasonable, indeed almost self-evident to contemporaries, was the revolution in productivity set off by Frederick W. Taylor in 1881, when he began to study the way a common laborer shoveled sand. Taylor himself worked in an iron foundry and was deeply shocked by the bitter animosity between the workers and managers. Fearful that this hatred would ultimately lead to class war, he set out to improve the efficiency of industrial work. His efforts, in turn, sparked the revolution that allowed industrial workers to earn middle-class wages and achieve middle-class status despite their lack of skill and education. By 1930 when, according to Marx, the revolution of the proletariat should have been a fait accompli, the proletariat had become the bourgeoisie.

Now it is time for another productivity revolution. This time, however, history is on our side. In the past century, we have learned a great deal about productivity and how to raise it—enough to know that we need a revolution, enough to know how to start one.

Knowledge and service workers range from research scientists and cardiac surgeons through draftswomen and store managers to sixteen-year-olds who flip hamburgers in fast-food restaurants on Saturday afternoons. Their ranks also include people whose work makes them "machine operators": dishwashers, janitors, and data-entry operators. Yet for all their diversity in knowledge, skill, responsibility, social status, and pay, knowledge and service workers are remarkably alike in two crucial respects: what does not work in raising their productivity and what does.

The first thing we have learned—and it came as a rude shock—is about what does not work. Capital cannot be substituted for labor. Nor will new technology by itself generate higher productivity. In making and moving things, capital and technology are *factors* of production, to use the economist's term. In knowledge and service work, they are tools of production. The difference is that a factor can replace labor, while a tool may or may not. Whether tools help productivity or harm it depends on what people do with them, on the purpose to which they are being put, for instance, or on the skill of the user. Thirty years ago, for example, we were sure the efficiency of the computer would lead to massive reductions in clerical and office staff. The promise of greater productivity led to massive investments in data-processing equipment that now rival those in materials-processing technology (that is, in conventional machinery). Yet office and clerical forces have grown at a much faster rate since the introduction of information technology than ever before. There has been virtually no increase in the productivity of service work.

Hospitals are a telling example. In the late 1940s they were entirely labor intensive, with little capital investment except in bricks, mortar, and beds. A good many perfectly respectable hospitals had not even invested in readily available, fairly old technologies: they provided neither x-ray departments nor clinical laboratories nor physical therapy. Today hospitals are hugely capital intensive, with enormous sums invested in ultrasound, body scanners, nuclear magnetic imagers, blood and tissue analyzers, clean rooms, and a dozen more new technologies. Each piece of equipment has brought with it the need for more highly paid people but has not reduced the existing staff by a single person. (In fact, the worldwide escalation of health care costs is largely the result of the hospital's having become a labor-intensive and capital-intensive monstrosity.) But hospitals, at least, have significantly increased their performance capacity. In other areas of knowledge or service work there are only higher costs, more investment, and more people.

Massive increases in productivity are the only way out of this morass. These increases can only come from what Taylor called "working smarter."[1] Simply, this means working more productively without working harder or longer. The economist sees capital investment as the key to productivity; the technologist gives star billing to new machines. Nevertheless, the main force behind the productivity explosion has been working smarter. Capital investment and technology were as copious in the developed economies during the first 100 years of the Industrial Revolution as they have been in its second 100 years. It was only with the advent of working smarter that productivity in making and moving things took off on its meteoric rise.

So it will be for knowledge and service work, with this difference: in manufacturing, working smarter is only one key to increased productivity. In knowledge and service work, working smarter is the only key. What is more, it is a more complex key, one that requires looking closely at work in ways that Taylor never dreamed of.

When Taylor studied the shoveling of sand, the only question that concerned him was, "How is it done?" Almost fifty years later, when Harvard's Elton Mayo set out to demolish Taylor's "scientific management" and replace it with what later came to be called "human relations," he focused on the same question. In his experiments at Western Electric's Hawthorne Works, Mayo asked, "How can wiring telephone equipment best be done?" The point is that in making and moving things, the task is always taken for granted.

In knowledge and service work, however, the first questions in increasing productivity—and working smarter—have to be, "What is the task? What are we trying to accomplish? Why do it at all?" The easiest, but perhaps also the greatest, productivity gains in such work will come from defining the task and especially from eliminating what does not need to be done.[2]

A very old example is still one of the best: mail-order processing at the early Sears, Roebuck. Between 1906 and 1908, Sears eliminated the time-consuming job of counting the money in incoming mail orders. Rather than open the money envelopes enclosed with the orders, Sears weighed them automatically. In those days, virtually all Sears customers paid with coins. If the weight of the envelope tallied with the amount of the order within fairly narrow limits, the envelope went unopened. Similarly, Sears eliminated the even more time-consuming task of recording each incoming order by scheduling order handling and shipping according to the weight of the incoming mail (assuming forty orders for each pound of mail). Within two years, these steps accounted for a tenfold increase in the productivity of the entire mail-order operation.[3]

A major insurance company recently increased the productivity of its claims-settlement department nearly fivefold—from an average of fifteen minutes per claim to three minutes—by eliminating detailed checking on all but very large claims. Instead of verifying thirty items as they had always done, the adjusters now check only four: whether the policy is still in force; whether the face amount matches the amount of the claim; whether the name of the policyholder matches the name on the death certificate; and whether the name of the beneficiary matches the name of the claimant. What provoked the change was asking, "What is the task?" and then answering, "To pay death claims as fast and as cheaply as possible." All that the company now requires to control the process is to work through a 2 percent sample, that is, every fiftieth claim, the traditional way.

Similarly, a few hospitals have taken most of the labor and expense out of their admissions process by admitting all patients the way they used to admit emergency cases who were brought in unconscious or bleeding and unable to fill out lengthy forms. These hospitals asked, "What is the task?" and answered, "To identify the patient's name, sex, age, address and how to bill"—information found on the insurance identification cards practically all patients carry.

These are both examples of service work. In knowledge work, defining the task and getting rid of what does not need to be done is even more necessary and produces even greater results. Consider how one multinational company redefined its strategic planning.

For many years, a planning staff of forty-five brilliant people carefully prepared strategic scenarios in minute detail. The documents were first-class works and made stimulating reading, everybody agreed. But they had a minimal impact on operations. Then a new CEO asked, "What is the task?" and answered, "To give our businesses direction and goals and the strategy to attain these goals." It took four years of hard work and several false starts. But now the planning people (still about the same number) work through only three questions for each of the company's businesses: What market standing does it need to maintain leadership? What innovative performance does it need to support that standing? What is the minimum rate of return needed to earn the cost of capital? Then the planning people work with the operating executives in each business to map out broad strategic guidelines for achieving these goals under various economic conditions. The results are far simpler and much less elegant, but they have become the "flight plans" that guide the company's businesses and its senior executives.

When people make or move things, they do one task at a time. Taylor's laborer shoveled sand; he did not also stoke the furnace. Mayo's wiring-room women soldered; they did not test finished telephones on the side. The Iowa farmer planting corn does not get off his tractor between rows to attend a meeting. Knowledge and service work, too, require concentration. The surgeon does not take telephone calls in the operating room, nor does the lawyer in consultation with a client.

But in organizations, where most knowledge and service work takes place, splintered attention is more and more the norm. The people at the very top can sometimes concentrate themselves (though far too few even try!). But the great majority of engineers, teachers, salespeople, nurses, middle managers, and the like must carry a steadily growing load of busywork, activities that contribute little if any value and that have little if anything to do with what these professionals are qualified and paid for.

The worst case may be that of nurses in U.S. hospitals. We hear a great deal about the shortage of nurses, but how could it possibly be true? The number of graduates entering the profession has gone up steadily for a good many years. At the same time, the number of bed patients has been dropping sharply. The explanation of the paradox: nurses now spend only half their time doing what they have learned and are paid to do—nursing. The other half is eaten up by activities that do not require their skill and knowledge, add neither health care nor economic value, and have little or nothing to do with patient care and patient well-being. Nurses are preoccupied, of course, with the avalanche of paperwork for Medicare, Medicaid, insurers, the billing office, and the prevention of malpractice suits.

The situation in higher education is not much different. Faculty in colleges and universities spend more and more hours in committee meetings instead of teaching in the classroom, advising students, or doing research. But few of these committees would ever be missed. They would do a better job in less time if they had three instead of seven members.

Salespeople are just as splintered. In department stores, they now spend so much time serving computers that they have little time for serving customers—the main reason, perhaps, for the steady decline in their productivity as producers of sales and revenues. Field-sales representatives spend up to one-third of their time filling out reports rather than calling on customers. Engineers sit through meeting after meeting when they should be busy at their workstations.

This is not job enrichment; it is job impoverishment. It destroys productivity. It saps motivation and morale. Nurses, every attitude survey shows, bitterly resent not being able to spend more time caring for patients. They also believe, understandably, that they are grossly underpaid for what they are capable of doing, while the hospital administrator, equally understandably, believes that they are grossly overpaid for the unskilled clerical work they are actually doing.

The cure is fairly easy, as a rule. It is to concentrate the work—in this case, nursing—on the task—caring for patients. This is the second step toward working smarter. A few hospitals, for example, have taken the paperwork out of the nurse's job and given it to a floor clerk who also answers telephone calls from relatives and friends and arranges the flowers they send in. The level of patient care and the hours nurses devote to it have risen sharply. Yet the hospitals have also been able to reduce their nursing staffs by one-quarter or one-third and so raise salaries without incurring a higher nursing payroll.

To make these kinds of improvements, we must ask a second set of questions about every knowledge and service job: "What do we pay for? What value is this job supposed to add?" The answer is not always obvious or noncontroversial. One department store looked at its sales force and answered "sales," while another in the same metropolitan area and with much the same clientele answered "customer service." Each answer led to a different restructuring of the jobs on the sales floor. But each store achieved, and fairly quickly, substantial growth in the revenues each salesperson and each department generated, that is, gains in both productivity and profitability.

For all its tremendous impact, Taylor's scientific management has had a bad press, especially in academia. Perhaps the main reason is the unrelenting campaign U.S. labor unions waged against it—and against Taylor himself— in the early years of this century. The unions did not oppose Taylor because they thought him antilabor or promanagement. He was neither. His unforgivable sin was his assertion that there is no such thing as "skill" in making and moving things. All such work was the same, Taylor asserted. All could be analyzed step by step, as a series of unskilled operations that could then be combined into any kind of job. Anyone willing to learn these operations would be a "first-class man," deserving "first-class pay." He could do the most advanced work and do it to perfection.

To the skill-based unions of 1900, this assertion represented a direct attack. This was especially true for the highly respected, extremely powerful unions that dominated what were then some of the country's most sophisticated manufacturing sites—the army arsenals and navy shipyards where nearly all peacetime production for the military took place until well after World War I. For these unions, each craft was a mystery whose secrets no member could divulge. Their power base was control of an apprenticeship that lasted five or seven years and admitted, as a rule, only relatives of members. Their workers were paid extremely well—more than most physicians of the day and triple what Taylor's first-class man could expect to get. No wonder that Taylor's assertions infuriated these aristocrats of labor.

Belief in the mystery of craft and skill persisted, as did the assumption that long years of apprenticeship were needed to acquire both. Indeed, Hitler went to war with the United States on the strength of that assumption. Convinced that it took five years or more to train optical craftsmen (whose skills are essential to modern warfare), he thought it would be at least that long before America could field an effective army and air force in Europe—and so declared war after the Japanese attack on Pearl Harbor.

We know now Taylor was right. The United States had almost no optical craftsmen in 1941. Modern warfare indeed requires precision optics in large quantities. But by applying Taylor's methods of scientific management, within a few months the United States trained semiskilled workers to turn out more highly advanced optics than even the Germans were producing, and on an assembly line to boot. By that time, Taylor's first-class men with their increased productivity were also making a great deal more money than any craftsman of 1911 had ever dreamed of.

Eventually, knowledge work and service work may turn out to be like the work of making and moving things, that is, "just work," to use an old scientific management slogan. (At least, this is what Taylor's true heirs, the more radical proponents of artificial intelligence, maintain.) But for the time being, we must not treat knowledge and service jobs as "just work." Nor can we assume they are homogeneous. Rather, these jobs can be divided into three distinct categories by looking at what productive performance in a given job actually represents. This process—defining performance—is the third step toward working smarter.

For some knowledge and service jobs, performance means quality. Take scientists in a research lab where quantity—the number of results—is quite secondary to their quality. One new drug that can generate annual sales of $500 million and dominate the market for a decade is infinitely more valuable than twenty "me too" drugs with annual sales of $20 million or $30 million each. The same principle applies to basic policy or strategic decisions, as well as to much less grandiose work, the physician's diagnosis, for example, or packaging design, or editing a magazine. In each of these instances, we do not yet know how to analyze the process that produces quality results. To raise productivity, therefore, we can only ask, "What works?"

The second category includes the majority of knowledge and service work, jobs in which quality and quantity together constitute performance. Department store sales are one example. Producing a "satisfied customer" is just as important as the dollar amount on the sales slip, but it is not so easy to define. Likewise, the quality of an architectural draftswoman's work is an integral part of her performance. But so is the number of drawings she can produce. The same holds true for engineers, sales reps in brokerage offices, medical technologists, branch bank managers, reporters, nurses, claims adjusters, and so on. Raising productivity in these jobs requires, asking, "What works?" but also analyzing the process step by step and operation by operation.

Finally, there are a good many service jobs (filing, handling death claims, making hospital beds) in which performance is defined much as it is in making and moving things, that is, largely by quantity (for example, the number of minutes it takes to make up a hospital bed properly). In these "production" jobs, quality is primarily a matter of external criteria rather than an attribute of performance itself. Defining standards and building them into the work process is essential. But once this has been done, real productivity improvements will come through conventional industrial engineering, that is, through analyzing the task and combining the individual simple operations into a complete job.

Defining the task, concentrating work on the task, and defining performance: by themselves, these three steps will produce substantial growth in productivity—perhaps most of what can be attained at any one time. They will need to be worked through again and again, maybe as often as every three or five years, and certainly whenever work or its organization changes. But then, according to all the experience we have, the resulting productivity increases will equal, if not exceed, whatever industrial engineering, scientific management, or human relations ever achieved in manufacturing. In other words, they should give us the productivity revolution we need in knowledge and service work, but on one condition only: that we apply what we have learned since World War II about increasing productivity in making and moving things. The fourth step toward working smarter, then, is for management to form a partnership with the people who hold the jobs, the people who are to become more productive. The goal has to be to build responsibility for productivity and performance into every knowledge and service job regardless of level, difficulty, or skill.

Frederick Taylor has often been criticized for never once asking the workers he studied how they thought their jobs could be improved; he told them. Nor did Elton Mayo ever ask; he also told. But Taylor's (and Mayo's, forty years later) methodology was simply a product of the times, when the wisdom of the expert prevailed. (Freud, after all, never asked his patients what they thought their problems might be. Nor do we have any record that either Marx or Lenin ever thought of asking the masses.) Taylor considered both workers and managers "dumb oxen." While Mayo had great respect for managers, he thought workers were "immature," "maladjusted," and deeply in need of the psychologist's expert guidance.

When World War II came, however, we had to ask the workers; we had no choice. U.S. factories had no engineers, psychologists, or foremen. They were all in uniform. To our immense surprise, as I still recollect, we discovered that the workers were neither dumb oxen nor immature nor maladjusted. They knew a great deal about the work they were doing—about its logic and rhythm, its quality, and its tools. Asking them what they thought was the way to address both productivity and quality.[4]

At first, only a few businesses accepted this novel proposition. (IBM was a pioneer and for a long time one of the few large companies to act on this idea.) But in the late 1950s and early 1960s, it was picked up by Japanese industrialists whose earlier attempts to return to prewar autocracy had collapsed in bloody strikes and near-civil war. Now, while still far from being widely practiced, it is at least generally accepted in theory that the workers' knowledge of their job is the starting point for improving productivity, quality, and performance.

## Notes

1. Among the few attempts to apply working smarter in health care are Roxanne Spitzer's *Nursing Productivity: The Hospital's Key to Survival and Profit* (Chicago: S-N Publications, 1986) and Regina Herzlinger's *Creating New Health Care Ventures* (Gaithersburg, Md.: Aspen Publishers, 1991).

2. See Michael Hammer, "Reengineering Work: Don't Automate, Obliterate," *HBR* (July-August 1990), and Peter F. Drucker, "Permanent Cost Cutting," *Wall Street Journal* (11 January 1991).
3. See Boris Emmet and John E. Jeuks, *Catalogues and Counters: A History of Sears, Roebuck, & Company* (Chicago: University of Chicago Press, 1965).
4. In my 1942 book, *The Future of Industrial Man* (Westport, Conn.: Greenwood, 1978 reprint of original), and my 1950 book, *The New Society* (Greenwood, 1982 reprint), I argued for the "responsible worker" as "part of management." Edwards W. Deming and Joseph M. Juran developed what we now call "quality circles" and "total quality management" as a result of their wartime experiences. Finally, the idea was forcefully presented by Douglas McGregor in his 1960 book, *The Human Side of Enterprise* (New York: McGraw Hill, 1985, twenty-fifth anniversary printing), with its "Theory X" and "Theory Y."

# 3

# The Service Imperative

*Karl Albrecht and Ron Zemke*

> *McDonald's has more employees than U.S. Steel.*
> *Golden arches, not blast furnaces, symbolize the*
> *American economy.*
> —George F. Will, *Newsweek*

Ours is a service economy, and it has been one for some time. Trend analyst John Naisbitt marks the beginning of this new period as the year 1956, when "for the first time in American history, white-collar workers in technical, managerial, and clerical positions outnumbered blue-collar workers. Industrial America was giving way to a new society."

Naisbitt labeled this new era the "information society." Earlier, Harvard sociologist Daniel Bell noted the same events and trends and pronounced us entered into the "postindustrial society." Call it what you will, the fact remains that we live in an America, perhaps in a world and time, dominated by industries that perform rather than produce.

According to the U.S. Department of Commerce, the forecast for the foreseeable future can be summed up in four words: more of the same. There will be continued fast growth in service industries and service jobs, with data processing and hospitality leading the way. Service is no longer an industrial byproduct, a sector that generates no wealth but "simply moves money around," as one economist has scoffed. Service has become a powerful economic engine in its own right—the fast track of the new American economy. *Newsweek* columnist George F. Will summarized the look of this new economy succinctly when he observed that "McDonald's has more employees than U.S. Steel. Golden arches, not blast furnaces, symbolize the American economy." We are only beginning to understand the significance of this change in the way we

Reprinted from Karl Albrecht and Ron Zemke's book, *Service America! Doing Business in the New Economy* (Dow Jones-Irwin 1985).

live and work. Let's be clear here. We aren't suggesting that U.S. Steel is about to convert its factories into laundries to survive, or that Chrysler Corp. should consider abandoning automobile manufacturing for condominium management. As Wharton School management professor Russell Ackoff has argued, this shift toward a service-centered economy does not mean that fewer goods will be produced and consumed, "any more than the end of the agricultural era meant that fewer agricultural products were produced and consumed. What it does mean is that fewer people will be required to produce manufactured goods."[1] To us, that implies the gold and the growth are in services. That's where the jobs are; that's where the energy is; that's where the opportunities will continue to be.

We are persuaded that a real and important shift is under way. The fabric of our economy and the way we do business in this country are changing. This change in thrust, this transformation from a marketplace focused on goods to one focused on services, this phenomenon that Ackoff calls the "second industrial revolution" and Naisbitt refers to as the "beginning of the information society," is real and important. It is our new competitive edge—both domestically and in the world at large. Already 20 percent of the world's need for services is filled by American exports. It is only a beginning.

We contend, however, that this shift from products to services, if it is to be fully leveraged as a driving force, requires a parallel transformation in the way organizations are conceptualized, structured, and, most importantly, managed. We contend that organizations that place a premium on the design, development, and delivery of services are as different from traditional industrial organizations as the factory is from the farm. The distinction applies not only to organizations that market pure service products (the traditional service industries), but also to manufacturers of hard goods and commodities who place a high strategic value on service and treat it as an integral part of the product they deliver. Whether service is valued simply because it is a useful strategy for product differentiation or because service is an ingrained organizational belief, the result is the same. In those organizations service isn't a function or a department. To them, service is product.

### Service Is...

What do we mean by service? Several things. Bureaucrats and economists traditionally have talked about the "service sector" and defined it as consisting of "industries whose output is intangible." To the Census Bureau and the Department of Commerce, that definition covers organizations that employ just short of 60 percent of all the people employed in the United States, and applies to four broad segments of the economy:

- transportation, communications, and utilities;
- wholesale and retail trade;

- finance, insurance, and real estate;
- services—the fastest growing part of the "service sector," which includes business services such as accounting, engineering, and legal firms; personal services such as housekeeping, barbering, and recreational services; and most of the nonprofit areas of the economy.

All four of these groups offer service in the classic "Help Me" sense: help me with my taxes, help me get from point A to point B, help me find a house, help me pick out a new pair of shoes. There is nothing intrinsically wrong with this traditional approach to defining who is and who isn't in the service business. It does, however, mask the full impact of service in today's marketplace. Management expert and social scientist Peter Drucker is even more emphatic that the term *services,* as used to describe the largest portion of our contemporary economy, is a singularly unhelpful description. In a recent column in *The Wall Street Journal,* he surveys the world economy, the slump in commodity prices, and the slow recovery of manufacturing compared to the rapid growth of the service sector and states:

> We may–and soon–have to rethink the way we look at economics and economies, and fairly radically. "Information" is now classed as "services," a 19th-century term for "miscellaneous." Actually it is no more service than electrical power (which is also classed under service). It is the primary material of an information-based economy.
>
> And in such an economy the schools are as much primary producers as the farmer— and their productivity perhaps more crucial. The same in the engineering lab, the newspaper and offices in general. (9 January 1985)

We heartily agree with Drucker's argument that service, as we know it today, is very much a primary product. It is, indeed, this argument that service is not a single-dimensioned "thing" that is at the core of our contention that service is as much a commodity as an automobile and as much in need of management and systematic study.

Harvard Business School professor Theodore Levitt agrees that the service and nonservice distinction becomes less and less meaningful as our understanding of service increases. "There are no such things as service industries. There are only industries whose service components are greater or less than those of other industries. Everybody is in service," he writes. At Citibank, half of the organization's 52,000 employees work in back rooms, never seen or heard by the public. They spend their time writing letters of credit, opening lockboxes, processing transactions, and scrutinizing everything done by the public contact people. Is Citicorp any less a manufacturer than International Business Machines Corp.? Is IBM, half of whose 340,000 employees deal directly with the public, any less a service provider? Service is everybody's business.

## "Fix It" Service

The second dimension—after "Help Me" service—is service in the "Fix It" sense. It sometimes seems we are a nation of broken toys. The car is in the shop, the phone is out of order, and this computer you sold me isn't working so well, either. Service in this sense is underaccounted for in the economy and marketplace, but seldom undervalued in the eye of the contemporary consumer.[2] The quality of a company's "Fix It" service is already a significant factor in its marketplace success. The capacity of an IBM, a General Electric (GE), or a Caterpillar Tractor to deliver high-quality "Fix It" service as a matter of routine—while others offer excuses, complex requirements, or failure—sets each apart in its industry and in the marketplace as a whole. We are not suggesting, of course, that manufactured goods have never before needed fixing. Far from it. But only recently have so many products become too complex for users to repair and maintain on their own. At the same time, consumers have come to expect—to demand really—that a manufacturer's obligation to guarantee the performance of a product should extend further past the point and date of purchase than ever before.

Such changes in consumer expectations can be both a bane and a blessing. It is the growing demand for high-caliber "Fix It" service in the personal computer business, falling on the deaf ears of most dealers and manufacturers, for example, that is behind the spate of start-up companies like Sorbus Service Inc. and Computer Doctor Inc., which specialize in servicing electronic products. The same demand is enticing large-computer manufacturers and the few service-savvy micro producers into the development of aggressive, third-party service subsidiaries.

What an opportunity it is! Every day a thousand Macintoshes come rolling off the Apple Computer assembly lines in Cupertino, California, while an equal number of IBM-PCs hit the road north from Florida. If we add the 3 to 5 million "orphaned" personal computers and computer peripherals in this country (which were gear-manufactured by companies that no longer exist but owned by users who do), then the need for quality "Fix It" service in the computer area alone is staggering.

According to a study by Arthur Andersen & Co. for the Association of Field Service Managers, the repair of information processing, telecommunications, and other diverse electronic products—dubbed the "electronic products service business" in the study—bills $20 billion annually, and this figure should grow to $46 billion a year by 1990.[3] Yet few manufacturers of high-tech gear are interested in the opportunities presented by this obvious void. This is so despite the fact that a well-run service operation can, by Andersen's estimates, contribute as much as 30 percent to a manufacturer's revenues. Is it any mystery that the few companies that do see the handwriting on the wall—TRW Inc., Control Data, Bell & Howell Co., Western Union Telegraph Co.—

are doubling their efforts to establish solid reputations and names for themselves in the service end of the electronic future while others are content only to manufacture?

This naïveté about the value of service among producers of hard goods may be glaringly obvious in the personal-computer world, but it is hardly confined to that world. Automobile manufacturers, big steel companies, machine-tool builders, and any number of consumer-product producers have suffered the same malady in the past. The attitude plainly has been, "This would be a great business if it weren't for all the damned customers." Such an attitude almost always proves to be a costly error in judgment, but it's becoming a more deadly mistake every day. Service, it increasingly turns out, can play a significant role in the economic well-being of an organization that produces hard goods. When your food processor is distinguishable from the competition's food processor by only a dime's worth of detailing and a dollar on the price tag, your customer service and service reputation become a critical discriminator. The GE commercial that promises, "We don't desert you after we deliver it" plucks a heartstring in a million frustrated consumers. You can count on GE.

An unusually incisive set of studies of consumer complaint behavior was carried out during the Carter administration for the While House Office of Consumer Affairs by a Washington, D.C. company called Technical Assistance Research Programs, Inc. (TARP). These studies spoke volumes about the positive economics of first-class service.[4] According to their findings, manufacturing organizations that don't just "handle" dissatisfied customers but go out of their way to encourage complaints and remedy them, reap significant rewards.

Among TARP's key findings are the following:

- The average business never hears from 96 percent of its unhappy customers. For every complaint received, the average company in fact has twenty-six customers with problems, six of which are "serious" problems.
- Complainers are more likely than noncomplainers to do business again with the company that upset them, even if the problem isn't satisfactorily resolved.
- Of the customers who register a complaint, between 54 and 70 percent will do business again with the organization if their complaint is resolved. That figure goes up to a staggering 95 percent if the customer feels that the complaint was resolved quickly.
- The average customer who has had a problem with an organization tells nine or ten people about it. Thirteen percent of people who have a problem with an organization recount the incident to more than twenty people.
- Customers who have complained to an organization and had their complaints satisfactorily resolved tell an average of five people about the treatment they received.

If automobile industry studies are correct that a brand-loyal customer represents a lifetime average revenue of at least $140,000, then the image of a
manufacturer or dealer in a bitter dispute with a customer over an $80 repair
bill or a $40 replacement part is plainly ludicrous. Similar logic holds for
almost every business sector. In banking, the average customer represents $80
a year in profit. Appliance manufacturers figure brand loyalty is worth $2,800
over a twenty-year period. Your local supermarket is counting on you for $4,400
this year and $22,000 for the five years you live in the same neighborhood.

As TARP president John Goodman put it in an address to the Nippon Cultural Broadcasting Company in Tokyo:

> The fundamental conclusion [of our studies] is that a customer is worth more than
> merely the value of the purchase a complaint concerns. A customer's worth in-
> cludes the long-term value of both the revenue and profit stream from all his pur-
> chases. This becomes particularly important if the customer could potentially
> purchase a range of different products from the same company.[5]

The Japanese, by the way, are only beginning to see service as important
and problematic. Decades of concentration on manufacturing quality products and exporting finished goods have left service basically unattended to.
The tendency in Japan is, as it has been here, to equate service with servitude
and face-to-face attention rather than with customer-centered management.

The pattern of consumer behavior TARP uncovered is as true for industrial sales as for retail sales. There really is no mystery, then, as to why a
heads-up company like Proctor & Gamble prints an 800 number on all eighty
of its products. This year, P & G, the nation's largest producer of consumer
product (Ivory soap, Folger's coffee, Crest toothpaste, Pamper's disposable
diapers, Tide detergent, and so on) expects to answer more than 750,000
telephone calls and letters from customers. A third of these replies will deal
with complaints of all kinds, including those about products, ads, and even
the plots of soap operas sponsored by the company. If only half of those
complaints are about a product with a thirty-cent margin, and only 85 percent are handled to the customer's satisfaction, the benefit to the company
in the year, according to a formula developed by TARP, could exceed half a
million dollars. Such a sum represents a return on investment (ROI) of almost 20 percent. The "Fix It" dimension of service is most surely an important economic force in its own right.

### Value-Added Service

The third service dimension shaping the way we do business is the most
intangible of all. Value-added service has the feel of simple civility when delivered in a face-to-face context, but it is more than that. When it shows itself
in such an ingenious and successful product as the American Express Plati-
num Card, it looks like perceptive marketing.

Value-added service is more easily understood in experience than in definition; you know it when you see it. Because a cabin attendant pushing the drink wagon on the Republic 507 flight out of Chicago is out of loose change, she gives you back three one-dollar bills from a five for a $2.50 drink. In response to an offhand comment you made, a calling officer from Wachovia Bank and Trust, who pitched factoring services to you last week, sends you an article on how to use limited trusts to help put your kids through college. A 3M visual-products representative setting up a seminar on how to use overhead projectors in sales presentations stays to help one of your salespeople rehearse for a next-day presentation. All those people are practicing the fine art of value-added service.

Each variation on the same theme is an example from, and an integral part of, the service revolution. The common thread is customer-focused service. None of these examples represents a new definition of what service means; it is rather the value and power they have in the marketplace that is new.

John Naisbitt's "high-tech/high-touch" concept has a lot to do with development of this need. As new technology is introduced into our society, there is a counterbalancing human response. For example, Naisbitt points out, "The high technology of heart transplants and brain scanners led to a new interest in the family doctor and neighborhood clinics." In that same vein we have noticed that the advance of automated tellers in banking gave rise to a countermand by many for access to a personal banker. The more we are faced with high tech, the more we want high touch. The fewer contacts we have with the people of an organization, the more important the quality of each contact becomes. All contacts with an organization are a critical part of our perceptions and judgments about that organization. The quality of the people contacts, however, are often the firmest and most lasting.

Russell Ackoff sees another dimension to the demand for value-added service: a shifting focus from concern for one's standard of living toward a concern for the quality of life. If some aspects of this phenomenon represent a shift away from materialism and the "I-can-have-it-all" credo, as some claim, other factors that fall under the quality-of-life umbrella certainly signal that with a secure standard of material life, the accessories become more important. A young person's need for a car gives way to a desire for the "right kind" of automobile. Access to discretionary funds sufficient to support frequent air travel gives way to a desire for first-class seating and the best possible amenities. The total experience of obtaining a product or service becomes integrated into a real and palpable quality of the product or service itself.

Warren Blanding, editor and publisher of "Customer Service Newsletter," suggests that several forces are at work here. Together they create a new understanding of service:

> The trend toward consumerism, the changing competitive climate and the recent recession all have forced companies to reexamine their relationships with customers. As a result, customer service has become a strategic tool. It used to be regarded

as an expense. Now it is seen as a positive force for increasing sales—and for reducing the cost of sales.

The constant quest for improvement in the quality of life is not a new phenomenon, only a new mass phenomenon. In the early industrial era of this country, only the wealthy few played tennis, summered in the mountains, or wintered in the Bahamas. Today these are mass cultural experiences. Our parents and grandparents were tickled to have a paid week off, once a year. The paid vacation was a great labor victory. We—or at least some of us—jet to London for a long weekend of shopping and theater in an almost casual manner. As the mass demand for a product or service increases, the ability to deliver it effectively, efficiently, and dependably is taxed. It must be managed. Thus, we find ourselves entering the service management era, the age of systematically designed, developed, and delivered services.

### Service as a Managed Endeavor

Historically, the terms *service* and *management* haven't rested easily side by side. Service delivery was something most self-respecting business school graduates shunned—with the exception perhaps of rising young bank officers. The concept of management seemed to encourage an orderly image antithetical to service in the traditional "Help Me" sense.

Ronald Kent Shelp, vice-president of American International Group (a New York-based multinational insurance company) and chairman of the federal advisory committee on service industries, attributes those perceptions to a confusion of personal services—such as those provided by housekeepers, barbers, and plumbers—with the concept of service as the provision of intangible products in general. Consequently, service has been misperceived as always involving a one-to-one relationship between provider and receiver, as labor-intensive, and as having productivity characteristics not readily increased by capital and technology.

Characterizing service in today's economy as servitude is as inaccurate as calling Francis C. Ronney, Jr., head of Melville Corp. (the $4 billion-a-year retail chain store conglomerate that started as Thom McAn), a shoe clerk. Today two thirds of the gross national product result from service production; and at the same time, personal service in the traditional sense accounts for less than 1 percent of all service jobs. Here is how Shelp sees it:

> While personal-service jobs were declining, industrialization was calling forth a whole range of new services. Some of these were the result of new found affluence, as more and more people could afford more and better health care, education, amusement, and recreation. Other services were needed to increase the productivity of production—wholesale trade, information processing, financial services, communications. These services and others like them (engineering, consulting, retailing and insurance) became highly productive when modern tech-

nology supplied them with computers, satellite and other rapid communications, and systems analysis.

Thus service jobs moved away from the low end of the economic spectrum toward the other extreme. Much of the service-oriented job growth in advanced nations has taken place in professional, managerial, administrative, and problem-solving categories. Increasingly, education became the name-of-the-game in service jobs.[6]

This change in the nature of what a service is leads to a situation where we see a number of quite different kinds of activities nestled under the umbrella of "service and service-related industries." Shelp sorts these into five types and suggests that each developed in response to a set of stages and parallel economic conditions through which Western society has passed and through which many developing countries are now passing.

### Unskilled Personal Service

Housekeeping services for females, military conscription for males, and street vending for both sexes are the primary type of service activity in traditional societies. Historically, these kinds of jobs have provided opportunities for excess population to become socialized into urban life. Though unskilled labor exists today in this country, it is on a very different scale. People plying the trades of housekeeping, street sweeping, janitoring, and the like do exist today, but it is more likely than not that the services they provide are through a corporation like Service Master International and not on a free-lance basis. It is also most likely that these organizations call on technology and mass-production techniques to assist in the delivery of the service rather than on simple brute force. But automated or not, it is a good bet that the effort is more effectively managed.[7]

### Skilled Personal Services

As productivity increases in agricultural societies and production exceeds subsistence levels, industrialization and trade begin to develop. Opportunities open for the kinds of services provided by skilled artisans, shopkeepers, wholesale and retail merchants, repair and maintenance people, and clerks. The need arises for complex government and government services to support both industry and the burgeoning urban population. This is the first stage of what we described above as service in the traditional sense. Yes, these services are also very much with us today, but as is the case for unskilled services, they are now organized and managed.

### Industrial Services

As industry becomes competitive, the need for marketplace support services arises. Industrial services are really organized groups of highly skilled specialists. Their services are, by and large, those that cannot be provided by individual contractors. They are the services offered by legal and accounting firms, banks and insurance firms, real estate brokers, and trading companies. We traditionally called such services the professions and did not consider them amenable to innovation and productivity improvement. But all that is changing. The marketing and management of *professional services,* as they are termed, are becoming hot topics. The creation of accounting, health, and legal franchise operations has, in effect, industrialized the industrial services.

## Mass Consumer Services

As wealth increases in a population, discretionary purchasing power is created. This gives rise to a consumer-service industry able to enjoy economies of scale while accommodating a growing consumer demand for discretionary services. The demand for travel has promoted growth in airlines, hotels, and auto-rental companies. The demand for dining (an average of nearly two meals a day is now consumed outside the home), both fancy and fast, has led to a highly-variegated restaurant industry. The demand for entertainment has created a broad base of services from movies to professional sports. A significant increase in the health and wellness industries can be attributed to the growth of discretionary dollars as well.

## High-Technology Business Services

The introduction of microchips, lasers, satellites, bioengineering, and the like create opportunities for large advances in both the creation of new services and the streamlining of existing ones. The automation of goods production, data processing, and hydroponics are creations of the special services of the knowledge worker, which result in a demand for new, highly technical services. The creation of industrial robots threatens production-line jobs; at the same time, a need for skilled robotic technicians is felt. Of course, it is not a one-for-one swap. Not every job lost to automation is replaced by a skill or craft job. All the same, every job that can be done by a robot will probably soon be replaced.

Another kind of service specialist created by the new technology is the knowledge consultant. Management consultants, university researchers, and software programmers are examples of such service providers. The tasks performed by each of these specialists are highly organized, integrated, and managed. This is service in its most vital and modern sense.

From this perspective it is obvious that as a society increases in sophistication and wealth, the demand for services outweighs the demand for commodities. As discretionary time and money make their presence felt in the marketplace, the ways in which one can satisfy basic needs are most likely to increase, not the basic needs themselves. Thus, the railroad has seen first the automobile and then the airplane rival it as a method of fulfilling travel needs. This means that competition for the dollars of travelers and shippers has increased both within and across industries. *Increased competition,* as Shelp notes, leads to an increased demand for services that create efficiencies which are the basis of effective competition. At every stage of the evolution of service, we see an increase in competition among service providers as well as an increased need to effectively and efficiently deliver such services. Increased also is the awareness that a service is managed differently than a commodity.

The idea that service is a unique product that has to be understood and managed differently from a manufactured commodity isn't news to everyone. In July, 1984, a *Business Week* feature, "Service as a Marketing Edge," hailed the upgrading of service from an onerous corporate chore to an important organizational strategy. Though the article focused primarily on the value-added dimension of service and not on service as a product per se, the title alone had implications that, we believe, will echo through the economy for years.

Louis V. Gerstner, Jr., newly named president of American Express, calls service his "most strategic marketing weapon." Though the 1984 tab for the communications lines, computers, data banks, salaries, and training that went into Am Ex's service centers ran to $150 million, the benefits in terms of customer satisfaction and market information are almost incalculable. Am Ex, along with companies like P & G, IBM, Sony, General Electric, and Whirlpool, is finding that service is an active marketing tool. Such companies are learning that aggressive service programs effectively allow them to discover the demographics of their marketplace, problems with new products, customer concerns and needs, the life expectancies of their products, the ability of consumers to effect their own repairs, and the potential of proposed new products.

At Procter & Gamble, the customer-service unit at the end of the 800 number not only acts as a problem solver and value-added service to consumers, but is also an effective data trap for information that can lead to other service improvements. During the 1960s, for example, P & G noticed that the average household's weekly laundry increased from 6.4 to 7.6 loads. At the same time the average wash temperature dropped fifteen degrees. Closer investigation revealed that the cause of this was a multitude of new fabrics, especially synthetics, requiring closer sorting and control of the weekly wash. The upshot for P & G was the creation of the All-Temperature Cheer laundry detergent, a product especially developed to solve another of consumers' ever-evolving needs.

Over the years P & G's phone lines gathered information that has led the company to develop many value-added services. On the basis of such hot-line data, the company now includes special cooking instructions for Duncan Hines brownies intended for distribution at high altitudes. It has added instructions for turning the average white cake into a wedding cake, and developed guidelines for defrosting Downy liquid fabric softener, which sometimes freezes in snow-belt states. C. Gibson Carey, a P & G advertising executive, has an explanation for the company's "knock-yourself-out-for-the-customer" approach to service that tells us something about both P & G and value-added service in general. "There is a whole lot of enlightened self-interest in this."

Managers in such mature industries as machine tools, chemicals, consumers, and electronics, as well as purveyors of formerly regulated services such as banking, communications, and air transportation, are facing challenges that require them to take a new look at the service dimensions of their products. Traditional goods purveyors are finding that the classic market-differentiation strategies of price, quality, and special features are not enough to ensure either customer satisfaction or repeat business.

Theodore Levitt likens the relationship between today's buyer and seller to a marriage. He observes that if the act of selling someone something was once a simple, "time-discrete, bare human interaction," it is most certainly not that today. Today's buyer, whether a purchaser of industrial or consumer products, expects significantly more from the seller than a "take-the-money-and-run" attitude. As Levitt puts it:

> Buyers of automated machinery (for example) do not, like buyers at a flea market, walk home with their purchases and take their chances. They expect installation services, application aids, parts, post-purchase repair and maintenance, retrofitted enhancements, and vendor R & D to keep the products effective and up to date for as long as possible and to help the company stay competitive.

> Thanks to increasing interdependence, more and more of the world's economic work gets done through long term relationships between sellers and buyers. It is not a matter of just getting and then holding onto your customers. It is more a matter of giving the buyers what they want. Buyers want vendors who keep promises, [and] who'll keep supplying and standing behind what they promised. The era of the one-night stand is gone. Marriage [between buyer and seller] is both necessary and more convenient. Products are too complicated, repeat negotiations too much of a hassle and too costly. Under these conditions, success in marketing is transformed into the inescapability of a relationship.[8]

Service, in the context discussed by Levitt, is an ongoing relationship between buyer and seller that focuses on keeping the buyer happy with the seller after the sale. This is a relationship undertaken not for vague public-image purposes, but for vital economic ones. The buyer-seller relationship is not a simple contract of trust between two individuals, but a promise of continuing contact between two economic entities for mutual benefit. In Levitt's words:

> During the era we are entering the emphasis will be on systems contracts, and buyer-seller relationships will be characterized by continuous contact and evolving relationships to effect the systems. The "sale" will be not just a system but a

system over time. The value at stake will be the advantages of that total system over time.[9]

Levitt's point is stated in simpler terms by Bill Cove, a motivational speaker who tells the following story about a businessman named Harry, the owner of a small general-appliance store in Phoenix, Arizona

> Harry is accustomed to being price-shopped by young couples looking for their first new refrigerator or washer-dryer or air conditioner. When a young couple comes into the store, pen and paper in hand, asking detailed questions about prices, features, and model numbers, Harry is pretty sure that their next move will be to trot off to a nearby discount appliance dealer to compare tags. When, after spending half an hour with such a couple and patiently answering all their questions, Harry suggests an order, he usually gets a firm, "We want to look around some other places." His rebuttal is to nod, smile, move up close, and deliver this little speech:
>
> "I understand that you are looking for the best deal you can find. I appreciate that because I do the same thing myself. And I know you'll probably head down to Discount Dan's and compare prices. I know I would.
>
> "But after you've done that, I want you to think of one thing. When you buy from Discount Dan's you get an appliance. A good one. I know because he sells the same appliances we do. But when you buy the same appliance here, you get one thing you can't get at Dan's: you get me. I come with the deal. I stand behind what I sell. I want you to be happy with what you buy. I've been here 30 years. I learned the business from my Dad, and I hope to be able to give the business over to my daughter and son-in-law in a few years. So you know one thing for sure: when you buy an appliance from me, you get me with the deal, and that means I do everything I can to be sure you never regret doing business with me. That's a guarantee."
>
> With that, Harry wishes the couple well and gives them a quart of ice cream in appreciation for their interest.

"Now," Cove asks his audience, "how far away do you think that young couple is going to get, with Harry's speech ringing in their ears and a quart of vanilla ice cream on their hands, in Phoenix, in August, when it's 125 degrees in the shade?"

Yes, it's a salesman's story, where the salesman gets cute and gets the order. But the point is exactly the same as Levitt's. Today, the buyer-seller relationship is more than a fleeting, face-to-face encounter. The product purchased isn't simply an item with a set, intrinsic value the buyer is invited to take or leave. It is rather a bundling of the item: the product, the seller, the organization the seller represents, the service reputation of the selling organization, the service personnel, the buyer, the organization he represents, and both organizations' images in the marketplace.

Service is a key differentiation in such a marketplace, especially when the choice is among products distinguishable along no other dimension meaningful to the customer. Let's assume that you tell us that your microcomputer is better than the competitor's microcomputer because yours has a thirty-two-bit microprocessor. But if we don't know a microprocessor from a food processor, and you don't do anything to help us see why that just might be important, then we are left not having the faintest idea why we should buy from you instead of the competitor. Or worse yet, if you tell us that your microcomputer has a thirty-two-bit microprocessor and that everyone's microcomputer has a thirty-two-bit microprocessor, you merely convince us that there isn't a dime's difference between yours and the competitor's. Let's assume you tell us that should anything go wrong with your computer—heaven forbid—a technician will be Johnny-on-the-spot in less than two hours to remedy the problem. By way of contrast, if something happens to the competitor's computer, we'll have to put it in a box and mail it back to the factory. If you then add that the factory closed up last week, you will have told us quite a lot about your computer that differentiates it from the competitor's.

Service is not a competitive edge, it is *the* competitive edge. People do not just buy things, they also buy expectations. One expectation is that the item they buy will produce the benefits the seller promised. Another is that if it doesn't, the seller will make good on the promise. When a company picks Xerox Corporation over Canon Inc. as a photocopy machine supplier, many considerations go into the decision. One is the dependability of the "Fix It" service reputation that accompanies the Xerox name. If the technician providing the "Fix It" service maintains the machine in line with the buyer's expectations, and does so in a way that gives an impression of competence and friendliness, the relationship is solidified along two additional dimensions. Should the technician prove to be either incompetent or offensive to the buyer's employees in the fulfillment of his duties, the relationship may be short-lived despite the fact that the initial conditions of the decision have not changed.

Let's consider why IBM's personal computer sells so well when a multitude of cheaper yet similar computers are available, and when the market contains several competitors, notably the Wang personal computer and Apple's Macintosh, that seemingly offer so much more of a machine for the same money? Indeed, why does IBM do so well in the big computer business when companies like NCR Corporation, Amdahl, and Tandem sell mainframe computers said to be faster, better, more reliable, and better maintained than IBM's?

To answer this question, we have to go back to the young couple at Harry's appliance store in Phoenix. If they can afford the purchase, they will return to Harry's to buy their air conditioner. When you buy from Harry, you buy from the best. If anything goes wrong, you can rely on good old Harry. In the same way, when you buy from IBM, you don't just get a computer, you get IBM with the deal—a value of considerable weight in any purchase decision. If the buyer buys and the computer doesn't work, there is no second guessing. "Hey, what more could we do? We went with IBM." IBM doesn't just design, build, and deliver the product; IBM is the product. IBM says so, just as loudly and as often as it can, and we get the message.

While most business schools still teach an approach to management and management science more appropriately described as "industrial management," this situation is changing today. The stunning success of corporations like McDonald's, Federal Express, ServiceMaster Industries, and ARA Services—all companies whose products are almost purely services—has caused academics, entrepreneurs, and eager business school graduates to look at service industries with a new respect. Those organizations, which are among the most profitable and fastest growing in the country, could never have achieved the results they have achieved without highly competent, sophisticated management. Managers in such companies as well as in financial services organizations like American Express, Citicorp, Phibro-Salomon, Allied Bancshares, and Dun & Bradstreet, as well as retailers like Wal-Mart, Melville, Super Valu Stores, Southland, Lucky Stores, and Dayton-Hudson, are proving that service is both big business and a challenge to the most demanding of management minds.[10]

## The Service Management Challenge

Economics and sociology have conspired. Carl Sandburg's "Stormy, husky, brawling, City of Big Shoulders" Chicago—which was America's "Hog Butcher for the World, Tool Maker, Stacker of Wheat, Player with Railroads"— is but a romantic memory today. Service is now the business of business in America. The capacity to serve customers effectively and efficiently is an issue every organization must face. No one can evade this challenge: manufacturers and traditional service providers, profit-making and nonprofit organizations, private-sector and public enterprises must all face the task of responding effectively and efficiently to customers and consumers who expect quality and service as a part of every purchase. Some organizations are well aware of this need and have responded to it. For others, the need to be customer focused and service preoccupied comes as a rude surprise. But it cannot be ignored; it is not a momentary fad that will suddenly go away. It is the new standard used by customers and consumers to measure organizational performance. Increasingly, the marketplace is opting to do business with those who serve, and declining involvement with those who merely supply.

Organization concerned with honing a competitive edge for the 1980s, 1990s, and beyond must develop two new capacities. The first is the ability to think strategically about service and to build a strong service orientation around and into the vision of their strategic future. The second capacity, which is perhaps more difficult to develop, is the ability to effectively and efficiently manage the design, development, and delivery of service. In our view the ability to manage the production and delivery of a service differs from the ability to manage the production and delivery of a commodity. It requires a familiarity with the idea of an intangible having economic value, and a deftness in conceptualizing intangible outcomes. It requires a tolerance for ambiguity, an ease in dealing with lack of direct control over every key process, and a finely tuned appreciation of the notion that the organization is equally dependent on soft (or people-related) skills and hard (or production-related) skills. Last but not least, it requires a tolerance for—perhaps even an enjoyment of—sudden and sometimes dramatic change. The only constant in service is change.

## Notes

1. Russell Ackoff, Paul Broholm, and Roberta Snow, *Revitalizing Western Economies* (San Francisco: Jossey-Bass, 1984), 2. Ackoff, Broholm, and Snow take issue with Naisbitt and others who use the term "postindustrial" to describe the current economy, and who spring from there to the argument that the shift in the economy's population base is from industrial to informational. They argue that postindustrial connotes the demise of industry rather than a shift in the employment base, which is clearly much more the case. They further argue that for Naisbitt and others to be correct, the shift in the employment would have to be toward jobs directly involved with information technology. This, according to all available statistics, is not the case. The data that exist clearly show that the employment shift in all of the more developing countries of the world is away from employment in manufacturing and toward employment in services. But there is also an equivocation to be observed. "Nevertheless, the changes occurring in both goods-producing and service industries are largely due to technological developments relating to the generation, processing, transmission, storage, and retrieval of information, particularly the microprocessor." Their point should not be lost. On the whole, most of the new jobs being created in the United States today are in the service sector and *not* directly related to information manipulation.

2. Several good books and essays make this point. The most critical is by Barbara Tuchman, "The Decline of Quality," *New York Times Magazine* (2 November 1980). A nice photo essay on the same subject was done by Jeremy Man, "Toward Service without a Snarl," *Fortune* (3 March 1981). You have to overlook a bit of "one-simply-can't-get-good-help" snobbishness in these laments of service quality, but they do make their point.

3. The Arthur Andersen & Co. study was a Delphic forecast effort that went two rounds and involved 100 people split into four panels—twenty-five service industry people, twenty-five business planners, twenty-five technology mavens, and twenty-five customers—DP and telecommunications executives. The report is available for $100 a copy from the Association of Field Service Managers, 7273 President Court, Fort Meyer, Fla. 33902.

   The report doesn't suggest that primary providers of computer service, the manufacturers, are about to get completely out of that part of the business. These providers "must keep offering service as part of their sales and marketing strategy," regardless of how minimal and shoddy that service may be.

   A friend of ours recently regaled us with the trials and tribulations she was experiencing trying to get a fix on a microcomputer hard disk storage device. It seems that the dealer who talked her into buying it, and who, coincidentally, advertises the fact that he has factory-trained technicians, had no one on staff qualified to service it. "A marginal product for us," the store manager told her, as if an understanding of his economics was going to convince her that the repair of this very expensive paperweight was not his problem. Frustrated on her first attempt at a remedy, our friend called the manufacturer. There she was told that she couldn't expect the manufacturer to deal with her problem—they were much too busy for that. "Go back to the dealer you bought it from," she was told. "The dealer won't help me," she replied. "Then you're in tough shape, Sweetie." Click! Eventually someone at the seller's store, who had experienced the same problem and solved it for himself, was able to repair the unit. But the damage was done. When the time came for our friend's department to plunge into full computerization, her horror story raised enough hackles that the offending equipment was considered too risky for adoption, and the dealer—despite a 25 percent corporate discount policy—was classified as too unreliable a supplier. Oh yes, that particular piece of hardware has recently joined the ranks of the orphaned. It is word of mouth like this that keeps some of us snug as a bug in the Apple/IBM rug.

4. Technical Assistance Research Programs Inc. (TARP) is located in Washington, D.C., if you are interested in more of their data, and there is certainly a lot more of it that we have shared with you here. They have done extensive work on a number of consumer satisfaction issues and their dollars-and-cents implications. They have studied the value of word of mouth in the soft drink industry, the use of 800 numbers as a consumer satisfaction tool, and the role of consumer satisfaction in automobile and auto parts purchase and repurchase.

The TARP formula for profits from complaint handling is an interesting exercise in logic. You buy the assumption and you will be happy with the way they come to the conclusion that a satisfied consumer is worth a lot of money.

Profit = Long-term profits from loyal customer
+ Word of Mouth
+ Regulatory response cost avoided
− Cost of handling

The half-million dollar figure was derived from data developed for the Clairol Corporation, not from P & G. The key variables are a five-year purchase history, 70 percent loyalty rate for satisfied customer complaints, one new sale for every complaint favorably handled, a $500 cost or regulatory response, a 1:200 complaint to an agency rate, and administrative costs of $5.50 for each company responded to.

5. Ibid.

6. Ronald Kent Shelp, John C. Stephenson, Nancy Sherwood Truitt, and Bernard Wasow, *Service Industries and Economic Development* (New York: Praeger Publishers, 1985), 3. Ron Shelp is an insurance executive who is one of the leading authorities on the role of services in the world economy. Several federal administrations have appointed him to commissions on service industries. Maybe he can get them to drop the system of classifying 60 percent of the GNP under the meaningless rubric of "services."

7. Ibid., 4–5. Actually, the stages we describe are derived or adapted from Shelp; his description is focused on the needs of developing nations today. The problem he looks at is a good one. How can a developing or less-developed nation move toward a well-managed service sector without repeating the stages Western countries have trekked through? This is no idle question in the face of the possibility that time and technology won't allow developing countries to take that route.

8. Theodore Levitt, "After the Sale is Over...," *Harvard Business Review* (September-October 1983): 88–89. An important point here is that Levitt is not talking about the idea of relationship selling. Relationship selling has been a buzz phrase in the sales and sales training game for many years. What Levitt describes

is relationship building between the buying *organization* and the selling *organization*. This is a more involved process than relationship selling, which can loosely be translated as, "Make the purchasing agent like you, and he'll buy from you." Perhaps the most descriptive phrase would be relationship marketing, the thrust of which is to form a long-term liaison with the customer rather than make a single sale. (Reprinted with permission of *Harvard Business Review*. Excerpt from "After the sale is over..." by the President and Fellows of Harvard College; all rights reserved.)

9. Ibid., 87

10. Probably the most instructive reading on the topic of new respectability for service sector companies is a pair of *Fortune* magazine articles, the first of which, "Ten Years of Bounding Profits" (11 June 1984) features profiles of the most successful Fortune Service 500 companies and compares their overall results with the more dismal performance of the Fortune Industrial 500 list. The second article is "Corporate Stars that Brightened a Dark Decade" (30 April 1984). Here we are treated to the stories of thirteen companies that had an average 20 percent ROE for the ten years 1974–1983. Number two on the list, Dow Jones & Company, Inc., is a service company, but more interesting is the fact that eight of the thirteen are organizations with a strong service reputation in their home industry.

# 4

# World War II and the Quality Movement

*J. M. Juran*

World War II was a major upheaval in human affairs. Its profound effects extended to the quality movement. It created discontinuities and a long train of aftershocks. The end of these is not yet in sight.

To understand these profound effects, it is not enough to look solely at events that took place during 1941 to 1945, the period during which the United States was a full combatant in the war. Neither is it enough to look just at that long train of aftershocks. It is necessary in addition to look at the convergence of forces that preceded the war.

As it happens, I have been a close observer of the quality movement for nearly seven decades. In addition I have been, to a modest degree, one of the architects of many of the changes that have taken place during our turbulent century. I will therefore deal with the full spectrum of events—the key events—that took place before, during, and after World War II.

## The Quality Movement Before World War II

Managing for quality in the United States has evolved as a series of distinct phases, with much overlap between phases.

### Craftsmanship

The early colonists brought with them the European concept of craftsmanship. A young man learned a skilled trade as a master's apprentice. The master instructed the apprentice in the production processes and in how to produce the finished product. The master also maintained a form of quality control by inspecting the finished goods before selling them to the client. In large shops, the master might assign an experienced craftsman to be a part-time inspector/instructor.

---

Once the apprentice had learned his trade, he became self-employed or employed by the master of a shop who hired many craftsmen. Either way, the craftsman was in a state of self-control and self-inspection.

Quality was usually in good hands—the hands of the craftsmen. Most goods were sold locally, which meant that the craftsman had a significant personal stake in meeting his customers' needs for quality.

## The Industrial Revolution

The Industrial Revolution created the factory system. It forced most craftsmen to become factory employees. The masters became production supervisors. The factories also employed semiskilled and unskilled people as well as craftsmen. Managing for quality remained largely a production department function, but use of inspectors was expanded. Large production departments employed full-time inspectors who reported to the respective production supervisors.

## The Taylor System

Late in the nineteenth century, the Taylor system of separating planning from execution emerged in the United States. It made possible a considerable increase in production and productivity without a corresponding increase in the number of skilled craftsmen. In my judgment, it was the Taylor system, more than any other factor, that brought the United States to world leadership in productivity. However, there was a price to be paid. The Taylor system had serious negative effects, notably on human relations and quality.

## Independent Inspection Departments

Of course, companies wanted quality as well as productivity. Their solution was to move the production inspectors into newly created independent inspection departments. These new departments were then headed by a chief inspector who reported either to the head of production or to the plant manager.

The major job of the new inspection departments was to keep defective products from reaching customers. This was done by various forms of inspection. Raw materials and goods in process were commonly sampled. The results of the sampling determined the disposition of the lot. Finished goods were usually inspected in detail to separate the good from the bad.

In many companies, the assignment of responsibility for quality took a curious turn. If defective goods did get out to clients, it was common for upper managers to ask the chief inspector, "Why did you let this get out?" It was less common to ask the production department, "Why did you make it this way?" In due course, there evolved a widely held belief that quality was the responsibility of the inspection department.

*The Obstacles to Prevention*

In those days, there was no debate about the merits of preventing defects from happening in the first place. A major limitation was the organizational barriers. I can recall an incident that took place in about 1926 that illustrates the then-prevailing views.

I was a young engineer in the Hawthorne Works of Western Electric Company, which was then the manufacturing arm of the Bell Telephone System. I was assigned to clear up a shop complaint involving high defect rates on electrical resistance of certain tiny, mass-produced circuit breakers. I collected data on the process performance and found that the process was inherently highly reproducible. I also identified the two critical variables that caused high defect rates. As it happened, the production supervisor was then able to provide remedies. Once these remedies were in place, it was virtually impossible for the process to make that type of defect.

I was impressed by the way a rather simple study made it possible to eliminate a costly chronic defect. I then proposed to my supervisors that we go after such chronic wastes on a large scale. They agreed on the need but not on my approach. In the culture of the factory, defect prevention was the responsibility of the production department, not the inspection department. So everything remained on dead center. Production had the responsibility but not the capability for making such studies. Inspection had the capability but could not act unless invited. The unwritten law was, "You do your job, and I'll do mine." The concept that some jobs required a team approach was only beginning to evolve.

*The Contributions of Science and Technology*

During the early decades of the twentieth century, the major contributions to quality came from expanded use of science and technology, replacing empiricism. Companies such as the Bell System and General Electric established laboratories to develop new materials and design new products. Synthetic materials began to replace natural materials. New product designs created new features to stimulate client interest. Competition in the marketplace prompted companies to develop better and better features. Additional advances were made in related fields, such as metrology.

In the factories, engineers were employed to develop new manufacturing processes. These engineered processes were needed to meet the greater precision and uniformity demanded by new product designs. As a result, the engineered processes began to replace those that had been handed down through generations of craftsmen.

While the advances in technology were impressive, the advancements in managing for quality were not. In particular, two major problems were not being addressed adequately:

- the unreliability of the products, resulting in extensive field failures, high costs of field service, and much customer dissatisfaction;
- the costs of factory waste due to relying on inspection and test, rather than preventing the defects from happening in the first place.

During those decades, the upper managers of companies made their contributions to quality mainly by supporting the technologists—by providing the funds for the laboratories and the engineering personnel. They regarded these funds as investments needed to sustain and increase sales. The upper managers made no contributions to the processes of managing for quality; they were detached from them. Quality had been delegated to the inspection departments. In turn, these departments were handicapped by the jurisdictional barriers prevailing in the functional organization structures.

The professional engineering societies of those early decades were primarily oriented to their respective technological specialties. The budding industrial engineering societies were oriented to productivity. There was no society oriented specifically to quality. My first published paper was presented at a quality-oriented session held during a regional conference of the American Society of Mechanical Engineers.[1] About fifty people attended this conference, which took place in Cincinnati, Ohio in 1935. The papers dealt mainly with inspection and test.

### The First Wave of Statistical Quality Control

The mid-1920s witnessed the first significant wave of so-called statistical quality control (SQC). It was initiated in 1926 when a team from the Bell Telephone Laboratories proposed that the Western Electric Company apply certain tools of statistical methodology to control the quality of manufactured telephone products. Those tools were:

- the newly invented Shewhart control chart;
- using probability theory to put sampling inspection on a scientific basis;
- implementing a demerits plan for evaluating outgoing quality of telephone products.

That initiative resulted in the creation of a Joint Committee on Inspection Statistics and Economy. At that time, the Hawthorne Works was notably lacking in people trained in statistical methodology. So Walter Bartky, a young professor from the University of Chicago, was brought in to conduct a statistics course for about fifteen or twenty managers and engineers. I attended that course. Then a new department—the inspection statistical department—was created, consisting of a boss and two engineers. I was one of those engineers. That department might well have been the first such department in American industrial history.

In this new job, I became closely involved with the premiere effort to apply statistical tools to quality control of manufacturing processes and products. I also became closely associated with the cognizant Bell Laboratories personnel: George Edwards, Walter Shewhart, Harold Dodge, and others.

The most fruitful activity of the Joint Committee on Inspection Statistics and Economy turned out to be the development of sampling tables. The inspection branch at Hawthorne had made extensive use of sampling, but in empirical and primitive ways. The joint efforts produced numerous innovations: the identification and terminology of sampling risks; an assortment of sampling plans—single, double, and continuous; the average outgoing quality limit (AOQL) concept; the process average concept, which was an early version of the process capability concept; and so on. In due course, derivatives of these sampling plans emerged as published sampling tables: MIL-STD-105, the Dodge-Romig tables, and many others.

In contrast, the control chart concept did not arouse much interest at Hawthorne. This lack of interest was simply due to the fact that the major quality problems at Hawthorne required remedies of a far more fundamental sort.

- The physical layout of that huge plant was like a colony resulting in long production intervals, huge process inventories, gridlocked transportation, chaotic paperwork, and other problems.
- Manufacturing planning was done empirically. The planners had no grasp of the concept of quantifying process variability. Measuring instruments were mostly of the go/nogo type to facilitate sorting of good products from bad.
- The priorities assigned to the production departments were to meet the schedules, achieve high productivity, and maintain piecework earnings. Quality was left to the inspection department.

During the 1920s, the committee activities had an impact on Bell System practices, notably with respect to sampling inspection. However, there was, at the time, hardly any impact on the U.S. economy. The latter had to await the events of World War II. During that war, the work done by the joint committee became the basis for the wartime training courses in SQC, the various published sampling tables, and other developments.

## Quality during World War II

U.S. involvement in World War II began during the late 1930s, as a supplier to the Allies. The attack on Pearl Harbor in December, 1941, brought the country into the war as a combatant. Legislation was then enacted to put the country on a war footing. A War Production Board was created to gear the civilian economy to the war machine. Regulations were established to give the war effort priority in the allocation of facilities, materials, skilled manpower, and services of all sorts. Production of a wide range of civilian products, including automobiles and household appliances, came to a halt. All the while defense factory employees were working overtime and building up a great hoard of purchasing power.

## The Effect on Quality of Mill Products

The effort to produce both guns and butter resulted in widespread shortages. The effect on quality was severe—quality always declines during a time of shortages. The top priority was on meeting the delivery schedules. This was underscored by the system of awarding the coveted Army-Navy "E" to government contractors for meeting delivery schedules.

The war greatly enlarged the armed forces' problem of ensuring that the products delivered by contractors were adequate for quality. The traditional government approach had been to award contracts based on competitive bidding. Ensuring quality was then based on inspection and testing for conformance to specifications. In many cases, this involved inspecting and testing every single product.

This same basic approach was retained during World War II. It required a huge expansion of the inspection forces, with massive problems in recruitment, training, and employee turnover. The armed forces tried to reduce these problems by greater use of sampling inspection. In doing so, it decided to replace its empirical ways of sampling with a method based on the laws of probability. With the aid of industry consultants, especially from the Bell Telephone laboratories, it adapted the sampling tables that had been devised by the Bell System.

The resulting tables were published as MIL-STD-105 and were incorporated into the contracts by reference. In turn, many contractors referenced these same tables in the contracts they made with their suppliers. This practice was extended to nonmilitary contracts and continues to this day.

## The Second Wave of SQC

One department of the War Production Board was given the mission of helping industrial companies contribute to the war effort. A section of that department was set up to help companies meet quality requirements. As it happened, two professors of statistics were appointed to lead that section. To no one's surprise, they decided to help industry by training companies in the tools of statistics. Their decision led to the famous eight-day courses on statistical quality control.

These free courses were held in many locations throughout the country. During the eight days, the attendees were trained mainly in probability theory, sampling theory, and the Shewhart control chart. The story of the eight-day courses has been well documented [2,3] (I was not involved in this training.

During the four years of the war, I was occupied as assistant lend-lease administrator and assistant foreign economic administrator.)

The course attendees included inspection supervisors and chief inspectors.
Some had difficulty grasping the subject matter. Others were skeptical about
being able to make practical use of the new tools in their culture.

The course attendees also included young engineers who could readily understand the subject matter. Many of them became enthusiastic about the possibility of using the new tools to help their companies improve the methods of
quality control.

## A New Job Category: Quality Control Engineering

On return to their companies, the young enthusiasts devised various ways
of putting their new tools to use.

- They prepared and published training manuals that included instructions
  for using the sampling tables and control charts. They also became the in-
  house SQC trainers.
- They organized data systems for preparing control charts.
- They investigated out-of-control conditions by using the factual approach—collecting and analyzing data.
- They prepared manuals that included procedures for inspection and test,
  control of accuracy of measuring instruments, and disposition of noncon-
  forming products.
- They introduced the concept of quality audits to ensure that procedures in
  quality manuals were followed.
- They began to evolve quality reports for use by the factory managers.

The conduct of these functions created a demand for a new job category for
the young enthusiasts. The companies responded positively, and amid a wel-
ter of new titles the term *quality control engineer* emerged dominant.

### Quality Control Departments

As quality control engineers came into being, there arose the question
"Where shall we put them on the organization chart?" The companies concluded not to make them subordinate to the chief inspectors. Instead, the companies created a new department for them. Common titles were "statistical
quality control department" and "quality engineering department."

A further question arose, "Where should we put the new department on the
organization chart?" Most companies decided to create a new managerial office, the "quality control department," to be headed by a quality control manager. This manager then presided over the old inspection department and the
new quality engineering department.

The new quality control department now occupied a higher place in the company hierarchy than any previous organizational unit had. This was not solely the result of the wave of interest in SQC. An even greater influence was the post-war decline of product quality due to shortages (see the post-World War II section that follows).

*Quality Control Societies*

One aspect of the eight-day courses appealed to all attendees: they relished the opportunity to meet for eight days with people who faced the problems of quality control in other companies. For many attendees, this opportunity for sharing experiences was unprecedented. In some areas, they proceeded to create local societies to enable such sharing to go on and on. These local societies then merged in 1946 to form the American Society for Quality Control.

## Post-World War II: The Aftershocks

When World War II ended in 1945, there was a massive shortage of and a great demand for consumer goods. It took many years to refill the pipelines. During those years, the quality of products declined severely. The old, experienced manufacturers gave top priority to volume of production; each wanted to secure maximum share of market. The shortages also attracted new competitors whose inexperience contributed further to the decline in quality.

*The Effect of the Shortages*

Shortages created a subtle habit among manufacturers; meeting schedules was given top priority. As the years went on, this priority found its way into the company policies and procedures. Companies then developed a vested interest in this habit and resisted change.

During the years of shortages, merchants didn't complain about quality. They feared that their suppliers might reduce their allocations. Then, as the pipelines filled up, the complaints about quality became intense. Unqualified suppliers soon disappeared, but poor quality still threatened the market share of the survivors. That threat then attracted the attention of the marketers and upper managers. The usual solution was to strengthen inspection and testing. In turn, this solution took two major forms. One was to create a new function of reliability engineering. The other was to raise the stature of the quality control department.

Reliability engineering was a response to the growing problem of field failures of durable goods. Conventional quality control had focused on inspection and test before shipment, but this did not ensure that the products would perform reliably during use in the field. Therefore, reliability engineering evolved to develop tools and procedures that would help supply additional guarantees that products would work.

Many companies recognized the need and proceeded to create a new job category of reliability engineer. Some went further and established a department of reliability engineering. In such cases, the new department became a part of the quality control department.

The quality control department, however, was changed as well. It now housed the functions of inspection and test, quality engineering, reliability engineering, and quality audit. In addition, there was a need to give it added organizational status to help it deal with the entrenched habit of giving top priority to meeting schedules. To provide this new status, the department name was typically changed to "quality assurance department." The chief was typically given the title of quality manager, and he typically reported to the vice-president of manufacturing. Considering that, early in the century, the organization charts were devoid of anything oriented to quality, this was high status indeed.

### The Decline of SQC

An important reason for the spread of SQC was that the wartime government paid the costs. Defense contracts were usually of cost-plus nature. The termination of defense contracts also ended the associated SQC programs; however, this was by no means universal. Many SQC departments had generated a momentum that sustained matters—for a while. These departments were producing visible outputs: sampling tables, control charts, training in statistical methods, inspection plans, quality manuals, audits, and reports.

Nevertheless, these departments were vulnerable to the next economic recession. Their vulnerability arose from the fact that most of their activities were tool oriented, not oriented to results as judged by the upper managers. The measures of progress were in terms of number of people trained, number of active control charts, and the like. The action was focused on sporadic blips as they appeared on the control charts. The major quality problems, however, were the chronic wastes that went on and on.

To make matters worse, too many of the SQC applications went to extremes. In some companies, control charts were placed at every machine, yet the production workers made no use of the charts because the concept had not been accepted by the production managers. (The charts were being maintained by the process inspectors.) In other companies, two worlds existed. One was the SQC office, its walls covered with control charts consisting of the vital few and the uneconomic many. The other world was the world of operations. It made the product. No effective link existed between the two worlds.

In due course, the recession came. As is customary, the companies reviewed each staff activity, "What value does this contribute to justify its existence?" Most of the SQC activities were judged to have failed the test of return on investment. The end result was a widespread downsizing. In many companies, the word "statistical" was dropped from department names—it had become a symbol of preoccupation with tools rather than problems and solutions.

In most companies, certain activities survived the downsizing: inspection planning, sampling tables, written procedures, and selective use of control charts. In some process industries, there was growing interest in design of experiments and analysis of variance. Central to all was the survival of the factual approach—the principle that decisions on quality should be based on data collection and analysis, rather than on empiricism.

## The Emergence of Assurance under Surveillance

Following World War II, the U.S. armed services reviewed their wartime activities to improve future performance. One of the Air Force reviews led to a major change in the approach to quality assurance, a change that affected the military sector and later the civilian sector.

The military approach to quality assurance had been mainly inspection and testing of the finished product. The Air Force review found that, to cope with the huge growth in wartime purchases, the response had been to increase the inspection force by about twelvefold. The associated problems of recruitment and training were severe, yet the use of inspection and testing did not provide adequate levels of quality assurance. The Air Force decided to create a new approach; assurance would come mainly from establishing not only criteria for a plan of quality assurance, but also government surveillance of contractors' conformance to the plan.

This new concept was described in Air Force standard AF 5923. In due course, the same concept was embodied in the Defense Department standard MIL-Q-9858. Subsequently, revised versions were adopted by numerous countries, NATO, and the International Organization for Standardization (ISO) in the ISO 9000 series of standards.

At the outset, this new assurance concept was applied only to military contracts and subcontracts. Then, as companies gained experience, they incorporated the concept into their civilian purchase contracts. The most recent development has been in Europe, where the trend has been to establish a register of companies that conform to the criteria for the ISO 9000 series of standards. In turn, conformance is to be judged by certified assessors.

## The Japanese Revolution

Some Japanese are convinced that a major reason behind their quality revolution was the fact that Japan lost the war. Their reasoning is that, had they won, they would have seen no need to change their approach to quality or to anything else. The traumatic shock of losing the war forced them to open their minds, to search for a new approach, and to be willing to put it into effect. This theory is quite logical in the light of historical events.

In the decades preceding the war, the militarists had enormous influence over the Japanese economy. They used that influence to secure the budgets needed to build a military machine able to achieve national goals through conquest. The armaments they built were competitive in quality to those of the West and did a lot of damage during World War II.

During those same decades, the Japanese civilian economy received low priorities for funds and materials, and this included the foreign trade sector. The country did try to earn foreign exchange through exports, but the low priorities seriously handicapped the efforts to make and export high-quality products. (An added problem was the lack of knowledge about the quality standards of the West.) The resulting export of poor-quality goods was so extensive that Japan became widely perceived as a producer of low-priced, shoddy goods.

The crushing defeat then forced Japan to choose a new direction. Now national goals would have to be met by peaceful means and especially through foreign trade. The major companies had all been suppliers to the military. To survive, they were forced to convert to civilian goods and exports. As they did so it became obvious that the national reputation for poor quality was a major obstacle to selling Japanese products to the West. To change that reputation required a revolution in quality. The shock of the military defeat opened up minds and contributed to the companies' willingness to undertake a revolutionary change in direction.

The Japanese quality revolution had an enormous impact on the U.S. economy. Numerous industries lost large shares of market to Japanese competitors, chiefly for reasons of quality. A huge trade imbalance developed. Millions of jobs were "exported" to Japan.

The impact of the new competition in quality required a response from the affected companies. They tested a wide variety of strategies; most were hopelessly inadequate. Then, during the 1980s, a few companies adopted a mixture of strategies that succeeded in achieving world-class quality. The strategies that produced those results have been identified, and the common success factors are well known. The likelihood is that these success factors will be widely adopted in the United States during the 1990s.

### The Deming Prize

A further outgrowth of the Japanese quality revolution was the Deming Prize, named for W. Edwards Deming who, starting in 1947, made significant contributions to the revolution by traveling to Japan to help revitalize industry. The prize had a modest beginning in the early 1950s. Then, with the passing of years, it attained national attention and influence through the cumulative publicity generated by the winning companies. The concept of a national quality award later became one of the stimuli for creating the Malcolm Baldrige National Quality Award in the United States.

## The Third Wave of SQC

In 1980, there emerged a widely viewed videocast, "If Japan Can, Why Can't We?" One segment discussed quality. It concluded that Japanese quality was due to their use of statistical methods taught to them by Deming. This conclusion had little relation to reality; however, the program was cleverly presented and was persuasive to many viewers. The effects were astonishing. Some major companies used statistical methods as a panacea for their quality problems and required their suppliers to do the same.

Collectively these initiatives converged to become a near-national movement. The media provided additional stimuli. The term "statistical process control" (SPC) became the popular label for the movement. An enormous demand arose for training of company personnel in the tools of statistical methods. This demand spawned a whole cottage industry of new consultants. The videocast had brought Deming out of obscurity and into national attention. It also enabled the new consultants to market their services by labeling themselves as Deming disciples.

This third wave has been much more results oriented than its predecessors. SPC seems likely to become a permanent addition to the tools of managing for quality. However, during the 1980s many companies limited their quality initiative to SPC, assuming it was the cure-all claimed by the advocates. Those companies lost precious years before learning that world-class quality comes from a broad spectrum of strategies, none of which is a panacea.

## Prognosis: The 1990s and Beyond

The U.S. quality crisis deepened during the 1980s despite the application of numerous remedies. Some of these were misguided efforts: political solutions, exhortation, and the like. Others were narrowly focused efforts, mostly the commonly administered training in statistical tools. There was little effect on the economy as a whole.

The lack of visible progress gave rise to a school of defeatism, which contended that the U.S. culture was not as well adapted to producing quality as the Japanese culture was. Ironically, the latter was the same culture that, before World War II, had a national reputation as a producer of shoddy goods.

However, during the 1980s a small number of U.S. companies distinguished themselves by raising their quality to world-class levels. (Some of these companies became winners of the Malcolm Baldrige National Quality Award.) The results they achieved and the methods they used to get those results have been published.

The fact that such results were achieved proves that world-class quality is achievable within the U.S. culture. (The logic being if those companies did it, it is doable.) The job ahead then becomes one of scaling up.[4]

In addition, there are lessons to be learned from the experiences of the successful companies. The common success factors are:

- focusing on customer needs;
- continuous quality improvement;
- upper managers in charge of quality;
- training the entire hierarchy to manage for quality;
- employee involvement.

The 1990s will also see an accelerated adoption of additional strategies that have been undergoing tests:

- applying quality improvement to business processes;
- planning for quality on a structured basis to replace empiricism;
- replacing the Taylor system with methods such as self-control and self-directing teams of workers;
- putting quality goals into the business plan and converting the goals into action through deployment.

Collectively, the successful strategies are labeled by names such as "total quality management" (TQM). TQM can be defined only by setting out the specific strategies in the collection.

The achievement of world-class quality has profoundly affected the outlook of upper managers. Some CEOs, both here and in Japan, have told me, "Our prime concern is about quality. If quality is right, then everything else will be right." No U.S. or Japanese CEO told me that in the early 1950s. They now do so because they have acquired the faith of the true believer—they have witnessed the miracle.

### Notes

1. "Inspectors' errors in quality control," *Mechanical Engineering* (October, 1935): 643–44.
2. An extensive account of the eight-day courses was given by Holbrook Working in the *Journal of the American Statistical Association* (December, 1945): 425–47. See also Eugene L. Grants's Shewhart Medal address in *Industrial Quality Control* (July, 1953): 31–35.
3. Additional information on World War II training courses is contained in the fourteen videocassettes published by AT&T as "A History of Quality Control and Assurance at AT&T, 1920-1970." These videocassettes contain interviews with Ralph Wareham, W. Edwards Deming, myself, and others. They are available from the AT&T Customer Information Center, phone 800-432-6600, select code 500-721.

4. Juran, J. M., "Strategies for World-Class Quality," *Quality Progress* (March, 1991): 81–85.

# 5

# History of the Malcolm Baldrige National Quality Award

*Neil J. DeCarlo and W. Kent Sterett*

The Malcolm Baldrige National Quality Improvement Act was signed by President Ronald Reagan on 20 August 1987. The act is part of a national campaign to improve the quality of goods and services in the United States. It demonstrates the growing cooperation of business and government to achieve this goal.

Named after the late secretary of commerce, the National Quality Award represents the highest level of recognition for quality that an American company can receive. The award program, however, did not simply appear overnight; it was the culmination of years of effort by a diverse coalition. The roots of the effort go back to the beginning of the 1980s.

## Initial Support

By the early 1980s, government and industry leaders in the United States had become concerned about the nation's ability to increase productivity and compete for world markets. With the intention of encouraging greater productivity and competitiveness, President Reagan signed legislation mandating a national study/conference on productivity in October, 1982.

The law stated that American productivity was declining. As a result, American goods were becoming more costly—and less competitive—in the international market and jobs were being lost. The bill also pointed to a possible solution to the problem of declining productivity, "Productivity improvement can be restored in the United States through the application of policies and management techniques which have brought substantial productivity on a broad scale in other countries and in some businesses within the United States."

This chapter is adapted from an article that appeared in *Quality, The Journal of the Japanese Society for Quality Control,* in July, 1989.

At the time of this legislation, an effort was already underway to advise labor, management, and government on ways to develop national quality awareness through a mutual spirit of commitment, consensus seeking, and cooperation. The effort began in late 1981 under the leadership of the American Society for Quality Control and Alvin O. Gunneson, then-corporate vice-president of quality for Revlon. The effort led to the formation in February, 1982 of the National Advisory Council for Quality (NACQ), a broad-based group of private- and public-sector executives committed to quality.

The goal of NACQ was to become the recognized center for training, publications, conferences, and research in the quality disciplines.

Parallel efforts were being driven by the American Productivity and Quality Center—a nonprofit organization committed to improving productivity, quality, and competitiveness. In preparation for the upcoming White House Conference on Productivity, APQC sponsored seven computer networking conferences from April to September, 1983. The organization raised $1 million to pay for the conferences, which received and coordinated input from about 175 corporate executive, business leaders, and academicians. The need for a national quality and productivity award was an idea that surfaced repeatedly during the computer networking sessions.

The final report on the computer conferences recommended that "a National Quality Award, similar to the Deming Prize Award in Japan, [should] be awarded annually to those firms that successfully challenge and meet the award requirements. These requirements and the accompanying examination process should be very similar to the Deming Prize system to be effective." A special task force, comprised of members of the computer conferences, had already begun examining ways to set up the award.

The report also recommended the creation of a national quality association to promote quality in American products and services, similar to the Union of Japanese Scientists and Engineers (JUSE). Association membership would consist of senior managers and CEOs drawn from a broad spectrum of industries, representatives from labor and academia, and senior government officials.

In the same month that the final report was issued (September, 1983) the White House Conference on Productivity was conducted. Keynote speakers were President Reagan; Vice-President George Bush; Treasure Secretary Donald Regan, counselor to the president Edwin Meese III; and Commerce Secretary Malcolm Baldrige.

In December, 1983, the National Productivity Advisory Committee (NPAC)—a group of corporate executives, academicians, labor leaders, and government officials appointed by the president—recommended the creation of a national medal for productivity achievement. The recommendation, however, was tabled by the Cabinet Council on Economic Affairs because the committee was unable to offer viable direction for funding, guidelines, criteria, and other details of award administration.

A report on the White House Conference on Productivity was published in April, 1984. The opening paragraph of the executive summary put the matter bluntly, "America is the most productive nation in the world, but its growth in productivity has faltered. Some of the factors contributing to slower productivity growth are within our control and some are not, but it is important that we respond to this challenge." Further on, the executive summary struck an optimistic note. "Leaders from business, labor, academia, and government assembled for the White House Conference concluded that we can attain a higher rate of productivity growth if management and labor, and business and government, will work together to do it."

The report called for a national medal for productivity achievement to be awarded annually by the president in recognition of high levels of productivity achievement by organizations. Also recommended was a quality-awareness campaign at the national level in both the public and private sectors to demonstrate the importance of improving quality, productivity, and international competitiveness.

## Ongoing Efforts

By the mid-1980s, business and government leaders had drawn considerable attention to concerns about productivity and quality. Groups in both the public and private sector made hundreds of recommendations to improve quality and productivity growth in America. Many of these recommendations called for a national award.

About this time Jackson Grayson, APQC's chairman of the board, contacted Roger Porter, deputy assistant to President Reagan, to solicit presidential involvement in the award program. Grayson proposed that the award be presented by the president to ensure its impact, visibility, and prestige. He was careful to point out, however, that winners should be selected by the private sector to avoid political influence.

Substantive work on the award was begun in September, 1985 with the formation of the Committee to Establish a National Quality Award, an entirely private-sector group of academicians and corporate quality business leaders from ASQC, APQC, NASA, Ford Motor Co., AVCO, McDonnell Douglas Corp., and other organizations.

The first matter that had to be settled was the name of the award. The committee—chaired by Frank Collins, rear admiral and executive of quality assurance for the Defense Logistics Agency—spent the first day of a meeting in Washington D.C., discussing that issue. The group was split among three choices: the National Quality-Productivity Award, the National Productivity-Quality Award, and the National Quality Award. The third option won out.

The effort had begun to gather momentum. In the ensuing months, basic structures for award administration, funding, and criteria began to take shape.

Sanford McDonnell of McDonnell Douglas made a preliminary funding commitment and agreed to line up other corporate support. A representative of Florida Power and Light (FPL)—which was already active in the concurrent effort to enact federal legislation for a national quality award—joined the committee's efforts in May, 1986.

By the fall of that year, draft criteria had been developed by the National Organization for the United States Quality Award, as the committee was now called. Meanwhile, White House officials had indicated support for the award, though no commitment was made for the president to present the award. By March, 1987, the committee received indications that Vice-President Bush might present the award.

The importance of these early efforts by ASQC, NACQ, APQC, and the award organization cannot be underestimated. Their work created the private sector mechanisms and laid the groundwork for a national quality award. But it was the legislation—the Malcolm Baldrige National Quality Improvement Act of 1987—that lifted the national quality award from idea to reality.

## Legislation for a National Quality Award

The effort to legislate a national quality award began on 20 January 1985. FPL's chairman and CEO, John J. Hudiburg, and FPL Group's chairman, Marshall McDonald, met with Congressman Don Fuqua (D-FL), then chairman of the House Committee on Science and Technology, and members of his staff. After hearing about the national revival in quality and the need for a national quality award, Fuqua asked FPL to work with his staff to draft legislation for the award. Subsequently, Hudiburg helped arrange for Fuqua and committee staff to visit Japan for the fourth meeting of the United States-Japan Parliamentary Committee on Science and Technology. There, Hudiburg explained the quality improvement program at FPL, while Kaoru Ishikawa explained the history and activities of JUSE.

In March, 1986, Fuqua sent staff members of the House Science, Research, and Technology Subcommittee to learn more about FPL's quality improvement program. The two-day visit with FPL's quality director W. Kent Sterett convinced the committee staff members that quality was worth their attention. The following six months were spent drafting legislation for a national quality award.

On 25 June 1986, Hudiburg, Joseph M. Juran, and John Hansel, ASQC's chairman of the board, testified before the subcommittee on "Strategies for Exploiting American Inventiveness in the World Marketplace." It was the first time a national quality award was discussed in a formal legislative meeting.

By this time legislation for a national quality award was written, and in August, 1986, Fuqua introduced House Bill 5321 "to establish a National Quality Improvement Award, with the objective of encouraging American business and industrial enterprises to practice effective quality control in the provision of their goods and services." Among the findings and purposes of the National Quality Improvement Act were that:

1. the leadership of the United States in product and process quality has been challenged strongly (and sometimes successfully) by foreign competition;
2. our Nation's productivity growth has decreased in relation to our competitors' over the last two decades as American business has grown more concerned about short-term profitability;
3. failure to alter this trend will lead to a lower standard of living and less opportunity for all Americans;
4. although several other factors may have contributed, the year 1985 saw Japan becoming the world's top creditor nation while the United States became a net debtor nation for the first time;
5. in Japan, the Union of Japanese Scientists and Engineers sponsors a national quality award—the Deming Prize—which provides a powerful incentive to Japanese companies to promote quality improvement;
6. American business and industry are beginning to understand that improved quality of goods and services goes hand in hand with improved productivity, lower costs, and increased profitability.

The bill also stated that the award program would help improve quality and productivity by:

- helping to stimulate American companies to improve quality and productivity for the pride of recognition while obtaining a competitive edge through increased profits;
- recognizing the achievements of those companies that improve the quality of their goods and services and providing an example to others;
- establishing guidelines and criteria that can be used by business, industrial, governmental, and other enterprises in evaluating their own quality improvement efforts;
- providing specific guidance for other American enterprises that wish to learn how to manage for high quality by making available detailed information on how winning enterprises were able to change their cultures and achieve eminence.

The bill called on the president or the secretary of commerce to present the award.

Although Congress took no further action on this bill and Fuqua left the House of Representatives, efforts continued to gain momentum. Congressman Doug Walgren (D-PA)—who had chaired the June, 1986, hearings on exploiting American inventiveness in the world marketplace—maintained the momentum by introducing House Bill 812, "National Quality Improvement Act of 1987." The bill was essentially the same as Fuqua's. Meanwhile, John Hudiburg tried to generate Senate support of the bill by contacting Senator Bob Graham (D-FL), former governor of Florida. This resulted in activity by Graham's staff that would later produce Senate Bill 1251, sponsored by Graham.

In March, 1987, the House Subcommittee on Science, Research, and Technology held hearings on Walgren's bill. Testifying were Hudiburg; Frank Gryna, of the Juran Institute; and William W. Eggleston, then-IBM corporate vice-president for quality.

On June 8 the measure passed the House and was sent to the Senate Committee on Commerce, Science, and Transportation. Before the Senate could act, a tragic accident occurred; Commerce Secretary Malcolm Baldrige was killed in a rodeo accident. Three days after Baldrige's death, the Senate committee renamed the legislation in his honor.

The bill was sent to the Senate floor and passed. The House unanimously agreed to he amendment, and on 20 August 1987 President Reagan signed the Malcolm Baldrige National Quality Improvement of 1987 into law.

## Award Organization and Funding

The National Institute of Standards and Technology (NIST), formerly the National Bureau of Standards, was chosen to direct and manage the award program. A well-respected organization, NIST was selected because of its reputation for impartiality.

The Baldrige legislation called for a Board of Overseers, consisting of at least five persons selected for their preeminence in the field of quality management. The board, which was appointed by the secretary of commerce in consultation with the director of NIST, provides broad direction to the program. It meets annually to review award activities and make recommendations for improvement.

Commerce Secretary C. William Verity asked John Hudiburg and Sanford N. McDonnell to raise money for the award program. The Foundation for the Malcolm Baldrige National Quality Award was created in February, 1988, with FPL and McDonnell-Douglas as its co-founders.

The foundation now has a forty-two-member Board of Trustees, a select group of CEOs, and presidents of major U.S. companies that strongly support total quality improvement.

The foundation and NIST have a mutual interest in soliciting gifts to support the program. However, every attempt is made to diminish the possibility of foundation contributors influencing the selection of winners. Information about contributors with respect to a particular award cycle is not furnished to NIST until all awards for that cycle have been granted. Moreover, information pertaining to contributions cannot be disclosed to a government employee or an individual serving on the Board of Examiners.

The foundation raised money by asking a broad cross-section of companies to make donations ranging from $25,000 to $150,000, payable in thirds over three years. Current pledges equal $10.4 million. Interest on that endowment, plus application fees, fund the program.

Day-to-day operations and administration of the award program are carried out by the Malcolm Baldrige National Quality Award Consortium—consisting of the American Society for Quality Control and the American Productivity and Quality Center—under contract with NIST. The consortium also designs and prepares instructional materials for use in the information transfer program and assists with award publicity.

The Board of Examiners is a three-tiered structure consisting of nine judges, twenty-eight senior examiners, and about one-hundred examiners. Selected on the basis of expertise, experience, and peer recognition by the director of NIST, in cooperation with the consortium judges and examiners, are quality experts. They come primarily from the private sector, but there is some representation from academia and government.

The judges were chosen by the director of NIST, Ernest Ambler, in consultation with consortium members; as government appointees, the judges underwent a White House clearance process. A slate of examiner nominees was developed by NIST with the aid of affiliated professional societies and miscellaneous recommendations.

The judges, in conjunction with NIST and Consortium members, selected the senior examiners and the examiners. Attention was paid, particularly at the judge and senior examiner level, to obtaining representation from different industries.

Affiliated organizations—such as professional societies, trade associations, and area councils—make award findings available for use in education and training throughout the United States.

## Criteria Development

The development of criteria for the 1988 award cycle was spearheaded by Curt Reimann of NIST, the award program director. Although Reimann reviewed the criteria developed by the National Organization for a United States Quality award, as well as Deming Prize and NASA criteria, the final set of criteria represented a break from any previous versions.

Reimann spoke with about seventy-five quality leaders in the United States to extract the main ideas for the examination categories. The result was a basic structure of seven examination categories intended to unite the quality community. Although much of the award program is expected to evolve through annual improvements, the seven examination categories are intended to remain static, giving the program a foundation and continuity. The relative weights and relationships of these seven basic categories are shown in figure 5.1.

With the seven basic categories were forty-four subcategories, within which were a total of sixty-two examination items. Within the sixty-two examination items were 278 scoring criteria, or areas to address, for 1988, the factors

**FIGURE 5.1**
**Relationship of National Quality Award Examination Categories 1988**

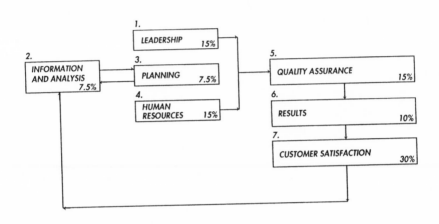

that the Board of Examiners considers in scoring the written responses to the examination items. An outline of the 1988 examination categories and subcategories and scoring weights is shown in figure 5.2.

### Improvement Process

With NIST in the middle listening to all sides, the award program's improvement cycle can turn without conflict and without major changes to the award's basic value system. The intention is to broaden the base of inputs each year to establish representation from more quality communities.

Feedback on virtually every aspect of the award program—criteria, application, examination, and examiner training—was collected throughout 1988. The feedback came from multiple sources. From February through May, after award criteria were made public, comments were collected from examiners just being selected and from companies in the application process. During the examiner training courses and the application review period, from May through

FIGURE 5.2
1988 Examination Categories/Subcategories

| Examination Categories / Items | Maximum Points |
|---|---|
| **Leadership** | 150 |
| 1  Senior corporate leadership | 50 |
| 2  Policy | 30 |
| 3  Management system and quality improvement process | 30 |
| 4  Resource allocation and utilization | 20 |
| 5  Public responsibility | 10 |
| 6  Unique and innovative leadership techniques | 10 |
| **Information and Analysis** | 75 |
| 1  Use of analytical techniques or systems | 15 |
| 2  Use of product or service quality data | 10 |
| 3  Customer data and analysis | 20 |
| 4  Supplier quality and data analysis | 10 |
| 5  Distributor and/or dealer quality and data analysis | 10 |
| 6  Employee-related data and analysis | 5 |
| 7  Unique and innovative information analysis | 5 |
| **Strategic Quality Planning** | 75 |
| 1  Operational and strategic goals | 20 |
| 2  Planning function | 20 |
| 3  Planning for quality improvement | 30 |
| 4  Unique and innovative planning | 5 |
| **Human Resource Utilization** | 150 |
| 1  Management and operations | 30 |
| 2  Employee quality awareness and involvement | 50 |
| 3  Quality training and education | 30 |
| 4  Evaluation, incentive, and recognition systems | 30 |
| 5  Unique and innovative approaches | 10 |
| **Quality Assurance of Products and Services** | 150 |
| 1  Customer input to products and services | 20 |
| 2  Planning for new or improved products and services | 20 |
| 3  Design of new or improved products and services | 30 |
| 4  Measurements, standards, and data system | 10 |
| 5  Technology | 10 |
| 6  Audit | 15 |
| 7  Documentation | 10 |
| 8  Safety, health, and environment | 10 |
| 9  Assurance/validation | 15 |
| 10  Unique or innovative indicators of quality improvements or economic gains | 10 |
| **Results from Quality Assurance of Products and Services** | 100 |
| 1  Reliability and performance of products or services | 25 |
| 2  Reductions in scrap, rework, and rejected products or services | 20 |
| 3  Reductions in claims, litigation, and complaints related to quality | 25 |
| 4  Reductions in warranty of field support | 20 |
| 5  Unique or innovative indicators of quality improvements or economic gains | 10 |
| **Customer Satisfaction** | 300 |
| 1  Customer views of quality of products or services | 100 |
| 2  Competitive comparison of products or services | 50 |
| 3  Customer service and complaint handling | 75 |
| 4  Customer views of guarantees/warranties | 50 |
| 5  Unique or innovative approaches assessing customer satisfaction | 25 |
| **Total Points:** | **1,000** |

September, comments were collected again from the examiners. Finally, after the application review process was over, comments were collected from examiners, companies that had applied for the award, and companies that had not applied but had been exposed to the program.

Based on these inputs, a draft of improved award criteria was prepared and reviewed in December at NIST. This version was sent out to about 200 people for review and comments, which were then incorporated in early 1989. After this, improvements to award criteria were made at the level of the examination item.

The relative weights and relationships of examination categories and an outline of examination categories, subcategories, and scoring weights for 1989 are shown in figures 5.3 and 5.4, respectively.

**FIGURE 5.3**
**Relationship of National Quality Award Examination Categories 1989**

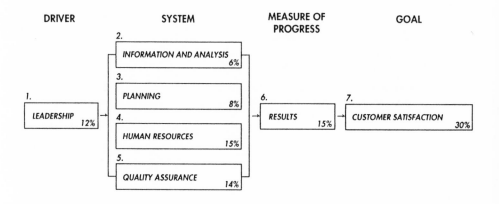

**FIGURE 5.4**
**1989 Examination Categories/Subcategories**

| Examination Categories / Items | | Maximum Points |
|---|---|---|
| **Leadership** | | 120 |
| 1 Senior management | 30 | |
| 2 Quality values | 20 | |
| 3 Management system | 50 | |
| 4 Public responsibility | 20 | |
| **Information and Analysis** | | 60 |
| 1 Scope of data and information | 25 | |
| 2 Data management | 15 | |
| 3 Analysis and use of data for decision making | 20 | |
| **Planning for Quality** | | 80 |
| 1 Planning process | 30 | |
| 2 Plans for quality leadership | 50 | |
| **Human Resource Utilization** | | 150 |
| 1 Management | 25 | |
| 2 Employee involvement | 40 | |
| 3 Quality education and training | 30 | |
| 4 Employment recognition | 20 | |
| 5 Quality of worklife | 35 | |
| **Quality Assurance of Products and Services** | | 140 |
| 1 Design and introduction of products and services | 25 | |
| 2 Operation of processes | 20 | |
| 3 Measurements and standards | 15 | |
| 4 Audit | 20 | |
| 5 Documentation | 10 | |
| 6 Quality assurance of operations business processes | 25 | |
| 7 Quality assurance of external providers of goods and services | 25 | |
| **Quality Results** | | 150 |
| 1 Quality of products and services | 70 | |
| 2 Operational and business process quality improvement | 60 | |
| 3 Quality improvement applications | 20 | |
| **Customer Satisfaction** | | 300 |
| 1 Knowledge of customer requirements and expectations | 40 | |
| 2 Customer relationship management | 125 | |
| 3 Customer satisfaction methods, measurements, and results | 75 | |
| **Total Points:** | | **1,000** |

The process of synthesizing improvement comments and recommendations for the 1989 award cycle took three months. The 1988–89 improvement process resulted not only in improved criteria, but also in:

- sharpened boundaries between categories;
- a more streamlined application review process;
- a more reliable scoring and reporting system;
- a tighter site visit system with more documentation of the on-site examination and better examiner consensus, enabling examiners to work together better.

All improvements were factored into the examiners' training program for 1989. Training materials from six cases were used to train the examiners in 1989, compared with materials from one case in 1988.

FIGURE 5.5
Relationship of National Quality Award Examination Categories 1990

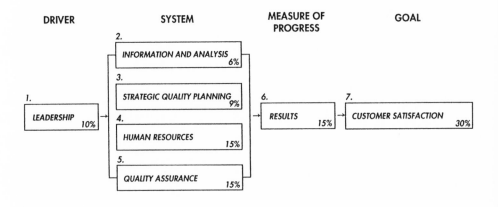

FIGURE 5.6
1990 Examination Categories/Subcategories

| Examination Categories / Items | | Maximum Points |
|---|---|---|
| **Leadership** | | 100 |
| 1 Senior executive leadership | 30 | |
| 2 Quality values | 20 | |
| 3 Management for quality | 30 | |
| 4 Public responsibility | 20 | |
| **Information and Analysis** | | 60 |
| 1 Scope and management of quality data and information | 35 | |
| 2 Analysis of quality data and information | 25 | |
| **Strategic Quality Planning** | | 90 |
| 1 Strategic quality planning process | 40 | |
| 2 Quality leadership indicators in planning | 25 | |
| 3 Quality priorities | 25 | |
| **Human Resource Utilization** | | 150 |
| 1 Human resource management | 30 | |
| 2 Employee involvement | 40 | |
| 3 Quality education and training | 40 | |
| 4 Employment recognition | 20 | |
| 5 Employee well-being and morale | 20 | |
| **Quality Assurance of Products and Services** | | 150 |
| 1 Design and introduction of quality products and services | 30 | |
| 2 Process and quality control | 25 | |
| 3 Continuous improvement of processes, products, and services | 25 | |
| 4 Quality assessment | 15 | |
| 5 Documentation | 10 | |
| 6 Quality assurance, quality assessment, and quality improvement of support services and business processes | 25 | |
| 7 Quality assurance, quality assessment, and quality improvement of suppliers | 20 | |
| **Quality Results** | | 150 |
| 1 Quality of products and services | 50 | |
| 2 Comparison of quality results | 35 | |
| 3 Business process, operational, and support service quality improvement | 35 | |
| 4 Supplier quality improvement | 30 | |
| **Customer Satisfaction** | | 300 |
| 1 Knowledge of customer requirements and expectations | 50 | |
| 2 Customer relationship management | 30 | |
| 3 Customer service standards | 20 | |
| 4 Commitments to customers | 20 | |
| 5 Complaint resolution for quality improvement | 30 | |
| 6 Customer satisfaction determination | 50 | |
| 7 Customer satisfaction results | 50 | |
| 8 Customer satisfaction comparison | 50 | |
| **Total Points:** | | **1,000** |

## 1989–90 Improvement Cycle

The 1989–90 improvement cycle went much as it had in 1988–89. Comments criteria were tightened by eliminating the award subcategories and reducing the number of examination items from forty-four to thirty-three. The areas to address were revised to provide clearer guidance for applicants. The relative weights and relationships examination categories and an outline of

FIGURE 5.7
Malcolm Baldrige National Quality Award

| 1995 Examination Categories / Items | Point Values |
|---|---|
| **1.0 Leadership** | **90** |
| 1.1 Senior Executive Leadership . . . . . . . . . . . . . . . . . . . . . . . 45 | |
| 1.2 Leadership System and Organization . . . . . . . . . . . . . . . . . 25 | |
| 1.3 Public Responsibility and Corporate Citizenship . . . . . . . . 20 | |
| **2.0 Information and Analysis** | **75** |
| 2.1 Management of Information and Data . . . . . . . . . . . . . . . . . 20 | |
| 2.2 Competitive Comparisons and Benchmarking . . . . . . . . . . 15 | |
| 2.3 Analysis and Uses of Company-Level Data . . . . . . . . . . . . 40 | |
| **3.0 Strategic Planning** | **55** |
| 3.1 Strategy Development . . . . . . . . . . . . . . . . . . . . . . . . . . . . . 35 | |
| 3.2 Strategy Deployment . . . . . . . . . . . . . . . . . . . . . . . . . . . . . 20 | |
| **4.0 Human Resource Development and Management** | **140** |
| 4.1 Human Resource Planning and Evaluation . . . . . . . . . . . . . 20 | |
| 4.2 High Performance Work Systems . . . . . . . . . . . . . . . . . . . . 45 | |
| 4.3 Employee Education, Training, and Development . . . . . . . 50 | |
| 4.4 Employee Well-Being and Satisfaction . . . . . . . . . . . . . . . 25 | |
| **5.0 Process Management** | **140** |
| 5.1 Design and Introduction of Products and Services . . . . . . . 40 | |
| 5.2 Process Management: Product and Service Production and Delivery . . . . . . . . . . . . . . . . . . . . . . . . . . . . . . . . . . . . . 40 | |
| 5.3 Process Management: Support Services . . . . . . . . . . . . . . . 30 | |
| 5.4 Management of Supplier Performance . . . . . . . . . . . . . . . . 30 | |
| **6.0 Business Result** | **250** |
| 6.1 Product and Service Quality Results . . . . . . . . . . . . . . . . . 75 | |
| 6.2 Company Operational and Financial Results . . . . . . . . . . . 130 | |
| 6.3 Supplier Performance Results . . . . . . . . . . . . . . . . . . . . . . . 45 | |
| **7.0 Customer Focus and Satisfaction** | **250** |
| 7.1 Customer and Market Knowledge . . . . . . . . . . . . . . . . . . . 30 | |
| 7.2 Customer Relationship Management . . . . . . . . . . . . . . . . . 30 | |
| 7.3 Customer Satisfaction Determination . . . . . . . . . . . . . . . . 30 | |
| 7.4 Customer Satisfaction Results . . . . . . . . . . . . . . . . . . . . . . 100 | |
| 7.5 Customer Satisfaction Comparison . . . . . . . . . . . . . . . . . . 60 | |
| **TOTAL POINTS** | **1000** |

examination categories, examination items, and scoring weights for 1990 are shown in figures 5.5 and 5.6, respectively.

As a result of the improvement process the 1990 award guidelines had cleaner instructions, more clarifying notes, and more information on the evaluation process for service companies and small businesses. The criteria have been reviewed and revised annually. The 1995 categories and scoring are provided in figure 5.7.

## The Award as Impetus

The Malcolm Baldrige National Quality Award Program is the result of cooperative efforts by business and government leaders concerned about the quality and competitiveness of American products and services. In its first two years, the award program exceeded the expectations of those who worked to establish and implement it. The task is to maintain the gains and continue to enhance the award's prestige and value.

The award program is intended to spark interest and involvement in quality programs, drive American products and services to higher levels of quality, and better equip companies to meet the challenges of world markets.

The Malcolm Baldrige National Quality Award is more than an annual presentation by the president. It is the driving force of a national movement, the hub around which the wheel of quality improvement in America turns.

# II

# The Context for Change in Higher Education

# 6

# The Lattice and the Ratchet

## Pew Higher Education Research Program

Since former Secretary of Education William Bennett discovered drugs, an uneasy calm has settled over public discussions about collegiate costs and prices. There is now less shouting, less institution bashing, with fewer personal attacks on college administrators and faculty—though among some there remains a well-honed instinct to make political hay at the expense of the nation's colleges and universities.

For their part, college and university presidents are less aggressive in their defense of current patterns of expenditure. There are fewer claims that what higher education needs is a good media campaign to remind the public of the inherently high cost of excellence.

At the same time, the focus has begun to shift from price to expenditure—from what students and their families pay, to what colleges and universities spend. Increasingly, colleges and universities are being asked to change the way they conduct their business: how decisions are made, how functions are staffed, how buildings are built, and with what amenities, and finally, how the energies of the institution are distributed between collective goals and individual pursuits.

The asking of these questions reflects two principles that are being applied with increasing frequency to higher education. First is the necessity for colleges and universities to abandon "cost-plus pricing." Like regulated industries of old, institutions of higher education have been practicing a kind of "bottom-up" budgeting, in which inflation is built into each unit's base budget and all quality enhancements are then added on. With the aggregate budget representing little more than the sum of these disaggregated decisions, the resulting price (tuition plus public appropriation) necessarily equals the amount needed to cover current operations plus elective and mandated improvements.

Reprinted from *Policy Perspectives,* Volume 2, Number 4, June 1990. *Policy Perspectives* is a publication of the Pew Higher Education Roundtable, sponsored by the Pew Charitable Trusts.

The alternative principle is "growth by substitution"—a term that implies the need to achieve institutional excellence by developing more focused missions. Colleges and universities are heading voices, from both within and without, saying that institutions must invest in what they do best, and that they should pay for those investments through savings generated by a combination of program reduction and administrative reorganization.

Still, these principles are limited in that they are descriptive without being diagnostic. They portray higher education's current condition without identifying either the factors that over time have defined the academic culture or processes for achieving necessary changes. Calling on institutions to "set revenues first" as "the best way to end higher education's reliance on cost-plus pricing," as we did in the September, 1989 issue of *Policy Perspectives,* is only the first step. It is, we think, important and perhaps necessary for change, but it provides precious little help in itself to an institution that is seeking to control costs in order to live within reduced means. For the president who proposes a voluntary revenue cap, the questions come in increasing fury. What is to be cut? Will there be reductions in academic as well as administrative departments? Will the cuts be across the board? Will there be layoffs? Hiring freezes? A year without salary raises? Will planned construction projects proceed even though they add substantially to physical plant costs? Can there be no relaxation in the amount of paperwork required to meet regulatory obligations? No temporary increase in the yield from endowment? No relaxation of the decision to hold the line on prices to give the institution a little more time to adjust to the new economic realities? Why even bother with voluntarily capping revenues as long as there are ample students ready to pay for a first-class education?

These questions suggest the real dilemma facing an institution seeking to reduce its costs in order to live within its means. They also suggest why solving the "problem" is not simply a matter of making less money available to operating units. Budget compression—the squeezing down of most operating budgets across an institution—works best in times of genuine crisis, as when a state suddenly cuts its appropriation to a public institution, or when a private institution experiences a sudden and dramatic shortfall in enrollment. At such times everyone pitches in, making whatever savings are possible. The danger is that once the crisis has passed, the tendency is to restore what was cut—to make up for lost salary increases, to fill positions that temporarily were left vacant, to provide some recompense for those units that bore the brunt of the cost reductions. The ironic result is that such budget compression simply reinforces the pressures for bottom-up budgeting, and hence cost-plus pricing, once the immediate need for expenditure constraint has passed.

We are left, then, with a fundamental question: How can colleges and universities redesign the way they conduct their business, without sacrificing their ability to invest in new ideas? We have come to believe that such a redesign will require a fuller diagnosis of how and why institutional costs have increased over the last decade. In this present essay, we provide a conceptual framework for understanding both the growth in administrative staffs and a shift in faculty functions that have caused the cost of an institution's operations to rise steadily. In subsequent issues of *Policy Perspectives*, we will address specific strategies for cost reduction and ways of making focused investments in instruction before returning to the question of prices, where we began our examination of the higher education economy in the essay "Double Trouble" (*Policy Perspectives*, September 1989).

## The Administrative Lattice

On most campuses there is an inherent tension between academic and administrative units, between faculty and staff. Sometimes that tension is genuinely creative, as each half of the institution strives to strengthen itself while recognizing the inherent value of the other. More often, that tension yields an unproductive competition for resources. The faculty remind themselves and the community that they are "the business" of the institution, all other activities being nonessential and frequently wasteful. For their part, the staff gleefully recount tales of faculty mismanagement and waste, secure in their sense that the only thing businesslike about the institution is their own ability to discharge increasingly complex management tasks.

We know now that it is the administrative function that has grown most over the last decade. In the 28 March 1990 issue of the *Chronicle of Higher Education*, Karen Grassmuck used data submitted by institutions to the U.S. Equal Employment Opportunity Commission to chart that growth. She found that "other professionals"—academic support personnel filling such roles as financial aid counselor, auditor, or systems analyst—rose in number by more than 60 percent between 1975 and 1985, a period during which the number of faculty rose on average less than 6 percent. Increases were also substantial for many institutions among the ranks of executive, administrative, and managerial personnel. No less telling than the data is Grassmuck's report of the impression among some higher education officials that, in spite of this growth, "many universities are making do with smaller staffs than they need."

The analysis in the *Chronicle* suggests that the growth of administrative personnel is pervasive; that it is not a case in which all of higher education receives blame for the profligacy of a few rich, largely private research universities. Just as most institutions enjoyed real revenue growth in the 1980s (see September, 1989 *Policy Perspectives*, "Profiles"), so apparently did most institutions substantially expand their administrative and academic support staffs. The result has been an extension of the scale and scope of an administrative lattice that has grown, much like a crystalline structure, to incorporate ever more elaborate and intricate linkages within itself. Controlling this lattice, perhaps even reducing its complexity and capacity for completing itself, means coming to terms with three principal causes of administrative growth.

## The Persistence of Regulation and Micromanagement

Though they often protest too much, college and university presidents are right when they claim that increased regulation and external micromanagement have resulted in substantially increased administrative staffs. OSHA, EEOC, EPA, FISAP, IPEDS, A21, OFCC—the lexicon of regulatory and reporting acronyms is all too familiar. Each new federal program carries with it substantial monitoring requirements that often lead to the establishment of new internal bureaucracies whose principal function is to create more work for others. Health and safety regulations are a prime example. Most research universities have had to increase their staff of health and safety inspectors fivefold or more. These inspectors then find problems that others must be hired to fix.

Micromanagement, principally by state agencies in the public sector and by energetic and sometimes intrusive boards of trustees, has had much the same result—more paper, more procedures, and more staff—without substantial increases in the quality of the product. Public commissions of higher education, either as coordinating or governing boards, have become increasingly insistent that they have a right to know, well in advance, what institutions under their purview intend to do. The filing of ever more detailed plans and the seeking of approval for each new certificate or degree program generates sufficient reporting requirements to keep small battalions of administrative staff busy. Boards of trustees are beginning to have the same effect, demanding that they be "kept in the loop" on all major administrative decisions. The result is more paper, more reporting, and, not surprisingly, more personnel, some of whom must explain to the trustees the continual rise in administrative costs.

## The Embrace of Consensus Management

In the 1980s, more and more American firms were persuaded to adopt new, explicitly participatory ways of making decisions. Across the span of business enterprises, efforts were made to get employees to buy into the decisions that affect their working lives and futures—to make the employees part of the process and hence, part of the solution. The rationale for this movement was drawn from both the work of human resource professionals and from a peculiarly American understanding of the use of quality circles in Japan to improve production. The ironic result was that increased participation was often purchased at the cost of decreased accountability and productivity.

On college campuses across the country, this commitment to consensus management was a natural complement to a renewed emphasis on community. Out of the turmoil of the 1960s and early 1970s there grew a distaste for hierarchy in any form, an affirmation by most institutions that they were, in fact, communities with equally important members. On most campuses, systems of governance were challenged to incorporate students and staff, in addition to faculty, as consulting partners whose opinions and preferences were to be sought and frequently heeded. Good communication became a goal in itself.

The next step was to extend to staff functions the consultative models that had historically dominated faculty deliberations. Without any demonstrable increase in coordination or planning, decisions were framed, reviewed, and ultimately made by working groups whose very representativeness substantially increased the probability that their recommendations would find broad acceptance—that is, a consensus—within the administrative community.

Colleges and universities, like businesses and service organizations, are just beginning to understand the scope of the direct and indirect costs associated with consensus management. Building a consensus, it turns out, takes time and extra personnel in the form of more and larger working groups that need to meet more frequently. Brokering between administrative groups becomes an explicit function, requiring additional personnel and introducing extra steps into the consultative process. Perhaps the most directly measurable costs associated with consensus management are represented by the amount of time administrative staff spend negotiating with one another. At more than one institution, senior staff, much to their chagrin, have come to view themselves as diplomats who are required to display the demeanor and the language of negotiators as they shuttle between the major officers each of them serves.

Indirect costs associated with consensus management have to do with the quality of the decisions that are reached. Because consensus management encourages collective judgement, it becomes increasingly less clear who is in charge of what—who is responsible, who gets the credit for success, who is accountable for failure. Consensus management thus becomes an attractive strategy for distributing to everyone the responsibility—and hence, the blame—for bad decisions.

Such risk aversion is not unique to higher education. In her study of managerial behavior, *Managers Managing: The Workings of an Administrative System* (1989), Jane Hannaway notes, for example, that "risk avoidance has been singled out as particularly problematic in the peacetime U.S. military bureaucracy. Stories are told of generals who were coming up for promotion and refused to take any actions in the weeks before the promotion boards met for fear of making a mistake." Hannaway argues that in the administrative systems of the private as well as the public sectors, "the chances of being held responsible for a negative outcome are greater than the chances of being rewarded for a success," and that this fact encourages managers to adopt risk-reducing behaviors.

Finally, consensus management inherently protects the organizational status quo. Since nearly every party is represented in the decision-making process, there is little chance that the group will decide to reorganize in response to changing circumstances, and thereby run the risk of finding itself without a viable assignment. The tendency instead is to solve problems by adding to the lattice—by elaborating staff functions, by creating extra steps in the process, and by building new functions that inevitably require further expansion of the administrative lattice.

## The Expansion of Administrative Entrepreneurism

Less understood is the pressure for growth created by the administrative staffs' own energies and the willingness of the faculty to consign to them traditionally academic service functions. Because colleges and universities were expanding administratively and had the reputation for being "good places to work," higher education attracted a new cohort of experts who brought an important sense of professionalism to the industry, and who expected energy and creativity to be rewarded with increased responsibility, enhanced status, and better pay.

One result was much better management. Colleges and universities have become better at managing their monies, at acquiring sophisticated technologies, at making their campuses more efficient in the use of utilities, and at servicing the needs of their students and staffs. A second, unforeseen result is that these experts have come to "own" their jobs, much as faculty "own" their appointments. This outcome was less a product of implied administrative tenure (though such understandings often accompanied the expansion of administrative services) as of the staffs' ability to define the content of their positions, much as faculty define the content of their teaching and research. Professional staff, precisely because they know what is best administratively, have acquired the capacity to put into place their visions of how a well-run institution should look. They define their goals, build their staffs, and use their successes to reach out for broader responsibilities, for opportunities to do their jobs even better.

The shift of responsibility for advising from faculty members to professional staff is one example of how such expansions feed on themselves. On most campuses where faculty have given up responsibility for undergraduate advising, there has been a corresponding shift in the scope and scale of advising now available. Having arrived in the hands of competent professionals whose sole job it is to develop and deliver academic advising, the advising function has come to require more and better computer support, greater flexibility of hours, and a broader range of services, including career placement, tutoring, and counseling. Where advising had once been subsumed within the faculty role, it has become instead an enterprise in itself with its own impulse for expansion.

Most administrative activities have become similarly complex, a development justified largely in terms of improved services and greater efficiencies at the unit level. The result has been a proliferation of increasingly independent agencies, each competing to be the very best at delivering its administrative specialty. The impulse at almost every turn has been to develop the lattice further, rewarding administrative personnel who show initiative with larger staffs and increased responsibilities.

At the same time, colleges and universities have seldom managed to apply the principle of growth by substitution to administrative personnel—to substitute one kind of administrative or support function for another. Most new problems are tackled separately; new groups are formed, new administrative functions are defined, more ad hoc relationships with on-going administrative functions are required. The more discretionary revenue an institution generates, the more likely it is to make further investments in administrative "add-ons," often with the implicit acceptance of a faculty who see substantial improvements in their work conditions deriving from quite visible improvements in administrative services.

## The Academic Ratchet

Ironically, some of the principal beneficiaries of administrative entrepreneurism have been the faculty members themselves. The four and one-half decades since the close of the Second World War have witnessed a fundamental transformation of the American professorate. In 1940 there were approximately 147,000 full-time faculty in just over 1,700 colleges and universities. By the mid-1980s, the number of institutions had nearly doubled, while the number of faculty members more than quadrupled. Over the decades, a shift has occurred in the focus of faculty's efforts. Because reliable quantitative data are maddeningly absent, our best guess is that professors in 1990 spend less time in the classroom than their counterparts before the Second World War. There is a general feeling that faculty today spend less time advising, teach fewer courses outside their specialties, and are less committed to a commonly defined curriculum.

These shifts are the visible evidence of a pervasive change in the definition of the academic task—what it is that faculty are formally paid to do and for whom. At work over these more than four decades is an "academic ratchet" that has loosened the faculty members' connection to their institution. Each turn of the ratchet has drawn the norm of faculty activity away from institutionally defined goals and toward the more specialized concerns of faculty research, publication, professional service, and personal pursuits.

Part of what makes the ratchet work is the uniformity with which faculty members expect to be treated with respect to work loads. It is almost impossible, for example, for there to be substantial differentiation of teaching loads within a single department. As long as a few faculty members are advantaged, there will be an irresistible pressure to lower the average load—advancing the ratchet by another click. No one wants to teach more general courses at the expense of the opportunity to teach one's specialty. Eventually everyone gets to teach his or her specialty. The number of general courses declines, the number of specialized offerings increases, and the ratchet turns again.

It is a process that has produced gains as well as losses—increased research productivity, a more expansive set of courses, and more freedom for students, particularly those prepared to join their faculty mentors in specialized study. Such gains have been achieved, however, at substantial costs—the need for academic support personnel to leverage faculty time, administrative staff to perform tasks once routinely assigned to the faculty, and a need to increase the size of the faculty. The larger cost, however, lies in the shift of faculty attention and effort away from institutionally defined goals and toward personally and professionally defined pursuits.

Before the Second World War, faculty were largely extensions of their institutions, identified with and part of a collectivity that linked them together in common endeavor. The curriculum was collectively developed. Students were guided through a series of courses in which there was a clear introduction, a variety of middle-level experiences, and a final set of advanced courses that constituted the major. Faculty members devoted as much, if not more, time to teaching general courses within the department as to teaching their own specialties. Teaching loads were heavier than now, but seldom onerous, leaving sufficient time for advising and mentoring, as well as the more limited amount of publication expected of most faculty.

A sad paradox has come to describe the changing responsibilities and perceptions of the American professorate. Many of those who chose an academic career did so as a result of having been taught well as an undergraduate, often at a smaller, teaching-oriented institution. After years of graduate training and experience in the academic profession, however, college faculty learn to seek "relief" from the responsibilities of teaching, mentoring, and developing their college's and department's curriculum; they soon realize that the real gainers are those faculty members who earn more discretionary time to pursue their own definitions of purposeful work. They understand that professional status depends as much, if not more, on one's standing within a discipline, and less on one's role as a master instructor within an increasingly complex institution.

Because of the growth of the administrative lattice, faculty no longer numerically dominate their institutions, are generally more concerned about their standing within their disciplines, and are more ready to move in search of better deals. The irony is that while administrative units have become more like academic departments—more committed to group processes and collective decision making—more and more faculty have become independent contractors largely unfettered by the constraints of institutional needs and community practices.

## A Framework for Redesign

Change will not come easily, or even purposefully, as long as higher education as an industry perceives itself to require neither greater efficiency nor a heightened sense of accountability. Absent a commitment to redesign, colleges and universities will likely presume that the process of incremental growth can be reversed, leading to decremental and largely across-the-board budget reductions. The resulting budget compression would neither dismantle the administrative lattice nor reverse the academic ratchet, largely because budget compression places a management premium on achieving reductions that affect as few people as possible. If, on the other hand, a college or university were prepared to proceed by design rather than by compression, what steps might it take?

### Take Account of Administrative Growth

The first step is to measure the dimensions of the administrative lattice and to note where and why it has grown over the last decade. This analysis will not be easy. For good and understandable reasons, the administrative staff will resist, citing the difficulty of making meaningful comparisons, the paucity of accurate data, and the extent to which actual growth has been a function of external regulation, the increased size of the physical plant, and faculty and student demands for increased services.

The key questions are those directed at identifying the extent of the lattice at all administrative levels: proliferation of administrative organizations, elaboration of decision-making processes, and redundancies among organizations that perform roughly similar tasks, but for different parts of the institution.

Simplify transactions and procedures. The analysis of the administrative lattice will show that growth has been accompanied by the adoption of increasingly complex transactions and procedures—more rules, forms, and reviews for hiring staff, for evaluating students, for tracking expenses, for monitoring contracts, for planning and constructing buildings, and for developing institutional policies and standards. Institutions must seek ways to combine steps, and to use better the power of modern data processing systems to monitor transactions. At every turn, the question that ought to be asked is, "Is this step necessary?"

Fundamentally, the administrative lattice can be scaled back only by redesigning administrative organizations, by redefining the nature of administrative authority and responsibility on the one hand and, on the other, the content of administrative tasks. Such redesigns and combinations will necessarily break down the barriers separating academic and administrative functions and, in larger, more complex institutions, those separating the central administration from that of the individual schools and centers.

## Shift the Focus of Incentives away from Individual Faculty Members and Toward Their Departments, Divisions, and Schools

Reversing the academic ratchet will prove even more difficult, in part because the looming shortage of research-trained scholars will substantially enhance the faculty's bargaining position. A first step available to most institutions is to focus less on individual faculty members and more on departments, divisions, and schools. Begin distributing resources less in terms of rewarding individual faculty members and more in terms of strengthening departments. Make the department rather than the individual instructor responsible for the quality of undergraduate instruction and the nature of the curriculum. Focus less on the teaching loads of individual faculty members and more on the aggregate amount of instruction expected from a department, and then leave to the department's members the distribution of individual assignments. If the department understood that it would be rewarded collectively—in terms of salary increases, tenure levels, new appointments, and support funds—for the quality of its instructional programs, it might allocate its own resources with an eye to achieving better outcomes. Such a shift in attitude would halt, and perhaps even begin reversing, the progress of the ratchet.

### Make Clear Who is in Charge

It has become fashionable to mourn the loss of educational leadership, to wish for bygone days when a Charles Eliot and Nicholas Murray Butler could single handedly recast Harvard and Columbia, and in the process change the nature of higher education. We recommend a more prosaic change. What institutions of higher education need now are effective decision makers—what in the old days were called men and women with vision and backbone—who feel empowered, often by their boards of trustees, to make choices for which they will be held accountable. Academic leaders and key administrative managers need to know that they can make a difference, that they will be demonstrably rewarded for their successes, and properly chastised, perhaps even retired, for their failures. Less time needs to be spent consulting and to getting everyone to "own" the outcome.

At the level of the academic department, such empowering means strengthening the hands of the department chairs. At the level of school deans and principal managers, taking accountability and responsibility implies a willingness to change personnel more easily and with less political consequence.

Any accounting of change must address both the administrative lattice and the academic ratchet. Some might observe that because reducing the former will prove easier than reversing the latter, savings will come principally from administrative budgets. For real reform to occur, however, institutions must check the advance of both mechanisms—the ratchet and the lattice.

## A Cautionary Note

Not one of these changes in itself is very novel. Indeed, one of the principal dangers facing colleges and universities will be the tendency of some both within and without the academy to say with malice, "I told you so!" There is a class of faculty politicos who are particularly prone to use studies of administrative growth to wage again that ancient battle between academic and administrative functions. These academics seldom note that they have been a primary beneficiary of administrative growth; that the administrative lattice is the natural complement to the academic ratchet.

Even friends in the business community are likely to say, "It's about time!" Yet to urge colleges and universities to be more "businesslike" will hardly be persuasive after a decade in which businesses too often engaged in a frenzy of mergers, acquisitions, leveraged buy-outs, and spectacular bankruptcies. It would not be churlish for higher education to note that, in terms of cost, the problem of student loan defaults nowhere approaches that of the federal bailout of the savings and loan industry. The $300 to $500 billion likely to be spent over the next thirty years cleaning up the S&L mess dwarfs higher education's most profligate demands for federal aid.

What is clear is that the challenge facing higher education is no different from that facing most American enterprises. The nation's colleges and universities need to become more competitive—leaner, perhaps meaner, certainly more focused—with simpler organizations and a greater ability to make collective investments in targeted programs and projects.

# 7

# Productivity or Quality? In Search of Higher Education's Yellow Brick Road

*Sean C. Rush*

During the past several years, the word productivity has crept into the lexicon of higher education with all the subtlety of a Kansas tornado. Previously anathema at most institutions, the term is now bandied about with considerable urgency as institution after institution grapples with shrinking resources and growing budget shortfalls. Downsizing, retrenchment, and doing more with less have become themes, if not necessities, for most institutions. However, despite the frequent use of the word productivity on many campuses, its actual meaning, acceptance, and application within higher education is less than clear.

The notion of productivity brings substantial baggage with it. All but the most steely hearts shudder at the thought of a productivity initiative in their workplace. For many the word conjures up images of Tayloresque time-and-motion studies, sweat-inducing taskmasters, or Charlie Chaplin, forever caught in the gears of a gargantuan machine in the 1936 movie *Modern Times*. For most people, productivity, like reading Tolstoy's *War and Peace,* is something more often talked about than actually done.

Within higher education, the practical implementation of the concept is especially nettlesome. How does one value the intellectual exchange between a student and teacher? A basic discovery in a campus laboratory? An institutional public service initiative? Because the primary purpose of colleges and universities is the creation and transfer of knowledge and not the maximization of shareholder wealth, many monetary measures of performance fall short.

### Previously Not a Concern

Part of the problem of productivity in higher education may be that colleges and universities have not had to cope with the issue. For the past forty-five years, higher education has been an incredible growth industry. Since 1950:

- total enrollment in American colleges and universities has grown more than 400 percent, from 2.7 million to the current 13 million;
- the total number of institutions has grown by more than 80 percent, from 1,800 to 3,300; and
- college and university facility space has increased by more than 500 percent, growing from 500 million to some 3 billion square feet of space.

Between 1955 and 1974, a new institution was opened at the rate of one every two weeks. More college and university space was constructed during this period than in the preceding 200 years. These statistics are not the telltale signs of an ailing industry. The main problem during this period was coping with incredible growth, not retrenchment.

During that four-decade stretch, a substantial number of institutions became large, highly complex businesses. Although many within the industry rail at the thought, higher education is a big business with some institutional budgets well in excess of $1 billion, easily cracking *Fortune* magazine's 500 companies in terms of financial size. In aggregate, American higher education:

- spends approximately $130 billion in operating expenses (excluding capital),
- has a physical-plant replacement value of some $330 billion,
- manages more than $75 billion in endowment funds, and
- employs millions of faculty members and staff.

Today's research university is a far cry from its ancestors, the small medieval colleges of masters, teachers, and students. It offers a dazzling array of classrooms, laboratories, housing, museums, galleries, gymnasia, technology, and support services. In short, many universities have become self-contained small cities as more and more functions become integrated into the enterprise.

## A New Environment

Despite the seeming prosperity of the late 1970s and early 1980s, higher education was also filled with a number of would-be Cassandras. Various doom-and-gloom scenarios were prophesied based on changing demographics and uncertain national economic performance. Yet, despite the dour forecasts, the 1980s proved to be a relatively prosperous time for higher education. Resourceful management tapped new student markets to increase the nontraditional-age student pool, robust economic performance bolstered endowments and spurred charitable giving, and low inflation kept at least some operating costs in line.

This period of prosperity, however, masked a number of fundamental problems. Expenses increased, enabled by revenue growth that has since proved unsustainable. New education program initiatives and burgeoning academic support were built while the ever-increasing cost of maintenance of educational facilities was deferred. The delicate balance between trends in institutional resources and needs, and between long- and short-term interests was tipped into financial disequilibrium at many institutions by the late 1980s. The Cassandras had finally hit pay dirt!

Administrators must now address budget gaps caused by constricted institutional resource growth and burgeoning needs. National and regional economic recessions make traditional external funding sources uncertain. Finally, changing student demographics present new concerns during a time of growing public concern and focus on the price and value of higher education.

## Finite Resources

Several factors contribute to the rising concern over resources and revenues in higher education, including tuition, federal and state aid, state tax revenues, federal research grants, and an ailing economy.

Tuition charges at private institutions grew by 127 percent between 1982 and 1992, well ahead of the 47 percent rise in the consumer price index, and outpacing increases in median family income. There is both a growing public resistance to the trend of steep tuition increases and a fairly pervasive sense in the education industry that the pace of tuition growth must slow down.

The problem of rapid tuition growth outstripping families' ability to pay has been compounded by declining federally funded student aid. The burden of financial aid has increasingly passed to the institutions, resulting in a 130 percent increase in institutionally funded student aid from 1980 to 1988. This institutionally funded aid directly offsets tuition revenue and causes institutions to retain less of each incremental tuition revenue dollar and further squeezes institutions' resources.

As state tax revenues diminish and the competition for funds among social programs, K-12 education, and prisons intensifies, funding for higher education will be stretched. Hence, colleges and universities can expect declining allocations of tax revenues as states struggle to do more with less.

In addition, competition for federal research dollars has grown. Although the government is still the most significant source of research funding, its largess slowed considerably in the 1980s, especially compared with the quickening pace of other research funding sources. Academic institutions and the private sector are assuming a greater share of the nation's research efforts. The shift away from federal funding hurts colleges in two ways. First, to the extent that institutions move toward self-funding the direct costs of research, their level of expenditure on research will rise. Second, research grants from private foundations and companies generally do not fund indirect costs. As institutions and the private sector fund more of the direct and indirect costs of research, fewer discretionary revenue sources are left to finance other educational activities.

Lastly, as the economy has slowed down, charitable giving has leveled in real terms. Further, erratic endowment performance has mirrored the economic uncertainty and market volatility that have prevailed since 1987.

These financial resource issues present real and immediate problems to college and university administrators, who also face problems of expanding needs.

## Expanding Needs

In an era when quality was defined under the more-is-better model, colleges and universities grew, expanding programs, scholarships, and student services as they went. Budgeting was at the margin: How much more can we do/offer this year? Now institutions are faced with an altogether different task—budgeting the core programs. The questions are different now: How will we fund the institution we've become? What is central to our mission? A number of needs have emerged as critical only recently in higher education.

An aging workforce, government intervention, sophisticated technology, declining enrollment, and long-deferred maintenance present unique demands to administrators. Generally, personnel costs comprise nearly 70 percent of an institution's operating budget. Over the last eight years, faculty salaries, one of the largest components of compensation expense, have risen faster than inflation.

Yet, despite high investment in this area in the 1980s, faculty still have not regained the salary purchasing power they had in the 1960s and early 1970s. Furthermore, while salaries have always been a large part of the university budget, its portion could grow dramatically as institutions are forced to offer more money to attract top candidates from the declining number of doctoral students.

Fringe benefits are also increasingly costly to institutions. Health care costs have escalated and increased the cost of medical benefits. In 1994, retirement benefits will prove to be particularly challenging as mandatory retirement will be eliminated by law. The aging faculty workforce not only will increase the duration of the institution's pension-fund contributions but also will preclude younger, less expensive faculty appointments.

Government regulation and taxation also present growing expenses to universities. For example, demonstrating and reporting compliance on such issues as primate care in biomedical research will increase the cost of doing that research. In addition, lawmakers increasingly view higher education as a potential source of new tax revenue. Changes to the unrelated business income tax (UBIT) will tax more directly activities run by colleges and universities, such as bookstores, travel and tour groups, food services, and hotels. Another area under review as a source of new tax revenue is endowment income. Legislation of this type would directly affect the institution's operating expenses.

Cost concerns have also increased in the areas of obtaining and maintaining scientific equipment, computers, and other technology. The growing sophistication of technology in recent years presents unique needs, often requiring special facilities, maintenance, and ongoing technical support. Institutions are called upon to provide the most up-to-date resources and associated support services as possible, as part of a high-quality education. Yet, the prohibitive cost of obtaining and maintaining these state-of-the-art technologies means that most institutions just haven't been able to keep up. Despite major investments in this area, most college and university labs are stacked with old equipment and technology that is generations out of date.

The declining applicant pool also presents unique requirements. Recruitment costs—including market analysis, marketing consultants, and direct-mail campaigns—are becoming significant cost factors. This is particularly true in minority recruiting. Recruitment for qualified minority students is intense. Furthermore, proportionally minority students have historically needed more financial aid. The greatest opportunities for maintaining enrollment levels lie in increasing minority enrollment, yet this presents even more financial challenges to institutions.

The thread of consistency among these issues is the rigorous challenge of maintaining or increasing quality while decreasing cost. Shrinking revenue streams and upward pressures on costs are forcing college and university leaders to think of ways to do more with less. For many people, this translates into achieving greater productivity, and therein lies the rub. Academics argue over how to define or measure productivity but feel that the concept of productivity should be left in the corporate sector.

## Predictable Response

Higher education's response to its budgetary shortfalls has been predictable. The most common reactions include:

- hiring and spending freezes,
- across-the-board budget cuts (usually by some percentage amount), and
- layoffs.

The difficulty with most of these approaches is that they are often short-term solutions; sometimes damaging to the institution and frequently harmful to morale. The words used to describe these initiatives connote failure. Downsizing and retrenchment are not words of optimism. However, despite the negative aura surrounding these activities, downsizing usually does occur. As William Massy and Robert Zemsky have pointed out in "The Lattice and the Rachet," published in the June, 1990 issue of *Policy Perspectives,* most departments will chip in with budget freezes or reductions to help address the problem at hand. When the problems appear to have passed, budgets quickly return to their original size as pent-up needs are funded and reintroduced into the operating budget. In most instances, institutions do not fundamentally re-think their current position and put in place lasting long-term corrective solutions. Too often, the issue is viewed as a short-term problem rather than an opportunity to change the culture and overcome inertia.

Any college or university that views the current issues and problems as short term has misread the socioeconomic tea leaves. Most of the problems predicted for the 1980s have come to pass, albeit ten years late. They key concern for higher education is to recognize the permanence of these issues. Short-term solutions to long-term problems will not suffice. The challenge is not how to merely survive with fewer funds in the future, but how to thrive with less money.

## Quality First

As institutions begin to cope with the many cost-reduction issues before them, the landscape has become littered with an alphabet soup of dueling cost-reduction methodologies. Total Quality Management (TQM), Just in Time (JIT), Overhead Budget Management (OBM), Total Quality Cost (TQC), and others all profess and, to varying degrees, provide useful responses to institutional concerns. However, underlying each of these methodologies is a concept that should resonate with all colleges and universities—quality. At every institution, student quality, faculty quality, teaching quality, and research quality are highly valued. Productivity may, in fact, be the wrong word to use regarding higher education. Instead of pursuing productivity, perhaps colleges and universities should pursue quality within realistic and appropriate financial parameters.

Many colleges and universities find themselves in the difficult position of trying to fund—with shrinking resources—the institutions they have become during the past forty years. For many, it will be impossible. Across-the-board budget cuts dilute the quality of existing programs and jeopardize the programs that aspire to greatness. In aggregate, higher education in the United States has reached a programmatic and cost size that can no longer be supported with available resources. As fewer and fewer resources are distributed across a broad programmatic base, institutions risk a slow deterioration in quality.

The pursuit of quality is not without peril, however. Massy has drawn a very important distinction between design quality and implementation quality, using an analogy of BMWs and Fords. He argues that while a BMW may have more design quality than a Ford, the Ford is less expensive and can still meet the quality needs of its owner. The key is that design quality must be measured against the task at hand. A cruise missile is an extremely well-designed weapon, but is inappropriate for taking out a mosquito on the back patio. Implementation quality, on the other hand addresses how well a product or service meets its design specifications. If a fly swatter is deemed to be the appropriate extermination device for the mosquito, then it should be a very good fly swatter. A high-quality implementation of the fly swatter production process should produce excellent fly swatters at the lowest reasonable costs. The distinction between design quality and implementation quality is critical. The unbridled pursuit of design quality may well yield the academic version of the cruise missile/mosquito analogy. Programmatic design quality must be bounded by institutional needs and resources and implemented in a high-quality manner.

## Toward Efficiency and Effectiveness

If quality is to be the driving force behind institutional change, then some important steps need to be taken.

### Determine Institutional Financial Equilibrium

Each institution must realistically calculate how much money is available to be spent currently and in the future. While seemingly self-evident, this has not been the practice within higher education. The concept of financial equilibrium broadly examines an institution's financial structure, given its mission, to ensure its short- and long-term financial health. A balanced budget does not necessarily mean that an institution is in a state of financial equilibrium. If the endowment spending rate is too high and no funds are being reinvested in facilities, the long-range financial health of the institution is in jeopardy. The budget may be balanced, but at what future cost? The purchasing power of the endowment and the functional value of the facilities are eroding. Yet, this is the tactic many schools use to balance budgets. In essence, these institutions have been living beyond their means and have invaded their capital to do it.

In determining financial equilibrium, each college and university must ask and realistically answer several questions.

- What is the appropriate market-based tuition price that it can afford to charge? Historically, the industry has utilized a cost-plus pricing strategy; Here's how much we need to spend; let's set prices accordingly. Most institutions were able to get away with this approach during the robust economic growth of the 1980s. However, this model has systematically outstripped parental and student ability to pay the bill and led to ever-growing financial aid budgets (in the form of tuition discounts). In the early 1990s, many institutions were netting only twenty-five to thirty cents of each marginal dollar of increased tuition. A market-based pricing approach focuses less on what the institution needs and more on people's willingness and ability to pay.
- How much should be reinvested in the physical plant to maintain its functional value to the institution? American colleges and universities have accumulated a staggering $60 billion backlog of capital renewal and de-

ferred maintenance. Programmatic growth and balanced budgets have been achieved in part at the expense of existing facilities.

• How much debt can the institution sustain?
• What endowment spending rate will preserve endowment purchasing power? A number of institutions have slowly increased spending rates as a short-term, budget-balancing measure. However, this is a slippery slope for most institutions because it is very easy to become addicted to those revenues.
• What is a realistic level of sponsored research given the growing competition for those dollars?
• What is a reasonable enrollment level for the institution given its standards and demographics?
• How much money can the institution realistically expect to raise from its donor base?

The answers to these questions will vary from institution to institution. In the end, however, realistic answers will identify an institution's unique financial equilibrium pressure points and determine how much money is available for programs and operations.

*Determine What can be Afforded*

Having determined the institution's point of financial equilibrium, faculty members and administrators must answer the fundamental question, What programs of appropriate quality can we afford? Answering this question is not a simple undertaking. During the growth period of the past forty years, many institutions have attempted to be all things to all people. Programs have grown topsy-turvy at many institutions, largely in response to competitive pressures. However, as student demand abates and costs continue to rise, numerous colleges and universities can no longer maintain program quality.

The concept of selective excellence will have to prevail throughout the industry if reasonable quality standards are to be maintained. Each institution will have to systematically address is programmatic strengths and weaknesses to identify what is worth keeping, what should be improved, and what should be discarded. Simply making the entire program base more productive is unrealistic and inappropriate. Traditional productivity concepts (i.e., more output, cost benefit analysis, etc.) have limited value. Colleges and universities should have a solid understanding of their program revenues and costs. However, merely increasing class size and ballooning student-faculty rations will only diminish quality. Costs may be controlled, but it is to the long-run detriment of the institution and its students. Education is a labor-intensive and capital-intensive industry. Although technology may play a greater role in the delivery of educational services in the future, the basic educational exchange still takes place between good faculty and good students. The challenge for institutions is to determine which of those exchanges they can afford to do best, remembering that they cannot afford all of them.

Design quality should play an important role in shaping programs. What is in the best interest of students, faculty, and the institution? As Massy and Zemsky argue, faculty activity has moved away from institutional goals toward the activities that enhance a faculty member's standing within his or her discipline (research, publishing, etc.). Consequently, program design and infrastructure often reflect BMW design quality when a Ford or Chevy would be more appropriate (i.e., departments that offer a broad range of specialty courses but have few or no majors). The BMW design quality should not be arbitrarily dismissed, but it must be tempered by institutional resource constraints, other programmatic needs, and student needs.

### Reconsider Administrative Activities

The basic challenge in this area is defining the outputs of administration. What exactly do administrators do? A scan of the typical institution will usually find people working hard. Paper is flowing. Approvals are granted. Reports are issued. Yet, is all of that work really needed? If it is necessary, is it done efficiently and effectively?

Anecdotes about cumbersome administrative processes and bureaucratic snafus abound. At one institution, five approvals are required for a faculty member's change of address to be entered into the personnel information system. At another, a labyrinthine purchasing process groans inexorably forward, turning tens of thousands of requisitions into tens of thousands of purchase orders. Throughout, stamps and signatures of approval are collected, adding mostly cost and little value to the transaction. In many ways, such administrative processes are control systems that happen to provide services to users rather than appropriately controlled service systems. Reorienting such processes around essential activities and focusing on customer service most often produces greater productivity and improved service quality. Administration should not be an end in itself.

To begin assessing administrative activities, each institution must answer several sets of questions.

- Does the institution need all of the administrative activities currently performed? What can be eliminated with non-perceptible harm to the college? What is nice to do but not essential?
- What are the key processes through which work gets done? How well designed are these processes? Does the work flow smoothly? How long does it take to get something done? How much does it cost to produce the desired output? Are needless and unnecessary steps involved? Does institutional decentralization produce redundancy and added cost in administrative activities?

- Can these work processes be designed from the bottom up? Most work processes typically start with noble goals—to better control and mobilize institutional purchasing power, to more effectively register students, or to more effectively produce payroll checks. Over time, however, layer upon layer of added tasks, steps, and controls are added to such processes. The end product of this evolved, rather than designed, approach is often a monster that devours its young. The process assumes a life of its own while its costs rise and the quality of its service declines. Pieces of the process are "owned" by individual departmental managers, but no one "owns" the overall process.

A more logically and rationally designed administrative infrastructure can yield lower costs overall and higher-quality service. Productivity becomes a by-product of good implementation quality, assuming the design quality is appropriate for the task at hand.

### Need for Change and Leadership

The preceding section speaks directly to the need for change in the way colleges and universities are managed. Much of the change is basic. It requires a rethinking of the financial management of the institution, a focus on academic quality in light of shrinking resources, and a reorienting of administrative efforts around essential task and activities. Yet, despite the seeming simplicity of the proposed changes, such undertakings are fraught with career-limiting implications for those initiating them. More than one job has been lost in challenging institutional culture and inertia.

The key to the basic change required in higher education is leadership. Without it, little can happen and institutional inertia will prevail. The exercise of strong leadership in higher education can be a Bermuda Triangle of sorts, a place where strange fates and disappearance occur. However, it is essential for effective change. Despite the cutting-edge thinking and research that takes place within colleges and universities, institutions themselves are not predisposed to change. When change occurs, it happens very slowly. Although consensus management has many positive attributes, it does not foster the dramatic change required at many institutions. Certainly, institutional leaders must work with and through faculty members and staff, but bold initiatives are seldom born in committees.

An appropriate starting point may well be the notion of reinventing the institution. Most people are familiar with the concept of zero-based budgeting. Perhaps the concept of zero-based operations needs to be invented. If an institution went out of business at 5 P.M. on a given day and started anew at 9 A.M. the following morning, would it do things the same way? Probably not. Certain programs would likely be jettisoned, administrative procedures simplified, and a tighter, higher-quality institution created. This is exactly the type of breakthrough thinking and return to basics so many schools need. The necessary changes will more likely occur if institutional leaders climb above the fray of institutional politics.

## Summary

The preceding discussion might appear to be more about strategy than about productivity and quality. However, it is important to recognize that productivity and quality have become strategic issues. Increased productivity is not a tactical response to a transient issue. It must become imbedded in institutional cultures for the long-term reasons of quality and robust survival. The primary challenge for all institutions is not downsizing but rightsizing. Each institution must be "sized" programmatically and administratively to fit its available resources given its mission and quality standards.

Business as usual is a highly risky mode of operation in this decade. Unless productivity is internalized and recognized as a strategic issue, colleges and universities may well be swept up in a tornado. Dorothy and Toto were also consumed by a Kansas whirlwind and embarked on an odyssey in search of home and the gentle Auntie Em. Institutions that continue to search for the comforts of their "home" of the past forty years may be in for a rude awakening. When they get there, they may well find that Auntie Em has moved.

# 8

# Building Responsive Universities: Some Challenges to Academic Leadership

*C. Warren Neel and William T. Snyder*

Universities face a difficult task in responding to societal problems. Information growth coupled with the rising tide of professionalism gives the individual professor personal identity while precluding any cross-discipline understanding of the broad problems of society. We have become an academy of researchers, not scholars, a faculty of highly trained specialists without concern for how the depth of our understanding applies between and among other disciplines. The challenge of university leaders is to foster an organizational climate that values breadth, not just depth.

### Building Responsive Universities:
### Some Challenges to Academic Leadership

Imagine this scenario: The guests at a cocktail party are community leaders and scholars from a nearby university. The conversation swirls around topics of local interest as well as those concerning the global village. One small group over in a corner of the room is involved in a discussion of careers and as you approach you hear a townsperson asking a distinguished professor about his career. Since he is new to the campus, the professor begins his response by speaking of his involvement in cutting-edge research of his field. He tries to give meaning to his studies by noting that his particular endeavor focuses on the spring offense of a particular Napoleonic battle. Since few people in the circle are familiar with that subject, he adds that he is a professor of Western European history with a specialty in the Napoleonic era. That, too, needs some explanation, or so it seems from the continuing discussion, so later he sug-

This chapter first appeared in Michael J. Stahl and Gregory M. Bounds (eds.) *Competing Globally Through Customer Value* (Westport, CT: Quorum Books, 1991). Reprinted with permission of Greenwood Publishing Group, Inc., Westport, CT. Copyright © 1991 by Michael J. Stahl and Gregory M. Bounds.

gests that he is a member of the distinguished faculty of the History Department and there upon elaborates on the quality of the faculty within the department. Still later, he suggests that he is part of a larger unit on campus referred to as the College of Liberal Arts. Finally, he announces himself as being a faculty member of the university. As the conversation continues, someone asks how he became an historian, to which he replies that he has always loved history and teaching.

This scene is symptomatic of a major set of problems facing universities today. In some measure these problems parallel the greater society problems, particularly those that face American business in a global economy. The professor at the cocktail party is a specialist, a professional, and a nationally recognized researcher in his field of endeavor. In the course of that particular evening he defined himself in very narrow, vertical terms, never once suggesting to his audience that he was an educator first. In the practice of his chosen field, he selected the field of history. Most complex businesses today have their own set of "professors" who profess a particular discipline for a particular function. They see the problems facing a particular company in highly structured vertical terms. Like the university, the manager of today is a well-trained specialist whose chief contribution has been largely determined by continual specialization of labor in highly fragmented hierarchical structures. Universities mirror that same dilemma. As a matter of fact, they may magnify the problem.

How did we get to this position? Wasn't it absolutely essential that we design this kind of structure in a modern university given the information explosion? Isn't it in keeping with the traditional land-grant mission of comprehensive universities in this country to have scholars pursuing the cutting edge of their field? The answers to all these questions is an obvious yes. But something has gone astray. The land-grant university concept is over one hundred years old, founded in a period of time when the dominant employment pattern was agriculture. It rose to a position of prominence by being responsive to the societal needs of an educated labor pool during the blossoming of the Industrial Revolution. Its growth paralleled the burst of energy that resulted in an exponential increase in new information. Now, over a hundred years later, its mission still intact, the public is asking the cadre of scholars who inherited the academic mantle, "Are we being responsive to societal needs at the turn of the twenty-first century?" Thoughtful leaders are suggesting that the answer is no.

When we look at the university as it is organized today, we find that its structure mirrors the information explosion. Naisbitt and Aberdeen (1990) say in *Megatrends 2000,* "[W]e are drowning in information and starved for knowledge." Each department is set up so as to accommodate a body of information and give identity to that body by way of a professorate and a degree. The department is comprised of a group of faculty members with specialties and subspecialties. Generally, all members of the field can get an independent evaluation of their scholarly output through journals or other publication media whose editorial boards are from similar departments and specialties. Getting published becomes the sign of success and the currency that is "spendable" in the job market. Furthermore, more often than not the editorial boards focus the area of interest and thus, the research agenda, by soliciting the articles for publication that address those areas of specialty already accepted as "interesting." The market plan for academic positions, particularly in comprehensive universities, places a high value on publications. They are countable, a sign of research capability if the research is funded, and there is independent judgment of quality.

All these elements are important to an academic community. But can that community value other equally important activities of the faculty, namely, teaching and service? Perhaps those leaders who are questioning the responsiveness of comprehensive universities and higher education in general are asking how institutions lost sight of who the customers are, of who the professorate really serves, and how. Thus, a university, if we dare draw an analogy, is a large community made up of small households, each often having a separate language, a separate set of goals and aspirations, and a separate sense of identity. Each house may be painted a different color, have a different roof pitch, and a different size family, but it is part of a larger community. Or is it? What makes a community is a common set of shared values, not a disparate group of houses lined along the street. So the question to the modern university is: How can we develop a common set of shared values, bridge the gap between our specialties, and develop breadth as well as depth in our body of information so that we do indeed have a community of scholarship rather than small independent households of narrow research?

Some would suggest that this analogy is counter to the information explosion era in which we need the specialist whose entire energies are devoted to a particular aspect of a field. That argument is certainly appropriate. However, not everyone pursuing those small glitches in the armor of a particular discipline will build a great university that is responsive to the larger needs of society. Thus, the challenge is to build breadth as well as depth, to get a common, shared set of values that build a community rather than a disparate group of houses.

That analogy is not totally unlike the problems that face American business. The huge American corporation, with its line and staff positions, each fragmented into highly specialized units, has been the hallmark of American economic dominance since World War II. Today most executives are finding that those same specialists no longer talk to one another, yet the problems are multidisciplinary, requiring individuals from different points of view to work together, debate together, and come to a common solution. That need, as well as the pressure to be responsive to that need, is driving American corporations to experiment with different models and different staffing needs for those models. There is no greater challenge to university leaders today or to those captains of industry than addressing the narrowness and the professionalism that have isolated and insulated both professor and manager from the major threats facing the country today.

It is often said that American business (or for that matter any business operating in a competitive environment) has as its force of change the need to make a profit in order to remain in business. That pressure of competition in the marketplace is supposed to exert sufficient influence on the structure of the corporation. But universities don't have the same set of market pressures. As a matter of fact, universities have generally been isolated from such pressures. Certainly, there is the public outcry to hold tuition costs down while admitting additional students to the academic programs. Generally, however, universities have been able to pass along the tuition costs. Tuition has actually risen far faster than the inflation rate in the last dozen years or so without any material change in the delivery system of education. Now, however, the pressures are mounting for public accountability, for the wise and frugal use of public funds. Those pressures suggest that large comprehensive universities must respond differently today than they have at any time in their history.

The public's increasing insistence on accountability by the American educational system was initially felt by the K-12 segment of education. The public perception of the quality of American education, what is right and what is wrong with education, is influenced primarily by the perception of the condition of this level of education. This is understandable, given the larger K-12 student population relative to higher education and the greater involvement of the public with K-12 rather than higher education.

It was natural, therefore, that the initial wave of dissatisfaction and insistence on accountability would be focused on K-12. The skill deficiencies of students certified by K-12 are initially more readily discernible in K-12 graduates than in higher education graduates. In looking for scapegoats for our educational problems, the public has centered on the school boards and on the preparation of teachers by colleges of education. While there is great need for improvement in the preparation of teachers, the public criticism has at times become unfair and oversimplified.

Criticism of colleges of education is the cutting edge of public insistence for more accountability by higher education, yet other professional disciplines are also experiencing increasing criticism and insistence on accountability. The law profession and law schools are being criticized for contributing to a more litigious society. Business schools are being criticized for producing graduates more interested in optimizing corporate quarterly profits than in issues of quality, customer satisfaction, value added, and international competitiveness. The engineering professions are being criticized for being insensitive to environmental issues and the social implications of technology.

The common thread of criticism centers on the inward focus that has come with excessive specialization and inadequate emphasis on cross-functional, interdisciplinary education. Universities, like American business, are being challenged to give greater attention to value added to the students they matriculate, to have more concern for customer satisfaction. This emphasis on accountability can be expected to increase in a future of finite financial resources as education competes with other societal needs for funding.

Interestingly, the proliferation of professionalism within the narrow distance of a modern university is detrimental not only to the quality of education, particularly at the undergraduate level, but also to achieving any economies. As disciplines are further fragmented, specialists are hired, teaching loads are reduced to enhance the image through research, and class sizes fall. The result is lack of responsiveness by comprehensive universities to their various constituencies (publics).

Several other elements suggest that the university is insulated from change. One is that in many instances the most important "currency" for enhancing the reputation of the individual faculty member and/or the department or college is that of research funding and publications. While indeed that is important to the continuing process of inquiry, the faculty member of a narrow specialty often picks an esoteric research agenda so as to appeal to a particular editorial board of a particular journal, not because the agenda item chosen is of national concern, and not because the students in the faculty member's charge have a need to understand both breadth and depth of a discipline. Imagine if you will a large comprehensive faculty of a major land-grant institution, say, one thousand or more professors, each seeking an outlet for their critical research in a narrow discipline as the major driving force behind their behavior. In such an environment, it becomes extremely difficult, if not impossible, for the leadership of a campus to materially affect, or for that matter, address multidisciplinary problems, the kind of problems that are generally those of society and the world marketplace. In such an environment it is left to the student to follow the path of the curriculum to gain breadth by being exposed to a host of highly vertical, narrow disciplines. Ironically, most major universities today leave that responsibility for gaining any disciplinary understanding and knowledge primarily to the student.

In many instances, especially in professional schools, faculty members (as in the cocktail party previously noted) view themselves as members of an academic household, that is, a very narrow specialty, and do not see themselves as educators or as members of a larger community. This of necessity means that the leadership of comprehensive universities today has the challenge of rebuilding a community of scholars, rather than producing narrow researchers.

The agriculture-dominated campus of the old A&M model of a hundred years ago was epitomized by large surrounding fields with handsome silos standing watch over the various research projects whose findings would ultimately benefit the farms of the citizens of that state. Today we don't see concrete silos; rather, they are functional silos representing every discipline on campus. There is no concrete or brick, but they are made even more durable. Today they have the same hardness and muscularity that they have always had, but the concrete is being replaced by a unique language, and the bricks by a set of understood acronyms. They are the professional silos. Clustered together, they stand watch over curricular and budget turf. The research outcome of these silos is often returned to the silo and recycled over and over and over. It may never get to the domain of public debate and use. The challenge to the leadership of the universities is, therefore, to break down the silos, to find the richness of inquiry (research and scholarship) matched by quality classroom teaching (professing) that collectively builds a mosaic of breadth and depth so as not to leave students responsible for breadth. Tomorrow's leaders who come from that cauldron of intellectual fervor will be capable of handling those problems that require the competence of depth with understanding of breadth. But first American higher education must value those traits and organize itself to engender them in the next graduating class.

## References

Naisbitt, J., and Aberdeen, P., *Megatrends 2000* (New York: Morrow Publishing Co., 1990).

# 9

# The Big Questions in Higher Education Today

## L. Edwin Coate

*"'The Change Masters'.... Those people and*
*organizations adept at the art of anticipating the*
*need for, and of leading, productive change. "*
—Rosabeth Moss Kanter, 1988

### Questions of Survival

By the year 2000, American colleges and universities will be lean and mean, service oriented and science minded, multicultural, and increasingly diverse— if they intend to survive.

In 1992, two-thirds of the nation's public institutions had operating budgets that were less than the previous year. Three years of revenue difficulties and poor public perception has led to increased tuition, higher fees, increased class size, layoffs, and reduced spending on maintenance, library acquisitions, and salaries. Over the next ten years, U.S. universities and colleges will continue to face profound revenue shortfalls. We must either increase productivity and effectiveness or the next generation of citizens will face significantly reduced educational opportunities.

What is happening? Why do we need to change now? The first problem, of course, is the current recession or state of the economy. In the public sector, legislators and governors struggle to balance budgets with less revenue. In the private sector, families struggle to pay higher tuition and/or fees.

The second problem is too many students. Demographic forces continue to press for more seats in colleges and universities and at the same time, more adults are trying to prepare for a new career as jobs of the past disappear.

The third area of concern is the credibility of higher education itself. We are under siege. We're told we cost too much, spend carelessly, plan myopically, teach poorly, and, when questioned, act defensively (Governor Thomas Kean, New Jersey). According to pollster Louis Harris, only 25 percent of the public have confidence in the "people running higher education."

It is apparent that the current system is simply breaking down—often in ways we don't like—and we must be open to change. But in this department we don't have a good track record; academia has structural difficulties in reacting to change. We are committed to shared governance, to manage by consensus, and we encounter strong resistance to reshaping institutional goals. Yet, governors, legislatures, business leaders, and tax payers are demanding change. They want and expect us to identify and pursue ways to reduce costs while increasing productivity and effectiveness. So change we must. The only question is whether we do it by design or by default.

### Questions of Quality

Today, many universities and colleges are looking at the "quality movement" to see if it can provide a template for change. Questions about quality in education get at the "business of the business." In the past, quality in education was linked to the quantity of resources and an institution's reputation. Now the dialogue has changed. How do we assess the outcomes of higher education? How do we measure quality in teaching, research, and service? Can we restructure our curriculums to be more effective? Can we reduce the time it takes for our students to earn a degree? In what ways can we improve our service internally? Can we process new hires more quickly? Can we pay our bills faster?

Money alone will not provide answers to the these questions. One solution that begins to address these issues is to become a customer-focused institution, using the quality tools introduced by Dr. Deming in Japan in 1950 and by Dr. Hammer here in the United States in 1990. This change to a customer-focused institution is touching the lives of almost everyone in our world; higher education seems to be one of the last bastions of resistance. But there is evidence that this revolution is touching higher education at last. Over 150 colleges and universities are now experimenting in some way with Total Quality Management (TQM) or Business Process Re-engineering (BPR).

These experiments with TQM and BPR in higher education raise a cadre of questions. Is there valid evidence that organizational change will have a lasting impact on the quality of our higher educational institutions? Are there really sincere efforts to change the culture, measurement, infrastructure, motivation, planning and technology systems in a comprehensive way? Are there serious efforts to be customer driven? Are we sincerely attempting to address the gap between customer expectations and our performance?

The answer is a cautious yes; not a resounding yes, but small steps are being taken by a few brave souls in community colleges and research universities across the nation. At Oregon State University (OSU) we attempted to answer these types of probing questions and currently at the University of

California, Santa Cruz (UCSC) we are attempting to address similar probing questions. This "peaceful revolution" is causing stress and strain in many aspects of our university lives. We are on the cutting edge of change, learning as we go, excited by new opportunities. Even though we are still uncomfortable using terms like "customer," "value added," "touch time," "processes," and "systems," we are trying to change and, in our own way, we are succeeding.

Historically changes occur when there is (1) sufficient dissatisfaction with things as they are; (2) a clear vision of an end goal; (3) a strategy for change to achieve the desired state; and (4) the knowledge and skills to achieve the change. This chapter discusses the need for change in higher education and provides a vision and a strategy as well as a summary of the knowledge and skills needed to achieve the desired change.

## The Vision

In 1776, Adam Smith described the roots of American work styles and organizational structures in his book, *The Wealth of Nations*. His division of labor embodied his observations that more products or services can be provided if specialized employees work in sequence, each performing a single task. This approach to work was improved upon by Frederick Taylor in 1916, but was not significantly changed in America until recently when we realized we were falling behind in world competition.

Today's universities and colleges, as well as private sector companies such as insurance firms and computer chip manufacturers, were all built around Smith and Taylor's central ideas; the division or specialization of labor and the consequent fragmentation of work. The larger the organization, the more specialized and fragmented is the work. For example, in higher education our registration, admission, purchasing, and facilities management offices typically assign separate staff to process standardized forms. They enter data and pass the forms on to supervisors for approval. The supervisor subsequently sends the form to another office for more data to be entered or sometimes for all the data to be re-entered. No one completes the entire job; they just perform piecemeal tasks. As these processes mature and evolve, we build in redundancy and control checks. Many processes now exceed 50 percent in nonvalue added work in our organizations.

In today's universities the staff may talk about serving customers, but the real job is still perceived as "keeping the boss happy." Many employees feel they're just a cog in the wheel. The best strategy is often seen as "keeping your head down and not making waves." When things go wrong it's the manager's job to solve the problem. After all, that's why he or she gets paid the big bucks. In turn, the manager is evaluated by the number of direct reports and the size of the budget he or she has; the one with the biggest empire wins. Sound familiar?

Dr. J. Edwards Deming realized that the way we in America were organizing work wasn't effective. He found in his research that 85 percent of the problems in organizations were occurring in processes, not people (*Out of the Crisis,* 1982). But his key idea of focusing on process improvement presented a problem for U.S. management because most work is managed by focusing on tasks, jobs, people, and structures, not processes.

Process management was introduced in Japan by Deming in the early 1950s, and is the one thing that is most often credited with Japan's business success since World War II. Process management asks us to realize that customers pay our salaries and that we must provide a product or service that meets or exceeds their expectations. We must recognize that we get paid for value created. All employees must accept ownership of problems and actively participate in resolving them. Employees belong on teams; they fail or succeed together.

This is change in a big way. Getting people to accept the idea that their work lives will undergo radical change is not easy. After providing them with a compelling argument for change, we must give them a clear goal or a vision statement on which to focus. The vision statement for our process management effort at UC Santa Cruz is:

> To be the campus known for quality in the best university system in the world. Our administrative goal at UCSC is to provide effective services to our students, faculty, staff and other constituencies. These services will employ modern technology at the lowest reasonable cost. UCSC's administration will be largely decentralized, placing responsibility and accountability at the appropriate level closest to the transaction or client/customer. Administrative processes will avoid needless redundancy. Technology will enhance communication at all levels of the institution. Staff, faculty, and students alike will save time and money from improved administrative functions.

## The Strategy

Without students to teach, research to conduct, or services to provide, there is no business for colleges and universities. Without value there is no reason for customers to choose our institution over an increasingly large number of similar institutions. The number of colleges and universities in the United States has grown from approximately 1800 to over 3300 in just forty years! Competition, market niche, empty seats, and empty beds are a new phenomenon to many of us, yet these are problems that have long been familiar to American businesses. What we must concentrate on now is continually increasing the value of our product—our teaching, research, and service—to our customers.

The concept of creating value and passing it along to our customers is an approach that can transform rigid institutions into responsive, world-class colleges and universities. We want our customers to feel that they have received exceptional value for their dollar. When tuition was heavily subsidized, almost any level of teaching was of value, but with the cost of tuition skyrocketing, the value is now being scrutinized and questioned.

To be customer driven, we must be able to read our customers' minds, give them caring, personalized service and provide them with the knowledge and skills they need to be successful. No small task!

So just who are our customers? Students, faculty, taxpayers, parents, legislators, citizens—the list goes on and on. The trick to being customer driven is to first recognize our customers, then identify their needs, wants, and desires, and subsequently meet or exceed their expectations.

Most institutions of higher education have developed around the bureaucratic organizational model. This model is hierarchial, procedural, and dependent on Adam Smith's specialization of labor, narrow delegation of authority, and complex procedures. The problems associated with this model include:

- substantial organization layering,
- a high reliance on paper and forms to document decisions and transactions,
- excessive points of control, and
- excessive redundancy of operations.

Within the bureaucratic model, productivity is significantly reduced by the proliferation of unnecessary tasks while communication is blocked by vertical functional silos.

To foster productivity and service, a new management model is evolving on campuses like OSU and UCSC. Built on the concepts of process control (Deming, *Out of the Crisis,* 1982), this new model has evolved from implementing the new management tools of Total Quality Management (TQM) and Business Process Re-engineering (BPR). This new model can be called "Quality Process Management."

Quality Process Management can be described as a disciplined, structural approach designed to meet or exceed the needs of the customer by improving the efficiency and effectiveness of our processes. This new model reflects the strategies of many industrial leaders, but only a very few campuses. It is meant to eliminate layers of hierarchy by decentralizing the authority for decision making, by increasing spans of control, and by imbedding minimal internal controls within integrated information systems. The model delegates responsibility and authority to the lowest possible organizational level where the customer first interacts with the institution. It encompasses a set of human resource strategies that specifies expected employee behavior and rewards risk taking, initiative, personal accountability, outcomes, collaboration, and customer service. Finally, the model uses process improvement teams to improve processes and rewards teams accordingly.

But what exactly are processes? A process is a sequence of activities that is intended to achieve a result (create added value) for a customer. There are over 150 processes in a typical college or university. There are *academic processes,* which include teaching, research, technology transfer, and tenure giving; there are *auxiliary processes* such as food service, child care, mail service, and book sales; and there are *business* and *administrative processes* such as fund-raising, hiring, assigning space, allocating money, cleaning and maintenance of buildings, and distribution of payments.

Quality Process Management is an exciting new way to improve the quality of work performed for our customers. It puts customers at the top of the organization and asks our leaders to provide direction, empowerment, and support for the people who create value for our customers.

Quality Process Management requires significant cultural changes that begin with leadership. It requires leadership to reduce fear of change, encourage open communications, push decision making to the lowest practical level, and build performance around systems that motivate people to grow and develop.

Leadership in a quality university or college is essential to create the vision and provide the direction that will unify and inspire these efforts. A compelling vision has the power to motivate. Clear communication of our campus direction focuses our energies and talents on the shared purpose and common goals of Quality Process Management.

Leadership helps set these shared goals and translate them into action. Quality Process Management provides the structure to planning and implementation that can help leaders focus and direct their energies to improve critical processes.

## Conclusions

Significant changes that have been experienced at UCSC and OSU include:

- Elimination of jobs (in some instances, several existing jobs were merged into one);
- Workers' roles changed from controlled to empowered;
- Work is now performed where it makes sense, work steps are performed in a logical order, and redundant tasks have been eliminated;
- Checks and controls were significantly reduced;
- Jobs changed from simple to complex;
- Work units changed from functional departments to process teams;
- Values changed from protective to productive;
- Organizational structures changed from hierarchical to flat;
- Salary structures are changing from salaries based on the size of budget and staff to salaries based on results;
- Systems changed from paving cow paths to enabling radical changes; and
- Work is performed for the customer, not the business.

As described above, this is a significant change from the bureaucratic management model currently in use at most colleges and universities today.

One of the enduring characteristics of our national university system has been its stability. But that stability has a tremendous downside: it becomes an excuse to resist change. To believe that we can preserve the American university as it is today is to ignore the reality of our rapidly changing world and its expectations of us. However, change of the magnitude required today can only be made with the use of new methodologies combined with strong leadership and administrative support. Quality Process Management is an exciting new management tool that offers significant improvement over the current bureaucratic model used by most institutions of higher education.

> *"There is nothing more difficult to carry out, nor more dangerous to handle than to initiate a new order of things. For the reformer has enemies in all those who profit from the old order and only lukewarm defenders in all those who would profit by the new order."*
>
> —Machiavelli, *The Prince*

## References

Deming, W. E. *Out of the Crisis.* Cambridge, Mass.: MIT Center for Advanced Engineering Study, 1982.

# III

# Applying the Quality Approach
# in Higher Education

# 10

# TQM: A Time for Ideas

*Ted Marchese*

It's fascinating to watch the arrival of Total Quality Management (TQM)—
or Continuous Quality Improvement (CQI), as it is called by its health care
practitioners—in higher education. A few campus pioneers began their TQM
effort in the 1980s; the big wave of interest kicked in during the 1991-92
academic year. By now, it's hard to find a campus without a knot of people
trying to implement the thing. On almost any campus, thin as the knowledge
may yet be, people are already either stoutly for Total Quality or deeply skeptical of it. What the quick-to-judge miss—what the early, triumphalist writing
about TQM in higher education also misses—is that Total Quality is complicated, important, difficult to implement, and far from figured out. Contrary to
the tool-driven, seven-step workshops that consultants are busily selling, we're
years away from knowing what academic versions of TQM will appropriately
look like.

TQM, as campuses are indeed discovering, is not some bite-sized management fad like MBO. Instead it's a code word for a big tentful of ideas aimed at
the transformation of the modern corporate enterprise. In the eyes of the quality movement, the late-twentieth-century corporation is bureaucratic, over-
sized, sluggish, self-absorbed, unresponsive, and repressive of initiative and
talent; worse, it is uncompetitive. To achieve its desired transformation, the
Total Quality movement over time has gathered in loose union ideas from
systems theory, humanistic and industrial psychology, management theory,
human-resource and organizational development, and statistical process control, plus lessons from earlier attempts at quality improvement, like quality
circles. All of these ideas, in many guises and combinations, aim to remake
organizations so they become more focused, disciplined, quick footed, humane, and competitive.

This chapter originally appeared in *Change: The Magazine of Higher Learning,* Vol-
ume 25, Issue 3, pp. 10-13, May/June, 1993. Reprinted with permission of the Helen
Dwight Reid Educational Foundation. Published by Heldref Publications, 1319 18th
St., N.W., Washington, D.C. 20036-1802. Copyright © 1993.

With this understanding of the quality movement, it's important to stand back from the particularist versions of the "it" being vended today. The danger is that we'll be put off by the fervor, the formulas, or the smell of fad and miss the fact that a very important set of ideas about the organizations we work in has made its way through the industrial, service, health care, and governmental sectors of society and is now at our doorstep. The issue, then, is less TQM itself than the appropriateness of the set of ideas behind it to problems we know we face.

What are those ideas? One could list dozens. Here are six important ones, with reflections on their applicability in higher education.

The first idea is *customer focus*. In earlier days, quality was defined as what the craftsman or the professional said it was; in industry, as the absence of defects. The new dispensation is that quality is what the customer says it is. The corporate objective is to provide goods or services that meet or exceed customer requirements; indeed that may surprise and delight the customer.

A customer focus impels organizations to be specific about the parties they serve. Who are your customers? The ultimate users of the good or service you produce, TQM says. Those users are both external and internal to the organization. The external customers of a college, for example, would likely include funders and donors, employers, and graduate schools; internally, customers would include students (in their academic roles, "learners"), but also, for any employee of the college, "the people down the hall who receive my work." Must you do everything the customer wants? No, good judgment applies as ever.

Writ large, the doctrine of customer focus is a call to everybody in the organization to get out of the cubbyholes they work in and talk with the real people they're serving. The concept especially challenges managers and professionals—the "experts" who run knowledge-intensive enterprises—to be clearer about whom they work for and systematically to listen to those parties.

It is a commonplace observation that all organizations, over time, tend more and more to be run for the people who work in them, and for the convenience and reward of their managers and professionals especially. Scholars tell us this is notably so in larger, older organizations dominated by professionals—hospitals, court systems, armies and navies, government bureaucracies, and universities. The customer orientation of Total Quality challenges that orientation; it asks, Who pays the bills here? What public is this profession supposed to serve? To whatever extent a university may be inward looking, its departments and disciplines peer focused and self-referential, the "customer" questions posed by the quality movement have a healthy air to them.

The focus on customers offers another advantage, that of demystifying quality. Over the decades, judgments about campus or departmental "quality" have often been settled by the presence or absence of certain resources, by citing the opinion of insiders and peers, or quality has been declared "ineffable" and therefore beyond discussion. The assessment movement broke through these closed-end ways of thinking with the insight that an institution's quality was a function of its contributions to student learning—contributions that are knowable and trackable. In the same spirit, the quality movement enters its own, new way of judging quality: the degree to which customer needs or expectations are met. Customer needs are knowable and trackable; "good outcomes for named parties we serve" becomes an additional, useful measure for campus and unit performance.

The second idea is *continuous improvement.* This is a simple idea, clear enough in its stating, sprung from the intensely competitive world of automotive, computer, and similar industries where any failure to push the boundaries of quality, each year out, can be fatal. Entire industries have come to learn that if you're standing still, you're dead; whatever quality level you've achieved today won't be good enough tomorrow.

Simple as the concept seems, the embrace of continuous improvement as an organizational imperative has profound consequences: to reach ever higher performance levels every year out, an organization needs to think systemically about the constant improvement of all processes that deliver value to its customers. It needs management, production, personnel, information, supplier, and reward systems that are in gear and geared to the task—in a word, all (or most) of TQM.

Continuous improvement, as idea and as imperative, is probably the stranger for the academy among Total Quality's tentful of ideas, especially when it comes to the daily tasks of undergraduate education. A community sense or ethic that teaching and learning need continuously to be improved—and all that would follow from that, notably assessment—is absent from our discourse. Quality assurance we do know, but continuous quality improvement, "well, that would take money," and "we're doing the best we can." The missing ethic is less personal than corporate: somehow, despite all the good will, talent, and effort of individual faculty, there's seldom a collective sense of obligation toward or avidness about the improvement of student learning. So it is that an organization full of learners doesn't add up to a learning organization.

This fact came home for me last summer reading Sheila Tobias's *Change* report on science programs that work (May/June, 1992). In most of the large universities she visited, the picture was one of business as usual in science classes, interrupted only every so often by some grand, externally funded innovation, which tended either not to work or be sustained. The programs that did work, on the other hand, were characterized by a "process model that focuses attention continuously on every aspect of the teaching-learning enterprise," where "faculty pay continuous attention to what we teach, whom we teach, and how we teach," and where "once a problem is identified, a solution is sought—locally, incrementally, quickly."

The discouraging circumstance about the Tobias finding is just how rare such an approach turns out to be. One recalls Derek Bok's remark in *Change* that—thousands of projects, task forces, foundation grants, and journal articles notwithstanding—the state of teaching and learning in American higher education seems no better than it was twenty years ago. When I look at college completion rates over those years, or at the standardized test scores of our graduates, or at campus assessment findings over time, I find little to refute Bok's observation. What's missing, again, is less the know-how or money than the felt need for improvement—an ethic and the aspiration that would impel a collegiate organization toward higher levels of student attainment year after year.

The third emphasis is *management by fact*. The notion of continuously improving the quality of an organization's goods or services implies that "quality" has to be specified and monitored. If you're serious about quality, corporate managers say, you have to be as specific as possible about what you mean by quality and systematically keep track of how you are doing. TQM wants everybody's focus on the organization's central missions; it deploys public, visible information systems to let each person and team know what's important and how we're doing.

More largely, the central idea here is to get managers and work teams to move beyond decision making by personal impression, anecdote, or complaint; keep track, dig out the facts, find the systemic problem or root cause, the idea says, and spend your time on that. TQM's statistical armamentarium includes dozens of relatively simple ways of tracking organizational or unit performance. Most of these tools—indeed, the habit of looking for and preferring data—would be entirely new to the informal, loosely coupled, problem-chasing world of academic administration.

These "be clear, keep track, use data to improve" injunctions are close in spirit to what higher education has come to learn from assessment. Assessment, of course, has been an uphill battle these last eight years; even now it's little more than an episodic veneer in most institutions. The reasons for this are several; not least among them is a general disinclination to specify and track the key processes of undergraduate education. But what is the point of the assessor's "knowledge for improvement" if continuous improvement isn't the aim?

A fourth idea is that of *benchmarking*. The word itself can be confusing; people think it implies a statistic or norm. In today's corporation, benchmarking means the "systematic search for best practice." Driven by the need to improve continuously, a corporation identifies its key work processes, large and small, then asks, What company in the world does this one the best? It searches out that "best practice," studies it, adapts it, and tries to do as well or better. Xerox, for example, improved its own handling of 1-800 phone orders by studying the way L. L. Bean responds to callers; at IBM's Baldrige-award facility in Rochester, Minnesota, some 360 processes have been benchmarked.

In undergraduate education, the same absence of ethic that constrains continuous improvement makes searching for "best practice" almost a nonexistent practice. One consequence is that even our best innovations don't spread. Over the past years, well-conceived, cost-effective approaches have been developed for scores of academic processes: for student advisement, for the teaching of writing, for the deployment of technology, for the doing of assessment, and on and on. The observable fact is that most of these innovations have gone nowhere. There must be 500 "successful" FIPSE projects that have never been replicated.

It doesn't take long on most campuses to figure out why: the first thing a visitor will be told is, "We're unique." If a committee can be persuaded to learn from another campus, the example better be from the tiny spectrum of institutions it aspires to be like—a likely dry well. In industry, this cobbled, localist attitude is derided with the phrase, "Not invented here." What is remarkable also is the degree to which companies, even entire industries, collaborate with one another in benchmarking for mutual improvement, a phenomenon all too rare in the inward-looking, status-driven world of higher education.

A fifth, very important emphasis in the quality movement is *people*. An organization avid for improvement sees people as its greatest resource. It does everything possible to give every employee the preparation, tools, and initiative to contribute to corporate goals. This emphasis starts with an organizational vision capable of giving power to each person's work, a vision carried forward in a hundred policies aimed at the empowerment of individuals and work teams. For employees, the watchwords become training, teamwork, responsibility taking, and mutual accountability. For leaders, the call is to provide vision and strategy, to coach, mentor, and be a team player, and to tend to what Peter Senge and others label "organizational learning." In TQM, 85 percent of the problems that arise in the course of work are attributable to the organization's systems; just 15 percent to the shortcomings of individual employees. The manager's job, then, is to improve constantly the work systems of the organization, to drive out blaming and fear, and to remove obstacles in the system that prevent persons or teams from doing their best work.

A lot of powerful ideas are packed into the preceding paragraph; many of them contradict prevailing norms on campuses where blaming and fear infect relationships, teamwork is rare, and managers know best. The good news, though, is that many of these "new" organizational teachings turn out to be ones the academic world is ready for. To the surprise and delight of many of its campus initiators, this "human side of TQM"—especially the idea of working in teams with real authority—has struck a positive chord, to the frequent happy improvement of work processes and morale.

The early success of a few teams, of course, does not a campus remake. Teamwork is only a first step on a longer, difficult journey the quality movement would have us undertake. At a deeper level, the barriers are cultural, attitudinal, and political. What trust, for example, do collegiate organizations vest in the broad range of their employees? What value is placed on their development? In companies like Motorola, Corning, or GM's Saturn Division, a remarkable 5 percent of the company's expenditures are devoted to employee education, training, and development. Motorola, which has realized 15 percent or greater productivity gains for eight years running, thinks its return on investment for employee training is 30 to 1. Why is it that in almost any university or college—organizations devoted to learning—the comparable expenditure will be a fraction of one percent?

The sixth insight has to do with organizational *structures*. Quality champions argue that, to assure the delivery of value in the marketplace, work has to be organized around the needs and preferences of customers, not those of the corporation or its employees.

In the bureaucratic world of old, the particulars of most work processes tended to be clustered within neatly tiered departments or disciplines ("silos"), each with its own turf and norms—manufacturing, sales, finance, R&D, purchasing, and so on. As the Cadillac Motor Car Company tells it in its Baldrige presentation, the consequence for the company (up until the mid-1980s) was "over the wall engineering." Car buffs in the design shop would draw up a new model, fins and all; they'd toss their drawings over the wall to engineers, who were supposed to figure out how to manufacture it; the engineers tossed their work over the wall to the factory floor, where workers were supposed to build it; upon which the car went to dealers, who were supposed to sell it; whence it was passed to the buyer, to whom they said, "Good luck."

Now that whole process is inverted, or at least turned on its side, and the walls disappear, customers, mechanics, dealers, assembly-line workers, engineers, designers, and even the finance people work together as a team to produce a car that is buildable, sellable, usable, fixable, and a delight to the customer. The entire process, as they say, has been re-engineered.

From a quality perspective, American colleges and universities seem incredibly vertical and compartmentalized, like a corporation of ten years ago. Indeed, we practice "over the wall teaching" as students traipse across loose collections of free-standing courses on the way to degrees of unspecified outcome. Anything that requires cross-unit collaboration, like student advisement or general education, never seems to be done well.

What, then, shall we make of the coming of TQM? There *are* powerful, relevant ideas here: wonderful stories of accomplishment have already been written in its name, as you'll see on the following pages. Even so, the transformations TQM wants are so great that the best one can say is that this, too, will be uphill.

The pessimism about TQM's arrival in higher education comes from a comparison with its adoption in industry. Motorola and Xerox remade themselves into "high-performing work organizations" because they absolutely had to; it was change now or die. Few institutions or people in higher education feel that's a reality for us now; there just isn't that "heat at the backside" that brought transformation elsewhere. Even if we felt that urgency, I'm not sure that a headlong, externally driven rush into this thing makes sense for us. Too much of value could be left behind.

Having said that, I return to the ideas that TQM has put in the air. One of those ideas is that organizations should be driven by the intrinsic motivation in all of us to do our best work. Might it be that a fine sense of our own possibilities—and of our obligations to students, knowledge, our publics, and to one another—could serve as impulse for a homegrown push for higher quality?

What vision might drive such a push? What is it we hope for from our work? Last winter in *Change*, Jane Tompkins listed what she wanted from her university work: a common enterprise, belonging, good feelings in the workplace, a community of hope, and an integrated life. Here's another answer, from Max DePree's *Leadership is an Art*, a little book written by the CEO of a quality-oriented furniture company:

> We would like to find the most effective, most productive, most rewarding way of working together. We would like to know that our work process uses all the appropriate and pertinent resources: human, physical, financial. We would like a work process and relationships that meet our personal needs for belonging, for contributing, for meaningful work, for the opportunity to make a commitment, for the opportunity to grow and be at least reasonably in control of our own destinies. Finally, we'd like someone to say "thank you."

# 11

# TQM: Focus on Performance, Not Resources

*Daniel Seymour*

The butter in my refrigerator has a banner across the bottom of the package—A Tradition of Quality. Earl Scheib, the king of auto painting, assures me that he offers Quality at an Affordable Price. The local hospital offers Quality Medical Care "at your convenience," and a nearby university advertises its MBA program with the nifty headline, Quality to the Highest Degree.

"Quality" may be the most overused word in the English language today. People are willing to pay for it; organizations are driven to invest in it. Workers are exhorted to produce it, and advertisers feel compelled to communicate it. Quality is a near universal goal. At the same time, it is one of the least understood concepts. Everyone wants it. But what is it? And once you decide what it is, how do you attain it?

Total Quality Management (TQM) is a philosophy and set of tools that enable an organization to pursue systematically a definition of quality and a means for attaining quality. Nearly seventy years ago, W. A. Shewart, a statistician at Bell Telephone Laboratories, began to recognize that variability in industry could be understood using probability and statistics. Since the 1930s, "statistical process control" in industry has evolved into a broad set of concepts that touches every aspect of an organization—product or service design, reward systems, market research, work flow, supplier relations, and leadership style.

It has also evolved in another important way. From the narrow confines of the industrial shop floor, it has been adapted to the work of government and the service industry. The city of Madison (Wisconsin), the U.S. Navy, Federal Express, and the Hospital Corporation of America, for example, have implemented quality management practices. Each organization seems to take what it needs. Some concepts require no translation; others are redesigned or reshaped to fit unique circumstances.

Quality management's track record, so far, has been spotty. In some organizations, it has transformed the culture and had a dramatic impact on efficiency and effectiveness. In others, it has been an outright failure. Virtually everyone says":"We've only been at this for a short time. We're still learning." For those of us in higher education, the question is: Can TQM help colleges and universities improve performance? I believe it can.

## Five Scenarios

This was Jody Krall's fourth stop. She was waiting for a signature on an authorization form that would allow her department to hire an adjunct instructor. A professor had become ill before the fall semester was to begin; there was a scramble to cover his classes. Once she got this signature, she would walk to the business and finance office. That would leave just two more signatures to get.

Any organization is a multitude of processes; that is, a series of activities performed to achieve a specific outcome. Healthy processes are effective (meet customer requirements), efficient (use minimal time and resources), under control (documented and well defined), and adaptable (able to respond to changing conditions). Unhealthy processes, in contrast, tend to generate customer complaints, problems that never get resolved, missed deadlines, low staff morale, excessive overtime, and so on. In Jody's case, the adjunct professor hiring process had evolved into a series of activities that required seven signatures. She was angry. It was a waste of her time.

Quality management experts suggest that 30 to 40 percent of service organizations' operating costs result from unhealthy processes that produce scrap, rework, and needless complexity. Scrap is the failure to convert input into output—grant proposals that don't get funded and students who flunk out, for example. Rework is fixing something that wasn't done correctly the first time. Remedial courses are rework, and the typical course scheduling system is a nightmare of rework. Every form that is returned for a correction or missing information is more rework.

Then there is needless complexity. Does it really require the wisdom of seven people to hire an adjunct faculty member? Should it take ninety-nine days to respond to a graduate school application? At the University of Wisconsin-Madison, a team has redesigned that process—eliminating steps, reordering others, and reducing the time to two days—and has saved more than $120,000 in overtime costs. A physical plant team at Oregon State University studied the institution's remodeling process and uncovered three causes of overlap, delay, and unnecessary paper flow. The cycle time to complete projects has been reduced by between 5 and 35 percent.

After almost twenty minutes, Gary Walter finally made it to the front of the financial aid line. He gave the woman his social security number and waited for her to find his check. Gary thanked her and headed down the hallway and through the breezeway to the bursar's office. With his registration forms in one hand and his check in the other, he took his place at the end of the line and settled in for a long wait.

The work in organizations flows from one person to the next until the product or service is delivered to the end user. The people in organizations, however, tend to think and act like their boxes in the organizational chart. Each person adds his or her contribution, then tosses the work over the wall.

This pigeonholing effect often results in the wasted time that Gary experienced; rarely does any single person have enough knowledge to understand the extended process. The financial aid people distribute funds. The bursar's office collects funds. Only students experience the extended process. A collaborative look at the extended process might reveal new ways to merge work, simplify the process, and better serve the student-customer.

Teamwork makes sense for several reasons. People with different perspectives can generate new insights and working in groups can be far more invigorating than working alone. In a quality management environment, teamwork not only makes good sense, it is an absolute necessity. At the core of the quality philosophy is the idea that processes reflect how work gets done and that the best way to improve performance is to increase the efficiency and effectiveness of organizational processes. One person cannot do that. It requires bringing together the people who work in those processes to work on those processes.

At Samford University, a team consisting of members from the biology department and the school of nursing has made a real difference. In order to improve scores on the National League of Nurses board exam for anatomy and physiology, the team gathered and analyzed data, and then used that information to redesign the anatomy and physiology competencies-acquisition process. Three years later, the team has met its goal: a 100 percent pass rate.

"New parking lot" was the agenda item. The vice-president for business said that they were going to "move up" the paving of an auxiliary parking lot on the master plan. There were more complaints this semester, and recently, a board member's car had been towed. The director of planning asked whether the school really needed the new lot, but everyone else agreed it needed to be done—and soon.

Quality management practitioners take a scientific approach to their work. They make decisions based on data rather than on hunches, look for root causes rather than react to superficial symptoms, and search for permanent solutions rather than rely on quick fixes. Quality management is, in effect, a systematic way to learn about processes.

Tools such as brainstorming, flowcharts, check sheets, experimental designs, focus groups, and user surveys help generate data. Scatter diagrams, pareto charts, and time series organize and analyze data, and multivoting and nominal group techniques facilitate decision making.

The parking lot scenario is fairly typical of how most decisions are made in organizations—a problem arises, anecdotes are swapped, and a decision is generated in the hopes of making the problem disappear. It doesn't have to be that way. At the University of Pennsylvania, the cost of trash removal increased by $350,000 in one year. A team studied the process, generated a hypothesis, collected and analyzed data, and then instituted a root-cause solution. Net savings are running at $15,000 per month. Student payroll was the problem at the University of Kansas. After flowcharting the process and collecting and analyzing data, the time to produce one student check was reduced from two months to two weeks.

Professor Susan Sullivan stopped by the department office to get her mail. She picked up the copies of her winter mid-term exams and a large manila envelope. Back in her office, she opened the envelope to find the end-of-term student evaluations for the Fall. She glanced over the Z scores. On most items, she was right around the departmental mean. "Looks okay," she thought.

A basic quality tenet is continuous improvement. "Good enough" is never good enough. There is always a better way, a simpler approach, a more elegant solution—always. This mind-set is best put in practice by setting ever-higher standards and devising tight feedback loops that reveal the gaps between where we are and where we want to be.

Does the reward system at Professor Sullivan's college create a continuous improvement environment? Probably not. Teaching skills at most institutions fall into a normal distribution, with 10 percent or the professors being truly "gifted," 10 percent being "inadequate," and 80 percent being "acceptable." The stars receive merit increases; the dullards are invited to attend Teaching 101. There is little or no incentive, however, for the majority of "acceptable" teachers to become better teachers.

Even if ever-higher standards are an explicitly stated expectation, adequate feedback mechanisms usually are not in place. Professor Sullivan's feedback arrived five weeks after the class was over. If improvement, not accountability, is the real goal, why not use evaluations developed by the professors themselves and send them back (for their eyes only) on a rush basis? That's what they are doing at the U.S. Air Force Academy. They collect, compute, and return 25,000 student evaluation forms in ten days. Some professors at the University of Maryland and Clemson University (among others) routinely administer mini- evaluations after three or four weeks of class. Why wait until the next semester to change a teaching style that isn't working?

Can continuous improvement be extended to other areas? The yield rate (the number of students who enroll versus the number accepted) at one college is 22 percent. What would need to be done to increase that to 30 percent? Or 0 percent? Less than 50 percent of students get four out of five course choices during registration. Why not 75 percent? Why shouldn't all students get all the courses they want—all the time?

Professor David Kaminsky is dismayed and depressed. It was only the third day of his microeconomics class. He wanted his students to calculate a series of "price elasticities" as part of a case study. But the request had drawn blank stares. Shouldn't they have learned how to do that in macroeconomics, the prerequisite course?

An organization is a series of linkages in which people transform input into output, adding value in the process. The provider of the input is the supplier; the recipient of the output is the customer. In a quality-driven environment, the customer defines quality by clearly expressing his or her input requirements or expectations. The supplier, in turn, delivers a quality product or service by adding value in such a way that it meets or exceeds customer expectations.

The macroeconomics professor in our scenario, Linda Marlin, did not perform quality work because she did not meet her customers' requirements— "price elasticities" competencies. The fault may be Professor Kaminsky's for not articulating his expectations, or it may be Professor Marlin's for thinking that "price elasticities" were unimportant. Finger-pointing aside, the value-adding process breaks down, and frustration skyrockets as Professor Kaminsky struggles to teach price elasticities (rework) to half the class, while the other students spend the hour doodling in the margins of their notebooks.

Extending this user-based definition of quality throughout an organization changes the dynamics of how people interact. Efforts begin to span boundaries, listening is more intense, and a lot more questions are asked. When a team from General Stores at Pennsylvania State University asked questions of its customers, they received a straightforward response, "The catalogue is too complicated, too difficult to use." The team redesigned the catalogue, made it more customer friendly and available electronically. After two months orders increased by 30 percent.

Finally, perhaps the most important quality concept is one that does not lend itself to a one-paragraph scenario. W. Edwards Deming, the key influential figure in the development of quality management, refers to it as "constancy of purpose." Organizations function best with a core philosophy and a set of unifying goals. Once you declare an "unshakable commitment to quality," you begin to realize tremendous synergy from the alignment of individual goals with both process and institutional goals.

Many professors and programs at many colleges and universities have achieved excellent results without the benefit of a TQM philosophy. But such excellence is often a solitary gem on the campus landscape. The quality paradigm offers a systematic and comprehensive way to change that landscape: quality becomes a commonplace occurrence rather than a pleasant surprise.

The formula is straightforward: Bring together the people who work in a process. Have them define the supplier-customer linkages and expectations. Provide them with the tools and techniques they need to gather data and approach problems systematically. Give them the incentive to challenge their own assumptions about how things have been done in the past. Then empower them to improve or reinvent the process—to change their own work lives—on a continuous basis.

The result is an institution that not only teaches, but learns. It is an institution that energetically engages itself in the business of expanding knowledge about its own purposes and processes.

## Cynics and Skeptics

One aspect of quality management that concerns some members of the academy is its business birthright and language. A recent letter to the editor in *The Chronicle of Higher Education* illustrates the level of discomfort. An administrator wrote: "Higher education simply cannot be forced into the narrow confines of business rhetoric" (Pederson 1992, B4).

It is understandable that some individuals react harshly to the rhetoric of the corporate world. Words like "customer," for example, can easily evoke the phrase, "The customer is always right." It is a short stretch from there to notions of "pandering" and lowered academic standards.

But when the debate never extends beyond language, then the battle may be about the primacy of the status quo, not the validity of new ideas. From our research training, we all are aware of the problems associated with closed systems. We also know the benefits to be derived from working at the intersections of disciplines. For example, some of the most interesting ideas regarding organizational theory and practice are coming from three different branches of science: quantum physics, self-organizing systems, and chaos theory.

### FIGURE 11.1
### Fundamental Questions That Drive Performance

**American Association for Higher Education's
"Implementing Successful Assessment"**
1. Who are our students, and why do they come here?
2. What should a graduate be like?
3. How do students change—and why?
4. How do students talk about their own learning?
5. Is there a better way to organize the curriculum?
6. How could we do better?

**Hewlett-Packard's "Quest for Total Quality"**
1. Who are my customers?
2. What do they need?
3. What is my product or service?
4. Does my product or service exceed their expectations?
5. What is my process for providing the need?
6. What corrective action is needed to improve the process?

Once you scratch beneath the surface of the language, the fundamental questions that drive performance in most organizations are essentially the same. A recent American Association for Higher Education monograph on the successful implementation of assessment asks a series of questions, from "Who are our students and why do they come here?" to "How could we do better?" Hewlett-Packard's pocket guide to TQM contains a number of questions, beginning with "Who are my customers?" and ending with "What corrective action is needed to improve the process?"

Finally, a certain amount of cynicism is associated with the rhetoric-based attack on quality management. But most quality management advocates are interested in improving their institutions. Most are not enthralled by acronyms like TQM and seek to avoid any orthodoxy that suggests there is "one right way." Indeed, there has been a steady shift away from the notion of "TQM in education" to more benign language emphasizing "continuous quality improvement."

### Caveats

I do think, however, that a healthy dose of skepticism is in order. My own skepticism runs deep. One of the most troubling issues concerns leadership. Futurist Joel Barker says that "you lead between paradigms" (Barker 1992, 159). That suggests two things: a clear vision of what the new paradigm looks like and a willingness to "stay the course" as the culture is transformed. The problem is that while new paradigms require unconventional thinking, studies show that the most important criterion in presidential searches is a "high degree of fit between the president and the institution" (Green 1989, 29). More than two-thirds of all presidents are recruited from the same or similar institutions. The process preserves tradition. Moreover, the average presidential tenure is seven years. Given the pace of change in higher education, seven years is scarcely enough time to nudge a culture, let alone transform it.

Another area worthy of skepticism is the flawed logic that confuses means with ends, activities with results. The driving force behind quality management should be the performance-related question, "What do I want to achieve?" This requires that individuals think hard about measurable objectives and then redesign processes and reallocate resources to meet those goals. Instead, more than a few organizations tend to stress activity-centered programs. They spend too much time debating grand, abstract visions, staffing a "Quality Office," developing comprehensive training programs, and producing newsletters, and they spend too little time focusing on achieving measurable operational improvements.

A final note of skepticism: In conducting quality management workshops and seminars on college campuses, I have begun to ask the question, "Why are we doing this?" I am trying to tease out the participants' level of discomfort. Change does not occur unless there is significant dissatisfaction with the status quo. As one professor recently said to me, "Few professors perceive there is a real crisis. Even though we have a futures committee and we are trying to figure out what to do with less money, I think my colleagues still perceive that there are going to be students coming through" (personal conversation). The boundaries that enable professors and students to pursue basic intellectual inquiry that is free from the vagaries of politics and society also insulate the institution and its members from the realities of competition and performance.

## So, Why Bother?

The foundation upon which excellence in education has been built is shifting from a resource model to a performance model. The traditional resource model is illustrated as an amplifying loop with three elements: resources, perceived quality, and public trust. For example, if a college or university is able to attract increased resources (more state support, more tuition revenue, more endowment, more National Merit Scholar freshmen, more "star" professors), its perceived quality increases. That leads to greater public trust and increased resources; students and parents are willing to pay higher tuition for a "quality" education. The continued reinforcement of the loop is driven by reputation, not educational excellence.

The problem is that while increased resources do have a positive influence on perceived quality, they ultimately have a negative influence on value (i.e., the amount of quality received relative to the resources invested). Once this value gap takes hold, the loop can produce an accelerating decline. Public trust falls, resulting in fewer resources, followed by a lowering of perceived quality, and so on.

At the 1990 annual meeting of the Education Commission of the States, lawmakers expressed dissatisfaction and frustration with spiraling college costs, inadequate teaching of undergraduates, and lackluster progress in helping minority students complete their education. More recently, Derek Bok remarked, "With the passage of time, the public is beginning to catch on to our shortcomings.... [T]hey are often wrong about the facts—but they are right about our priorities, and they do not like what they see" (Bok 1992). The public may not actually distrust us, but it is safe to say it has its doubts.

Under stable conditions, professional bureaucracies like colleges and universities are highly autonomous, with individual "professionals" operating in pigeonholes, perfecting their skills. But when conditions destabilize, society at large and its representatives in government see the problems as resulting from a lack of external control.

So they do the obvious: they try to control the work. Some states have been enacting "accountability" laws and policies that require colleges to file effi-

**FIGURE 11.2**
Resources Model

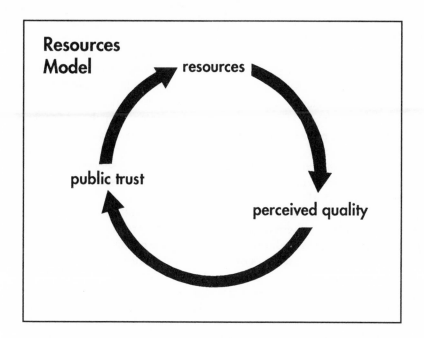

ciency reports. Other states have been conducting productivity studies and have been pushing for "performance-based" funding. One Texas senator was quoted in a recent *Chronicle* article as saying the public is tired of ivory-tower explanations of what universities do. "Educators need to become attuned to the fact that, whether they like it or not, they are public employees and accountable to the great unwashed" (Lively 1992).

With public trust waning, the depressed economy only amplifies the decline. Richard Heydinger, head of the Alliance for Higher Education, predicted last year that the scrutiny of higher education would only intensify. The numbers seem to support him. State appropriations for higher education in the 1992–93 academic year are one percent less than they were two years ago— the first two-year drop in the country's history. Higher education has been relegated to the back of the budgetary line.

Unfortunately, many educators have looked to the resource model—the source of the problem—for the solution. One tack is to reinforce the resource/perceived quality link by making public statements about the disastrous effects budget cuts will have on quality. Local newspapers dutifully run articles that suggest the institution will lose top-notch faculty and will be forced to eliminate academic programs. The president of one institution declared recently, "What we're witnessing is the abandonment of public higher education" (Mercer 1992, A23).

Another tack is to push hard to increase resources. In 1992–93, private college tuition rose by 7 percent—twice the rate of inflation—bringing 100 institutions to the $15,000-per-year mark. Tuition at public institutions climbed by 10 percent. In states such as California and New York, increases ranged from 20 to 40 percent as the systems tried desperately to make up for shortfalls in state support. Shrinking state support also has been used to justify billion-dollar campaign drives. The University of Michigan recently announced a five-year, $1 billion capital campaign. That follows closely on the heels of Yale's $1.5 billion campaign and a host of other highly visible efforts to generate private support.

While in the short run these resource-enhancement efforts may balance budgets, their long-run effect may be a further increase in the value gap. Recent student protests at California campuses have a common theme, "Explain to me why my tuition increases by one-third but I still can't get the courses I need to graduate—and why the classes I do get are taught by teaching assistants." One education writer suggested that campaigns could have some backlash because a number of the same institutions who had high-profile campaigns were also having budget problems. His conclusion: "It makes people wonder where all the money is going" (Nicklin 1992, A33).

A final response has been various types of belt-tightening exercises—from controlling telephone costs and reducing library hours, to introducing early retirement programs. While many of these efforts are laudable, they do nothing to reshape or rethink how the institution operates. Early retirement programs usually just transform a larger inefficient institution into a smaller inefficient institution. Simply cutting, without rethinking how colleges operate, will not lead to better-run or more educationally productive organizations.

I believe that a new paradigm, the performance model, represents what is required to thrive in an environment in which budget shortfalls are probable and public trust questions remain unanswered. The "quality" goal of this model is achieved through the interaction of resources and performance. As has been shown, this solution is enticing, but ultimately inadequate to sustain quality. The bottom loop, in contrast, is a fundamental response to achieving the quality goal through high performance.

The best approach to working in such a model is a combination of strengthening the fundamental response and weakening the ever-appealing symptomatic response—that is, relying more on performance and less on resources to effect perceived quality. As performance soars relative to resources, the value

**FIGURE 11.3**
Performance Model

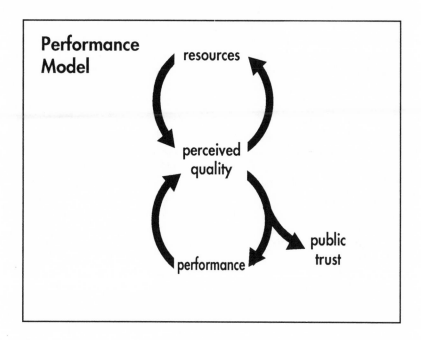

gap that caused the decline in the resource model disappears. Increased public trust is a necessary byproduct.

How can this be accomplished? The key to enhancing performance is to continuously improve the efficiency and effectiveness of operational processes. That is precisely what the University of Wisconsin-Madison, Samford University, the U.S. Air Force Academy, and other institutions are doing through the application of quality management principles. We must swim, too.

According to Aesop, a rich man was on a voyage across the sea when a terrible storm blew up. The ship capsized, and everyone was thrown into the sea. All the passengers began to swim for their lives, except the rich man, who raised his arms to heaven and called to the goddess Athena, offering her all kinds of riches if she would save him. The other passengers soon reached pieces of wreckage, and, clinging to them, shouted back to the praying man, "Don't leave it all to the goddess; you must swim, too."

By relying on a resource model, higher education has adopted a passive approach to its own salvation. In the fall of last year, Trenton State asked its students to pay a $500 "fee for quality" so that the college could "hire new faculty members, thereby ensuring quality" (Mercer 1992, A33). On the west coast earlier this year, the chancellor of the University of California system proposed a 5 percent faculty and staff pay cut to go along with a 33 percent increase in undergraduate fees. One newspaper source said that the pay-reduction proposal was floated in order to show the governor and the legislature that "we are bleeding" (Gordon 1993, A23). As we continue to plead for more funding, we have surrendered the locus of control to off-campus constituencies—that is, to the resource providers. We have left it all to the goddess.

The quality management philosophy is a systematic way to focus on educational and organizational processes. It is a way to regain control of our own destiny by actively and aggressively focusing on the continuous improvement of performance. The methods are not easy, and the work is time consuming. The language can be frustrating, and the results slow to come. conspiracy theorists and cynics will fire their shots. Nonetheless, the time has come for us to realize that we must swim, too.

## References

Barker, J., *Future Edge: Discovering the new Paradigms of Success* (New York: William Morrow and Company, 1992).

Bok, D., "Reclaiming the Public Trust." Speech delivered at the American Association for Higher Education National Conference, Chicago (April, 1992).

Gordon, L., "UC Plans to Hike Fees, Slice Pay 5%," *Los Angeles Times* (12 March, 1993): A23.

Green, M. F., *The American College President* (Washington, D.C.: American Council on Education, 1989).

Lively, K., "Accountability of Colleges Gets Renewed Scrutiny from State Officials," *The Chronicle of Higher Education* (1992).

Mercer, J., "Drop in State Support Leaves Ohio Colleges Wondering how much Farther they can Fall," *The Chronicle of Higher Education* (1992a): A23.

———, "New Jersey College Pitted against State in Struggle over Autonomy," *The Chronicle of Higher Education* (1992b): A33.

Nicklin, J. L., "Fund Drives Flourish, but how much do they Really Raise?" *The Chronicle of Higher Education* (1992): A33.

Pederson, R., "The Perils of Total Quality Management: Bringing Business Rhetoric to Academe," *The Chronicle of Higher Education* (1992): B4.

# 12

# Defining and Assessing "Quality" in Higher Education: Beyond TQM

*Brent D. Ruben*

From the perspective of higher education, the popularity and pervasiveness of the corporate quality approach may actually be a mixed blessing. On the one hand, it signals excitement about a new way of thinking that has potential applicability in wide-range organizational settings, colleges and universities among them. On the other hand, the popularity also brings alien and exclusionary terminology, and a missionary zeal that is often unaccompanied by a theoretical perspective.

In the rush to investigate the relevance of the quality approach for higher education, a good deal has been said about how to *apply, cause, implement,* and *improve* quality in colleges and universities. Much less has been written, however, about how to *define* and *assess* quality in higher education, and it is upon these issues that the significance of the approach will ultimately depend.

### Applying the Quality Approach in Higher Education

Clearly, higher education can be viewed as a service industry, and as such, it faces many of the same service quality challenges as do other types of institutions. Moreover, colleges and universities are influenced by the same organizational dynamics that have often led other organizations to become insulated from the needs and concerns of the publics they serve.[1] If the quality approach offers a way of addressing deficiencies in service quality and organizational process, shouldn't the approach be as applicable for higher education as it is for private-sector institutions? Rather than being only a query about the mechanics of implementing the quality approach, the question turns out to be a very basic one. It raises fundamental issues about the nature of higher education, and a meaningful answer requires consideration of: (1) What, exactly, is meant by *quality;* (2) how quality is defined and assessed in the context of corporate quality programs; and (3) whether these concepts are appropriate for in higher education.

*Defining "Quality"*

The idea of *quality*—the core concept in TQM, the Malcolm Baldrige award, and other derivative approaches to management and organizational theory—has evolved considerably over the years. Conventional definitions of quality emphasized inherent characteristics and attributes of a product or service, and the professional judgments of experts. Quality products and services—whether computer programs, automobiles, architectural design, or electronic devices—were those developed by experts according to technically exacting industry standards of design and production excellence. This approach emphasized the perspective, judgment, and assessment criteria of organizational and industry "insiders"—management, professional staff, and technicians.

Enter the contemporary approach to quality, and with it the persuasive argument that customer expectations and requirements must be central in the definition of quality. The older definition, it was suggested, was limited theoretically and practically. Ultimately, after all, is it not the tastes, appetites, needs, expectations, and evaluations of customers that determine which products and services will be valued and successful, and which will not? Computer programs, automobiles, architectural design, or electronic devices developed without regard for consumer expectations, requirements, and needs are unlikely to do well in the marketplace. Such products or services, it is argued, can be said to be of "high quality" only in a very limited and hollow sense.

In the context of this contemporary perspective, with its emphasis on consumer satisfaction, quality quite literally begins and ends with customer expectations, requirements, and value. The quality approach challenges organizations to put customers first, and to engage in a continuous process that involves:

1. Determining how well needs and expectations are being met; and
2. Identifying where improvements are needed.[2]

Emphasizing this point, Timothy Marvil, director of product planning and development at Ames Rubber, winner of the 1993 Malcolm Baldrige National Quality Award in the small business category, indicates: "Quality in any area begins by determining customer requirements." Explains Joel Marvil, president and CEO at Ames, to emphasize this point their organization has "turned their organizational chart upside down"—customers and their expectations are at the top and management is on the bottom.[3] The paradigm shift, as it has sometimes been termed, has been apparent in thinking about quality in the manufacturing, as well as the service sector, where if anything the change has been more dramatic and more widely heralded.

Thus, in its contemporary context, a focus on customers—whether termed *stakeholders, constituencies, consumers, publics, clients, users, audiences, or*

**FIGURE 12.1**
The Contemporary Organizational Quality Approach

# Assess Customer Requirements, Expectations & Satisfaction Levels

# Assess Organizational Performance

# Identify Gaps

# Plan Improvements

**FIGURE 12.2**
Concepts of Quality: A Comparison

| Traditional Quality Concept | Contemporary Quality Concept |
| --- | --- |
| Internal focus | External focus |
| Emphasis on product and service characteristics | Emphasis on customer requirements and expectations |
| Technical experts define quality criteria | Customers define quality criteria |
| Use of insider experience, intuition, and anecdote in assessing consumer expectations and requirements | Use of measurement and quantitative information in assessing customer expectations and requirements |

*beneficiaries*—is central to defining, assessing, and improving quality. The key questions are: Who are our customers? What do they need, require, want, expect, and value? How does an organization's performance measure up against these customer-based criteria? Whether the aim is to be the leading computer software developer, the most competitive steel producer, or best legal service, the definition of *leading, competitive, or best* is seen as conceptually and pragmatically dependent upon meeting and exceeding customer expectations and requirements as compared to competitors.

As illustrated in figure 12.1, this way of thinking about the quality improvement process begins with an assessment of customer requirements and expectations, and moves next to an assessment of current levels of organizational performance. Gaps between performance and customer expectations guide the quality improvement process, as organizations strive to enhance customer satisfaction.

Figure 12.2 presents an overview of differences between this contemporary definition of quality and the traditional concept.

## The Critique of "Quality" in Higher Education

Much of the interest in applying quality approaches to higher education carries with it an explicit or implicit critique. The argument articulated most clearly, most frequently, and most forcefully within the private sector is that higher education suffers from many of the same problems that a number corporations have faced as a consequence of embracing the older, traditional view of quality. Surely the contemporary approaches to quality assessment and improvement that have been widely utilized in industry could be applied as well to the many problems facing higher education.

The older approach to quality that is viewed as leading to the present deficiencies is illustrated in figure 12.3. The pursuit of quality traditionally involves an institution-centered review of the mission, vision, and goals of a college or university, and its various academic and administrative units. Assessment efforts consist of evaluations of current performance based on self-studies, external reviews, strategic planning and/or accreditation visits by colleagues from peer institutions. Gaps that are identified between institutional or unit mission, vision, and goals on the one hand, and current performance levels on the other, provide the agenda for the quality improvement. In this approach, assessment can be seen as relying largely on professional judgments of the inherent attributes of educational programs and services by higher education "insiders." Quality enhancement initiatives are then directed toward closing these expert-defined gaps.

Problems that are viewed as by-products of this traditional quality approach—and its relative inattention to the needs, expectations, and judgments of key external constituency groups—include:

**FIGURE 12.3**
The Traditional Quality Approach in Higher Education

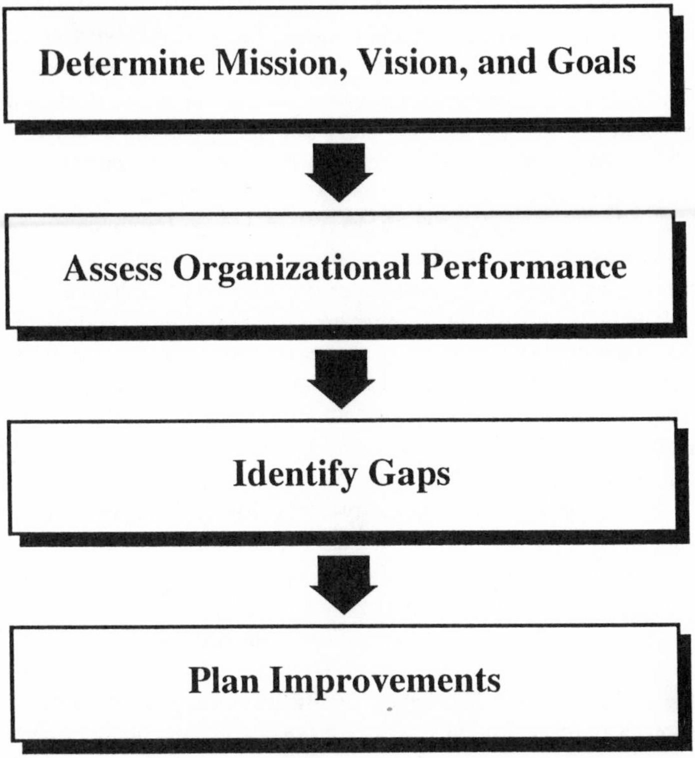

Determine Mission, Vision, and Goals

Assess Organizational Performance

Identify Gaps

Plan Improvements

- minimal concern with identifying and meeting the educational and service expectations and requirements of customers—especially students and parents;
- rising costs without corresponding increases in value;
- inefficiency, waste, and unnecessary bureaucracy;
- little interest in determining or meeting educational needs of the contemporary workplace, as defined by employers;
- preoccupation with internal—institutionally- and especially faculty-based—definitions and assessments of instructional quality;
- over reliance on anecdotal assessment and too little effort to measure instructional processes and outcomes quantitatively;
- insufficient accountability;
- short-term planning and reactivity versus long-term planning and proactive anticipation of need;
- institutional defensiveness, denial, deflection, rigidity, resistance to change, and smugness in the face of environmental, societal, and marketplace needs.

There are, no doubt, elements in this list of allegations that strike resonant chords among most higher-education administrators, faculty, staff, and certainly students. Specific examples that support each category abound. A partial list in the area of instruction and access to instructional services includes: limited parking, difficulty enrolling in required or desired courses, multiple stops and occasionally long wait lines for basic services, an uneven level of courtesy and concern shown by faculty and staff, undefined course and instructor requirements, inadequate classroom facilities, language barriers in instruction, courses required in sequence with content that is uncoordinated, extensive delays in providing feedback on classroom performance, major variations in coursework and evaluative criteria across multiple sections of the same course, defensive and sometimes condescending attitudes toward the suggestions or criticism from "higher-education outsiders," and so on.

While none of these problems occurs everywhere all the time, they do occur with sufficient frequency at most colleges and universities that higher education has become an increasingly attractive target for criticism even by organizational "insiders."[4] In these and other areas, most higher-education institutions have substantial room for improvement, and in each the value of the contemporary approach to quality—with its emphasis on external constituencies and their perceptions, needs, expectations, satisfaction, and values—seems clear.

## Applying Contemporary Definitions

If the quality approach is to have a significant and lasting influence in higher education, it must also be able to move beyond critique to provide new insights and strategies that relate to the primary processes of higher education—those involved with the creation, integration, communication, and application of knowledge. To date, most applications of the approach in been in administrative and support areas such as purchasing, facilities, financial aid, and admissions. These are important areas, and they are often an important source of dissatisfaction among students and other key constituencies. In these areas fundamental definitional and assessment issues regarding the meaning of quality in higher education need not be addressed in order to proceed.

In efforts to apply quality in the areas of instruction, research, and service/ outreach, however, issues of definition and criteria become quite complex. For purposes of illustration, consider the area curriculum development, delivery, and evaluation. The traditional approach has been for faculty members with expertise in the respective field to create, deliver, and evaluate courses, generally with little systematic attention to the expectations or satisfaction levels of nonacademic, external constituencies. Essentially, in this approach students, parents, and other stakeholders are given "what they need" by knowledgeable faculty members whose academic training, experience, and network-

**FIGURE 12.4**
**The Contemporary Quality Approach to Higher Education Improvement**

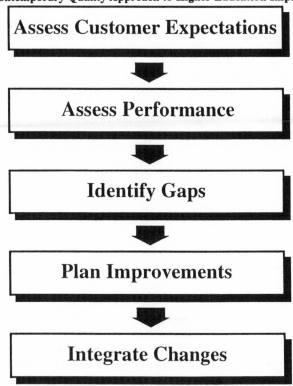

ing within their fields equips them to render expert judgments about curricular content and method.

The alternative, suggested by the contemporary quality approach, is the consumer-centered method illustrated in figure 12.4. This approach emphasizes the perspectives and judgments of nonacademic, external constituency groups: students, parents, and potential employers.

In this approach curriculum development and delivery—and other university processes—are guided by the needs, expectations, values, and satisfaction/dissatisfaction of students and other external stakeholders. As illustrated in figure 12.4, with this approach, gaps between institutional performance and stakeholder needs and expectations are identified, appropriate improvement strategies are implemented, and outcomes are evaluated and standardized. The process is recursive; when these steps are complete, the cycle begins again. In adopting this approach, one leaves behind the problems associated with the internal expert-driven strategy whereby "we decide what they need." Eliminated also are the roots of alleged "ivory-tower detachment," faculty arrogance, and institutional insensitivity.

But, unfortunately, the shift to a wholly customer-driven approach to curriculum development and delivery simply trades one set of problems for another:

- To what extent can we rely on the expectations and requirements students-as-consumer as indicators of quality?
- Will students (parents, and other stakeholders) necessarily require, expect, or "delight" in courses that push their thinking beyond familiar limits, compel them to examine their own beliefs and assumptions, require them to assume new heights of responsibility and organization, or nudge them into more active and collaborative participation in the classroom?
- Will students, parents, potential employers, or other stakeholders be able to determine if a course or the instructor is effectively preparing them for subsequent courses? For the workplace? For graduate or professional school? For community and family life today and in the decades ahead?

## The Problem

While quality may be usefully viewed as beginning and ending with the customer requirements in some contexts, higher education and health care are areas where caution is required in applying the contemporary quality framework. Like patients, students and other consumers of higher education research, instruction, and public service/outreach activities do not always know what is in their best interest. Research in the area of higher education, for instance, shows that when students are asked to recall their most memorable positive and negative experiences, the events they recall often have little to do with the academic elements of their experience.[5]

Comparable studies of patients-as-consumers produce analogous conclusions.[6] Patients' most-remembered experiences do *not* most often have to do with aspects of the quality of clinical/technical care provided, but rather with the interpersonal relationships and communication.

On one hand, these studies point out how important it is to better understand the student-as-customer (and the patient-as-customer) and the nature and complexity of the learning (and health care) experience, and underscore the need to apply that knowledge. On the other hand, these studies also point out how ill equipped these consumers are to fully assess the quality or the value of the professional and technical services they receive. In such contexts, customer expectations and requirements alone are not sufficient indicators of quality.

Further thought reveals that higher education and health care are actually two of a number of service industries where this potential problem is present. The limitations of the customer-driven quality approach appear in any domain where there is a substantial knowledge gap between professionals providing services and lay consumers receiving them. Other examples come to mind in law, journalism, counseling, engineering, and government.

## The Higher Education Approach to Quality

*Integrating the Consumer-Driven and Mission-Driven Approaches*

It is not difficult to argue that the traditional approach to defining and assessing quality in higher education has limitations. However, the traditional approach to quality in higher education has also produced the world standard in the industry. By the same token, the newer quality approach, with its primary focus on meeting customer expectations, is certainly not a simple, quick-fix panacea to the myriad of difficulties facing industry, let alone higher education.

From the perspective of higher education at least, neither the traditional nor the contemporary approach alone is fully adequate. What is needed is a concept and approach to defining, assessing, and improving quality that integrates both the corporate *customer-driven approach* and a more traditional *mission-driven approach*, preserving the strengths of each.

A framework that accomplishes this integration is illustrated in figure 12.5. This approach emphasizes: (1) internal mission/vision-based quality assessment; (2) external constituent expectations/satisfaction-based quality assessment, and, most importantly; (3) the relationship between these two.

Stated in another way, the framework underscores the interdependence of institutional mission/vision/goals relative to instruction, scholarship, outreach, support, and operational services on the one hand, and the evolving needs and expectations of key constituencies for whom these services are being provided on the other.

*Higher Education Quality Gaps*

Beyond its value as a way of conceptualizing quality in higher education, this approach is useful because it helps to differentiate three different kinds of quality gaps of concern, as illustrated in figure 12.6.

*Type 1 gaps: mission/vision <–> performance.* Many of the critical challenges facing higher education can be seen as resulting from—and reflecting—gaps between institutional mission and internal vision as compared with current levels of performance. In such instances, our internal sense of "what we want to be" does not square with assessments of "who we are." To give a very simple example, an institution's mission and vision may call for balanced attention to instruction and research, while available evidence suggests that performance is unbalanced in one direction or another. Or, mission/vision statements may suggest the need for attention to minority recruitment and retention, while available performance data indicates that this goal has not been achieved.

*Type 2 gaps: constituency expectation/satisfaction <–> performance.* The second type of higher-education quality gap is between external service ex-

FIGURE 12.5
A Higher Education Approach to Quality

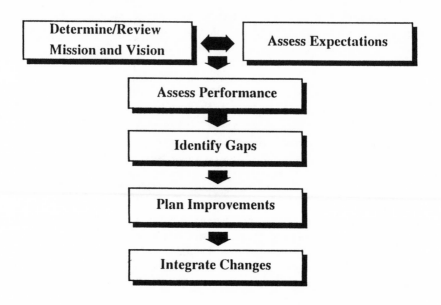

FIGURE 12.5
A Higher Education Approach to Quality

pectation/satisfaction on the one hand, and college or university performance on the other. Here the gap is between the expectations and/or satisfaction levels of external consumers in comparison with current performance levels. The dissatisfaction of students at not being able to enroll in oversubscribed courses is one example of this kind of gap; an expectation that all courses would be taught by tenure-track faculty is another.

*Type 3 gaps: mission/vision <-> constituency expectations/satisfaction levels.* Other gaps of concern in higher education are between an institution's mission/vision and the expectations/satisfaction levels of external constituency groups. In this case, our internal sense of "who we are" or "who we want to be" does not correspond to the external expectations and satisfaction levels of those for whom we provide instructional, research, outreach, or other services. For instance, a college or university mission and vision may call for achieving excellence as a research institution, but this direction may be at odds with the stated needs or expectations of students, parents or potential employers.

**FIGURE 12.6**
**Quality Gaps in Higher Education**

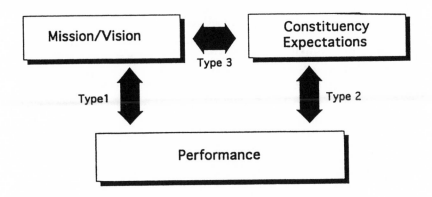

Type 1 Gaps: Mission/Vision<->Performance
Type 2 Gaps: Constituency Expectation/Satisfaction Level<->Performance
Type 3 Gaps: Mission/Vision<->Constituency Expectations/Satisfaction Levels

## Work-Process and Communication-Process Gaps

As the contemporary quality approach emphasizes, many type 1 and 2 gaps of concern in higher education can be seen as the result of problems in our internal *performance*. Long registration lines, multiple stops at multiple offices to securing basic student services information, inadequate recruitment, faculty time devoted to cutting and pasting and photocopying several versions of exams for large lecture courses are examples. Where the underlying problems arise from the way we do our work, these gaps are best addressed by developing new or refined work processes, systems, procedures, and policies.

However, many type 1 and 2 gaps, and perhaps all type 3 gaps, may also be the result of problems in our *communication*, and in these cases, improvements in communication and information processes provide a second important strategy for quality gap improvement. (See figure 12.7.)

In higher education, to a greater extent than in most other sectors, an emphasis on communication process improvement is as vital a component of a comprehensive quality initiative as attention to work process improvement. Generally speaking, the objectives would include increasing our visibility, telling our story more effectively, educating our consumers, working more cooperatively, and showing more concern for those we serve and one another.

In the case of type 1 gaps—gaps between mission/vision and performance—for instance, inadequacies in communication may isolate administrators, faculty, and staff, and thereby preclude meaningful dialogue and the development of consensus relative to mission and vision. Gaps of this type may be reduced by revisions of the mission/vision or the performance of the institution. The gap can also be addressed by refinements in internal communication processes or through a combination of these two strategies.

Type 2 gaps—service gaps between expectations/satisfaction levels and performance, may be a consequence of inadequate work processes, inadequate communication, or both. In efforts to reduce or eliminate such gaps, both strategies are available. To illustrate, dissatisfaction among students (and their parents) because of limited openings in some courses in which they would like enroll, or waiting in lines at peak times of the year are gaps that, in theory, can be reduced by changes in work processes and increased resources. However, in the short term, such changes may not always be possible or, in some cases, may even be undesirable. In such instances, attention to improved communication can help students and parents anticipate, understand, and cope with the situation.

One compelling example of this process is provided by the Disney Corporation's approach to wait management. Long waits in line is a potential source of dissatisfaction among visitors to Disney theme parks. One way to avoid such quality gaps would be to devise systems and allocate resources such that guests never needed to wait to enter an attraction. However, there are always financial and physical limits to the extent to which this expectation/satisfaction level gap can be reduced through improved work processes. Therefore, Disney supplements work process improvement strategies with a number of ingenious communication strategies aimed at expectation management. These include posting signs to inform guests of how long waits will be so that they may choose to wait or not, systematically overstating the wait time estimates so that patrons' expectations are exceeded, providing entertainment and diversionary activities during the wait, and arranging queue lines so that movement is continual and the distance to the entrance appears close at hand.

In higher education, many type 3 gaps—gaps between our mission/vision and the expectations/satisfactions of external constituencies—can be traced to inadequacies in explaining the nature of our institutions and the role they play. Evidence for this contention is apparent in the popular view that faculty productivity can be equated to hours teaching in the classroom, and a frequent failure of the public to understand the economic contribution of colleges and universities to a community, region, or state.

**FIGURE 12.7**
**Strategies for Reducing Higher Education Gaps**

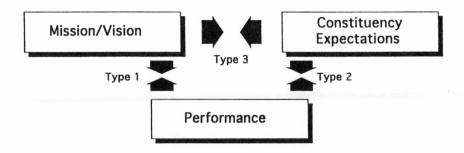

Type 1 Gaps: Work Process Improvement and/or Communication-Process Improvement
Type 2 Gaps: Work Process Improvement and/or Communication-Process Improvement
Type 3 Gaps: Communication Process Improvement

*The Gap Assessment and Improvement Process*

College and university quality leaders might think of themselves as being in the "gaps business." Perhaps it is more accurate to describe the role as that of a "gap consultant." The role involves working with university and unit administrators, faculty, and staff to gather and analyze information in order to *identify* gaps, provide assistance in efforts to *analyze* and *prioritize* these gaps, work with the individuals involved to *reduce* gaps, and *standardize improvements,* as illustrated in figure 12.5. As shown in figure 12.8, the process involves six steps, each defined by a series of fundamental questions to answer and issues to address.

**Concluding Comments**

If the quality approach is to make meaningful contributions to higher education, it must move beyond critique and simple prescriptions for application.

**FIGURE 12.8**
**Quality Assessment and Improvement Process**

1) Development, refinement, and/or review of the institution's /unit's mission, vision, and goals.
   - Why does the institution/unit exist?
   - What services do we provide?
   - What products do we create?
   - How do we fit with and contribute to the overall mission of the institution and/or the unit in which we are located?
   - What goals and/or values guide our activities?
   - How would we ideally like to be seen?
   - To what extent do faculty and staff share a common understanding of our institution's/unit's mission, vision, and goals?

2) Identification of key consumer groups for each of the academic and service components of the institution/unit, and assessment of their needs and expectations.
   - For whom do we provide services and/or products (for instance, students, faculty, staff, alumni, potential employers, boards, taxpayers, funding sources, donors)?
   - Are there other constituency groups upon whose judgment we depend (for example, colleagues at other institutions, accreditation and regulatory bodies)?
   - What does each of these external constituency groups expect from us? How do we know?
   - What criteria do they use in assessing the services and/or products we provide?

3) Assessment of current levels of performance in each mission/vision/goal area.
   - How well does our unit do?
   - How do we assess our performance? What criteria do we use?
   - What are our strengths? Our weaknesses? Our limitations?
   - How do consumers for our services and/or products assess our performance?
   - What are the major sources of satisfaction and dissatisfaction with our services or products?
   - How does our performance compare to that at peer institutions? To other types of institutions?

4) Identification, analysis, and prioritization of gaps between: (a) mission/vision and current performance levels; (b) mission/vision and consumer expectations/ satisfaction levels; and/or (c) consumer expectations and current performance levels.
   - What gaps exist between our performance and our vision of what we would like to be?
   - What gaps exist between our performance and the expectations of key constituency groups?
   - What gaps exist between our vision and expectations of key constituencies?
   - Which of these gaps have the greatest impact on key constituencies?
   - Which gaps are the result of performance problems?
   - Which gaps are a consequence of communication problems? Both?

5) Development of improvement strategies for eliminating or reducing selected gaps.
   - What options are available for reducing critical gaps?
   - What are the barriers and facilitators for each possibility?
   - What resources are required? (time, dollars, expertise)
   - What should the plan of action be? (How does it fit with and contribute to the overall mission of the unit and University?)
   - How will we know if the effort is successful?

6) Integration of changes into normal work processes.
   - What can be done to ensure continuation of the improvements (short term and long term)?
   - How can the changes be integrated into an improved work flow?
   - What needs to be done to ensure regular evaluation and improvement?

Our approaches to quality must be uniquely suited to addressing primary academic processes as well as services and operational processes. To do so, our thinking and our action strategies should integrate both customer- and mission-driven concepts of quality.

As contemporary quality approaches focus attention increasingly on identifying constituencies and assessing their expectations and satisfaction levels, we in higher education also need to put similar emphasis on the development and meaningful assessment/review of our mission and vision for our institutions, the identification of indicators of present achievements and progress toward envisioned goals, the articulation of our mission and vision to key internal and external constituencies, and where appropriate, the modification and refinement of our mission, vision, and goals in light of needs and expectations of key constituencies.

In our efforts to assess and improve the quality gaps that confront higher education, it is vital to consider the impact and potential for improvements in communication processes, as well as work processes.

The enthusiasm regarding the application of quality approaches in industry, government, health care, and higher education makes for exciting times. To the valuable experiences of quality practitioners, higher education can and should contribute—as is its tradition—an analytic, theoretical, and critical perspective. This contribution will be useful for the advancement of understanding of the quality approach in general, and essential for its meaningful application in higher education.

## Notes

1. See discussion in Brent D. Ruben, chapter one, this book.
2. See, for instance, *AT&T Quality Improvement Cycle* (1988): 4 and 5.
3. Presentation by Timothy Marvil and Joel Marvil, 1993 Malcolm Baldrige National Quality Awards Conference, Washington, D.C. (February, 1994).
4. See, for instance, C. J. Sykes, *ProfScam* (Washington, D.C.: Regnery Gateway): 1988; Martin Anderson, *Impostors in the Temple* (New York: Simon & Schuster, 1992; Bruce Wilshire, *The Moral Collapse of the University* (Albany, NY: State University of New York Press, 1990); Page Smith, *Killing the Spirit* (New York: Penguin Books, 1990); and Laurence A. Weinstein, *Moving A Battleship with Your Bare Hands* (Madison, Wis.: Magna Publications, 1993).
5. See discussion in Brent D. Ruben, chapter 14, this book.
6. See also, See Brent D. Ruben, *Communicating with Patients* (Dubuque, Iowa: Kendall-Hunt, 1992); Brent D. Ruben, "What Patients Remember: A Content Analysis of Critical Incidents in Health Care, *Health Communication* 5, 2 (1993): 99–112; Brent D. Ruben, ed., "The Health Caregiver-Patient Relationship: Pathology, Etiology, Treatment," in *Communication and Health: Systems and Applications*, ed. E. B. Ray and L. Donohew (Hillsdale, N.J.: 1990), 51–68; Brent D. Ruben, "Building Effective Client and Colleague Relationships: Insights from Patients, the Factory, the Classroom, and the Pet Shop," in *Caregiver-Patient Communication: Readings*, ed. B. D. Ruben and N. Guttman (Dubuque, Iowa: Kendall-Hunt, 1993), 197–214.

# 13

# Quality Improvement in Higher Education: TQM in Administrative Functions

*Eugene H. Melan*

### Growth in Quality Improvement

Interest in quality improvement has exploded in recent years in virtually all sectors of our economy. An increasing number of organizations in the private and public sectors in the U.S. have embarked on quality improvement programs. In 1988, a survey of firms in the private sector showed that nearly 50 percent have quality improvement programs (GOAL/QPC 1990). All industries surveyed predicted continued growth of improvement efforts. Recognition activity has become an indicator of these efforts. Twenty-four states now have established quality awards for products and services—many patterned after the federally administered Malcolm Baldrige National Quality Award (Bemowski 1993).

A significant amount of improvement activity has developed in higher education. A study by Henderson shows at least 126 institutions of higher learning were involved in various aspects of quality improvement in 1990 (Henderson 1991). Of 220 colleges and universities reporting in 1992, 150 were in various stages of implementing quality practices in administration (Axland 1992). The specter of budget reductions, reduced funding, and cost containment pressures appear to be primary motivators for higher education to examine TQM (*Chronicle* 1991). TQM is also serving as a means for responding to criticism concerning the quality of its education processes (Henderson 1991).

### Origins of TQM

Although the concept is nearly forty years old, it is only in recent years that quality improvement has taken a more pervasive form. TQM has its origins in

Reprinted with permission of the College and University Personnel Association, 1233 20th St., N.W., Washington, D.C. 20036.

the work of Armand Feigenbaum. In his book, *Total Quality Control*, he points out that improving the quality of a product is a multifunctional matter and is not exclusively the responsibility of the manufacturing operations of a firm (Feigenbaum 1956). His systems approach was subsequently adopted and modified by the Japanese and called both Total Quality Control (TQC) and company-wide quality control (CWQC). In the last decade, this notion was reactivated in this country as American firms began to realize that improving product quality requires the participation of all major functions involved in producing a product or providing a service. TQC then became known here as total quality improvement or total quality management and given the acronym TQM.[1]

Today, TQM is broader in scope than originally visualized as TQC. It now encompasses improvement activity in both the primary functions that produce a product or service and the various supporting functions of an organization, such as human resources and information systems. The implication of this for higher education is that TQM should be deployed throughout the organization and include administrative, academic, and research functions.

## Definition

At present, there is no standard or widely accepted definition of TQM. By examining its various features as they appear in practice, the following definition emerges:

A philosophy and set of concepts and methods employed throughout an organization by individuals with a view towards continually improving the product or service provided to customers.

Implied in this definition is that TQM consists of a duality of both view and methodology that is employed by providers on an ongoing basis to achieve an objective—namely, an improved product or service. The two key elements of TQM are improvement and customer orientation.

Because of the organizational, cultural, and behavioral variables of improvement, there is no model that is universally applicable. TQM, as we know it today, does not demand a special methodology or prescription for improvement. It contains a philosophy and a set of operational concepts. However, understanding its features can lead one to deduce certain requirements for successful implementation.

## TQM Features

Based on experience with various TQM efforts, it has been found that effective and sustained improvement contains the following features:

- Organizational leadership and commitment

- Strategy
- Deployment and participation
- Customer orientation
- Continuous improvement
- Progress assessment

These features form the primary elements of a quality system. In addition, there are ancillary features that facilitate the improvement process, such as communication, training, and recognition.

### Organizational Leadership and Commitment

Since TQM represents a change in the way organizations operate, the hierarchical arrangement of many organizational entities suggest that the governing structure must provide leadership to initiate, promote, and sustain change. The administrative functions of institutions of higher education are, for the most part, organized in a manner similar to businesses. Management, therefore, is the primary agent for initiating and promulgating change.

As with any new philosophy or way of thinking, TQM is subject to various degrees of acceptance ranging from complete and enthusiastic adoption to total rejection. Resistance to change and cultural conflicts within the organization are factors that must be understood and dealt with. For this reason, demonstrated commitment and involvement by the leaders of the organization are necessary to facilitate and maintain the change process. The existence of a champion among the leaders tends to smooth and even accelerate change.

On the one hand, successful TQM efforts have consistently shown that leadership, on-going support, and involvement by the principals of the power structure exist (Schein 1990). Even organizations mature in TQM practices find upper management involvement necessary to maintain improvement momentum (Troy 1991). On the other hand, many failed or flagging TQM initiatives are attributable to lack of management commitment and what can be termed a lack of "constancy of purpose" (Deming 1982).

### Strategy

A strategy is a game plan for transforming policy, philosophy, and goals into action within an organization. In some organizations, strategy is established by top management or a committee of key people. In others, it is a result of a consensus of participants after a period of discussion and debate. In essence, a strategic plan provides direction to the participants, synchronizes the implementation of TQM throughout the organization, and provides time lines to measure progress towards stated objectives.

A typical TQM strategic plan for an organization contains a statement of the role of TQM in relation to the basic mission of the organization, a set of goals or objectives, an outline of the method of implementation, a description of how the strategy is to be deployed, and a statement of the overall time horizon for the strategy.

## Deployment and Participation

Deployment and participation are inherent in a well-executed TQM strategy. By definition, an organization successfully engaged in total quality management can also demonstrate that all functions of the organization are participating, including its suppliers. If, for example, one examines the administrative and support functions of a college or university, coordinated quality improvement efforts among admissions, registration, student services, facilities, finance, human resources, and information systems should be readily apparent if it is engaged in TQM.

In addition to functional deployment, TQM requires both commitment and participation of all members of an organization, management and nonmanagement alike. Since TQM represents a paradigm shift—a change in the way an organization conducts business—it is essential that the rationale for the change be communicated to everyone in order to achieve acceptance and support of the participants. In any organization, the support of the people involved is a crucial factor in quality improvement. Hence, it is important that the leadership assure that goal congruence is achieved.

## Customer Orientation

Another key aspect of TQM is its customer orientation. In higher education, the tuition-paying, education-seeking student is the primary reason for the institution's existence. TQM not only reminds us of this but also implies that customer focus must continually take into account the determination and satisfaction of needs. Consequently, a necessary step in the progression of improvement activity in a TQM environment is the establishment of constituent requirements in providing a service.

In many administrative activities, TQM also involves adopting an internal customer focus as well. As a result, business operations can be examined and improved by taking into account internal customer needs (Melan 1985). For many internal operations, the needs of internal customers are ultimately a reflection of requirements of the external customer(s). In this sense, the concept of a customer-provider relationship is of fundamental importance. A logical extension of this notion is the customer-producer-supplier (CPS) model (Melan 1993). The CPS model provides a construct to depict all of the internal and external customer requirements necessary to provide a product or service.

## Continuous Improvement

The notion of continuous improvement is another essential feature of TQM. Given that improvement is to be achieved, a system or mechanism must be in place to enable improvement to continue on an ongoing basis. Quality improvement is viewed by practitioners as a journey—a never-ending journey.

There are various methods for achieving continuity. A vision statement that may be developed during the planning phase of TQM can serve as a means for obtaining continuity by setting long-term objectives. The concept of annual target setting first proposed by Juran is another method (Juran 1964). Here, a target quality level is set for a product, a service, or an operation at the beginning of the year. Improvements are made and measurements performed and compared with the target. By the end of the year, the improvements made are intended to achieve the target. If it is achieved, a new target is set for the following year and the improvement process begins again. Customer satisfaction and response times are typical measures used for target setting.

Other continuous improvement techniques involve the notion of the "ratcheting" target and the zero defect goal approach. Similar to the yearly target method, ratcheting involves setting a quality target, improving the output to achieve the target, and then resetting the target to a higher quality level (Melan 1993). The new level should be aggressive, but not unachievable. The zero defect method involves setting an objective of zero (or near zero) defects initially. Interim targets are set to provide realistic and reasonable levels that can be achieved. Improvement activities are put in place to achieve these levels on a progressive basis (McFadden 1993).

Regardless of the method, goal setting provides improvement teams with a quantitative objective. Without this, improvement efforts become exploratory in nature, results may not achieve potential, and discontinuity may occur.

## Assessing Progress

A corollary to having a system for continuous improvement is providing a means for measuring results. Having goals or targets in place is a necessary first step; measuring improvement is a necessary second step. The primary external measures are customer satisfaction, response or cycle time, and defects or errors. Because customer focus is a key element in TQM, satisfaction measures become important in assessing improvement. Internal measures are primarily process measures such as errors and the time taken to progress through various steps of a process. Other internal measures may include human resource parameters such as morale, turnover rates, employee satisfaction, and costs.

In higher education administration, typical measures include:

- registrar—registration wait time;
- physical plant—response time to a service request, maintenance costs;

- admissions—response time to an application;
- library—retrieval of a published item, response time to a request;
- human resources—satisfaction with staff services, response time;
- food service—satisfaction with food quality, variety, and service.

In addition to having measures, it is important to have a means for assessing results. Progress reviews either by management or a governing body such as a council act as a forcing function for sustaining activity and resolving issues. Without regularly scheduled reviews, TQM will, in many organizations, receive a low priority in the daily activity schedule and, consequently, will either be forgotten or postponed. Reviews also serve to demonstrate management's involvement as well as its interest.

### Ancillary Features

In addition to the key features already discussed, TQM contains certain ancillary elements that facilitate and sustain it. These are: training, recognition, and communication. Training of managers and workers in both job-specific and quality-related matters is an integral part of TQM. Job-related training has been found to be an excellent investment for obtaining a productive work force and helping to achieve quality products and services.

Quality-related training for both management and employees has been found to be essential in TQM and ranges from courses in awareness to quality tools and problem-solving methods. Quality awareness training comprises an introduction to TQM, its rationale, organization, strategy and direction, fundamental concepts, and management expectations of the employee. In contrast, TQM-specific training involves training in the methodology to be used whether it be project or process, or a multiple-step, prescriptive approach.

Recognition has been found to be an essential motivator for sustaining continuous improvement. There are no standards or rules for recognizing individual or team accomplishments. Recognition, however, should be timely and given as close as possible to the time at which the improvement effort was completed. Recognition can be tangible as well as intangible and may take the form of both peer and management cognizance of contribution. The appropriateness of a specific type of recognition varies from one organization to another and even within an organization. Culture and values, wage and salary levels, employee needs, individual and team perceptions of reward, and standardization and equity of awards are among the factors that need to be considered in developing a recognition plan.

For any concept that involves a change in personal and organizational behavior communication is vital. It is no different with TQM. It is important that all key aspects of TQM, as well as ongoing status and achievement, be communicated to the participants of the organization. Communication is also necessary so that everyone knows the direction that has been established for the organization and the reasons for it. Communication is accomplished by newsletters, special memoranda, group meetings, video, and organization-wide conferences.

These features form the basic elements of a quality system integral to TQM. We now turn to the application of these elements in administration.

## Application to Administration

If one examines the initiatives taken by higher education in the implementation of TQM, there are three areas of application in addition to research that are readily apparent: course offerings, teaching methodology, and administration. This article focuses on improvement in administrative and staff functions. Staff and administrative areas of higher education provide the most expedient application of TQM at the present time. These areas include human resources, information systems, finance, registration, physical plant and grounds, security, and student services. As noted previously, these operations are similar in many respects to those of a firm. The primary difference is that in educational institutions, many activities are calendar driven and, therefore, cyclical in nature. Registration, student housing, and food services are prominent examples of activities governed by academic calendars.

**TABLE 13.1**
**Principle Administrative Functions in Higher Education**

| | |
|---|---|
| Admissions | Library |
| Alumni Relations | Mail Distribution |
| Bookstore | Physical Plant |
| Career Planning | Placement |
| Finance | Purchasing |
|   Accounts Receivable | Registrar |
|   Accounts Payable/Disbursements |   Course Scheduling |
|   Payroll |   Graduation |
|   Research Administration |   Registration |
|   Student Aid |   Room Scheduling |
|   Treasury (Cash Management) |   Degree Audits |
| Food Services |   Diplomas |
| Grounds |   Transcripts |
| Human Resources |   Research Contracts |
|   Benefits Administration | Security |
|   Hiring | Student |
|   Separation |   Affairs |
|   Equal Opportunity |   Counseling |
| Information Systems |   Health Services |
| Institutional Research |   Housing |
| Legal |   Special Services |

Table 13.1 is a listing of the principal administrative functions of a higher education facility. These functions are organized in a command structure similar to that of firms and contain many of its shortcomings. It is not surprising to encounter suboptimization, lack of communication, and parochialism in these organizations—characteristics that inhibit their effectiveness. The term "segmentalism" has been applied to describe the stovepipe phenomenon of this type of structure (Kanter 1983). Consequently, an improvement methodology that is systemic in nature and addresses barriers to work flow can serve as a means for achieving significant changes in the way an organization operates.

For many organizations, changes that affect the functioning of the system itself are often facilitated and managed by a group or committee of representatives of the functions involved—usually management. In TQM parlance, this group is known as a quality council, an interfunctional body of selected representatives of the organization charged with managing and overseeing the implementation of TQM. In application, the first order of business, then, is the establishment of a governing council.

Implementing TQM means introducing a paradigm shift to an organization. The result of this shift is a change in the manner by which an organization functions. In order to accomplish this change, the organizational climate or environment in which this change is to occur must be understood. The environment of the organization consists of, among other elements, a set of shared values and beliefs, a process or mechanism by which decisions are made, the stability and constraints of the organization, and motivating factors to promulgate change—preconditions for creating the paradigm shift. After these preconditions are examined, understood, and taken into account by the agents of change, the planning phase of implementation can be addressed.

*Planning Phase*

Experience has shown that a comprehensive, well-thought-out plan is key to successful execution. The elements of a strategic plan (noted earlier) that need to be addressed are: mission, goals and objectives, manner of implementation, deployment, and schedules. Early in the planning phase and prior to developing a plan for the organization, time should be devoted by the planning group or committee to acquiring an understanding of the nature of TQM, elements of its successful execution, and the prevailing methodologies of choice. This can be accomplished through readings, attending lectures and seminars, and training consultants.

At the present time, few sources exist that present TQM in an unbiased and balanced manner. The variations and apparent contradictions among the methodologies—each with its own set of success stories—tend to create confusion in the minds of the uninitiated who are often under pressure to begin implementation within their own organization.

TABLE 13.2
Malcolm Baldridge National Quality Award
1993 Examination Categories and Items

---

**1.0 Leadership**
1.1 Senior Executive Leadership
1.2 Management for Quality
1.3 Public Responsibility and Corporate Leadership
**2.0 Information and Analysis**
2.1 Scope and Management of Quality and Performance Data and Information
2.2 Competitive Comparisons and Benchmarks
2.3 Analysis and Uses of Company-Level Data
**3.0 Strategic Quality Planning**
3.1 Strategic Quality and Company Performance Planning Process
3.2 Quality and Performance Plans
**4.0 Human Resource Development and Management**
4.1 Human Resource Management
4.2 Employee Involvement
4.3 Employee Education and Training
4.4 Employee Performance and Recognition
4.5 Employee Well-Being and Satisfaction
**5.0 Management of Process Quality**
5.1 Design and Introduction of Quality Products and services
5.2 Process Management: Product and Service Production and Delivery Processes
5.3 Process Management: Business Processes and Support Services
5.4 Supplier Quality
5.5 Quality Assessment
**6.0 Quality and Operational Results**
6.1 Product and Service Quality Results
6.2 Company Operational Results
6.3 Business Process and Support Service Results
6.4 Supplier Quality Results
**7.0 Customer Focus and Satisfaction**
7.1 Customer Expectations: Current and Future
7.2 Customer Relationship Management
7.3 Commitment to Customers
7.4 Customer Satisfaction Determination
7.5 Customer Satisfaction Results
7.6 Customer Satisfaction Comparison

---

*Source: 1993 Award Criteria, Malcolm Baldridge National Quality Award, National Institute of Standards and Technology, Gaithersburg, MD.*

Survey data on firms applying current TQM methodologies show that sustained and significant improvement can be achieved regardless of the methodology used, provided that a system is in place to create it (GAO 1991). A system transcends methodology; lacking a system, results are transient at best. Criteria for national and state awards for quality such as the Malcolm Baldrige National Quality Award reflect the elements of a quality system (see table 13.2). The six features described in the beginning of this article comprise the main elements of a system needed to provide a foundation for improvement.

Once the members of the planning group have completed their education, attention should be given to the manner in which TQM is to be introduced into the organization and the approach to be used. This can be accomplished in one of two ways. The first (and most frequently used) is by embarking on a pilot program, which involves selection of a small number of departments or work groups (or interfunctional process teams) for implementation on a trial basis. After assessment of results, a determination as to whether or not to proceed on a larger scale is made.

The other is to proceed with full-scale implementation at the onset. This approach usually requires a significant commitment of resources by all of the participating functions. For organizations where resource constraints or uncertainties affecting implementation exist (as is often the case), it is desirable to establish a pilot program first even though it may add as much as a year or more to this phase.

Because of the multifaceted nature of work activity, much of the improvement effort is conducted by teams often guided by the quality council or a management committee. Quality circles, empowered teams, quality improvement (or QIT teams), and process teams are examples of implementation groups. Training in terms of a sound understanding of group dynamics, interpersonal relationships, team leadership, and facilitation and problem solving is of primary importance for the successful execution of team-based improvement activity.

*Methodology*

Given that the method of progression has been resolved, the planning group may then devote attention to the issue of how the implementation groups or TQM teams should approach improvement. The main approaches used are:

- Problem Solving
- Process Improvement
- Process Redesign

Problem solving entails addressing an issue, complaint, or some specific operational problem. This approach is generally of shorter duration than the other types and is task specific. Training requirements are problem- rather than process-oriented and are directed toward tools and techniques. Problem or issue selection may be performed by management, by a steering group, or may be generated by the team itself. An example of a problem-solving approach used at the University of Pennsylvania will be described later.

Process improvement is systemic in nature and addresses the manner in which a product or service is created and delivered. Process improvement is a method for examining work processes across the organization and improving upon them (Melan 1993). Oregon State is illustrative of process improvement (Coate 1990). A timing examination of the remodeling process in the physical plant function resulted in a reduction in project completion time of forty-five days. Process teams are generally cross functional and have typically a longer duration than problem-solving teams. Depending on the magnitude of the process, the frequency of team meetings, and the degree of involvement of the teams in the improvement phase, the duration of existence may be as long as two years. Training requirements are process and tools oriented rather than problem-solving in nature.

Hillenmeyer has employed a five-step method used to improve processes in the administrative departments at Belmont University (Harris and Baggett 1992):

1. Select a process to improve.
2. Organize a process improvement team.
3. Learn the present process.
4. Determine and verify causes of variation.
5. Develop an improved process.

After the fifth step, the Shewhart plan-do-check-act (PDCA) cycle, a popular improvement technique, is used to implement the improved process.

In contrast, process redesign involves the establishment of a cross-functional, process-oriented team with the objective of completely redefining the methods used to produce a product or service. It is a form of reengineering or breakthrough thinking with a focus on innovative ways of performing work and delivering the end item—often with the application of information technology. This approach has resulted in dramatic improvements in productivity and reduction in staffing. Redesign frequently employs outside consultants in conjunction with members of the organization. Teams are highly task oriented and have specific objectives and time schedules. Ford's reengineering of its accounts payable process, resulting in a reduction of several hundred people, is a frequently cited example of process redesign (Hammer 1990). In several cases, the concept of benchmarking has initiated and enhanced process redesign (Camp 1989; Shafer and Coate 1992).

For organizations first adopting TQM, these three improvement alternatives narrow down to either the problem solving or the process approach. Redesign is usually considered later as the organization matures in TQM or is done independently of the improvement effort. Taking the problem-solving approach first may provide the organization with some immediate, short-term results that may be useful in convincing skeptics of the value of TQM. The process approach, however, being systemic in nature, provides an integrating force and yields both incremental and breakthrough improvements (Melan 1989).

In addition to resolving the means by which TQM is introduced and the approach to be used, the planning phase should also address aspects of leadership involvement, deployment, communication, training, and recognition— features of TQM which have been described earlier. Having done this, the organization is ready to enter the execution or implementation phase.

## Execution Phase

Assuming that a strategy and plan have been developed, approved, and supported by the leadership of the organization, the execution phase may begin. This phase consists of two subphases: training and doing. The early stages of TQM execution involve awareness training, which is generally devoted to familiarizing the participants with the philosophy, concepts, and benefits of quality management.

## Training Subphase

Typical quality awareness seminars range widely from a few hours to a few days, depending on the depth of coverage and the type of audience. The basic objectives of awareness training are to apprise the various members of the organization with strategy, plans, and rationale for TQM. Participation in these sessions by leaders of the organization tends to increase buy in, as do external speakers of prominence. Examples of TQM implementation and results of similar organizations promotes identification and role modeling. Training may be done with either internal or external resources, depending on skills availability and budget considerations. The time span for awareness training may range from a few months with small organizations to as much as two or more years for large organizations numbering thousands of people.

The next part of this subphase involves what may be called tools and techniques training. This type of training is generally provided to the various team members (potential or actual) including facilitators, team members, and sometimes the leaders of the organization. A fundamental precept in training is that it's most effective when provided at the time of need. This is why tools and techniques training should be given shortly after the formation of the teams or assignment of individuals. Troy points out that "training many people is less important than training the right people" (Troy 1991).

Tools training typically includes concepts of quality management, problem solving and/or process analysis methods, elementary statistical methods for data analysis, and training in group dynamics or team concepts. As the need arises, more advanced training may be provided as the team matures and new needs are identified.

*Doing Subphase*

As the teams complete the training subphase, they are ready to undertake the "doing," or improvement, subphase. In the planning phase, issues of a pilot or trial effort versus full-scale implementation and the methodology (problem versus process) have been addressed. Since the improvement subphase can last for several months and represent hundreds of hours of team work in addition to the normal work activity of the individual members, an official launch of the team by the leadership of the organization is often valuable in impressing upon the members the importance of the undertaking for the organization and shows visible signs of support by the leaders. Following the inauguration of the teams, each will go through an initial team progression phase that involves meeting housekeeping, protocol, and discussion of objectives and scope of work. Subsequent progression phases involve problem solving or process analysis, fact finding, and improvement determination and implementation.

Included in these phases is communicating status and results to peers and leaders. With the understanding that continuous improvement implies a journey for the organization, the execution phase, when considered in aggregate, lasts for the life of the organization or as long as the organization is committed.

*Example*

The University of Pennsylvania illustrates all three approaches to improvement. First initiated in 1990 in the operations area of the university by its vice-president (who assumed the role of leader and champion), the original (and exploratory) approach taken was problem solving. Key managers and selected staff members of the area were trained by outside consultants in this method after which four teams, under the guidance of a management council, were constituted to address specific operational problems selected by management. One such problem was a postage rate increase that caused the budget of the mail room to be exceeded. This prompted the initiation of a problem-solving team, which found lower-cost ways of mailing and resulted in savings of nearly $100,000 a year (Maser 1991). Another team addressed the cost of waste paper removal and determined that regularly scheduled removal could be replaced by removal on a demand basis (Iannece and Topper 1991). This resulted in savings of $175,000 a year.

As these problem-solving teams progressed, staff personnel associated with improvement examined the process methodology approach. Finding it more advantageous to the organization in terms of integrating improvement activity, a strategy was developed to implement the process approach. Starting first in the Division of Finance, a series of training classes for management, staff, and process teams were held by the author starting in the summer of 1991. During a two-year period, over twenty process improvement teams were launched in central administration and the various schools comprising the university.

Eleven of these teams addressed business processes in the Division of Finance. Processes such as student financial services, purchasing, sponsored research, and treasury were examined over a period of one year. Eight of the teams that completed the execution phase developed sixty recommendations for improvement (Real 1993). Many of these have been adopted or are currently being worked on. As the teams proceeded through the execution phase, several function-wide meetings were held, during which teams communicated the status of their progress to both management and other teams. During this phase, the operations council developed recognition guidelines to be used as the teams completed their work.

Approaching the latter stages of the execution phase, a university-wide initiative began to address a broader issue of a total information architecture, including a financial management information system. As a result, efforts are now underway in the Division of Finance to reengineer various financial processes to serve as a basis for a new information system. Meanwhile, the administrative operations of the various schools comprising the University of Pennsylvania have begun to implement the process approach. Teams from Wharton, Engineering, and the Graduate School of Fine Arts are working on improving such processes as advising, classroom scheduling, payroll, facilities, and admissions. The author estimates that well over 100 improvement recommendations will result from all of these teams. Other recent examples of improvement in administration utilizing both project and process approaches have been published (Coate 1990; Chaffee and Sherr 1992).

## Conclusions

In the implementation of TQM in administration several key factors must be considered. Survey results, anecdotal evidence, and the author's personal experience show that successful TQM effort is initiated and committed at the higher levels of an organization and requires consistent and continual involvement by its leadership (Schein 1990). This has been confirmed in the Henderson study (Henderson 1991). A phrase often echoed among TQM practitioners is that management should "walk the talk."

Strategic planning is a second important factor in implementing TQM effectively. Without a clearly thought-out plan of action, the probability of erring increases with negative effects on the perceptions and attitudes of those involved. The inventory of experience with TQM has increased dramatically within the last decade. Higher education can, and should, take advantage of the empirical knowledge gained in business of what works and does not work in guiding the planning and execution of improvement.

Since improvement implies a change in the manner in which an organization conducts activities, an understanding of its processes, its structure, the environment, and the culture in which they are practiced is vital to successful execution. Finally, for TQM to be viable, it must be based on a system possessing an interlocking set of elements that nurture and sustain improvement.

## Note

1. The acronym was believed to have originated in 1985 with the Naval Air Systems Command. However, recent research suggests that it may have originated in 1983 by the Allen-Bradley Company (*Quality Progress,* August 1992, p. 8).

## References

Axland, S., "A Higher Degree of Quality," *Quality Progress* (October 1992).

Bemowski, K., "The State of the States," *Quality Progress* (May 1993).

Camp, R. C., *Benchmarking* (Milwaukee, Wis.: ASQC Quality Press, 1989).

Chaffee, E., and Sherr, L., *Quality: Transforming Post-Secondary Education* (Ashe-Eric Higher Education Report Series, George Washington University Press, 1992).

Coate, L. E., "TQM on Campus," *NACUBO Business Officer* (November 1990).

Deming, W. E., *Quality, Productivity and Competitive Position* (Cambridge, Mass.: MIT Center for Advanced Engineering Study, 1982).

Feigenbaum, A. V., *Total Quality Control* (New York: McGraw-Hill, 1956).

GAO, *Management Practices: U.S. Companies Improve Performance through Quality Efforts* (Washington, D.C.: U.S. General Accounting Office, 1991). Report, GAO/NSIAD-91-190.

GOAL/QPC, "Research Report No. 90-04-01," GOAL/QPC (Methuen, Mass.: (1990).

Harris, J. W., and Baggett, J. M., *Quality Quest in the Academic Process* (Birmingham, Ala.: Samford University,1992), 28.

Hammer, M., "Reengineering Work: Don't Automate, Obliterate," *Harvard Business Review* (July—August 1990).

Henderson, R. L., *An Analysis of the State of Total Quality in Academia,* Report No. AD-A246966 (U.S. Dept. of Commerce. Springfield, Va.: National Technical Information Service 1991): 45.

Iannece, S. H., and Topper, F. L., *Reducing the Cost of Trash Removal,* Proceedings IMPRO 91 (Juran Institute, Wilton, Conn.: October 1991).

Juran, J., *Managerial Breakthrough* (New York: McGraw-Hill, 1964).

Kanter, R., *The Change Masters* (Old Tappan, NJ: Simon & Schuster, 1983).

Maser, J., *Applying Juran in a University Environment: Reducing the Cost of Mailing at the University of Pennsylvania* (Wilton, Conn.: Proceedings, IMPRO 91, Juran Institute, October 1991).

McFadden, F. R., "Six Sigma Quality Programs," *Quality Progress* (June 1993).

Melan, E., *Process Management: Methods for Improving Products and Services* (New York: McGraw-Hill, 1993).

———, "Process Management: A Unifying Framework for Improvement," *National Productivity Review,* vol. 8, no. 4 (1989).

———, "Process Management in Service and Administrative Operations," *Quality Progress* (June 1985).

Real, S., Unpublished communication to the author (February 1993).

Schein, L., "The Road to Total Quality: Views of Industry Experts," *The Conference Board Research Bulletin* 239 (1990).

Shafer, B. S., and Coate, L. E., "Benchmarking in Higher Education," *NACUBO Business Officer* (November 1992).

"To Boost Quality and Cut Costs, Oregon State University Adopts a Customer-Oriented Approach to Campus Services," *The Chronicle of Higher Education* (6 February 1991): A27.

Troy, K., "Quality Training: What Top Companies Have Learned," *The Conference Board Report*, no. 959 (1991).

# 14

# What Students Remember: Teaching, Learning, and Human Communication

*Brent D. Ruben*

If the quality approach is to make a significant contribution to higher education, it must help us think differently about academic as well as administrative, support, and operational processes. To the extent that it guides us to a better understanding of our most primary process, teaching and learning, and focuses attention on students as consumers in the instructional process, the contribution to academics can be significant.

There is no question that much can be learned about the teaching and learning process from students themselves, *if* we ask the right questions, and listen carefully to the responses.[1]

One method that is promising in this regard utilizes the critical incident approach.[2] Using this approach, a survey of 165 undergraduate students was conducted. The students were in an introductory social science course at Rutgers University. The course enrolls students from a variety of majors and colleges. Most students in the course were first- and second-year students, but there was also a smaller number of third- and fourth-year students in the course.

Each student was given a sheet of paper with the following open-ended question:

> Think back on all your experiences as an undergraduate student. *What one experience most stands out in your mind?* This can be any experience related to college life, involving classes, social activities, students, faculty, or administrators, or any other aspect of your life at RU. (Please describe the experience in several sentences below.)

The experiences they described—of which there were 205 in all—were content analyzed to determine their *valence* (whether they were positive or negative) and to identify common *themes*.

The valence analysis is presented in Table 14.1. Based on a preliminary analysis of the narratives, four recurrent themes were identified. (See Table 14.2.) Each student's reported experiences were then categorized based on the

**TABLE 14.1**
Valences of Most Memorable Experiences of Undergraduates

| Valence | Responses | Percent |
|---|---|---|
| Positive | 76 | 37 |
| Negative | 120 | 59 |
| Undetermined | 9 | 4 |
| Total | 205 | 100 |

**TABLE 14.2**
Themes of Most Memorable Experiences of Undergraduates

*Academics*
Experiences involving academic aspects of college life such as classes, instruction, exams, library use, lectures, studying, content learning.

*Policies/Procedures*
Experiences involving university policies, regulations, rules, and procedures

*Facility/Accommodations/Environment*
Experiences involving university facilities, accommodations, or the physical environment.

*Interpersonal Communication/Relationships*
Experiences Involving interpersonal communication, relationships, and/or social aspects including encounters with faculty, TAs, administrators, other students, tour guides, etc.

**TABLE 14.3**
Themes of Most Memorable Experiences of Undergraduates

| Factor | Responses | Percent | Rank |
|---|---|---|---|
| Academics | 26 | 12.7 | 4 |
| Facilities/Accomm/Environ | 53 | 25.8 | 2 |
| Policies/Procedures | 35 | 17.1 | 3 |
| Interpersonal Comm/Relationships | 91 | 44.4 | 1 |
| Total | 205 | 100.0 | |

## TABLE 14.4
### Representative Experiences Related to Academics

---

#### Positive

"The one thing that stands out in my mind the most was when I got my first 'A' for a final grade...After working so hard all semester, it was...nice...to see that I received the grade that I worked for. It gave me the confidence to work harder in all my other classes."

"The experience that most stands out in my mind occurred at the end of my first semester. I had returned to college after 12 years away from school. My level of self confidence was extremely low. I felt that I could not compete academically....In preparing for the final I became overwhelmed with the amount of material. However, I persevered and (when)...I checked my grade—with my 5-year old daughter at my side—I was euphoric. I received an 'A,' and went to register for the next semester!"

"My most memorable experience...was getting an 'A' on my mid-term exam. I am taking _____, and was really confused...When I started studying I began to realize how much I knew without realizing it. To me this was a great experience...."

"My most memorable moment was when I received a certificate in recognition of my class standing at an awards ceremony my junior year...."

---

#### Negative

"Failing my first class. I had never failed any class before. It was a very new experience."

"Taking Professor _____'s final....He might as well have asked us to memorize every word in the dictionary—it would probably have been easier."

"...in a class with 275 students....I felt very small, sort of like a number, being in such a large room. ... I not only felt uncomfortable, but I felt I was far away from the professor mentally."

---

theme it emphasized. Frequencies were calculated for each category, and an overall ranking was developed. The results are presented in Table 14.3.

As shown in Table 14.3, experiences related to interpersonal communication and relationships ranked first, accounting for 44.4 percent of all memorable experiences reported. Experiences related to facilities, accommodations, and the environment ranked second (25.8 percent); experiences that involved policies and procedures, third (17.1 percent); and experiences related to academics, last, accounting for only 12.7 percent of experiences reported. Tables 14.4–14.7 provide selected examples of positive and negative responses in each category.

## Interpreting the Findings:
## The Importance of Interpersonal Communication

The results tell us about the richness and range of students' experiences as undergraduates, about what students most remember, and about the kinds of

## TABLE 14.5
### Representative Experiences Related to Facilities, Accommodations, and Environment

| Positive |
| --- |

"Seeing the student body just hanging out at "Bishop Beach," Voorhees Mall, and the Passion Puddle on a nice day. It's amazing to see how nice weather can bring people together—that is what college life is all about. Whenever I'm hanging outside with a lot of people, I say to myself, 'This is college.'"

"...when I got lost...the first time that I tried to find my way to Hickman (Hall). Then, I stumbled (literally) on a bridge which I had never seen on the tour....Because it is rustic and beautiful, I felt like I really could enjoy Rutgers...it wouldn't just be four years full of teeming hustle and bustle...."

"I felt an almost instant sense of pride when I first visited Rutgers. It felt like a piece of history along side of a modern city. I liked being right down town. I felt like a part of the world...."

"Last year when the basketball team won the Atlantic 10 championship game...everyone rushed onto the floor...."

"Freshman orientation...(I was) amazed how many students there were that I may someday meet. My face lit up with excitement. I was so proud to be attending this University...."

| Negative |
| --- |

"I thought I was on the 'E' bus and ended up on (the wrong) campus. Sometimes they don't change the letters on the back of the bus, so you have no idea where you are going."

"When I first walked into my dorm room, I hated it. I thought it was small, gray, and institutional. My first reaction was to cry. Looking back, the room wasn't really gray, it wasn't that small, and it actually looks pretty good now. I guess I just did not want to leave my family, friends, and house."

"I am an international student and I come from a country that is small....The thing I remember most vividly about Rutgers was its size...50,000 students...I found it difficult to adjust to such a vast environment...."

## TABLE 14.6
### Representative Experiences Related to Policies and Procedures

| Negative |
| --- |

"Standing in line for late registration. I left my house early in the morning...The line was already wrapped halfway around the building. I wound up waiting in this line for a little over six hours."

"The frustration I went through trying to get my schedule fixed. It took me five hours to get into this class. I just couldn't believe that I was paying for this education."

"On my first day of school, I showed up for my first class to find that the entire section had been cancelled and we had to register for another class. I was sent to different advisors and the registrar's office, and...had to rearrange my entire schedule and take a...class that I didn't want to take. It was pretty awful. I was already scared to death about starting college, and then everything went wrong...."

**TABLE 14.7**
**Representative Experiences Related to Interpersonal**
**Communication and Relationships**

| Positive |
| --- |

"On the first day of school last year, my first class, the professor greeted the class by saying, 'Welcome to Rutgers University' ....He seemed to really care about making us feel as comfortable as possible in a new school...."

"Director of the _____ Program. I felt down and low, heavily burdened with financial matters. Ms. _____ was wonderful to me, helped me out and was, overall, generously pleasant."

"When I called on the phone to ask for information about a tour before my freshman year, I was surprised at how nice they were on the phone. Then when I did come for the actual tour, everyone was nice and friendly."

"Going to Band Camp in August, even before school started. It was new but scary to be with a bunch of college kids that I didn't know. The best thing was that they were not judgmental or degrading towards me in any way. It was a great feeling to be accepted and liked the very first day there.... You learn a great sense of family from an experience like this."

"My most memorable moment...was on my first day. My roommate and I had just finished moving in and our parents had left....We looked around and saw the chaotic mess our room was in. We then sat down on our bed and cried....After a few minutes we stopped, looked at each other and laughed. It was then that I knew everything was going to be all right."

"The experience that really stands out in my mind...is being in a group and doing things together such as going to a frat party or just hanging out in front of Bishop Hall and socializing. All and all, college for me is a time for socializing and understanding myself."

| Negative |
| --- |

"I most remember...asking one of my professors a question and getting a rude answer."

"I remember my first meeting with my advisor. He asked me what I was contemplating as a major. I told him _____. His response was '_____ isn't exactly an intellectual major.' He attempted to encourage me in another direction. I was...offended."

"At the Orientation...an unkept, overweight (but light-hearted) dean who shall remain nameless, wearing multi-colored suspenders promised us a year of utter and total confusion and misery, mingled with anonymity and meaninglessness, interspersed with a few instances of personal contact which would involve the transfer of money."

"I commute....I often sit outside the...Student Center and watch people. It is what I enjoy most doing (since I feel no allegiance to home or the university—only my car)....I look everyone in the eyes attempting some sort of contact or recognition. And I receive none. I feel as though I am in port authority....If I could only hold one gaze—perhaps even elicit a smile!—I would be happier with commuting an hour and a half each way."

"The one most shocking thing I can remember was the ability to just walk out of a class while the teacher was conducting a lecture. It seemed so shockingly rude, and it indeed it was. When I first tried it, guilt overcame me, but that didn't stop me from repeating the procedure often over the length of the semester."

"The day I was given a tour, I sat with the young female student who was giving the tour during our lunch, and I asked her every question I could possibly think of... Where's the mall, hours the bus runs, nearest convenience store, etc. When we returned and my father picked me up, the girl turned to my father and said, "Please, take her to look at different schools!""

themes that are common across experiences and students. The findings indicate the variety of thoughts, expectations, and orientations of this group of students, the complexity and diversity of the teaching and learning environment.

By implication, the study also tells us about probable sources of satisfaction and dissatisfaction among students, and it contributes to our understanding of the criteria upon which images of educational institutions are formed. More generally, the findings remind us of the difficult process of adjusting to campus life; entering students are beset by new surroundings, new freedoms, new colleagues, new rules and regulations, new procedures, new responsibilities, and new risks.

The results also underscore the importance students attach to significant human encounters, to affiliation, and to experiences that confirm their sense of identity and worth. They also highlight the importance of the university *community* (in a literal and figurative sense), campus organizations, and campus activities in fostering the sense of connection and belonging that is basic to the adjustment process. (See Appendix).

Given these dynamics, it is understandable that students place a very high premium on quality interpersonal communication and relationships with faculty, staff, administration, and peers. Note that we are not only referring to communication in formal academic contexts such as lectures, discussion sections, or labs, but rather of the full range of human contact, about which more will be said later.

Lest one begin to look condescendingly upon the plight of undergraduates, it is important to remind ourselves of the vital role of interpersonal communication and relationships in a wide variety of human circumstances. Interestingly, results of a comparable study conducted with an entering class of thirteen doctoral students closely corresponded to those for undergraduates. (See Figure 14.1.)

Moreover, my research in the area of doctor-patient interaction, which includes analysis of narratives of more than 4,000 patients, indicates that interpersonal communication and relationships are also the most frequent themes of memorable experiences from hospital stays and visits to ambulatory care facilities. Communication and relationships are referenced far more often than any other factor, more often even than clinical and technical issues.[3] (See Table 14.8.)

## Human Communication Theory and Education

As interesting as the findings of this study may be in their own right, it is important to consider their broader implications for teaching and learning. Often the words *teaching* and *learning* are uttered in a single breath, as if they were wedded to one another conceptually. Actually, from the perspective of human communication, teaching and learning are probably more appropriately viewed as separate and distinct.

**FIGURE 14.1**
**Themes of Most Memorable Experiences Among Doctoral Students**

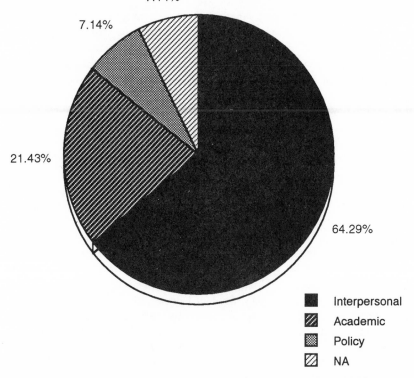

One of the most familiar ways of thinking about communication is the S->M->C->R = E approach.[3] The "S" refers to a *source*—the initiator of a communication encounter. In a classroom context, the source is a teacher. "M" signifies *messages*—the content, information, or knowledge of a lecture, textbook, or lab assignment. "C" denotes *channel*—the print or vocal means by which the messages are transmitted. Students are "R"s—*receivers*. The arrows and equal signs are meant to suggest that the S->M->C->R sequence predictably results in the achievement of particular goals, outcome, or *effects*— the "E." Thus, given this framework, the process of instruction would be described as a teacher preparing and delivering messages to students through various channels, and thereby bringing about learning.

In this way of thinking about human communication, tremendous power and influence is attributed to a source and his or her intentions, to messages, and to the channels through which messages are conveyed from a source to intended recipients. Moreover, it is assumed that the natural state of affairs in communication is for the received message and meaning to correspond to the message and meaning that was intended by the sender. In other words, it is assumed that the message received will correspond to the message sent—MR = MS.

If only communication were that simple. Nowhere is the inadequacy of the S->M->C->R = E view of communication and its dysfunctional implications more apparent than in education. The model implies that learning is controlled by teachers who transmit instructional messages to students through lectures, books, and other channels. It implies further that when messages are well formed, delivery articulate, and channels carefully selected, the desired learning outcomes will naturally follow.

This way of thinking leads to the conclusion that a teacher's preoccupation should be *subject-matter content, information* or *knowledge,* and the construction and delivery of quality messages through appropriate channels: Is the information in lectures, texts, discussions, and labs factually correct and up to date? Is the mode of delivery effective and efficient? Can technology be used to facilitate the teaching process? Are tests and other evaluative mechanisms valid and reliable?

These are certainly vital concerns, and it is not the intent here to suggest otherwise. However, a review of memorable experiences of undergraduates also reminds us that the dynamics of student learning is complex, and that it does not correspond in any lock-step fashion to the dynamics of teaching—MR seldom corresponds to MS. Student learning may occur relative to the intentional instructional messages provided by teachers, and it also can occur relative to the many *unintentional* messages provided by instructors and also by policies, by the environment, by staff, and by peers. (See Appendix, "Roles Associated with Most Memorable Experiences of Undergraduates").

Student learning involves the basics of chemistry and the basics of living away from home. It involves lessons on how to get to the library and lessons on how to get to the dinner line on time, on how to begin new class and how to begin new relationships, on how to locate research sources and how to locate buses, and on how to write a paper and how to right a relationship. Sometimes learning takes place in a classroom, for credit, and inspired by teachers; but learning also occurs outside a classroom, for no credit—from friends in a class, staff in the library, receptionists in an administrative office, campus polices and procedures, even from the appearance and maintenance of buildings on campus.

When we think about education and human communication not so much in terms of *teachers,* but rather, in terms of *learners,* we find ourselves implicitly utilizing a different model of communication—one that is consistent with the emphasis on the consumer advocated by the quality approach. We begin not so much with a focus on information sources—teachers—on what they intend, what they say or write, how they do it, or the books and materials they utilize. We begin by looking at the receivers, the learners, the consumers and their goals, their expectations, their environments, and the messages that become important to them.

From this perspective, learning is a perpetual, self-initiating and self-sustaining activity. As contemporary systems theories of communication remind us, communication and learning occur every time an individual processes messages in the environment in order to adapt to the challenges and opportunities that present themselves. We are continually surrounded by messages that compete for our attention, and which present challenges and opportunities to which we react.[4] Thus, communication is a natural, subtle, adaptive process, characteristic of all living systems. Learning occurs all the time.

## The Issue of Quality Teaching

What are the implications of these findings and concepts for what we do as teachers? The research suggests that we would do well to take a hard look at ourselves as information providers—and as people. We might begin by asking ourselves: What are the implicit as well as explicit lessons we teach by our lectures and by our behavior—about knowledge, inquiry, our disciplines, human behavior, diversity, community, our institutions, and about higher education.

It reminds us also that the transmission of information is only a part of the teaching process, and that the content of our classes, books, and assignments is only part of what makes a difference to students' learning and to their lasting impressions. By implication, it suggests, also, that students, parents, and the public at large are often unable to judge the quality of the knowledge and information we provide. Instead, their images may be based on what they can more easily see and comprehend—the way we respond to their questions, the kind of comments we write on their papers, the way we react when they approach us outside class, and the way we treat them as people.

Thus, the preoccupied teacher who seems indifferent and patronizing when a student asks a question during class, who writes what are perceived as condescending comments on a class paper, or who misses office hours when students travel substantial distances to meet, unknowingly and unintentionally creates an experience that interferes with intended learning outcomes, creates dissatisfaction, and damages the image of the institution. Even one incident that seems irrelevant to the instructor can become the basis for the student's lasting impression of the professor and the course, even to the point where it overshadows the impact of academic quality of lectures, discussions, labs, or readings.

From this perspective, every contact with a student is an encounter that either contributes to or detracts from quality teaching and learning. Each interpersonal encounter—even the fleeting exchange between an instructor and student before or after class—plays a role in the creation of relationships that are vital to the perception, and the reality, of teaching excellence.

TABLE 14.8
Frequency of Sports, Parties, Organizations, and Fraternities/Sororities in
Most Remembered Experiences of Undergraduates

| Factor | Responses | Percent |
|---|---|---|
| Sports (participant/spectator) | 13 | 6.3 |
| Parties | 8 | 3.9 |
| Organizations & Activities | 8 | 3.9 |
| Fraternities/Sororities | 7 | 3.4 |
| All Other Factors | 169 | 82.4 |
| Total | 205 | 99.9 |

The point is simply that faculty members play a central part in creating the experience and lasting impression of the thousands of students with whom they collectively come into contact during their years of service. Faculty members create images and the windows through which students come to view the course, the discipline, the department, the institution, and higher education in general. It is a complex challenge and an incredible responsibility.

To the extent that the quality perspective can enrich our understanding and vision of faculty as the "owners and managers" of the primary business of higher education—the teaching-and-learning process—the contribution of the approach will have been substantial.

## Notes

1. Adaptation of the Keynote Address presented at the 1992 Annual Teaching Assistant Orientation The Graduate School-New Brunswick, Rutgers University.
2. The critical incident method was first described by J. C. Flanagan in "The Critical Incident Technique," *Psychological Bulletin* 51 (July 1954): 327-57. It was popularized in management studies through the work of F. Herzberg, B. Mauzner, and B. Snyderman, *The Motivation to Work* (New York: John Wiley, 1959), and has subsequently been used in a variety of fields, including the following publications by the author in health and intercultural communication: "What Patients Remember: A Content Analysis of Critical Incidents in Health Care," *Health Communication* 5(2) (1993): 99-112; "Building Effective Client and Colleague Relationships: Insights from Patients, the Factory, the Classroom, and the Pet Shop," in *Caregiver-Patient Communication: Readings,* ed. B. D. Ruben and N. Guttman (Dubuque, Iowa: Kendall-Hunt, 1993), 197-214; *Communicating with Patients* (Dubuque, Iowa: Kendall-Hunt, 1992); "Patient Satisfaction: Critical Issues in the Theory and Design of Patient Relations Training," in *Journal of Healthcare Education and Training,* 1 (1), ed. B. D. Ruben and J. Bowman (1986): 1-5; and "Behavioral Assessment of Communication Competency and the Prediction of Cross-Cultural Adaptation," in *The International Journal of Intercultural Relations* 3(1), ed. B. D. Ruben and D. J. Kealey (1979): 133.
3. See Ruben, B. D., *Communicating with Patients* (Dubuque, Iowa: Kendall-Hunt, 1992); Ruben, B. D., "What Patients Remember: A Content Analysis of Critical

## APPENDIX
### Roles Associated With Most Memorable Experiences of Undergraduates

| Role | Responses | Percent |
|---|---|---|
| Faculty, Instructors, TAs | 12 | 6 |
| Staff | 33 | 16 |
| Administration | 7 | 3 |
| Other Students | 60 | 29 |
| Other | 12 | 6 |
| Collective Reference | 36 | 18 |
| No Roles Mentioned | 45 | 22 |
| Total | 205 | 100 |

Incidents in Health Care," *Health Communication* 5 (2) (1993), 99–112; B. D. Ruben, "The Health Caregiver-Patient Relationship: Pathology, Etiology, Treatment," in *Communication and Health: Systems and Applications,* ed. E. B. Ray and L. Donohew (1990), 51–68; and Ruben, B. D., "Building Effective Client and Colleague Relationships: Insights from Patients, the Factory, the Classroom, and the Pet Shop," in *Caregiver-Patient Communication: Readings,* ed. B. D. Ruben and N. Guttman (Dubuque, Iowa: Kendall-Hunt, 1993), 197–214.
4. For a more detailed discussion of the basic concepts and models of communication upon which this framework is based, see Ruben, B. D., *Communication and Human Behavior, third edition* (Englewood Cliffs, NJ: Prentice-Hall, 1992), chap. 2; Ruben, B. D., "Integrating Concepts for the Information Age: Communication, Information, Mediation, and Institutions, in *Information and Behavior: volume 4. Between Communication and Information* ed. J. R. Schement and B. D. Ruben (New Brunswick, NJ: Transaction Books, 1993), 219–39; or Ruben, B. D. and J. Y. Kim, eds., *General Systems and Human Communication Theory* (Rochelle Park, NJ: Hayden, 1975).

# 15

# Universities, Competitiveness, and TQM: A Plan for the Year 2000

*Richard M. Cyert*

## Introduction

The concept of competitiveness is one that is gripping our society and indeed societies all over the world. Universities must be relevant to the society and that means they must grapple with the problems that are significant to the society. Being relevant means facing up, in a number of ways, to the whole question of competitiveness. Universities can do this in three different ways—in their education, in their research, and in their internal management behavior.

## Education

The crux of competitiveness comes down to productivity. Those companies and those countries that are going to be the most productive are going to be the companies and countries that survive most effectively in the international markets that we have now developed and are developing in the world. Productivity is not a simple matter to measure, nor is it a simple phenomenon for which to prescribe appropriate behavior. Productivity, of course, is meaningful only in relationship to some standard of quality.

What happens in our society is that consulting firms and consultants have developed a number of techniques and systems that they believe can increase productivity for firms. Most of the systems that are being sold to corporations involve a good deal of education of the work force, as well as the executives, and are generally based on some variant of the Japanese "just in time" inventory system. Great effort is being made to reduce cycle times for production of different models and for the development of new models. Again, we are influenced by the Japanese ability, particularly in automobiles, to go to the whole cycle from designing to manufacturing automobiles in a time period that seems

Reprinted from *Public Administration Quarterly*, 17(1), pp. 11–18, Spring, 1993.

to be one-half or less of the time that it takes American automobile manufacturers. This phenomenon seems to exist in a number of modules.

One of the themes that has become extremely widespread is the whole notion of total quality management, or TQM. TQM is particularly interesting because it requires a change in culture and is almost a management philosophy in itself.

The heart of the philosophy is a recognition of the extreme importance of the consumer. Firms embracing TQM want to be the preferred supplier of customers that they deal with, whether they be other firms or retail customers. That means that more study is being given to what the consumer wants and to show more basic consideration for the customer. Such a shift, for most American firms, requires a significant change in attitudes. The customer and quality must become ingrained in each employee from the assembly line to the front office.

It is a philosophy that requires a great deal of attention to the employees. The employees must understand the objective of TQM and this means that they must understand their jobs well and how their particular jobs fit into the total manufacturing process. This kind or understanding requires management dedicated to communicating effectively with employees throughout the organization and it requires a management attitude that recognizes the tremendous importance of employee contributions, both in terms of ideas and actual competence.

Different firms become imbued with different aspects of TQM and view the process differently. In all firms, however, it is clear that a change in the culture of the organization is required and that top management must have the vision of what is involved in TQM and in the kinds of things that must be done in order to portray the vision of this new approach properly. There has to be a change in attitude on the part of management itself with respect to the role of the workers in the organization. There clearly is a decentralized aspect of TQM that is not necessarily consistent with traditional management attitudes.

It is also clear that other relationships of the supplier-customer nature in the organization must be recognized and nurtured. These relationships include the connection between school systems and corporations. Much can be done in a school system to change attitudes of students who are eventually going to become members of the work force. The concept of quality and of doing things right the first time is something that can be incorporated into the education of students from kindergarten through the twelfth grade. A process of this kind eventually changes the culture of the whole country.

Unfortunately, in most universities this revolutionary change, which is underway, goes unrecognized in the curricula of university business schools, public administration programs, and engineering schools. Instead of providing leadership to business firms in this area, the American academic institutions, including most business, public affairs, and engineering schools, are tending to follow practice rather than lead it. There is a belief that the kinds of actions involved in TQM are not the proper business of academics. There is a feeling that this activity is not proper material for a curriculum or even a course at an institution of higher learning.

Clearly, this position is in marked contrast to the kind of leadership that universities have been able to exert in the past. In the computer area, for example, academic research for the most part was ahead of practice. In areas involving the service and manufacturing process, however, universities are playing a less and less important role. We have to find ways of changing this state of affairs. This author thinks it requires a couple of different kinds of changes in our own attitudes. We have to look for the generalizations and the substance in the kinds of activities that consulting firms are teaching our corporate managers and we have to learn from the corporate managers themselves about these activities. We then have to be able to translate these kinds of changes into material that is appropriate to teach at a university. We must distill out of this activity generalizations relating to human behavior and try to embed these generalizations in a broader framework, such as organizational theory. We need to have a body of theory from which prospective public and private managers can develop their own systems.

In a real sense it is the kind of distinction that we have between a system that teaches you how to interact successfully with other people through a series of rules of thumb, and psychological theory, which can give a framework that helps students improve their human relations skills through an understanding of human behavior. We have to strive in this area of TQM for the kind of framework and theory that will enable students and prospective managers in the economy to understand the basic elements that are involved so they can design their own systems and modify their own behavior.

## Research

In view of the previous discussion, it is not surprising that research activities have not radically changed in universities despite the concern in society over the competitiveness of our economy. There is certainly more awareness of the whole area of competitiveness and there are now, through the activity of Sloan Foundation, several industry studies underway that are designed to determine the competitiveness of a series of American industries such as automobiles, steel, pharmaceuticals, textiles, and others. This research tends to be positive research in the sense that the approach is to determine what is going on and to evaluate the competitiveness of the industry in the light of knowledge about foreign competition.

There is, however, no series of research projects underway that might be viewed as normative. Such research would attempt to show how firms should be operated to be more competitive. Clearly, we need normative studies of this type so that we can feed the results of such studies to students through the educational process and change the way in which our students are being educated.

Activities of this kind take time. Agencies such as the National Science Foundation do not change their programs rapidly and researchers do not quickly modify their research in order to take on a topic that is more current. Nevertheless, this author thinks it is clear that we are giving increased attention to the competitiveness issue, particularly through the interest in manufacturing. More progress has been made on such topics as design for manufacturability in the manufacturing process than had been made on the management methods for increasing productivity. The research on the management topics is not taking place as it should.

Two factors that have improved the relevancy to competitiveness of some of the academic research have been the centers for excellence in engineering of the National Science Foundation and the federal government's sponsorship of the Federal Quality Institute. These organizations have enabled many more faculty members to interact in important areas with industry both to gain knowledge about what is going on and to transfer technology. The NSF centers, in particular, are models that could be used in the management area to a great advantage.

## Internal Management

The third way that universities can contribute to the increased competitiveness of the U.S. is through their own management. There are two parts to this suggestion. In the first case, the universities can hopefully serve as role models by showing other service industries, and industry in general, how to increase productivity and improve the competitiveness of the economy. In the second place, universities need to move in this direction in order to remain competitive themselves with universities around the world as we move to the future.

Universities have long resisted any effort to increase productivity in their functions. Anyone who has worked in a university recognizes the existence of many forms of inefficiency and indifference in both the organizational structure and the behavior of the participants in the organization. Efforts to eliminate the pockets of inefficiency and to increase productivity, however, are extremely difficult to implement. There are numerous reasons why it becomes difficult to increase productivity, but the biggest reason is the lack of desire. Most faculty members and others in the organization believe the universities are as efficient as they should be. Concentration is clearly on quality and productivity tends to be somewhat ignored unless there is tremendous leadership at the central level.

One hope for increased productivity is through the application of increased capital to the teaching process. With campuswide networks, the possibility of utilizing the computer to a much greater extent, particularly in the teaching process, is certainly one method for improving the productivity of the university. Thus, in general, universities become poor role models for taking actions that will show other firms in the economy—particularly the service firms— how to increase productivity and become more competitive.

This area becomes significantly more important when one looks hard at the future of universities. At the moment American universities—particularly the American research universities—are the best in the world. It is clear, however, that the relationship between universities and firms, one that is strong in the United States, must become stronger all over the world. The Japanese and the German universities in particular will be urged to become better research universities and to work in closer harmony with industry. The impact of the successful university-business relationships in the U.S. and the fact that the U.S. becomes international will drive businessmen in other countries to put pressure on their own governments to improve universities.

Thus, this author sees a future in which American universities are going to have to worry significantly about their own competitiveness. At the moment our quality is so high that we are drawing people from all over the world, even though we do not operate in the most efficient manner and are relatively high cost. There will come a time in the future when we will not have the same quality advantage that we now have and when we will have to pay closer attention to the productivity of out faculty and our nonfaculty, and to be more seriously concerned about controlling costs and streamlining processes.

## Initiating TQM in American Institutions

The application of TQM to a university or a single college is, perhaps, even more difficult that the application to a business firm. There is likely to be more skepticism among faculty members and a feeling that everything possible is being done to achieve excellence.

This attitude must be overcome by increased knowledge of TQM and why it works as a philosophy of management. The first step may be taken in the process of application by the formation of a Quality Improvement Council. Obviously, the name is not crucial, but it should convey the attitude the management wants it to implant. To simplify the exposition, the author will assume that we are discussing a professional school within a university. The council should be chaired by the dean and should include representatives from each grade of faculty and members of the staff. Through this council a series of seminars with outside speakers should be started with the objective of educating everybody in the school on TQM. Speakers initially should be academics at other universities. After the initial seminars, internal speakers can be used, preferably influential faculty knowledgeable on TQM.

As the council becomes educated and in parallel with the education, it should focus on a definition of quality, how it can be measured, and how it can be achieved. This work must then be subjected to criticism and modification by the rest of the organization. Clearly, it is necessary to have agreement through-out the organization on the desired objectives, their measurement, and the ways to achieve them. The net effect of this process is to focus the attention of each member of the organization on excellence and its achievement. The capture of the "attention focus," as the concept has been named by the organization theorists, is the objective of the council. Only if all members of the organization are focused in this manner will the organization achieve excellence. In reality, TQM works because of this fact. It is an organized effort to stimulate everyone to focus attention on improving the organization.

## Definition of the Organization under TQM

One characteristic of TQM is that it suggests a broad definition of the organization. The organization would include faculty, staff, students, applicants, alumni, vendors, central administration members, donors, professionals in the media, and local and federal government office holders, elected and appointed. This list is long and probably needs to be extended, but all of these groups need some attention and should be regarded as part of the organization to some degree. For certain participants periodic information meetings may be enough, but the needs of each group must be thought about in detail.

Many firms have made vendors a part of the organization. In some cases, vendors are brought into discussion of design changes and, in other cases, the firm has gone to the vendor's location to help solve production or quality problems. Media and governmental people are made privy to future building plans and given information about the organization on a regular basis. Recognizing that these various groups are members of the organization enables management to develop relationships that are more meaningful and useful for both the groups and the organizations.

Treating customers as members of the organization is particularly meaningful for an academic organization. Students are customers and can become a major source of feedback while they are in school and as alumni. Students can also be thought of as the product that is being developed by the school. Then another set of customers become the firms who hire the students. Surveying the "bosses" of the ex-students becomes a source of important information for improvement. Getting feedback of this kind is a key part of TQM.

## The Organization as a System

The essence of TQM is the recognition that the management of an organization is the management of a system. It is critical for the manager to take a broad perspective and to see the organization as a system of interrelated parts. Each of these parts has a significant and unique role to play in the organization for it to attain its objectives. If a function is not significant, it should be dropped. At the same time because the organization is an interrelated system, one cannot say that one function is more important than another. Frequently in an academic organization faculty are viewed as being more important than staff—teaching is more important than admissions. Such views can be held only by people who do not understand the nature of an interrelated system.

Because the organization is a system, the manager is forced to deal with all aspects of the firm. The notion that a dean or president can deal with only the fundraising, for example, is patently false when the systems concept is understood. Feedback from students is as important to an organization as feedback on an article to a faculty member from an editor of a professional journal. When these ideas are understood, TQM can be seen as a philosophy of management and the managers as integrators of the significant parts of the total organization. The manager has to see that all parts are functioning properly and working together to achieve the same objectives. Thus, a professional school curriculum must bring the various parts of the curriculum together and emphasize to the students that *management* is integration.

## Summary and Conclusion

In concluding, the author has to end on a rather pessimistic note. He does not believe that American universities at this point are playing the kind of role that they can and should play in improving the competitiveness of American corporations. Part of the reason is our own concept of what proper knowledge to teach at a university level, but more important is the way in which we tend to do research. American research, particularly in management and social sciences, has moved toward a more rigorous format and we tend to be highly concerned with mathematical models rather than necessarily with the short-run relevancy of research.

Under normal circumstances, this point of view is a fine one and is to be applauded. In the current circumstances that we find ourselves in this country, the author believes it is the obligation of all of us to look for ways in which we can increase the productivity of our society and, in particular, improve the competitiveness of American industry. American universities are the greatest source of new ideas and of knowledge that will eventually come to fruition in the marketplace, and, therefore, must be concerned about the ability of American firms to compete in the international marketplace.

Fortunately, firms are beginning to take action in many areas without the help of the university and it may be that that is the way the economy will again attain a level of competitiveness that will enable our standard of living to be maintained. This author personally believes, however, that universities can do more and, if they enter this area, progress will be firmer and more rapid.

## References

Crosby, P. B., *Quality is Free* (New York: Mentor, 1979).

Grayson, C. J., and O'Dell, C., *American Business, A Two-Minute Warning: Ten Changes Managers Must Make to Survive in the 21st Century* (New York: Free Press, 1988).

Juran, J. M., *Juran on Leadership for Quality: An Executive Handbook* (New York: Free Press, 1988).

Scherkenback, W. W., *The Deming Route to Quality and Productivity* (Rockville, Md.: Mercury Press, 1988).

Sensenbrenner, J., "Quality Comes to City Hall," *Harvard Business Review* (March/ April 1991): 64–75.

# 16

# Is There Hope for TQM in the Academy?

*Trudy W. Banta*

In his book *On Q, Causing Quality in Higher Education,* Dan Seymour (1991) cites four driving forces behind the current inclination of colleges and universities to be concerned about quality: competition, costs, accountability and service orientation. He describes each as follows:

*Competition.* For all but the most elite institutions, it is a buyer's market in higher education. Both public and private institutions have to worry about preserving head-count enrollment: privates need tuition dollars, and publics need both tuition and state subsidies based on enrollment. In some markets, there is open and blatant competition for students among institutions.

*Costs.* Throughout the 1980s, tuition rose faster than the consumer price index, and now students and the public want to know what more they are getting for their education dollar. In Indiana, public universities requested a 32 percent increase in state funds for the 1993–95 biennium and the legislature responded with the collective question, "What did you do with the last increase we gave you?"

*Accountability.* Those who support higher education want to know how the dollars are being spent, and have therefore instituted regulations and reporting requirements to ensure accountability. My own career includes ten years of dealing with Tennessee's performance funding program, which bases 5.5 percent of each public institution's budget on the results of a prescribed set of evaluation procedures, including testing students in general education and their major, as well as surveying alumni.

*Service orientation.* Professionals in higher education have set their own standards and have said, in effect, "Leave the money on the stump, and trust us." Those days are over. Now the public wants to be involved in structuring its public institutions to deliver better services by setting standards of quality and determining costs, and we are compelled to respond.

---

Reprinted with permission of Prescott Publishing Company, 1994.

In 1989, I received a three-year grant from the Fund for the Improvement of Postsecondary Education (FIPSE) to work with seven institutions, both two- and four-year, to study the implications of Deming's quality improvement principles for higher education. We met for joint discussions twice a year for three years and established study groups on our individual campuses. In 1989, we felt there was a great need for a translation of Total Quality Management (TQM) principles from the language of business and industry to that of the academy, and thus, over the course of the project we produced a brief overview of quality improvement principles as they can be applied to higher education. Now, nearly five years since we wrote the FIPSE proposal, there are hundreds of articles and several books on the topic.

The FIPSE project culminated in a meeting that took place in May, 1992, in Knoxville. We invited the quality improvement coordinators of several universities that were acquiring some reputation for implementing TQM. The group of institutions included Samford University and the universities of Maryland, Michigan, Minnesota, Pennsylvania, Tennessee, Wisconsin, and Virginia Tech. We considered at that meeting four topics:

1. The features of a quality-oriented institution;
2. Barriers to achieving that vision;
3. Ways to overcome the barriers;
4. Target areas for future work.

In this chapter, I would like to consider an extended list of the features of a quality-oriented institution that we identified on that occasion and identify some of the barriers we face in achieving these. I believe there is some hope for overcoming the barriers to continuous improvement within the academy, but nothing less than a culture change is required to do so.

## Features of a Quality-Oriented Institution

To most academics, a list of characteristics of a college concerned about quality will sound simplistic, like a Dale Carnegie recipe for success. Yet, the philosophy underlying TQM, or Continuous Quality Improvement (CQI), is profound. Its implementation requires a fundamental change in the culture of higher-education institutions.

An institution with a serious commitment to quality:

1. Is committed to the need for *continuous improvement—forever*. Its people are always thinking about how to get better.
2. Identifies *whom it wishes to serve* and what these potential clients want and need. Client groups include students, recipients of faculty research and service activities, and members of the community.
3. Addresses the *needs of its clients* in its mission statement.
4. Identifies the *values* that guide its actions.

5. Develops a *vision* of what it would like to be in the future.
6. Has *strong leadership* that *communicates* the mission, goals, values, and the vision of the institution continuously to faculty, staff and students.
7. Identifies its *critical processes:* teaching, research, and service.
8. *Aligns* the implementation of its activities with its mission and values.
9. Provides *continuing educational opportunities* for all employees, both in group process and in job-related skills.
10. Uses cross-functional *teams* to improve processes: works with its *suppliers,* builds quality into each process, and ceases dependence on inspection to achieve quality.
11. Pushes decision making to the lowest appropriate level, thus *creating* an *attitude of interdependence and trust* throughout the institution.
12. Bases *decisions* about the allocation of resources on *data.* Uses quantitative thinking, along with competence in group problem-solving skills and relevant statistical procedures. These should be in widespread use throughout the institution.
13. Views itself as a *learning organization,* one that:
    • Produces student learning, research, and service
    • Studies, monitors, and evaluates the processes that produce the products
    • Makes active collaborators in the improvement process of all concerned, including faculty, staff and students, parents, suppliers, employers, and community members
14. Recognizes and rewards those who conscientiously work to improve quality.

(I think it is interesting that my list of features includes fourteen points. It just turned out that way; I did not begin with the intention of addressing each of Deming's fourteen points, and I have not done so. But like so many others working in this field, my thinking has been profoundly influenced by Deming's work.)

## Barriers to Achieving the Vision of a Quality-Oriented Institution

Daily we hear and read diatribes against TQM. In an article entitled "What's Wrong with TQM?," Boyett and Conn have described ten mistakes that organizations investing heavily in training and TQM consultants often make. In effect, they say it's tough to change a culture based on individualism.

Within most colleges and universities, there are many faculty and administrators who hold views that provide an environment that is not conducive to establishing the concept of continuous improvement. Some of these views can be cited in connection with each of the fourteen points just identified.

The first argument advanced by many is that American higher education is generally regarded as the best in the world. Faculty and administrators are often overheard saying things like, "We have excellent faculty, all doing their best. How can we improve on perfection?"

Many faculty assert, "We don't have customers. We know best what students need and how to do our research, so why should we ask anyone else? How dare anyone try to tell us how to do our work? We have academic freedom. Moreover, creative work cannot and should not be managed."

In considering the need for statements of values and vision, the campus argument goes: the strength of American higher education is its diversity. Breadth is important. The whole student experience is the sum of parts; that is, individual courses. There is no compelling need to agree on comprehensive program objectives for students because they can and should put their knowledge together themselves in their own way. What we hope to promote in students is critical thinking, which can neither be defined or measured. Faculty cannot, and therefore should not, try to agree on specific goals for student learning in college.

Communication is not very effective in most institutions. Faculty in many departments communicate with similar specialists in their discipline on distant campuses more often than with colleagues in their own department. Administrators think they do well by absorbing outside flack so that faculty can do their jobs. In fact, faculty may have been shielded so effectively that they don't know the wolf is at the door. Most don't recognize that the questions being asked by the public (about how and how much faculty work) are serious and are not likely to go away.

Within every institution, there are critical processes such as student recruitment and admission, orientation, teaching, and evaluation. Crossfunctional teams could be established to effect improvement in each of these areas. But how many universities actually approach their critical processes in this way?

An overall campus plan must guide college and departmental plans so that all work together. Few institutions have a set of plans that really guides day-to-day decision making.

Most universities train secretaries in word processing and in the use of new software. Some training in human relations issues such as team building is being offered through human resources departments, but often we do not provide the structure for immediate use of the concepts being taught. The opportunity to practice what is learned is as important as the instruction itself.

By virtue of their training and tradition, academics tend to work alone. Despite the fact that we carefully collect and analyze data in conducting our disciplinary research, we ignore data and use intuition in reaching conclusions about the impact of our work with students. We have few explicit goals for this work and therefore little direction for evaluating it. In general, we offer few rewards for studying or evaluating the processes of teaching and learning.

We say that we want good teachers, then we reward faculty for doing research as reflected in grants and publications. Jim Fairwether, at the Center for the Study of Higher Education at Penn State, has analyzed massive faculty databases supplied by the National Center for Education Statistics and has demonstrated clearly that the more faculty teach, the less they are paid.

To outsiders, colleges and universities are viewed as big, bureaucratic places. Faculty are arrogant and unresponsive, not at all interested in evaluating their effectiveness. Both administrators and faculty pay far more attention to re-cruiting and ensuring the welfare of faculty than of students. We are seen as not interested in focusing our efforts, working together to set goals, or assess-ing our own progress. We teach the scientific method, but we don't practice it. When asked to explain what we are doing for students, we make it sound almost mystical. We say, in effect, "You put students and great minds together in periods of exposure of fifty minutes for four to six years, and out will come an educated student." "How do we know?" "Don't ask! We just know."

We are asked by parents and potential students, "Do your graduates get better jobs and make more money?" We reply, "Don't ask! We are not train-ing people for jobs. Many of our students go on to the best graduate schools!" "How do you know which schools are best?" We reply, "Don't ask. We just know." "Are you one of the best schools?" Again we reply, "Don't ask! Those rating systems they use are flawed. Our graduates live fuller, richer lives as a result of their education." "How do you know?" We respond, "Don't ask— it's immeasurable."

I want to emphasize that this is not a call to give up creativity and intuition and go to a recipe-like, step-by-step plan, just filling in the cells. Nor am I describing a quick fix. Managing for quality is not for short-term gain; it's a way of life. Simply stated, it will give more focus than we currently have to the doing and to the evaluation of our work in the academy.

### The Need for Change in the Culture of Higher Education

Which of the fourteen aspects of a quality-oriented institution are so im-portant that we must do something about them? I believe that all fourteen must be addressed, because they are conceptually interrelated. The need to provide evidence of accountability is not going to go away—it's well into its second decade and stronger than ever in Tennessee. Too many other pub-lic goods and services are competing with higher education for public dol-lars, and there are too many educational providers. Two- and four-year institutions, training firms, businesses, and industry are all in competition for today's learner. Colleges and universities must use the resources they have to do fewer things better.

According to Roger Chaufournier, the quality leader at George Washing-ton University, if TQM is to be accepted in higher education, faculty must recognize the need for change, acknowledge that new learning must take place, and be willing to take risks (*FYI* column 1992). Relinquishing control to an empowered workforce can be threatening. Finally, and perhaps most importantly for faculty, there must be a willingness for faculty to support the whole, even if this exacts a cost from the individual.

We can improve what we now do and we must. We do not necessarily need to adopt the philosophy of Kaizen—the Japanese concept of continuous improvement with a 200-year view of the future—but we could certainly learn from studies of Kaizen.

We must identify the individuals and groups that we serve, learn more about them, and be more responsive to their needs. We need to know the learning styles of our students and how to address those. Their goals should help to shape our approaches to courses and curricula. If we think of a customer as someone with whom we exchange something of value, it may be easier to recognize students as customers. We may know what students need to know, but they know how they learn best. They can help faculty become better teachers by providing continuous feedback about teaching strategies that work or don't work.

At Samford University in Birmingham, and now at Belmont University in Nashville, Kathy Baugher has had enormous success teaching student teams to work with instructors to continuously improve teaching and learning. Students from quality teams help instructors make changes in their courses that will enable more students to comprehend the material being covered. Baugher has published a manual entitled "LEARN: Student Quality Team Manual" (Baugher 1992) that guides student-team members to: (1) locate an opportunity for improvement; (2) establish a team; (3) assess the current process; (4) research causes; and (5) nominate a solution. In contrast to traditional course evaluations that furnish generic information for use in future classes and are given at the end of a class, student teams provide continuous evaluation throughout the class that can assist the instructor in improving learning opportunities for current students.

Bateman and Roberts (1992), professors in the Graduate School of Business at the University of Chicago, ask students to complete a "fast feedback" at the end of every class. Questions include those from the "one-minute paper" strategy described by Angelo and Cross (1993): "What was the most important thing you learned today?" and "What was the muddiest point?" The questionnaire also asks about the helpfulness of the advance reading assignments for the class in preparing the students for the day's work. In response to open-ended questions, students suggest how the instructor could improve the assignments as well as what went on in class.

Bateman and Roberts report that their questionnaires have produced immediate responses by professors. When students in one class said they were having trouble hearing the instructor, a portable microphone was installed. Students wanted larger type on overhead transparencies and asked that the lights be left on while the overhead projector was in use. Students said they did not need to cover material read in advance in detail in class, so instructors were encouraged to move more rapidly to other material. Students also asked for more examples in class, and instructors have acted on that suggestion.

Faculty complain about the poor preparation of the students they must teach. We need to get closer to our suppliers–teachers in grades K-12 and other professors who teach the introductory and general education courses in our own institutions. We need to set our specifications carefully, communicate them, and hold to our standards. We can help our suppliers by providing training for them.

We must focus our statements of purpose (our mission) and our goals. We can emphasize our unique strengths in determining what the goals will be and, thus, be distinctive. Many faculty say it will weaken rather than strengthen higher education to specify goals for student learning. Yet, we work hard to delimit problem statements to guide our own research. We decry "fishing expeditions." We prize purposefulness. Why should we expect student learning to proceed without any sort of plan?

We must articulate the values that shape our behavior. Do these include religious beliefs, civic participation, and honesty? How do we define and defend academic freedom? Does every faculty member simply teach his or her specialty in whatever way he or she likes? Is there any responsibility for what colleagues expect students to know after they complete one of these specialty courses? Do we ever discuss that with them?

We need a vision of the kind of institution we would like to create in the future. Here we could use Alexander Astin's (1991) concept of talent development, emphasizing the institution's responsibility to nurture and promote the personal growth of each student toward his or her maximum potential. In addition, Peter Senge's (1990) ideas about the learning organization can be instructive: the notion that there are five disciplines, or bodies of knowledge, that a successful organization must adopt. The five disciplines are systems thinking, personal mastery, mental models or images, shared vision, and team learning.

We need strong leadership. Often the commitment of a college president comes from contact with government, business, and industrial leaders outside academe. If we can't get help from outside the institution in persuading the CEO, respected, internal people who are convinced of the need to change should try to influence the leadership. In the final analysis, we may need to recruit someone else for the job. Leaders need to communicate broadly in person and in writing. One must not shield faculty from problems. All need to be involved in finding solutions.

Collaboration on critical processes is important. Cross-functional teams of faculty and staff need to be trained to work together to improve every aspect of the services colleges provide.

Decisions about how we will spend our time—the activities we will undertake—should be made within the context of our mission, values, and vision. We must be more concerned about education and training, both to do our own jobs and to help us become better collaborators. Then we need opportunities to practice the collaborative skills we learn in our training.

We must define our critical processes, work on them in crossdisciplinary teams, set our standards, and work with suppliers to help them meet them. They need feedback about their performance just as we do. Faced with underprepared students, we should not lower our standards. We need to build quality into each process, not simply announce at the end of the process that we have failed with a particular student. Students need assessment, with feedback at many points along the way in their education.

We must involve everyone in problem solving by giving everyone in the academy the pride of responsibility for quality. If we believe higher education can improve society then we ought to pledge to help more people complete their studies. This means working together to figure out how to do that.

We must cease to rely on intuition alone and begin to be systematic in using data to direct improvements. This is the contribution of outcomes assessment in higher education. The process of reviewing assessment colleagues' chapters for a book (Banta 1993) has convinced me that, despite the fact that few campus leaders who have guided assessment programs have background in educational research, the improvements undertaken in response to assessment findings are the very actions that decades of research show are most likely to improve student learning.

We must set goals in higher education and evaluate our progress in meeting them. We must also recognize and reward those who participate conscientiously in this process.

## What Chance Has CQI in the Academy?

In a letter written in December, 1992, to the president of Indiana University, the Executive Committee of the Bloomington chapter of the American Association of University Professors stated, "Any university, but most of all a major research institution, is a collection of specialists having expertise that extends beyond the knowledge of anyone else in the world. These specialists push forward the frontiers of knowledge by extending their own. Specialists do not thrive if managed closely by nonspecialists. At best they are slowed in their efforts to learn by having to drag along, by explanation, those who are not thinking at the same advanced level. At worst, specialists are stymied by the disapproval of their non-specialist evaluators."

In an article in the *Chronicle of Higher Education*, Michael McGerr (1993) argues that today America stands out among advanced industrial societies for its cultural resistance to organization. In the 1950s, Reisman's *Lonely Crowd* and Whyte's *The Organization Man* painted a picture of post-World War II Americans as victims of large-scale organizations that promoted a centralized, impersonal, homogeneous social system, with little room for individuals and individualism. But what has actually happened, according to McGerr, is that the fundamental value of individualism on which this country was founded has prevailed. Corporations have had little impact on our heterogeneous society, on the way we live our lives. "Managers, engineers and advertisers have not spoken the same language, and they have not drowned out other voices." Our society is "less organized, less modern, less susceptible to change than we have assumed." This suggests that TQM too shall pass because Americans cannot be comfortable collaborating to solve our problems.

But there are other voices. Bob Zemsky, director of the Institute for Research on Higher Education at the University of Pennsylvania, has said, "More and more higher-education institutions are coming to see themselves as enterprises that need direction. A college or university is not a gathering place. It needs purpose and discipline" (see Lively 1993.) In the future, external forces such as demands from students, public agencies, and industry, are more likely to shape colleges than are internal deliberations. College is a service industry, and education experience is its product. Zemsky asks, "How do you re-engineer that experience so that it is more flexible and adaptable and meets the needs of its customers; so that it takes advantage of assets and doesn't become so costly that the market evaporates? We are in the business of re-engineering the education experience."

Estela Bensimon and Anna Neumann (1993) studied top administrative leaders in fifteen colleges and universities by going to live on the campuses for a few weeks and interviewing presidents and their staffs. They found CEOs relying on close associates to help them make decisions because "the combined expertise of multiple minds" is needed to address the tensions of contemporary campus life. Bensimon and Neumann believe that the most important feature of a successful team is its ability to act like a social brain. Team members pool their intelligence in forging multiple perspectives; questioning, challenging, and arguing; and monitoring and providing feedback. The team becomes a source of creativity and can serve to correct institutional dysfunction.

What does the future hold? Are we individualists valuing academic freedom who cannot or will not be brought together around a common set of goals? Or will we combine our brain power to collaborate in teaching and in accomplishing all our other responsibilities?

## References

Angelo, T. A ., and Cross, K. P., *Classroom Assessment Techniques, 2nd ed.* (San Francisco: Jossey-Bass, 1993).

Astin, A. W., *Assessment for Excellence* (New York: ACE MacMillian, 1991).

Banta, T. W., and Associates, *Making a Difference: Outcomes of a Decade of Assessment in Higher Education* (San Francisco: Jossey-Bass, 1993).

Banta, T. W., Phillipi, R. H., Pike, G R., and Stuhl, J. H., *Applying Deming's Quality Improvement Strategies to Assessment in Higher Education,* final report (Knoxville: University of Tennessee, Knoxville, Center for Assessment Research Development, 1992).

Bateman, G., and Roberts, H., "TQM for Professors and Students," unpublished manuscript (1992).

Baugher, K., *LEARN Student Quality Team Manual* (Birmingham, Ala.: Author, 1992).

Bensimon, E., and Neumann, A., *Redesigning Collegiate Leadership: Teams and Teamwork in Higher Education* (Baltimore, Md.: The Johns Hopkins University Press, 1993).

Boyett, J. H., and Conn, H. P., "What's Wrong with Total Quality Management?" (unpublished manuscript).

"TQM in Higher Education," *FYI* 1 (2) (1992): 6.

Lively, K., "State Colleges Grapple With Tough Decisions on How to Downsize," *The Chronicle of Higher Education* (1993): A23, A28.

McGerr, M., "The Persistence of Individualism," *The Chronicle of Higher Education* (1993): A48.

Senge, P. M., *The Fifth Discipline: The Art Practice of the Learning Organization* (New York: Doubleday, 1990).

Seymour, D., *On Q: Causing Quality in Higher Education* (New York: ACE MacMillian, 1991).

# 17

# An American Approach to Quality

*Marilyn R. Zuckerman and Lewis J. Hatala*

Late in 1985 the AT&T Network Systems quality leaders embarked on an expedition to understand why the quality renaissance they believed in so deeply was not taking root. They had benchmarked the current best practices and tried to install them into the mainstream of their business. They faced what medical doctors face when trying to revive someone's life with an organ transplant and the patient's body has rejected their good work and heartfelt intentions.

Undaunted by this rejection, the pioneers launched a cultural study of quality in America. Their findings are documented in our book, *Incredibly American: Releasing the Heart of Quality*. This chapter is excerpted from our book.

## About Archetypes

Our work focuses on the transitional years of early childhood, roughly between the ages of one and six. During these years, children are shaped by the forces and people around them and begin to take on the qualities of the men and women they gradually become. Some of the most interesting and valuable aspects of our research concerns the learning of language during this period.

As people learn a particular language, they acquire a distinctive set of tools to relate, analyze, and function in the world. Language lets people grasp the meaning of objects, actions, or qualities and the relationships among them. Learning these relationships is not passive, experienced simply as information received by the mind. It's an active process, relying on personal discovery and grounded in emotion.

An *imprint structure* is the mind's permanent record of the imprinting experience—the complex sensory, emotional, and verbal episode converted to a form the mind can store and reuse. Think of channels and riverbeds eroded in the desert. They exist, and will continue to exist, whether or not any water flows in them. They were created by a flood, but when the flood is over, the structure of channels and riverbeds remains. This is the nature of an imprint structure: it's the riverbed, not the river. After a flood of emotion has passed,

**FIGURE 17.1**
The Conscious and Unconscious

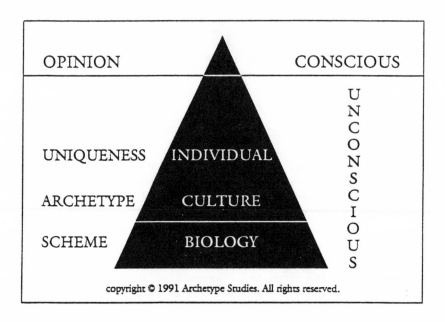

the imprint structure remains in place, full of potential for later experiences. These archetypes exist at multiple levels as shown in figure 17.1.

When Carl Jung first described the structure of a universal archetype in 1902, he depicted it as a field of forces created by the tension between points in opposition. Cultural archetypes, as well, can be depicted using a field of forces.

## The Study

To determine the source of a cultural archetype, something having a strong impact on our behavior, you would look for a certain pattern, a distinctive sort of emotional logic surrounding a particular word. This would lead you to an examination of the memories, perceptions, and connotations of that word that grow directly from a given culture.

The AT&T Network Systems quality study utilized focus groups conducted with fifteen to twenty people. Participants in the focus group were asked to recall and discuss their first and subsequent experiences and associations with

## FIGURE 17.2
### American Quality Archetype

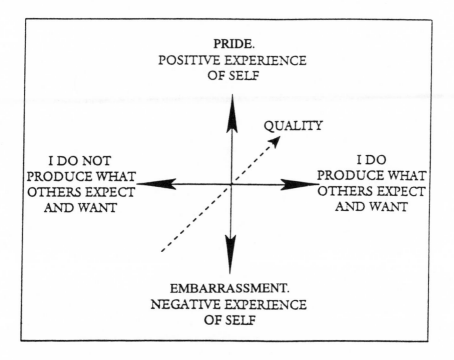

the word "quality." There experiences were written down, collected, and analyzed to identify patterns for individual participants, and collectively, for cultural patterns.

The *quality* archetype study revealed tension created by the opposing forces of actions and feelings. In the action area, tension exists between the states of doing what others expect or want and not doing what others expect or want—two opposite extremes. In the emotion area, the tension exists between the emotional states of feeling good about ourselves, having a strong sense of self-esteem, and feeling bad about ourselves, embarrassed. A graphic depiction of these relationships is shown in figure 17.2. Jung called this four-cornered archetype structure a quaternity.

This remarkably simple diagram shows the states of emotion and action for an American's first learning about *quality*. Typically, Americans start out in their quality learning somewhere in the lower left quadrant: they don't do what others expect or want, and they feel bad about it. Fortunately, that's not the complete archetype. The diagonal arrow represents a transformation. It indicates a change from the time when people don't do what others expect or want, and feel bad, to the time when they do produce what others expect or want, and feel good; this usually means "proud" and "satisfied." The success of this transformation depends on very specific roles being performed at certain times.

With this information alone, one can see that some of the messages typically used to stimulate quality behavior conflict with the archetype, and may actually produce the opposite response. Messages like "do it right the first time" and "zero defects" by their very nature are not consistent with the American quality archetype. "Doing it right the first time" and "zero defects" may be expectations, but as messages to Americans they are more debilitating than motivating; they contribute to feelings of being controlled and restricted.

Another discovery from the study concerned the word "perfection." In America, perfection isn't synonymous with quality, but instead has unpleasant connotations. For Americans, perfection is the end. Beyond perfection, there is nothing; perfection is death itself.

Figure 17.3 shows another quality quaternity. The opposing forces here create tension between the beginning and the end of something, and between failing and succeeding. Remember, in the beginning, the imprint of quality is associated with failure. This is characterized as "only human." For Americans, this is what it means to be normal and to be associated with life—in the beginning, you're not expected to succeed. You fail, or at least stumble, and certainly don't achieve ultimate success; but that's okay, you're only human. If you succeed in the beginning, there's no glory for you, and no reward.

This aspect of adult life reflects early childhood education. Many people received report cards that gave separate grades for effort and achievement. If you brought home a report card that indicated high achievement as a result of high effort (shown in figure 17.4a), you were proud, and your parents were proud, too. You had worked hard and had succeeded very appropriately, the greatest effort for the highest grade.

If you brought home the report card in figure 17.4b your parents would react as though something were out of whack. They would probably think the work was too easy, or the teacher had marked the card unfairly, perhaps being too lenient in the achievement grading. High achievement with low effort doesn't feel right or make sense to Americans. If effort is low, achievement should be low. This report card is a signal that something is wrong. This attitude is also manifested in modern business; many managers express a desire for their people to work smarter and harder, to put both more thought and more effort into their work. But in spite of much lip service to working smarter, these same managers tend to reward those who visibly work harder. The employee who leaves work at 5 P.M. every day, because he or she is so efficient and well-organized, just doesn't seem to be doing as much as the one who's in the office until 7 P.M. every night, sorting through heaps of paperwork with rolled-up sleeves.

**FIGURE 17.3**
**American Quality Archetype**

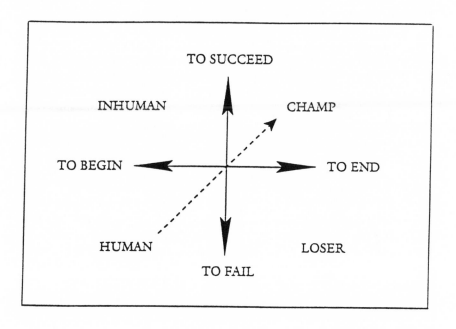

Very early, Americans learn that for their achievements to be valued, they must put in maximum effort. They must at least look like they are working their hardest, even if it's just a smoke screen. In our culture, achievement with minimum effort will never bring the same accolades as when maximum effort is expended. Achievement without effort conveys arrogance or unfair superiority.

Back to figure 17.3—our winner/loser quaternity. If you fail at the end, you are typically regarded as a loser, and land in the lower right quadrant. Americans don't like losers, or losing at the end, but it's preferable to succeeding at the beginning. If you lose, you always get another chance. Consider bankruptcy; it gives you a chance to end a failure and start over. This characteristic lies very deep in the American archetype. Everyone who immigrates to America comes for a new start, a second chance, and they know they have an unlimited number of times to try.

Now consider the place where all Americans want to be: the upper right quadrant of our diagram, where people achieve success at the end of something. When you succeed at the right time in a project (when it's over) you're

FIGURE 17.4a

| REPORT CARD | |
| --- | --- |
| ACHIEVEMENT | EFFORT |
| (A) | (1) |
| B | 2 |
| C | 3 |
| D | 4 |
| F | 5 |

FIGURE 17.4b

| REPORT CARD | |
| --- | --- |
| ACHIEVEMENT | EFFORT |
| (A) | 1 |
| B | 2 |
| C | 3 |
| D | 4 |
| F | (5) |

a champion, a winner. This is the classic story of the American hero. An American hero or heroine is someone who begins in the lower left quadrant, an underdog, with no advantage, no help, nothing. American champions overcome all adversity, withstand all pressures, and penetrate all barriers. They rise to their feet whenever they're knocked down, no matter how many times. American champions persevere against all odds, and finally, only in the very end, they win.

Every American athletic team that's ever had a big following started out as an underdog—the Dodgers, the Mets, the U.S. hockey team at the Lake Placid Olympics in 1980. The members of this hockey team were classic underdogs. They had never played together before, were relatively inexperienced as a team, and had no hope of winning. They spent a mere six months training together. They weren't star players, just good team players; but they won the gold medal.

Their magic came from their shared dream. It was a magic conjured up by people coming together out of nowhere with no advantage and working intensely, fighting against all odds, against a professional Russian team, overcoming every setback, but winning at the end. They became heroes and inspired the entire nation. This story is the archetype, the timeless story of success in America.

Many successful American movies tell the story of an underdog who becomes a champion, and reflect the basic pattern of the archetype. If Rocky had knocked out Apollo Creed in the first round few would have been interested in the story, and the film would have vanished shortly after release. The classic American success story is what provides this film's energy. It appears again in *The Karate Kid*, which captured the hearts of Americans and inspired two sequels. These films work because they're built on the American archetype. The people who wrote them may not have been aware of this fact, but they intuitively knew the pattern. They knew what would work for Americans.

Besides showing why Americans react favorably to certain stories, the archetype study also shed light on the American emotional reactions to certain words. The study revealed that words often used in conjunction with quality initiatives stimulate negative feelings, very much like the word "perfection." Words like "standards," "specifications," "control," and "maintenance" tend not to motivate Americans. They shut down people's energy, rather than feed their hunger for new possibilities. They contribute to Americans' feelings of being controlled rather than empowered. All these concepts are important, but they must be put into perspective. Certainly Americans must meet appropriate standards, conform to customers' specifications, control their processes, and maintain their equipment, operations, and software. But when work is described using these or similar words, Americans are rarely motivated to do it with the spirit or enthusiasm needed to be number one.

The study also found that some words stimulate very strong, positive feelings. "New," "change," "possibility," "opportunity," and "breakthrough" are all words that excite us. Americans associate them with creativity and innovation. Something new, something different, an adventure, a change, finding untapped resources, exploring unknown territory—these are the concepts that excite, energize and motivate Americans.

## Starring Roles

For virtually all Americans, the beginning of the imprint experience for "quality" was a time when they did not produce what others expected or wanted and, thus, felt bad. Their self-esteem was lowered—they were embarrassed. There's good news about this painful beginning: a successful completion results from transforming this negative emotion into positive energy, so the pain felt at the start actually fuels the ultimate drive to succeed.

The transformation of negative emotion into positive energy is not automatic, and may not happen at all. The study showed that a successful transformation occurs in three clearly defined phases and depends on specific roles being played during each phase. The fundamentals of this process, the most basic template of American quality, are discussed in the three sections that follow.

### Phase I: Crisis and Failure

The archetype story and its associated transformation begin in a state of crisis, what we simply characterize as a "Mess," shown in figure 17.5. For example, at work, you are often faced with a Mess when you receive an assignment, and the only thing clear about it is its urgency. Its details and parameters, the rules, are poorly defined; they may have seemed completely clear at first, but when you start getting to work on the assignment, you find that the rules no longer make sense. This extraordinarily common situation introduces the first role in the process: the Lawgiver.

The Lawgiver is the person, group, or phenomenon that creates the crisis; in this example its the person who gave you the assignment and communicated the sense of urgency. You need to take action, you want to succeed, to do it right, but the rules aren't clear.

The Lawgiver creates the pressure, forces you to move, and insists on results. You're still unsure of the rules, but because of the pressure, the urgency, you begin anyway. You leap into action, despite your vast amount of training and counseling to plan first.

This bias can either be a source of weakness or a source of strength. By following the archetype and transforming the Mess, it becomes our greatest strength. Americans are action oriented, and pay only lip service to planning first. They would much rather do first, plan later. For Americans, it's not "Ready, Aim, Fire," but more often "Ready, Fire, Aim." Regardless of how much planning they do, at some point in time mistakes occur and problems result, usu-

**FIGURE 17.5**
**Phase I—Crisis and Failure**

... Pain ... Guilt ... "I Quit" ...

**THE LAWGIVER**

- Communicates the Crisis and Urgency
- Creates Pressure and Forces Movement
- Insists on Results and Benefits

ally from not understanding the rules, or not believing them; when this happens, Americans often feel bad.

This sense of failure begins the transformation—it can happen relatively early or late in the cycle, and several failures may occur on a single pathway to success. The natural inclination is to try to avoid failure at all costs, but within failure lies the source of energy needed to fuel the transformation. This source of energy is emotion, particularly the emotional response to failing.

This time of emotional pain is as delicate as it is crucial. People must begin the cycle of transformation that brings them out of their initial pain and pulls them toward success. If the pain is too great, they can fall into other cycles that are tragic and debilitating, preserving the pain instead of transforming it.

**FIGURE 17.6**
**Emotional Cycles**

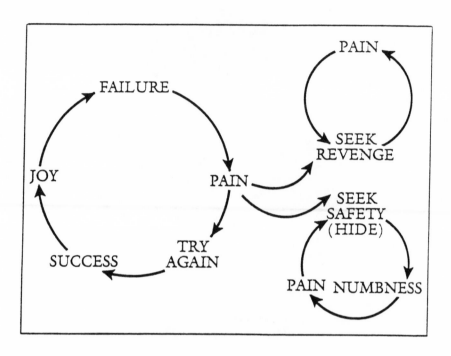

People often wear masks, deceiving themselves and everyone around them, and may not even be consciously aware of their pain; they will almost never show it in any obvious fashion. Looking at the emotional cycles in figure 17.6, you can see that the most critical point occurs just after experiencing failure and being overcome with pain. The first impulse is to cover up the failure and hide; but this is no escape. Even with an effective cover-up, the pain associated with failing is still experienced.

When people feel pain and move out of the healthy cycle pictured on the left in figure 17.6, they often move into another cycle to seek safety. Another common reaction to the pain of failing is to seek revenge. All of us have experienced times when we've escaped to one of these alternate cycles. Some are more prone to seek one cycle over the other, but both are destructive, to themselves and their organizations. These alternate cycles waste time, energy, and money. But worst of all, they waste people's talent. When people escape to these other cycles, they become noncontributing members of their organizations. It's not just a matter of giving less than their best—they're giving their worst.

**FIGURE 17.7**
Phase II—Support

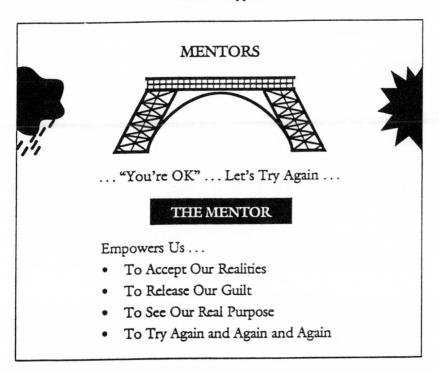

> MENTORS
>
> ... "You're OK" ... Let's Try Again ...
>
> THE MENTOR
>
> Empowers Us ...
> * To Accept Our Realities
> * To Release Our Guilt
> * To See Our Real Purpose
> * To Try Again and Again and Again

Perhaps the most important aspect of Phase I, the Crisis, is this: during a state of emotional crisis, people are closed to learning. They are in pain, and find it difficult to listen. Even the most precious advice from the wisest person around may roll right off someone in the midst of Phase I.

*Phase II: Support*

As Phase I is characterized by a Mess, Phase II is characterized by Support. In Phase I, you have been thrown into a crisis because the rules from the lawgiver were not clear. You burst into action, not asking for a plan or clarification. You were well intentioned and wanted to do it right. You took risks and gave an honest effort, but it didn't work. You failed, and by now you are probably feeling a certain amount of guilt. This phase, Phase II–Support, introduces the second important role in the cycle of transformation: the Mentor, described with some key characteristics in figure 17.7.

Listening to their problems, and acknowledging the way they feel about them, the Mentor helps people accept the reality of their situation, and in so doing helps them release any guilt they may feel. In this way, the Mentor helps them renew their sense of purpose. With the Mentor's help, people become willing to try again and again, as often as necessary, to continue along this path, until they achieve success. Cycling through failure several times is certainly not uncommon, but the Mentor must be there every time to offer the necessary emotional support.

In Phase II, the Mentor is accompanied by another very important role, the Coach. While they may sound like the same role, the study showed that Coach and Mentor are noticeably different roles, even though they're occasionally performed by the same person. Note that while one person can act as both Mentor and Coach, it is inadvisable for a Coach or Mentor to also be a Lawgiver. It is recommended that the Lawgiver be some outside force, like your competition or your customer, although a business leader may need to become a lawgiver to insure the competitive threat or the voice of the customer is heard before it is too late.

The role of the archetype Coach corresponds to the coach of an athletic team, an analogy we follow in figure 17.8. The Coach works with people to break projects down into smaller, more manageable steps and helps them develop their skills and acquire whatever resources they need to do the job. The Coach helps people achieve small, measurable successes, one at a time, build on them, and eventually achieve the larger success of the whole project. The Coach also sets deadlines and insists that people practice. When was the last time your business team practiced or trained together as a team?

In business, people use sports analogies all the time. They look for examples in football or baseball that are clear and obvious, and then translate them into the language of the business world. But there's one glaring difference in the sports versus business analogy, a difference managers never talk about when encouraging their staff to "go team go." Of the total time an athletic team spends together on the field, 80 to 90 percent of it is spent in practice, learning how to do it right, doing it wrong the first time. Only 10 to 20 percent of their time is spent actually doing it right—competing. In contrast, business teams spend nearly all their time trying to compete in the real world, with real customers and real money, and spend only 2 to 3 percent of their time practicing, if in fact they ever practice. Business teams compete far better when they get a reasonable amount of practice; this is why they need coaches.

In the course of Phase II, the Mentor provides emotional recognition that relieves people's pain, helps them release their guilt, and opens them to learning. Then the Coach steps in to teach them, deepen their understanding, provide the right tools for the job, keep them on schedule, and make them experiment and practice safely, away from the real world. This helps people refine their plans and methods to eventually do the job right.

**FIGURE 17.8**
**Phase II—Support**

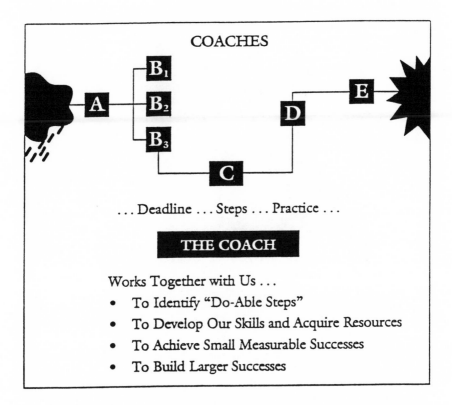

... Deadline ... Steps ... Practice ...

**THE COACH**

Works Together with Us ...

- To Identify "Do-Able Steps"
- To Develop Our Skills and Acquire Resources
- To Achieve Small Measurable Successes
- To Build Larger Successes

*Phase III: Celebration*

When Americans persevere long enough, and receive the right kind of support from Coaches and Mentors, the transformation ends in success. This third phase of the archetype is a Celebration of the quality performance, shown with supporting details in figure 17.9. Phase III introduces the last key role in the archetype structure: the Champion. The Champion is the worker or player who has been struggling to beat the odds, to make the deadline, to win the contract, to finish the job, to ultimately overcome the pain of initial failure and finally succeed.

**FIGURE 17.9**
**Phase III—Celebration**

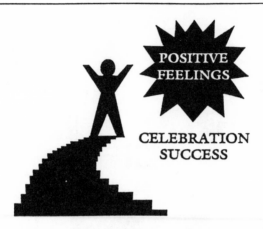

... Action ... Result ... Gold Medal ...

Celebrating **THE CHAMPIONS**

- Recognizes Their Journey and Accomplishment
- Reaffirms Their Worth
- Creates a Memory
- Refreshes All of Our Energy

The first thing to understand about a Celebration is that it's not a party, but it may have a party feeling or atmosphere. It is more like a ceremony, and sometimes acquires the flavor of ritual. It's a time to acknowledge the Champion or Champions who have achieved their success. The ceremony must recognize not merely the Champions' wonderful accomplishment at the end, but their entire journey, including all the failures, all the pain, the desire to quit, and the struggle to persevere. When people recognize the whole journey, they acknowledge that this experience is human. Parents, teachers, managers, and executives must show their Champions that they accept the Champions' initial failure, accelerating progress and ultimate success as a single, nurturing process, not discrete events to be analyzed individually. By reliving their jour-

**FIGURE 17.10**
**The Quality Transformation**

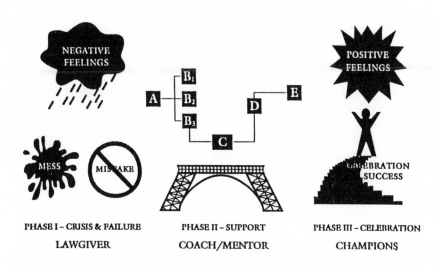

ney through storytelling and sharing their feelings, the Champions prepare for their next challenge.

The Celebration should be planned so that all the people attending can identify with the Champions' story. Remember, the Champions weren't always winning. Sometimes they were getting knocked down, sometimes stumbling and falling, sometimes making mistakes and feeling horrible. During the Celebration, the audience relives this journey with the Champions. Even though it doesn't focus on their own experience, they will still identify with it. When the last part of the story, the successful part, is the only story told, the champion is set up as a super human. The audience feels separated from the champion, rather than seeing that they also could be in the spotlight.

In all likelihood, the people in the audience are cycling somewhere in journeys of their own, perhaps still in pain, perhaps in failure, maybe wanting to give up. Attending the Celebration of another group or individual can provide them with tremendous emotional energy. A Celebration reaffirms the worth of the Champions, and a subliminal echo of this acknowledgment tends to spread to all the people in attendance. The event makes it clear to the audience that the Champions are considered people of outstanding value, people who are respected for having lived through the whole transformation, and that means respected even for their initial failures: at least they tried.

Through the Celebration of Phase III, the Champions internalize their learning from Phases I and II. The Celebration reinforces the structure of the archetype, and releases the energy needed for Champions to take on new challenges. Over time, this sort of recognition can accomplish the priceless task of reducing people's fear of failure and their immobilizing reluctance to take risks.

Figure 17.10 shows the complete transformation during the three phases, and the learning that occurs during each phase. Notice that the negative feelings in Phase I are balanced by the positive feelings in Phase III. This is not merely a graphic designer's trick. Americans must achieve this balance. Each of these elements is part of the American quality archetype. Each element must be present for any American quality initiative to be successful. It's a simple model and a powerful nurturing process, one that offers enormous potential.

## Americans and Perfection

We can demonstrate another critical element of the American quality archetype by relating typical American behavior to the "Q" line, shown in figure 17.11. The Q line is a simple graphic depiction representing marketplace expectations. It moves up because customer expectations of quality, as set or demanded by the marketplace, are always moving to a higher level. As new products, services, technologies, or levels of quality are achieved, these expectations continue to rise. This line therefore symbolizes quality as a constantly moving, evolving thing. The study showed that for Americans, the quality of goods and services is most often associated with the phrase "It works," meaning that a product or service does what it's supposed to in the way people expect.

Contrast this American idea of simple functionality with perfection. You've read what perfection means to Americans: the end, death. But for the Japanese, the Q line appears to be more closely aligned with true perfection—the results of this difference are quite striking and have a remarkable effect on their performance as producers.

In both the United States and Japan, the farther you are from the Q line, the farther you are from meeting marketplace expectations; your processes, products, and services are full of defects and deficiencies. This means you are in a greater state of crisis and have a greater awareness of the need for urgency. The big difference between Japan and the U.S. at this critical stage is the length of time before the reality of the situation is fully acknowledged. It often takes death or imminent disaster to shake Americans, which leads to tragedies like the Challenger explosion, the Exxon Valdez oil spill, or Three-

**FIGURE 17.11**
The "Q" Line

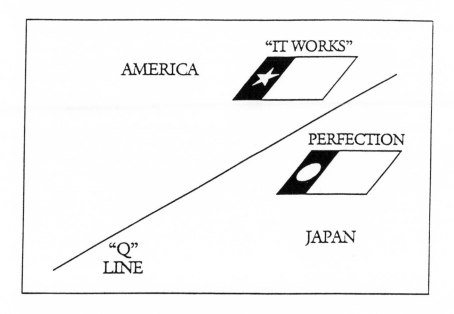

Mile Island. The Japanese appear to be more open to feedback and less likely to cover up problems and hide from criticism.

When awakened to a crisis, whether sooner or later, both Japanese and Americans rapidly take action to approach the Q line. Because of cultural differences, the Japanese can and will continue to work with great diligence, dedication, and constancy of purpose to get closer and closer to this market-place expectation, as shown in figure 17.12. The consistent discipline of the Japanese enables them to squeeze out every last bug, problem, and deviation to ultimately achieve close to zero defects. In fact, they are very likely to push past the point of exceeding current market expectations, thereby setting new thresholds.

For the Japanese, constantly approaching the Q line is the equivalent of striving for perfection, in their culture, a wonderful source of positive energy. When people in Japan achieve excellence or set a new standard, they become highly respected and are often revered as masters. Such people achieve a position of the highest regard in Japan and receive tremendous respect, status,

**FIGURE 17.12**
The "Q" Line

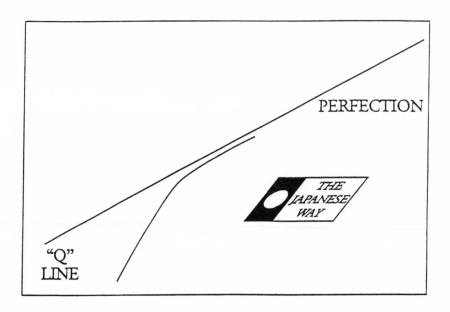

and recognition. As a reward, masters are permitted to deepen their wisdom by pursuing their work for the rest of their lives and are expected to teach other people their priceless skills and knowledge.

In this country, it's quite different. Once Americans achieve the highest level of excellence, they certainly don't want to continue doing "it" for the rest of their lives; they get hopelessly bored. For Americans, getting closer and closer to the Q line is anything but a source of positive energy. Americans don't like being methodical. There is little recognition for the diligence and perseverance required to maintain quality in the same task or product. In figure 17.13, the dotted line shows what happens to Americans when they try. Instead of getting closer and closer to the Q line, boredom sets in, defects multiply, and the curve falls off.

In America, if people are losing enough market share, if they are in pain and crisis and are willing to admit it, then they will move. They will feel the urgency and the crisis, and they will begin trying to reach the Q line. But once again, as they get closer and the end is in sight, they lose interest. Why? Be-

**FIGURE 17.13**
**The "Q" Line**

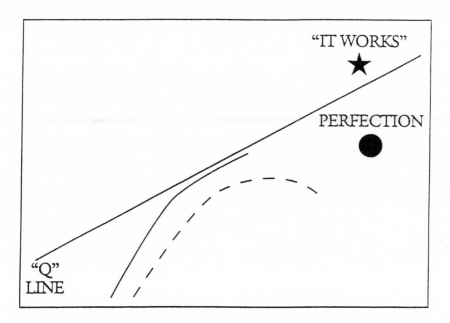

cause to reach the line and maintain a position there requires precision, control, discipline, squeezing out every last defect, an ongoing task that holds little excitement or reward. When Americans get close to the line, they're likely to say, "Well, looks like we're almost there. We can make it." They relax and begin looking for something new, something more exciting. Itching to move on to a new challenge, Americans get sloppy. Their interest and discipline wane, and they start to fall.

Figure 17.14 illustrates the way quality works in America—quality the American way. It begins with a great push from the crisis position, the low point full of defects and mistakes. With a feeling of urgency, Americans begin to move forward. What is needed to pull them up to the Q line is actually something that lies well beyond it—an impossible dream. This can't be just any dream, thrown at people like some emotional panacea. The right impossible dream for Americans must bear certain characteristics.

First, it must be something that seems almost impossible to achieve but is eminently worth striving for, like an Olympic gold medal. Second, it must

### FIGURE 17.14
### The "Q" Line

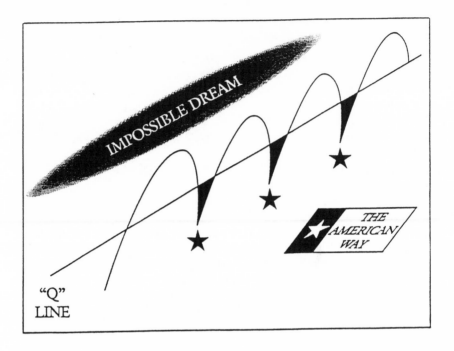

inspire that itchy, tantalizing feeling that in spite of its loftiness maybe, just maybe, the goal can be reached. A dream can't be too far fetched.

Individual's personal dreams are easily connected to this greater impossible dream, which can appeal to many. It's the challenge that excites people, and it must be a significant and distinctive challenge, preferably something unique. Meeting the specification that already exists is boring; doing the impossible, that's another story. But for Americans, the energy from such a dream has its limits and its pitfalls.

Even with the addition of an impossible dream, figure 17.13 shows basically the same pattern as figure 17.14. As Americans get closer and closer to the dream, maybe even reaching it, they lose interest. They see they are almost there, so they get overconfident and sloppy, and become more interested in finding something new, something more challenging. With this overconfidence, a lack of precision and discipline creep into their work, and it falls away from quality, sometimes disastrously.

How far below the Q line the work will fall is critical. How much market share did American auto makers have to lose to the Japanese before they took action and tried to implement change? How much pain do Americans have to feel before they're willing to admit that they are failing, that they are in a state of crisis? The archetype study showed that a crisis creates negative, painful emotions that can be redirected into the positive energy needed for tackling the next challenge. But what most Americans tend to do instead is dissipate the negative energy by calming the crisis, searching for the smallest crumb of good news buried in the bad to make us feel better.

The vital step here is to create a sense of urgency before performance falls below the Q line. Channel this negative emotional energy by connecting it to a new impossible dream. This can rekindle people's spirits. In such an effort, the crisis ignites people's emotional fuel, driving them forward, Mentors help them connect with the new and exciting purpose, and the impossible dream pulls them on to win.

Today, as American parents, teachers, managers, executives, and officials struggle for success in home, education, business, and government, they move from peak to valley, from highs to lows, lows to highs. It's a persistent roller coaster, and it has to be, at least to some extent. If Americans are to maintain consistent improvement in products and services, this variation is absolutely essential. Whenever those in charge of a project try to flatten the emotional curves, believing that this is what is needed to maintain some sort of "controlled quality," people lose their excitement, their energy, and finally, their interest. This is exactly the way to destroy the value of the greatest resource in the American workplace—Americans.

The American space program is a perfect illustration of this quality process. When the Russians launched Sputnik in 1957, they set a new standard for achievements in aerospace. The Q line for that particular arena moved up, and Americans were no longer the leaders; the Russians were. The gap that existed between the two countries was enormous. America was the underdog, very much behind; that was very painful for us. But actually, this is the best position in which Americans can find themselves. We don't like being second, and don't want to stay there any longer than necessary.

In 1960 and right on cue, President Kennedy stepped in with an impossible dream: putting a man on the moon and returning him safely to earth before the end of the decade. With Americans' drive fueled by the pain and embarrassment of being the underdog and their will and determination inspired by Kennedy's vision, they set out on a mission to be the first to conquer space, and they did! America left Sputnik near the starting line, landed a man on the moon, and returned him safely to earth in July, 1969.

Sadly, even with these glorious circumstances, space exploration followed the pattern of the archetype. Sloppiness crept in, and gradually the precision and the discipline were lost. The program's quality slipped, then fell. First, a fuel cell explosion crippled the Apollo 13 spacecraft in April, 1970. The three astronauts barely managed to improvise control and environmental systems to stay alive and return to earth. In 1979, due to an inaccurate long-term mission plan, Skylab's orbit began to decay earlier than expected. As the space-craft began to break up, the whole world wondered anxiously where the possibly large chunks of metal would fall. Through nothing but luck, no damage was done.

But that still wasn't enough to fix the space program; it continued to sink below the Q line. Urgency and crisis were felt, but the need to stay on schedule was the primary driver, and more people had to die before NASA would admit a state of crisis. It took the Challenger tragedy to bring everything to a stop.

### Mobilizing for Quality American Style

Phase I is a time to *generate emotional energy.* Emotional energy flows from the tension that exists between the crisis and the dream; in other quality language, the gap between the current state and the desired future state. The conventional quality language is accurate, but it is not fully engaging. Emotion is required to achieve engagement. Engagement that builds commitment is based on full engagement, the head, heart, and hands. Attempts to engage that are only "head" too often yield compliance only, not commitment. It is next to impossible to sustain compliance unless you institute punitive measures. This builds fear, and fear is often the enemy of quality. Dr. Deming's eighth point, "Drive Out Fear" is the cornerstone of the human side of quality.

During the Olympics, Dan Janson generated emotional energy in all of us when he lost every race he entered. As the olympic games progressed, we learned more about his story and how he had lost at three previous olympic games even though he had broken all records in his trails. In his last race his dream came true when, despite a near miss, he won the gold medal. We all seemed to know what Dan was thinking as he looked up, tipped his hand toward the sky, a tear rolling down his cheek, and sent a message to his sister, Jane, who had died hours before a previous olympic game in which he raced.

Phase II is the time to *stimulate innovation.* In Phase I our creativity is often directed toward covering up mistakes, creating alibis, or finding someone or something to blame for the fact that things did not go right the first time. If we are supported by mentoring and coaching when things are not going well, we are more likely to continue to try again. The emotional energy from Phase I drives us towards more constructive creativity—where real innovation can occur. Here we build on an idea, confident that the first idea is simply an element of a solution. If we keep going we will find solutions that are more than continuous incremental improvement, but are breakthrough ideas yielding discontinuous change.

Phase III is a time for *encouraging renewal.* A celebration that tells the whole story of someone's accomplishments—what it took to achieve the results—is a renewing experience for not only the recipient, but all those in attendance. Renewal prepares us for a new challenge and gets us ready for facing another struggle where, once again, we feel the tensions between a new crisis and another dream. Celebrations do not have to be elaborate; they must be sincere and heartfelt.

At a recent celebration for a man who was retiring after thirty years of service, a heartfelt experience was shared by all in attendance. The memory of this experience will stay with them for the rest of their lives. He received many lovely gifts, but one in particular, he will cherish always. In one box was a somewhat aged note, wrinkled and yellowed at the edges. At first he was baffled. Then a smile came over his face and a tear rolled down his cheek as he recognized his own handwriting on the note. He read the note out loud. When he was the supervisor of one of his guests, he had written the note. It was a simple note to thank his subordinate for all his extra effort he gave to complete a job successfully. It had meant so much to the man that he had kept it in his wallet all these years. In giving it back as a gift, he was saying, "You had the power to make a difference in my life—thank you for the gift of confidence and trust." These gifts have no price tag and they never go out of style. They have enormous power—they are the gifts that keep giving!

## Conclusion

It is widely known that the contemporary approaches to corporate quality were greatly influenced by developments in Japan. To a large extent, quality leaders in this country have sought to study, adopt, and adapt these approaches.

As valuable as this model may be, our work suggests that it is also vital to be mindful of cultural differences related to "quality"—the word and the concept. An awareness of the unique meaning and motivational character of "quality" for Americans can be of great value in planning and implementing quality initiatives in business, government, and education.

# 18

# Total Quality and the Academy: Problems and Opportunities

*Judy D. Olian*

### The Maryland TQ Experience

The University of Maryland began its total quality (TQ) initiative in 1990. Our interest in the total quality approach was prompted by the same economic, political, and competitive pressures experienced by most of higher education. Since then we have designed and initiated a total quality culture change process in both academic and administrative support functions, and we have learned from our successes and failures. The conditions compelling change in our environment, and our experiences in attempting to bring about cultural change, most probably can be generalized to many other institutions of higher education. This chapter describes our efforts and shares the lessons we are learning as we travel.

### The Need for Change

*Competing over Resources*

Universities have entered an unprecedented era of competition over resources. Declining federal and state budgets, exacerbated by the economic recession, have caused major cutbacks in the resources available to higher education funding sources.

> In growing numbers of states, 80–85 percent of the budget is now tied up in entitlements, court ordered spending, and restrictions of one kind or another; in this context, higher education has become the "budget balancer"—the last-in-line piece of discretionary spending remaining after mandatory expenditures are accounted for.

---

This article benefits greatly from the ideas and input of Dr. William E. Kirwin who, as president of the University of Maryland, leads the campus continuous improvement strategy.

A second element of the problem is that taxpayers simply will not support further increases, however worthy the cause.... These conditions, together with more general trends in the economy, suggest strongly that higher education will need to do what it does for less for the foreseeable future. (Ewell 1993, 50)

Whether it is state legislatures, granting agencies, or private donors, all are forced to reduce the number of programs they fund. The net result is that there is a larger number of institutions of higher education competing over a shrinking funding pie. As a case in point, the University of Maryland experienced a 20 percent cut in state support over the last three years as the state of Maryland endured its worst budget crisis in recent history. Tuition increases are no longer the answer to these increasingly severe financial shortfalls. Prospective students are finally saying "enough" to tuition rate hikes equivalent to two or three times the rate of inflation, and the vast majority believe that college costs are rising at a pace that will put college education out of the reach of most families (Edgerton 1993).

Universities are not only experiencing shrinking funding sources, they are also expecting a declining customer base. In 1995, we will reach a fifteen-year low in the number of high school graduates. This has already had an impact on admission patterns. For the first time in its history, the University of Michigan re-opened its enrollment process in the summer of 1994 for the 1994/95 school year because of a smaller-than-expected pool of confirmed incoming students. One can only imagine the last-minute scramble to lure freshmen in institutions less prestigious and recognized than Michigan. Universities also compete for star faculty, frequently offering compensation, benefit, and research packages rivaling those dangled by top consulting, Wall Street, or corporate employers. Colleges compete against each other for donors who are becoming more discerning in their giving and more demanding of observable returns on their contributions.

Competition is even coming from the corporate sector. Corporate America now spends over $30 billion annually on training and education for employees (Cascio 1992), and the number of individuals trained by corporations rivals the total number of enrollees in conventional U.S. four-year colleges and universities (Scarpello and Ledvinka 1988). Frequently, companies design basic college courses that duplicate university offerings because their programs are customized to fit the firm's needs and delivered at a cost lower than that offered by universities.

### Demonstrating Accountability

If these competitive pressures are not significant enough, we are also being asked, in no uncertain terms, to demonstrate performance results as a condition of continuing funding. This is a legitimate request, akin to shareholder demands for corporate demonstration of return on investment. Over twenty states have issued accountability requirements for their state-funded institutions of higher education. Some thirty states will soon mandate various levels of faculty work loads. Regents, alumni, and donors ask for data demonstrating learning, graduation, and diversity results before they make funding decisions. Federal funding for university research is the subject of frequent Congressional investigation, and the country's primary research funding agency—the National Science Foundation—will focus 60 percent of its funding on research that demonstrates value added against nationally determined agenda. Basic researchers can no longer view funding as an entitlement; they too are accountable.

*Delighting Customers*

With many more and variable higher education options available to them, students and their families are savvy consumers, demanding high-quality services in their interactions with universities and demonstrated results in terms of learning and returns on education. As is true in every service relationship, customer expectations for quality in every type of service delivery—from admissions to library resources, to small class size—have gone up, sometimes radically. By the year 2,000, over 50 percent of the student body will be over twenty-five years old (Lewis and Smith 1994). This older, increasingly part-time student population will require a different portfolio of educational services and will be an even more discerning customer to universities than the "traditional" student. Laments about declining resources are of no interest to our customers. They want and deserve better quality, regardless of the institution's financial predicament. Each contact between the university and a prospective student or family member is a "moment of truth," a litmus test for the university, and a single failed interaction often results in the student going elsewhere.

*The Total Quality Promise*

Universities must be responsive to these changing conditions, public perceptions, and expectations. It is not the values of universities that are doubted. It is the choices over operationalization of these values that raise questions. The only way to be responsive to a public that is increasingly skeptical of the value added of the higher education experience is to change, in quite fundamental ways. Change must be brought into the academic core that facilitates learning and teaching, and into the administrative services that are the backbone of the academic core. The quality approach offers a framework within which institutional change can occur. It is a management and leadership philosophy, and it provides a menu of systematic tools and procedures to permeate the institution's goals through all processes.

The University of Maryland began its cultural change agenda in response to these growing pressures. Given our rapidly declining financial situation, we had no choice but to search for a different operating philosophy that would reach every corner of the university. It was fairly obvious that to keep operating as we had been, with a declining resource base, would at best allow us to tread water and stay where we were. However, our peer institutions were not standing still. If we kept doing the same thing with declining resources, the more realistic outcome was a slide into mediocrity that would inevitably escalate with time.

Something had to change. With committed leadership, TQ enables the top management team to systematically control the agenda for change, and it provides a philosophical framework and structure that can reach and propel uniform change across all parts of the university. TQ tools provide a means to translate a vision into measurable actions, it helps shed unnecessary bureaucracy, it facilitates the design of simpler and faster processes, and it creates shared and consistent operating approaches so that every "moment of truth," no matter where it happens in the institution, is a good one. Whether exemplified by a president, a dormitory counselor, an English professor, or a physical plant maintenance specialist, all share a common objective of performance excellence and each continuously seeks strategies for streamlining and improving his or her customer-oriented behaviors. The goal is constancy in the commitment to improve, and uniform excellence in the level of performance.

Obviously, we are not there yet and after all, as proponents of TQ frequently note, the journey never ends. However, since launching our TQ efforts some three years ago, the University of Maryland has made significant strides in improving a variety of academic and administrative processes, improvements that would have been unlikely without the quality framework as an organizing philosophy and set of tools. We are now expanding our TQ efforts across divisional lines, with the potential to dramatically improve the experiences of our applicants, students, and alumni. Our initiative has resulted in some insights into what works and what should be avoided when a university launches a TQ effort in its administrative and academic processes. The remainder of this chapter describes highlights of the chronology of the University of Maryland's TQ design and implementation process, and the lessons we have learned about features that help or hinder the change process.

## The Chronology of TQ at Maryland

In 1990, the president—prompted by effusive first-hand reports of private sector successes with TQM—decided to examine the potential for similar applications in the university. Over the next twelve months or so, the president and the top management team spent over thirty hours in formal training to learn about TQ and to determine whether the quality philosophy and culture change process fit the university. Given the crisis we were experiencing, the team decided to adopt a TQ approach. We needed to change to cope with budget cuts, and our customers were demanding significant improvements in service quality (e.g., registration) and in the way academic support functions are performed (such as advising). The state legislature was demanding accountability, companies of all forms and sizes in the U.S. and globally were transforming into quality-driven enterprises, and enrollments were steadily declining due to economic pressures and demographic trends.

In 1991, the president appointed a broadly representative planning committee to develop a strategy for implementation. The unique feature of the plan was that, unlike most other universities that have focused on administrative and support services, this plan focused also on the quality of delivery of academic and pedagogical processes. The committee decided that delaying or excluding the academic core of the institution from the culture change effort would run the risk of creating a destructive cleavage within the university's culture change process.

The planning committee was comprised of representatives from administrative support functions, academic departments, and key customer groups such as students and alumni, and was chaired by the dean of engineering. After much discussion, the campus TQ goals were couched in the language of "continuous improvement" in order to circumvent faculty opposition often evoked by the language of corporate quality programs.

The campus plan covered the imperatives for and general goals of the culture change process. The implementation process was as follows: units initially involved in TQ efforts would volunteer for continuous improvement training and support; would be role modeled at the top with projects undertaken by the President; and, over time, vice-presidents would be increasingly accountable for measurable improvements in key results areas within their divisions.

At the same time, the top management team formulated a vision for the campus, accompanied by measures of quality for each of the university's goals. "How will we know if we have reached the goals we intended, what measures will inform us of our success or failure one, two, or five years hence?" It was not enough to craft lofty goals. We had to have tangible yardsticks that would anchor these goals in measurable results, and would therefore inform us on our continuing progress toward realizing the goals.

The primary TQ planning group is the campus "Continuous Quality Council," chaired by the president, with the participation of all vice-presidents and representatives from key internal and external customer groups. This is the group that plans the quality agenda for the university, and evaluates progress against measurable yardsticks. Pilot projects continue in a variety of campus processes, such as enhancing the freshman experience by improving all of the cross-functional elements that affect first-year students' quality of life, or improving the quality of learning in large classes. Change agents are identified within each unit implementing TQ, and they receive facilitator training and supporting materials. In turn, they serve as the unit facilitators who keep the process moving. Periodically, these facilitators receive help from a small unit on campus that is the central "Office for Continuous Improvement."

A critical success factor in the university's quality initiative has been partnerships with corporate friends of the university who themselves are benchmarks in the implementation of TQ. These partnerships and the knowledge, skill, and resources they have provided have been essential to our program. Companies such as IBM, Xerox, AT&T, and Westinghouse have allowed us to borrow their training and implementation approaches, thereby shortening the cycle time for learning about TQ culture change processes. We were fortunate to have a Xerox executive on loan for a year who played a critical role in the earliest TQ plan design and training stages. In addition, we were a winner of the "TQ Challenge" that pairs a university with a corporation in order to train a critical mass of university faculty and administrators in TQ. In our case, Westinghouse Corporation hosted a quality orientation program for over 120 business, computer science, and engineering faculty and administrators, thereby creating a core of trained change agents from a variety of academic programs. This was an important milestone in the diffusion of TQM across the university community, especially in light of the continuing participation of the residents in this three-day event. AT&T has also provided funding for the dissemination of our TQ experiences inside and outside the university.

About eighteen months into our continuous improvement effort, the IBM Corporation announced a funding program to challenge U.S. universities to "deliver better prepared graduates capable of adding value in a TQ culture, trained in cross functional thinking (especially across engineering and business), effective performers in teams. Act as TQ institutions, thereby providing students the opportunity to experience a TQ role model within their institutions of higher education." According to IBM, this would enhance the competitiveness of the U.S. economy by supplying better graduates to American businesses. The attraction of the IBM grant program was that it emphasized the academic side of TQ implementation—an area traditionally neglected in most culture change processes—and that it provided a framework for accountability. The University of Maryland was a winner of the IBM-TQ competition, and the award generously supports the implementation of TQ in academic programs, pedagogy, and administrative support processes. The essence of the project is to develop an education prototype that provides students with cross-functional skills across business and engineering. Quality principles are applied to the teaching and learning processes. Application of these principles is facilitated in a fully interactive, electronic (computer-based) classroom that is also linked to the information highway via teleconferencing. For that reason, we call it a "virtual classroom" since the learning environment is extremely flexible and can take advantage of any worldwide teleconferencing opportunities. As part of this educational prototype, faculty team teach courses, frequent student feedback regarding design and delivery features of courses are employed, team-based projects capitalize on skill diversity within teams, class agenda are customized around student learning needs, and team-based peer evaluations are used as a component of course grades. These pedagogical features are integrated into radical revisions of the entire business and engineering curricula. The objective is to build on the experiences developed within the IBM-TQ Program and to create similar learning and teaching models for students across a variety of programs (e.g., honors) and colleges (e.g., education).

Many of the quality pilot processes created by departmental teams have been very successful; for example, in the health center (reducing wait times and client ambiguity about medical procedures), financial aid office (reducing processing time from twenty-four hours to twenty minutes for emergency financial aid approval), payroll department (faculty appointments can be done electronically), and registration (on-line, remote access class registration). These projects were designed to address important customer problems (e.g., terribly long lines of students waiting to register) and our customers are truly delighted when we end up delivering solutions in areas that matter to them. There have also been some failures in teams that have had to restart because they lacked the right leadership support, facilitator assistance, or realistic improvement goals. We have now progressed to larger-scope, cross-divisional project teams that address improvement goals impacting most or all divisions of the university. Among these cross-functional projects is a team developing strategies to improve the balance between student learning and employment needs, or another to streamline the financial aid process. Each cross-functional process has a vice-president taking responsibility for the process improvement effort, strict time lines, and associated measures of success.

## Lessons Learned

There are many parallels between TQ culture change processes in industry and in higher education. Universities are service providers, just like industry—we invoice, register, purchase, manage personnel systems, maintain large data bases, respond to public inquiries, and manage building projects, restaurants, parking facilities, and so on. There are also some crucial differences, or some areas (like teaching and learning) that are rarely the focus of firms in the private sector. Our experience since 1990 offers lessons about TQ process implementation features that are critical to success. At the same time, we have had to circumvent several challenges to the implementation of TQ within a university, some of which are unique to higher education, while others are fairly generic barriers to the implementation of any culture change process.

*What Works and Helps?*

*Discussing language and philosophy.* The applicability of quality concepts is intensely debated in academia. Isn't the notion of "customer" too passive a label for the student who is partner to the creation of the product (knowledge and personal development) by participating in collaborative learning? Does student involvement in defining requirements undermine the role of the teacher who is there to help students discover their knowledge and skill requirements? Does the adjective "total" in TQ reflect an impossible search for the holy grail? Is introduction of a TQ culture an admission that to date we lack quality? Is the goal of cultural consistency across the institution anathema to the academic ideal of creative diversity and intellectual freedom? Isn't TQ in conflict with the traditional reward structure of research-oriented institutions, where there is no room to recognize teaching and service leaders, only research winners?

Debates over these issues are as inevitable as they are necessary. They are a critical step in the process of achieving a comfort level with quality concepts that, once dealt with, no longer pose a barrier. We invited discussion over these issues and were open to modifying the language to meet the needs of the culture. The term "continuous improvement" (and later "continuous quality improvement") was a product of these discussions. We use "student" to refer to our primary customer in order to avoid the sometimes vitriolic opposition evoked in an educational setting by the generic terminology of "customers" and "suppliers." In our experience, pragmatic flexibility to fit the users is an important enabler of progress toward the next implementation stage, and it does not compromise the systematic implementation of TQ processes.

*Involving the academic core.* TQ is designed to improve all processes that affect our customers. Students interact with administrative support personnel and clearly this group of suppliers must be included in the quality improvement effort. Indeed, this is where most higher education quality processes begin and end. As noted previously, we recognized that the quality of our students' experiences on campus depends heavily on the caliber of their interactions with the faculty. The faculty represent the soul of the institution; they are the purveyors of its core educational and developmental mission. If they are left out of the TQ effort, we are missing the opportunity to improve the essential component of our primary customers' relationship with the university. Moreover, the TQ efforts involving the administrative support staff would be undermined if they observed, with skepticism, that "quality does not apply to faculty."

The campus TQ planning committee included faculty. As a starting point for introducing TQ into the academic core, all deans received two days of TQ training and faculty members were included in the campus quality planning committee. Deans were expected to lead the administrative and academic process improvement efforts within their own colleges. Being close to the action, it was felt they were in the position to recognize and reinforce the TQ champions in teaching and service delivery.

*Introducing TQ incrementally.* TQ should not come as a frontal assault. This invites opposition from the skeptics, and when there is anything less than wholesale success, it sets the stage for very visible failure.

Our approach is slow, incremental introduction of TQ. When we began, there were few peer institutions whose implementation experiences could serve as a model. It was important to test the boundaries of application of the corporate TQ model to higher education without dooming the effort to failure. Our initial forays were designed to maximize the probability of success by picking off the "low hanging fruit." Participation of a few experienced quality leaders was invited with the intention of building on these successes and expanding into less committed environments. By then we expected to have developed skills in anticipating and overcoming the barriers to applying TQ models to higher education.

This is the primary reason for incrementalism. The other reason is that university cultures respond violently to hierarchical edicts, and in some cases have the power to "just say no." University faculty must become personally committed to the change process. Certainly, the university leadership can assist this process by making a convincing case for change. Evidence of successes from the pilot projects is also a way to soften opposition to change. Frontal assaults are not the way to thaw attitudes among empowered university faculty.

*No "guru" model.* Frequently, when organizations launch TQ efforts, they follow the approach of a particular quality authority or "guru" like Deming or Crosby, or the model of a benchmark organization (e.g., Xerox, IBM, AT&T, or that of a particular consulting firm). In addition, many institutions and corporations devise a structured rule book when implementing TQ, and use a very systematic, tool-based sequence of steps. We elected to do neither and undoubtedly, some observers will quibble with the appropriateness of our "loose" strategy, especially since the ultimate goal is to achieve consistent, organization-wide culture change.

There were several reasons for our decision to implement TQ principles without following a guru model or step-by-step strategy. Our corporate partnerships helped us implement TQ by supporting a number of pilot teams. Each corporate partner was trained under a different guru model, and brought with them a slightly different set of tools from their TQ organization. As long as the strategy was implemented within the framework of the university's overarching TQ values and goals, slight differences in implementation strategies were less important than moving ahead with the appropriate support. Moreover, since our approach was to integrate TQ through inducements and voluntary buy in, it was important that the initial implementors be fully committed to their own process and adapt it around their local needs. Force fitting a particular TQ model or set of tools might have hindered pilot teams' progress efforts and adjustment of processes around their own needs. Finally, since our goal from the beginning was to implement TQ in academic processes, we were especially sensitive to the translation difficulties of guru models and implementation strategies developed for entirely different application purposes.

*Setting realistic expectations.* Culture change takes years. This is especially true in large organizations with only weak hierarchical authority to enforce rules, as is the case for universities. It is easy to become discouraged. Early on, we were visited by David Kearns, then chairman and CEO of the Xerox Corporation and one of the true beacons of quality in American industry. Xerox was a company that had been involved in TQ for at least ten years, had won the Baldrige award, and successfully recaptured market share and profits from its competitors. He cautioned us, "It will take you ten years to get to the end of stage one. That's how long it took us." As daunting as those words were, they helped us understand the depth of commitment necessary for the long term in order to reap the comprehensive, institution-wide benefits of culture change at the core.

*The president's involvement and continuing focus.* The biggest challenge in any complex institution is to select a lean agenda and to stick with it over an extended period despite the daily and sometimes hourly distractions that come up and compete—in time and resources—with the culture change efforts. To quote John LeCarré in *The Russia House:*

> If we see one goal clearly, we may advance one step. If we contemplate all goals at once, we shall not advance at all.

Since results of culture changes are not immediately evident, it is easy to become diverted into other, seemingly more pressing priorities. The only way cultures change, especially in complex and nonhierarchical organizations like universities, is if the president and top leadership doggedly persist in their commitment to TQ principles in reminding the institution that the quality approach is here to stay, and in their role modeling of relevant behaviors. This is easy to do in the first three months of the effort. What about in the second or fifth years? Is the leadership able to remain committed in words as well as actions? Are resource allocation decisions consistent with TQ as a priority, especially when the university resources are strained? Unless the top leadership remains focused and committed, the rest of the institution will not be willing to invest in a risky and effort-consuming change process.

To counter this tendency, the president has acted periodically to refocus and re-energize the institution around the TQ goals and processes. This happens through the president's role in chairing the Continuous Quality Improvement Council, participation in campus recognition events, TQ-related op-ed pieces in the student and campus newspapers, TQ training that the president attends with particular groups on campus, or quality-focused speeches in the business community that are reported back through the campus and popular press.

*Appointing a senior TQ advocate.* The president is the leader of TQ. However, given the competing demands on a president's calendar, there must be a full-time advocate who can focus on quality improvement and provide counsel regarding the TQ direction for the campus. The campus will infer the importance of the quality initiative from the type of individual appointed as its advocate. This individual must have the leadership skill and credibility to symbolize to the campus that the quality approach is central to the top management team's agenda.

Maryland has a three-person Office of Continuous Quality Improvement that supports the president in his TQ activities, facilitates the activities of the Continuous Quality Improvement Council, organizes and delivers training for facilitators, and periodically reminds the campus of the TQ effort through newsletters and events. The director of this function, the dean of engineering, also serves as the campus Director of Continuous Quality Improvement. Given the intention to permeate TQ through the entire university—both academic and support functions—the appointment of a senior individual with high credibility among all constituencies was deliberate. Our Director of Continuous Quality Improvement is the most senior dean and is also perceived as one of the most effective. He had originally spearheaded the planning committee that developed the campus TQ planning document, and was obviously committed to the goals of the effort. With his retirement from the deanship, he is moving into the full-time role of Director of Continuous Quality Improvement. The Director of Continuous Quality Improvement has executive status and participates in the weekly executive meeting of the president and vice-presidents, thereby incorporating TQ into the strategic agenda of the university. Such personal credibility and executive access is a powerful and important symbol. Conversely, a campus community will react skeptically to a TQ effort relegated to a junior staff function.

*What are the Challenges?*

Implementation of TQ is not without challenge in a higher education setting. Although we have achieved notable successes in certain aspects of our quality infusion efforts, we still struggle with many barriers to the culture change efforts.

*Continuing budget crises.* Economic difficulties and job insecurity frequently exhaust the energies and emotions of incumbents, leaving them unable to tackle new ventures or creative processes. In some instances, job losses occur as a product of budget crises. Employees must be given iron-clad guarantees that no jobs will be lost because of process improvements. The more likely scenario is that process improvements will become a survival necessity given contraction of the work force with no parallel reduction in the volume of work.

Transforming economic hardships into opportunities is where leadership makes a difference. At Maryland, the financial duress was *the catalyst* for change, the event that shattered the status quo and forced people to realize that we could ill afford to continue as before. If times are good, there is no compelling reason to change. Bad times are not "the best of times," yet they are the *best times* to bring about change.

*Agreeing on "the customer."* It is common for university groups to reach an early impasse when attempting to reach consensus on the identity of "the" customer. There are so many customers laying claims to universities' services, from students and parents to faculty and employees, prospective students and their families, alumni, researchers at peer institutions, athletic program supporters and fans, business partners, granting agencies and donors, accrediting bodies, citizens in surrounding communities, the legislature and tax-paying public, community groups, and on and on. This multiplicity of customers is readily dealt with when their interests magically converge. However, this happy solution is rare. More often than not, interests of one constituency must be balanced against divergent needs of another customer group.

We first experienced the "who is the customer" dilemma at a retreat at the president's house. The top management team was asked by our AT&T executive-on-loan to generate the answer to the question. Very quickly, a ten-by-five-foot wall was covered with yellow Post-it™ Notes as each member of the team added his or her view of the university's primary customer. After much debate, the group finally converged on "the student" as the primary service recipient of most of the university's core academic and administrative processes. Once a customer focus on the student was accepted, many competing priorities could be rank ordered more clearly, with resources allocated accordingly.

*Avoiding measurement.* Universities are often not disciplined in accountability processes. Most universities have few ongoing and systematic measurement systems that track reactions from key customer groups (students, alumni, parents, citizens). Introduction of the most basic customer measurement systems—teaching evaluations—still evokes resistance and sometimes howls of protest, especially when instituted at multiple points over the course of the semester. This may be attributable to a philosophical antipathy to any measurement of the value of education since, some would agree, stretching the mind through education is a moral good. Yet, the absence of measurement is no longer tolerable to our constituencies and it can be argued that it is not good for us, either. Unless we understand how to meet the expectations of the huge range of customers we serve, we will lose their business. Measurement—of the multitude of customer requirements and of performance against these requirements—is the only way to guide interventions as we attempt to move forward.

Although state legislatures have long encouraged and even demanded various accountability reports, these requests are often seen as just more bureaucratic paper chases. The real catalysts for the development of an accountability system are our industry partners, especially financial backers such as IBM and AT&T. These partners demonstrate in their own operations how to enforce accountability even when it is uncomfortable, and alternate between offering us developmental help and threatened loss of support as we continue our debates over the merits of measurement. In their minds, there is no debate. A stake has to go into the ground, no matter how far back we end up relative to where we thought we were. Progress is then measured against this starting point. How else can improvement be gauged? Understandably, we encounter anxiety and sometimes pain when individuals and units discover the bad news first hand, but that is exactly the point. Unless we recognize where we are now, force ourselves to prioritize our improvement foci, and then very deliberately track improvements, our efforts will be disorganized and diluted, and we will also miss the opportunity to celebrate successes because they are hidden.

*Re-engineering teaching and learning around TQ.* Most teachers end up having to alter their teaching style and, sometimes, their philosophy once they make a decision to apply the quality approach in the classroom. The change is usually incremental. Before any changes are made, however, a critical and common concern that must be laid to rest is the claim that TQ undermines academic integrity.

TQ is not intended to compromise academic goals and standards. On the contrary. Its application in this context is intended to enhance the learning process between teachers and students each of whom is a customer to the other, and to stretch the goals of learning. How? By treating students with respect, soliciting their input and feedback around most issues in the class such as questions on how learning might be improved, what points were covered in the class (to provide feedback to the instructor on how well students are learning), preferences around topic sequencing, the pace of the class, choice of guest lecturers, materials and learning aids, etc. The feedback is then used to improve the teaching and learning processes on an ongoing basis, as the course progresses. TQ also means clear articulation of requirements for every piece of the course, collaborative learning though team projects, student peer evaluations, a student quality committee to work with the professor on class design, and integration of cross-functional themes into the material by having teams of instructors from multiple disciplines introduce a topic from their different perspectives. TQ also represents a shift in emphasis from the inspection mode of giving quizzes and exams where all that is tested is recall to using tests and papers as value-added learning and knowledge-integration opportunities. Teachers reduce the fear of exams by providing complete preview of and preparation for the exams, thereby turning them into constructive learning prompts.

There are some teachers who are "naturals" and have always taught this way without calling it TQ. For most of us, this requires a significant adjustment in our behaviors in the classroom and when it really takes hold, a change in the definition of our identity as teachers. Status and power are no longer the distinguishing features of the teacher's role. The role is recast as an enabler of learning by better meeting the needs of end users (employers) and of our student customers. This is another area where frontal assault does not work.

*Becoming a TQ student.* Students are the primary customer of the university's administrative services, and they have a critical voice in improving these processes. In the tradition of TQ, many universities use student voice mechanisms for these purposes.

Improvements in learning and teaching processes cannot occur unless students are partners to the improvement processes, see themselves as empowered because their suggestions are enacted, and are respectful of their fellow students and professors. Obviously, if students invest effort in providing feedback and their improvement suggestions are consistently ignored, they will become quickly disillusioned. But even the best-intentioned faculty members will periodically receive student suggestions that lack merit for pedagogical, academic, or equity reasons. To avoid student disappointment when their suggestions are tabled, clear expectations must be established regarding the meaning of TQ in the classroom. It means that the teacher will: create an environment that fosters learning, clearly articulate expectations and requirements, practice and expect respect in relating to others, draw on students' input and team work as learning stimuli, and make efforts to improve based on ongoing student feedback. It does not mean that all suggestions will be enacted; some will be implemented immediately, some may warrant further discussion in the student's quality council, and others will not be implemented because of reasons that will be explained. In addition, TQ does not mean any relaxation of the expectations for excellence; the same goals for learning apply, with the same expected benchmarks of learning within an environment committed to students' success.

There is a challenge in helping students appreciate the nuances of both sides of the message—that they are and should feel empowered to have a voice in the design of many features of the learning process, but that empowerment does not go as far as setting the academic rules. This is not an easy message to communicate. On the one hand, telling students that they should feel involved and empowered, but not too empowered, is seen as a "teaser," while going too far the other way creates unrealizable expectations and subsequent frustrations.

*Encountering the university's core values.* Sources of universities' strength and distinctiveness in society may at the same time pose challenges to culture changes. First of all, universities are not hierarchical. The tenure system flattens the organizational pyramid. The participatory structure of governance in the academic arena is the fuel that powers the creative engine of the academic enterprise, and it removes the pressure to conform. Those who do not want to change might be persuaded to adopt TQ with compelling arguments or convincing leadership. For those who continue to refuse change, the institution tolerates the refusal and congratulates itself for promoting diversity of opinion and actions. Culture change is not easily advanced in such conditions.

The reward system at many research-oriented universities adds to the challenge by emphasizing research over any other forms of teaching or service contributions. As a complement to this value system, most faculty have much stronger allegiance to their academic discipline than to their university or department (Boyer 1990). The importance of research contributions will not and should not be downgraded in order to accelerate TQ implementation. However, the second-class status of TQ-based teaching and service contributions must be elevated to recognize the leaders in these areas that compare with the recognition afforded excellence in research. These ideas very much parallel Ernest Boyer's thesis in *Scholarship Reconsidered,* where he admonishes leaders of universities to nurture alternative (discovery, integration, application, and teaching), but equally valued, forms of scholarly contributions to student lives (Boyer 1990). This is a major challenge to the cultural fabric of universities. Management research tells us that organizations' implicit and explicit reward systems are the most potent influences on behavior. Unless leaders reward behaviors that are consonant with a TQ culture change process, TQ will not happen. It is that simple, yet that difficult.

*Waiting for Godot.* It is folly to wait for unanimous support for learning about and initiating a quality improvement effort. No culture change process is ever uniform, even in exemplary, private-sector, TQ-based organizations. But that should not be cause for reticence before starting the TQ process, nor for abandonment of efforts once they are started. Even units that are among the trail blazers suffer internal setbacks, especially when they interact with other units that have not yet bought into the change process. There are always going to be individuals who refuse to consider any changes to their behaviors.

Rather than focusing on the areas where change has been less than successful, it is worth noting the impact of results in areas where improvements are measurable. These are areas where progress would not otherwise have occurred, and the processes that have improved—whether in key administrative support areas or major curriculum and pedagogical changes in a selected number of departments—are clearly servicing the needs of customers better than before. Over time, positive results are a compelling reason for other departments to sit up and take notice, and slowly TQ processes spread by example. The process is continually re-energized through the enthusiasm of the people reaping the intrinsic rewards of documented positive results and customer appreciation.

## References

Boyer, E. L., *Scholarship Reconsidered: Priorities for the Professoriate* (Princeton, N.J.: The Carnegie Foundation, 1990).

Cascio, W. F., *Managing Human Resources: Productivity, Quality of Work Life, Profits* (New York: McGraw-Hill, 1992).

Edgerton, R., " The New Public Mood and What it Means to Higher Education," *AAHE Bulletin 45*(10) (June 1993).

Ewell, P., "Total Quality and Academic Practice," *Change 25*(3) (May-June 1993).

Lewis, R. G., and Smith, D. H., *Total Quality in Higher Education* (Delray Beach, Fla.: St. Lucie Press, 1994).

Scarpello, V. G., and Ledvinka, J., *Personnel/Human Resource Management: Environment and Functions* (Boston: PWS-Kent, 1988).

# 19

# Translating Quality for the Academy

*Robert L. Carothers*

Much of the criticism we hear on campuses of the quality movement and its applicability to higher education focuses on a mismatch of cultures, the inappropriateness of transplanting a set of practices designed on the shop floor to the halls of academe. Much of this debate, as you'd expect, revolves around language—around the specialized vocabulary of Deming, Crosby, and Juran, and now of the hundreds of quality consultants doing campus workshops—jargon heard in sessions at nearly every national higher education conference this year.

But even if the language of TQM can seem threatening to those of us who live our lives in the academy, the philosophy of quality is not an alien presence in our academic culture. In fact, the quality movement itself can learn a great deal from the way we do things on campuses. But we have things to learn from TQM, as well; to learn those lessons, however, we have to be open to its messages and do the hard work of translating that language so that strange words don't stand in the way of meaningful change.

## Quality on Campus

Of all the products and services America offers in the international marketplace, none is more desired than an American college education, certainly an American graduate degree. So if the "response of the marketplace over time" is the test of quality, it is hard to dispute that American higher education has been and continues to be what TQM calls a "benchmark" for the rest of the world.

Some of my colleagues in business find laughable my assertion that they should visit campuses to study quality in action. They doubt they could learn much of value about quality processes from studying how universities do busi-

Reprinted by permission of the author.

ness: They regard our structures and processes as essentially unchanged since Heidelberg and the fifteenth century.

Universities, they say, are the least efficient and most disorganized institutions in our society, chaotic collections of eccentric people held together by a common grievance about parking. Aren't the faculty essentially a loose collection of prima donnas, characterized by large egos, quarrelsome and myopic, trained to challenge authority, whether scientific or scholarly, or political, and just generally impossible to manage? Isn't the definition of a professor "one who won't take *yes* for an answer?"

They know, too, that universities are intensely political institutions. Woodrow Wilson is said to have remarked that he learned the art of politics on the faculty at Princeton and later went to Washington to practice among the amateurs.

Yes, let's agree that universities are difficult organizations to manage in the conventional sense, with management practices that rely on authority and power. On a campus, authority and power—those traditional mainstays of corporate culture—are, as any university president will tell you, purely illusory. I'm told that Charles William Eliot once made a remark at Harvard regarding "his" faculty. In the morning, he found a delegation of professors at his office door to remind him that the president of Harvard does not have a faculty; rather, the faculty of Harvard has a president. It is a lesson I try to remember.

But colleges and universities offer important lessons about what it will mean to lead and manage in the new knowledge era; an era in which free inquiry, creativity, and the entrepreneurial spirit are much more important to America than ever before, and in which concepts of authority and power are swiftly being supplanted by networks and influence.

Authority, the assumed right to give commands, does not ensure that the commands will be carried out. In fact, a leader must rely on either power or influence to assure that his or her decisions are implemented. Power, as I want to define it here, is the ability to cause change; but, at least for most of us, the word connotes force or intimidation. Leading though influence, on the other hand, requires us to invoke the classic Aristotelian definition of leadership, which includes ethos, understanding and the moral character to persuade; pathos, the ability to excite the emotions; and *logos,* the intellectual ability to give people logical reasons for a given course of action.

So a university, like most emerging and successful enterprises, is not a hierarchy—no matter what it says on the chart of organization. Rather, a university is a pluralistic enterprise, with multiple centers of influence and interest held together by a shared vision and by shared values. Despite its seeming chaos, a university is a purposeful community, and it employs powerful symbols to bind that community together. The academic regalia at commencement, for example, remind us of our common and ancient heritage; our passionate protests of fidelity to alma mater on sunny Saturday afternoons in autumn express a loyalty enjoyed by no enterprise this side of the Pacific.

In its operation, a university is highly reliant on the individual talents and motivation of its faculty, who must take independent actions that at the same time are consistent with the unifying vision of the organization as a whole. The university places great emphasis on the continuing development of its employees and supports professional development through devices such as sabbatical leaves and individually directed research at a level unheard of in most enterprises.

In short, an American college or university is centered on a vision; its culture is rich with values that shape behavior largely without coercion; its employees, particularly the faculty, are empowered people, independent actors whose activities generally advance the institutional mission. The organization invests heavily in developing these empowered employees, and it recognizes and rewards those who advance that mission and vision.

Now, at least to me, these sound like many of the characteristics of a "total quality organization," which is why I have come to believe that introducing lessons learned in the TQM movement to the academy is not to bring an alien presence into our culture. Rather, it is to give form and clarity to values that are already very much a part of our community.

## A Language of Our Own

Among our faculties, particularly those in the liberal arts, TQM (or CQI, "continuous quality improvement") is most often understood, if at all, as a response to fierce competitive pressures, chiefly from the Japanese in the manufacturing sector. Often they know as well that the tools of TQM include sophisticated methods of quantitative analysis. But today, TQM is not restricted to manufacturing, or even to business. It is spreading rapidly through all fields of enterprise, to the service sector, to government, to health care, and now to education.

TQM is spreading so rapidly and being so well received, not just because it increases efficiency and productivity in difficult times, but also because it incorporates a philosophy about work, people, and relationships built around humane values and shared vision. It is a philosophy that helps fulfill a need that so many Americans feel so strongly, on campuses as elsewhere, for a clearer sense of purpose in our work.

That sense of purpose, I believe, is the reason TQM has enlisted disciples whose commitment to the philosophy is downright evangelical. But that very evangelism often triggers the finely honed skepticism of our faculties, trained as they are to test ideas in a crucible of doubt. Their antennae up, faculty members encounter in TQM the words of commerce and the marketplace. While much of TQM's conceptual base might be consistent with academic culture, its language seems foreign, at least at first blush; it reflects a world many faculty hoped to escape by choosing the academic life.

Faculty members evaluate TQM's ideas and language in a context of their own loyal membership in the academic community and its value system. Discussions of "standards" are commonplace in faculty coffee lounges across the nation; but talk of "conformance to standards," the TQM phrase, seems somehow wrong. Most faculty are frustrated with the remedial work required throughout the university and would support enthusiastically a system that "did things right the first time." But "zero defects," a term loaded with powerful connotations when applied to people, is not how the idea would (or should) be expressed. Faculty may do quantitative analysis in their research and understand its value and importance there. But "statistical process control" applied to teaching and research in the history or art department sounds hostile, an affront to academic mores, if not academic freedom.

These strange terms reinforce the faculty's worst fears about this new effort called TQM, "The administration is about to turn our university over to the Philistines!" and they begin mobilizing to resist. It is a critical moment in the quality voyage.

At such a moment, it is important to emphasize the common ground—to move the discussion away from words "owned" by the corporate quality movement and toward a process that allows the university to find its own language for change.

## Two Examples

Earlier I claimed for America's colleges and universities many of the characteristics of quality organizations. An important and critical ingredient too often missing from that quality recipe is one TQM would bring us—a focus on customers. Since it's hard to imagine a quality improvement process without a "customer" focus, let's take that as an example.

TQM embodies an ethic of service. One of our janitorial workers told me in a quality workshop recently that all she had heard simply added up to the Golden Rule: that we should do unto others as we would have them do unto us. Clearly, one of the philosophical keys to the quality movement lies in the definition of the relationship between those served and those serving.

In the academy, one such relationship is that between students and faculty, and it is a complex one. Although students sometimes complain that they did not "get what they paid for," the relationship between a student and a faculty member is not the same as the relationship between me and the shop owner who sold me a table saw last week. Some similarities exist, of course, but the differences are greater. In what sense is a student a customer? When should we assess whether a student-customer is being well served by our academic programs? At registration? At the end of the first week of classes? At the end of a course? At commencement? At ten-year intervals following graduation? The answer is probably "all of the above."

Perhaps the student is really our *product*. If so, then who are really our customers, and how can we best serve them? What are their needs and expectations, and how are they to be balanced against the needs of students or their parents, who often are paying the bills? Is who pays even relevant? If paying is the test, then, in the case of public universities, perhaps the state legislature is our customer.

These are very important questions, ones with which we must yet wrestle. But their value to us lies chiefly in the process by which we set out to answer them. Our challenge is not to fit colleges and universities into some "customer" paradigm or language model derived from IBM or Xerox or PPG or Kodak, but rather, to answer the questions in our own way so as to gain the self-knowledge that will help us to improve. Our challenge is to change our habits, to adopt new ways of behaving so that we indeed better serve those whose needs we now better understand. In struggling with these questions on our own terms, the necessary language will emerge, and that language will be ours, authentic and not derivative.

Let's consider a second example; Deming's admonition to drive out fear. An organization on the quality voyage—armed with an understanding of its customers' needs and significant new self-knowledge—seeks to use fully the creative force of its members by empowering them. It gives them the authority to act on the ideas and strategies they develop, thus allowing the organization to be both more efficient and effective. To free members of an organization to be creative, Deming tells us, we must drive out the fear of failure. Such fear prevents people from taking risks and acting on the new ideas they have about how better to meet customer expectations. The quality organization steadfastly refuses to blame its people for the errors or faults that occur, since these most typically arise from "system" factors outside the individual's control. The quality organization instead encourages initiative and imagination in the interest of better service, free from the inhibiting force of fear.

But TQM also emphasizes setting clear standards of organizational performance. While achieving such standards can very well stress an organization, that stress can be necessary, since the alternative is a lot worse—lost business, with negative consequences for both individual members and the organization as a whole. "Driving out fear" never meant that everyone in the organization would be happy all the time or that hard decisions would not be made. Instead, what the university must do is change the way it responds to people who take initiative, who take risks in the interest of better service, and who advance the university's vision. It must change its habits. Once it does that, the language to describe these new habits will spring not from a TQM bible, but authentically from the changed circumstance. That new language will gain currency and institutional meaning when it is articulated and consistently acted upon by the organization's leaders.

## A New Style of Leadership

For me, then, TQM seems a natural fit for organizations such as universities that rely heavily on the intellectual and creative abilities of their people. It is also a tool for managing and leading such organizations. The leadership skills it would evoke are rooted in the concept described by the word *administration,* that is, "to minister" to the enterprise. To be successful, leaders of quality-focused enterprises will not be the authoritarian managers of traditional hierarchies; instead they will understand their role as envisioner, as interpreter, as facilitator of the living enterprise itself, one with its own language developed to give form to the effort.

Specifically, successful leaders in this new environment will:

- Believe in the enterprise. They will resist cynicism; they will dig for the strengths of the organization and give voice to them. They will learn and celebrate what the organization does right; they will find the best in co-workers and remember the good in even the most trying circumstance; they will defend the enterprise, not with the narrow parochialism of self-interest but with a loyalty born of genuine commitment.

- Give purpose to the enterprise. The new leaders will articulate its vision; they will shape its mythology; they will find and celebrate its heroes, the people whose acts embody the organization's values.

- Set standards by listening to those the organization serves. They will analyze the obstacles to meeting those standards and design and implement in a planned, systematic way a strategy for overcoming them. That is, they will use the TQM tools.

- Communicate often and effectively. The great leaders today are the great communicators. More of the organization's work must be done in public, in full view, so that people will understand the decision making process and the assumptions behind it. Trust is a key component of effective communication, because the message must be not only heard and understood; it also must be believed.

- Teach the enterprise to succeed. Increasingly, our institutions will be organized into "self-managed" teams, groups responsible for and capable of proceeding on their own to accomplish a defined mission. In such groups, the manager's role evolves from supervisor to coach, from giving direction to giving advice, from focusing on the task at hand to focusing on the future. As new leaders share knowledge and empower the team, they make their associates' personal and professional growth a goal in itself, and help the enterprise as a whole to grow in confidence. They themselves strive to model creative problem solving and in a sense become teachers, seeing each problem or crisis as an opportunity to teach the lessons that will make the organization succeed.

These are the qualities—believing, envisioning, analyzing, communicating, and teaching—that are critical for leaders in the long journey of continuous quality improvement.

## A Voyage Inward

The quest for quality is often described as a voyage, and the metaphor is an apt one. But like many voyages out, this one is also a voyage in. It's a trip that leads us to affirm many values and virtues of the academy and the moral purposes that brought us into community in the first place.

We are not alone on this voyage, of course; thousands of corporate, government, and health care enterprises precede us in TQM. Just as they are learning to serve, we must remember to serve. As others are learning to set high standards of performance, we must remember, affirm, and articulate more clearly those standards of achievement we set for ourselves and our students. As others learn the value of self-study and critical analysis, we must remind ourselves of the need to resist the comfortable and the habitual, to subject our university lives to the same scrutiny with which we ourselves approach our own scholarly work.

As others learn to respect the dignity and creativity of each member of the "team" and to promote collaboration and cooperation, we must reexamine the degree to which our organizations foster a debilitating and demoralizing class system, in which real collaboration is limited both by rank and privilege and by disciplinary structures that set territorial limits on who may study or teach certain pieces of the intellectual terrain.

Like Chaucer's Clerke, if we can both gladly learn and gladly teach the lessons of quality, we will be good—and then better—stewards of our important mission. Our lives, as well, will be more fulfilled.

# Suggested Research,
# Readings and Resources

# 20

# Ten Areas for Future Research in Total Quality Management

*A. Blanton Godfrey*

In the past fifteen years, many companies in the United States have made significant changes in the management of quality. For some, these changes have helped the companies achieve stunning results. Other companies are now implementing the same strategies and methods and are achieving similar results.

In this article, ten of these emerging trends are identified. Although much has already been learned and many of these lessons are summarized here, much work is needed to further the knowledge about the theory and implementation of these means. Several research opportunities for each of these emerging trends will be identified.

## Introduction

There has been much progress in the application of quality management methods in the past fifteen years. Companies have in some ways radically changed their management philosophies. Total quality management (TQM) has become far more than a set of useful tools; it has become a new management philosophy leading to radical changes in the ways that people, companies, and even entire societies are working together.

In this article, some of the recent trends—and where they may lead—will be examined. Some unexplored or partially explored research areas will also be identified. From this author's vantage point, there are ten clear trends for quality management over the next ten years.

1. Revolutionary rates of improvement
2. Expansion to all industries and all functions

---

3. Product design and process engineering
4. Intense education and training
5. Information systems and technology
6. Self-directing work teams
7. Partnering
8. Self-assessment and benchmarking
9. Customer focus
10. Strategic quality management

Some of these trends are quite obvious and need little comment. Some are more difficult to see and may need further explanation.

### Revolutionary Rates of Improvement

For many companies to compete in the next decade, rapid quality improvement may not provide a competitive edge; it may be a necessary skill. Some of the most impressive results have been achieved by Malcolm Baldrige National Quality Award (MBNQA) winners in the years after they won the award. Since 1988 when it won the award, Motorola has reduced defects another 150 times (Reimann 1992).

In many companies, quality improvement has become a way of life. Recently this author spent several hours talking with the winning team from a fossil fuel power plant's internal quality team competition. The team's project was the reduction of down time in the plant due to pump failure. The team had plotted the pump's reliability using a standard Weibull Analysis. Team members had estimated the parameters using maximum likelihood estimation and finally found the root-cause culprit by using a three-by-three-by-three-inch Latin square experimental design.

The culprit was an O-ring made from a material that could not withstand corrosive liquids at high temperatures. The results of the team's experiments convinced the manufacturer of the O-rings to change the materials used. To expand the data collection and proof of the improvement, the team shared its results with the other nine plants in its company and twenty other fossil fuel plants in the United States.

The quality team's project earned its members first place in their plant, in all fossil fuel plants, then in all power plants in the company. The prize included a first-class trip with spouses to Japan for two weeks to share results with Kansai Electrical and the International Congress on Quality Control Circles (ICQCC90).

During a conversation with a team leader, this author expressed surprise at the team's participation at ICQCC90 since the rumors of lack of support for quality at Florida Power & Light indicated a decrease in quality improvement activity. The team leader was surprised. He states, "No one here could kill quality improvement. Now that we know how to solve problems that have been bothering us for years, why would we stop just because some manager doesn't support it?" The recognition this team has already received and its sharing of results at ICQCC90 indicate far more support than some companies are giving their teams.

For many companies, quality improvement at a revolutionary pace is now becoming simply good management. Companies are now routinely averaging more than one improvement per person per year; some are even approaching one improvement per person per week. These improvements take many forms. Some are simple ideas. Arising from people all over the company, they are collected, processed, and put in the hands of the right person for quick action. Some companies manage this whole process in less than two hours.

Other improvements are intradepartmental. These ideas can be handled by people during their normal workday. Companies sometimes call these activities quality in daily work, or other names, but the concept is the same. Every week, or even every day, set aside time to examine the daily work processes. Explore ways to improve these processes. Select some of these ideas for quick action.

But the large improvements are usually the result of interdepartmental or even cross-functional quality improvement teams. These teams tackle the chronic problems that have been in the way of company progress for a long time. These are the vital few problems whose solutions create the breakthroughs in quality by reducing waste and by dramatically improving customer satisfaction.

*Research Challenges*

There are many areas to explore here; a few may be technical, but more are probably organizational. The companies achieving remarkable rates of improvement appear to have solved the daunting problem of transferring successes across organizations. As in the example, the quality improvement team managed to take the solution to a problem, or seize an opportunity, and apply it in ten, twenty, or thirty different places. The team overcame the dreaded not-invented-here syndrome. But other organizations are still struggling with this. In one health care company, startling improvements had been made in one clinic, and yet few of the improvements were used in the other nineteen clinics in the same organization, much less by other health care providers. In a manufacturing company, a series of improvements in one process plant led to almost $2 million a year in savings, but the company has yet to apply these same improvements in any of its more than fifty similar plants around the world.

Hooper (1990) indicates the directions this research could go in his study of Bell Laboratories best-in-class practices. But far too little has been explored in this area; companies all over the world are still struggling with this issue. Many companies are making some progress with annual meetings of quality facilitators and coaches. Honda is an example of a company making excellent progress in sharing and cloning (Sugiura 1992).

Kaihatsu (1990) provides a good example of how Fuji Xerox has changed its structure and management systems to promote cross-functional and cross-product-line cooperation. During the development of the Fuji Xerox 3500 copier, product planners and engineers working on other copiers, fax machines, and printers closely monitored progress. Then they quickly adopted the 3500 team's findings and improvements to other products.

But so far the progress across companies seems to be limited to open conferences like Juran Institute's IMPRO, ASQC's Annual Quality Congress, the MBNQA winners' conferences, the National Forum of the Institute for Healthcare Improvement, and many other similar conferences and workshops continually springing up. One of the exciting new ideas is open software networks to share details of quality improvement projects similar to the Institute for Healthcare Improvement's Quality Management Network's QUISS system.

How much is actually learned at these conferences? Are there more efficient ways of sharing this information? What do the participants actually implement when they return to their organizations? Are there better ways to help them learn and support the implementation?

What is the role of storyboards? Are they an effective means of transferring knowledge at least within a location? Can electronic storyboards help transfer knowledge, improvement processes, and results across the entire company? Should stricter standardization policies be adopted? What is lost in creativity and team spirit with standardization? What is gained ?

## Expansion to All Industries and All Functions

This may be the most obvious of all the trends. Consider the attendees at the 1990 IMPRO, Juran Institute's annual conference on quality management. Law firms, accounting practices, medical services, government agencies, military services, engineering construction firms, manufacturing companies, aerospace companies, universities, farmers, oil companies, dentists' offices, and transportation companies were all represented. Conference attendees also covered almost every function imaginable in a company: marketing and sales, research and development (R&D), production, accounting, finance, clerical support, laboratories, transportation, distribution, and especially senior management.

The expansion of quality management concepts, methods, and tools to all industries is easily shown by considering the 1992 winners of the MBNQA or New York's or other states' quality awards. Winners included a hotel, a rock supplier, the New York State Police, a school system, land surveyors, and architects as well as a wide variety of other manufacturing and service companies.

*Research Challenges*

The spread of TQM philosophy across industries has been painfully slow. Far too often, one industry is considered "different." For many managers, it appears that only examples from within their own industry will help them understand where to start, or even why to start.

There have been some planned experiments to stimulate cross-industry learning. One is the National Demonstration Project for Quality Improvement in Health Care (NDP).

In the fall of 1987, leaders from twenty-one health care organizations and an equal number of industrial experts came together at a meeting in Boston. Funded by the John A. Hartford Foundation and hosted by the Harvard Community Health Plan, this project was an experiment to explore whether the tools of modern quality improvement, with which other industries had achieved breakthroughs in performance, would also help n health care as well.

The participant health care organizations, assisted by their assigned quality experts, formed teams to tackle this question in their own real-world operations through specific pilot projects. In June, 1988, they reported back. Berwick, Godfrey, and Roessner (1990) provide an extended interpretation of their experience in *Curing Health Care: New Strategies for Quality Improvement.* The success of the NDP has now led to the creation of a new nonprofit organization, the Institute for Healthcare Improvement, which will become a permanent focal point for health care quality management activities.

Some similar efforts have been made in law, secondary education, and university education. Perhaps the most noteworthy of these endeavors has been the University TQM Challenge Grant, in which five of the United States' leading companies are directly supporting eight leading universities (Galvin 1992).

In secondary education, GOAL/QPC, the Juran Institute, Bill Golomski, Ray Wachniak, and others have created alliances for common learning and sharing. Some of the early results are quite promising. One of the earliest of these endeavors was the Quantitative Literacy project, jointly conducted by the American Statistical Association and the National Council of Teachers of Mathematics and funded by the National Science Foundation.

Some interesting and useful books have been written documenting this quality expansion into different industries. For the electric power industry, read Hudiberg's *Winning with Quality: The FPL Story* (1991). For banking, look at Aubrey's *Quality Management in Financial Services* (1988), and Aubrey and Felkins' *Teamwork: Involving People in Quality and Productivity Improvement* (1988). For the insurance industry, read Berry's *Managing the Total Quality Transformation* (1991).

What is the best way to transfer what one industry has learned to another industry? This is still an open question. What has worked in these experiments? What has not worked? What other approaches are there? What approaches have failed? Why?

Companies have, for the most part, taken the lead in expanding TQM philosophies, concepts, methods, and tools across their many functions. One notable exception is the trailbreaking experiment carried out at Fordham University. Here, a group of graduate business students, led by their professors, explored how leading quality companies were extending their knowledge of TQM into financial functions. Chief finance officers of award-winning companies and from other recognized leaders were asked to explain how their jobs were changing and how they were applying these ideas within their functions. The documentation (Stoner, Werner, and the Corporate Finance-IBM Study Group 1991) from these presentations and interviews was a major contribution to TQM research.

Rochester Institute of Technology and Juran Institute have brought together the heads of marketing organizations from leading companies for the past two years to share their ideas and applications in TQM and marketing. For the past three years, Juran Institute has hosted an annual conference on the application of TQM in the R&D function. Vice-presidents and other research leaders from outstanding U.S. and international companies have shared their progress and plans.

There is much to be learned from these and other efforts. There are still many untold stories of successes and disappointments from companies taking TQM methods into uncharted waters. Fordham University has started a second effort in the legal function and is now planning work in a similar way in the information systems area. There are enough questions to fuel tens, if not hundreds, of similar efforts.

## Product Design and Process Engineering

For many years in the United States and other western countries, efforts have been focused on product design. Process design has received only secondary emphasis. Today, the focus is rapidly shifting as companies discover the importance of not just coming up with new products, but designing new processes by which those products are manufactured. Thurow (1992) explains in *Head to Head: The Coming Economic Battle Among Japan, Europe, and America:*

> What was a good American strategy thirty years ago, a focus on new product technologies, is today a poor strategy. Levels of technical sophistication in Germany, Japan, and the United States are now very different, and reverse engineering has become a highly developed art form. The nature of the change can be seen in the economic history of three leading new products introduced into the mass consumer market in the past two decades—the video camera and recorder, the fax, and the CD player. Americans invented the video camera and recorder and the fax; Euro-

peans (the Dutch) invented the CD player. But measured in terms of sales, employ-ment, and profits, all three have become Japanese products (47).

Results from the inception of the process quality focus have been stunning. For example, product development cycle times are being improved from 50 percent to 90 percent, thus generating major revenue increases through ear-lier, more timely product introductions. AT&T has reduced development times for telephones from twenty-four to twelve months. Hewlett-Packard has cut the time to develop computer printers from fifty-four months to twenty-two months. Manufacturing process reengineering efforts are also crashing through previously undreamed-of cycle time barriers, routinely cutting overhead and resultant product costs. Companies are increasing inventory turns from the once-respectable two or three times per year to ten or more turns.

Process engineering and process reengineering are bringing TQM, with its wealth of cultural and technical tools and techniques, to the organization with an ongoing laserlike management focus. Consequently, processes critical to the organization, and more importantly to its customers, are rapidly improving.

Product reengineering, cloning, and reverse engineering are driving the prod-uct technology advantage out and the process technology advantage in. One of the stunning facts that many have recently discovered is that the typical Japa-nese company spends one-third of its R&D budget on product design and two-thirds on process design. The typical American company's spending is just the reverse—one-third on process design and two-thirds on product design.

At the Global Quality Conference in June, 1992, in Singapore, this point was driven home. The Sony presentation demonstrated how far some compa-nies have gone. Sony representatives described their designs for the new, very small CD player. For this product, the designers had to contrive the manufac-turing process at the same time they designed the product. There was no pro-cess in existence in the world that could make a product that small and that accurate. By continually redesigning their manufacturing process, Sony has managed to take over 50 percent of the labor out of many of its high-tech products in the last four years.

A case study in these new design methods is found in IBM's new Think Pad® laptop computer. A cross-country design team of fifteen labs operated as a virtual product development team (Nussbaum 1993). The team roamed IBM research and design labs worldwide looking for ideas and technologies for the new laptop. At one U.S. lab, the team found the TrackPoint™ cursor. In Japan, where the team was working in alliance with Toshiba, it found a 10.4-inch color liquid crystal display screen. As Tom Hardy, manager of the IBM design program at Stamford, Connecticut, states, "We transferred new tech-nology, went into prototyping quickly, defined the product early, and under-stood the cost constraints before moving to manufacturing. But the key was bridging the gap between technology and the user."

General Motors' new Northstar® engine is another excellent example of a combination of the emerging quality trends. Early in the design process it was obvious to the General Motors and Cadillac engineers that the Northstar had to match or beat the world's best engines (Kerwin and Woodruff 1993). The engineers tore apart and studied everything they could find, from four-cylinder Honda engines to V-12 BMWs. New computer design tools helped the designers rapidly simulate many possible configurations and performance conditions. Design-for-manufacturability techniques helped reduce the number of parts to 1,200 versus 1,700 for the competitive Lexus V-8 engine. The simpler design is a key for the 60 percent reduction in manufacturing time per engine compared to that of Lexus.

As process technologies increasingly become the heart of the competitive equation, it becomes necessary to have senior executives, middle managers, professional staff, and work force members who understand modern process technologies.

Also note that process management skills are not just necessary for production lines. These same skills must be applied to all key business processes. It is in these areas that many U.S. companies have not made significant strides in the past few years. If these key business processes in most companies are examined, it becomes obvious that the processes have become hopelessly bureaucratic, inefficient, ineffective, defect laden, and obsolete.

*Research Challenges*

There is many years' worth of interesting research in the areas of product design and process engineering. The American Statistical Association's Quality and Productivity Research Conference, now in its tenth year, started to explore one specific area in process engineering and product design, that is, robust design. The first Mohonk Conference was planned and run by a small group of Bell Laboratories' quality researchers who thought it would be a good idea to get professors, applied researchers, and engineers together to thrash out some of the issues surrounding robust design methods (or, as some call them, Taguchi methods). By the third conference, supported by the Ford Motor Company, the gathering had created such interest that the participants were Sir David Cox, Professor John Tukey, Dr. W. Edwards Deming, and Dr. Genichi Taguchi.

Much research in companies, universities, and other organizations was stimulated by these and other conferences. The following papers give a glimpse into this still-promising research area: Box (1988, 1986a, and 1986b); Taguchi (1985); Kacker (1990); Kacker and Shoemaker (1986); Kacker and Tsui (1989); Phadke (1986); Leon, Shoemaker, and Kacker (1987); Phadke et al. (1983); Godfrey, Phadke, and Shoemaker (1986); and Godfrey (November 1992). The book *Quality Engineering Using Robust Design* by

Phadke (1989) gives an excellent introduction to the practical application of robust design methods.

There are many other promising areas in product design and process engineering waiting to be explored. Far too little has been done in product design, value engineering, and product and process joint design and engineering. Most companies have applied little of what has been done. Some researchers are making good starts. Wheelwright and Clark (1992) and Clark and Fujimoto (1990) are notable examples in describing some of the new ideas in project management.

Must reading in this area, and a pristine example of the type of research so badly needed, is summarized by Womack, Jones, and Roos (1990) in their book *The Machine That Changed the World*. They report results of the International Motor Vehicle Program's study of the worldwide automobile industry. This $5 million, five-year, one-country study is the largest and most thorough study ever undertaken in any industry.

While much effort has been focused on product design and manufacturing process engineering, an entirely new area of business process quality management has been emerging. One of the early books in this field (Pall 1987) describes the basic concepts and methods. Articles by Papay (1990) give insight into IBM's application. The entertaining and informative AT&T guides (1990a and 1990b) make the basic principles available to hundreds of thousands of readers. Snee (1993) gives an excellent review article on robust work processes and many examples of creating work process ruggedness.

Business process quality management, or business process reengineering, as it is sometimes called, has become an entire industry in its own right. Numerous workshops have been held, and articles and books have been published. But little solid research has been conducted about how companies are identifying the key business processes, what processes are common across companies, what changes have been made, what the effects of these changes have been, or how companies have been able to hold the gains. Or, perhaps, have many of these reengineering efforts been like many diet programs: quick initial results with few lasting effects?

## Intense Education and Training

In the past few years, many companies have instituted intense education and training programs in quality methods, tools, and concepts. These courses and workshops are becoming key parts of company strategies. "The ability to learn faster than your competitors is the only sustainable competitive edge," according to Senge (1990).

Any company that has been actively engaged in moving toward TQM knows how important education and training are. The concepts, methods, and tools for modern quality management are new for most members of the company—managers, professionals, and workers. Thurow (1992) points out the following:

> The skills of the work force are going to be the key competitive weapon in the twenty-first century. Brain-power will create new technologies, but skilled labor will be the arms and legs that allow one to employ—to be the low-cost masters of—the new product and process technologies that are being generated. Skilled people become the only sustainable competitive advantage. (51-52)

The investment in education and training is high, but the rewards are great. Reports from companies show just how high this investment is. One company reports 105 hours of training per manufacturing employee per year and 169 hours per R&D employee. One of the MBNQA winners is averaging almost 100 hours of training per employee per year now, but expects to increase that to 150 hours within the next five years.

For many companies, this investment in training and education is already 1 to 2 percent of total revenue, and one of the high-tech MBNQA winners expects its investment to be as high as 5 percent of revenue. Other companies are reporting similar investments. According to Boyett and Conn (1991),

> Thomas Lindem, vice president for technology at Ingersall Milling Machine Company, estimated in 1988 that as many as four to six out of every 40 hours employees work in the future might have to be devoted to training and retraining. (271)

This necessary investment in people may have been best expressed by George Gilder in *Microcosm: The Quantum Revolution in Economics and Technology,* as quoted in Boyett and Conn (1991):

> The central event of the 20th century is the overthrow of matter. In technology, economics, and the politics of nations, wealth in the form of physical resources is steadily declining in value and significance. The powers of mind are everywhere ascendant over the brute force of things.... Today, the ascendant nations and corporations are masters not of land and material resources, but of ideas and technologies.... Wealth comes not to the rulers of slave labor but to the liberators of human creativity; not to conquerors of land but to the emancipators of mind. (278)

*Research Challenges*

Although quality education and training needs in most companies are among the most critical, time consuming, and expensive, little research has gone into defining just what is needed and when. Quality curricula in most organizations still reflect some great desire to train everybody in everything as soon as possible. This sheep-dip training has been responsible for many of the media's TQM-bashing articles and the low (or even negative) returns on investment that some companies have endured. Although it is obvious that the jobs performed by the chief executive officer (CEO) and senior management team are far different from the jobs performed by frontline workers, many organizations have persisted in delivering identical training courses to all personnel. It is far more difficult to carefully develop specific workshops and learning opportunities for different job levels and functions, but this is exactly what is needed.

There is probably a basic core of knowledge and skills needed by all, but what is this core? There are also specific tools and methods needed by special groups. But what, for estimation, and reliability growth models? Or should these basic skills be broken down and taught to specific sets of designers according to their roles in the process?

Some companies, such as AT&T, have made good starts in addressing these questions (Godfrey 1985 and 1988). The work in universities to define a core curriculum is still embryonic. Little progress is likely until the needs of business majors are separated from those of engineers. Perhaps the needs of engineers by type of specialty and level (undergraduate and graduate) should be separated. So far, no consensus on the introductory course has even been reached. Much progress was made in the summer of 1992 by the core curriculum committee under the auspices of the TQM Challenge Grant.

Other underexplored areas in training and education in the quality field include understanding how adults learn. Are examples and case studies closely related to the individual's job needed for learning to happen quickly? What should be the mix of learning and doing? Several companies—Boeing is a superb example—have coupled training in quality improvement methods with actual project work. By the time a team has completed its initial training in quality improvement, it has solved its first problem. Many other companies are using similar just-in-time training methods with outstanding results. Should this be the standard practice? Are there better ways?

Many companies have used cascade training, in which senior managers actively participate in training their direct reports, who then actively participate in training the next layer, and so on. This definitely shows commitment and leads to great learning opportunities for each level of teacher. But how effective is this? Some claim it is just the blind leading the blind or a modern version of the children's game of whispering a set phrase into the next person's ear and going down the line until the phrase comes out the other end as an unrecognizable mess. Others claim it is the only way to couple company strategy, key objectives, and business plans with quality training. What is the best way? Why?

## Information Systems and Technology

A key element of the TQM infrastructure is measurement work and information. Donald Peterson, former chairman of Ford Motor Company, stresses how important having the right information is. When Ford benchmarked

Mazda, it was quite impressed with how well Mazda managed this part of the business. Peterson (1992) states, "Perhaps, most important, Mazda had been able to identify the types of information and records that were truly useful. It didn't bother with any other data. [At Ford] we were burdened with mountains of useless data and stifled by far too many levels of control over them."

Information systems are a key part of the infrastructure for TQM. Yet, in far too many companies, they are still embryonic or, worse yet, they exist and are not used. At IMPRO91, Tim Schlange presented a remarkable paper describing his research on quality information systems. During his research at St. Gallens University in Switzerland, Schlange had studied quality information systems in two Swiss companies. Then, on a visiting scholarship at Columbia University and Juran Institute funded by the Swiss government, he studied quality information systems in four U.S. companies.

The remarkable finding in this research was that Schlange (1991) was able to discover in only one company evidence that people were actually *using* the quality information. The one company, Xerox, actually closed the loop and turned the data collected into useful information and then turned the information into action. The information was used to improve the next generation of products, improve business processes, reduce cycle times, improve distribution, improve field service, better understand the needs of customers, and design products and services to meet those needs. The other five companies had the data and the information, but Schlange found no evidence that it was being used.

*Research Challenges*

This is an almost untapped area. In many ways, Schlange's work was a pioneering effort. Few researchers have looked at data and information needs of companies engaged in serious TQM efforts. A Fordham University team has recently undertaken a study in TQM and information systems. If this in any way approaches the usefulness of the previous study in TQM and the finance department, it will make a major contribution.

Recently there has been some excellent work on the quality of information and data—a related area. Redman's book, *Data Quality: Management and Technology* (1992), is a definite plus in the field. Godfrey (1993 and 1991) summarizes some of these efforts and gives a simplified way to look at some of the critical issues. Early (1989a and 1989b) and Early and Dmytrow (1986) describe some of the pioneering work at the Bureau of Labor Statistics. Iau (1992) describes some of the critical questions in using information technology and the need to manage the quality dimensions. Sprague (1992) also describes many of the challenges facing companies in the next few years as information technology becomes one of the essential success factors.

One of the pioneering studies in information quality was done by the National Research Council (Kester 1992). This study focused on the systems for collecting and analyzing trade and other international economic data. The panel made several recommendations for new approaches to accuracy and usefulness and gave specific steps for improving the accuracy of trade data.

## Self-Directing Work Teams

Companies are moving quickly toward control by the work force, by the professionals, by the engineers, and by the entire company working together beyond what was ever dreamed possible. Work scheduling, hiring, training, salary, administration, tool design, process improvement, process design, redesign, and reengineering are being done by teams of people working across the company instead of external planners telling workers what to do, setting standards, and reviewing their performance. These teams are achieving continuous improvement on a remarkable scale.

The concept of empowered employees embraces many new ideas. Empowered employees are in control. They have the means to measure the quality of their own work processes, to interpret the measurements and compare them to goals, and to take action when the processes are not in control.

But the concept of empowered employees goes far beyond self-control. Employees also know how to change the process and improve performance, enhancing both the effectiveness and the efficiency of the process. They also understand how to plan for quality. They understand who their customers are; what the customers need, want, and expect; how to design new goods and services to meet those needs; how to develop the necessary work processes; how to develop and use the necessary quality measurements; and how to continuously improve those processes.

In summary, empowered employees understand and use daily the three basic processes for managing quality: planning, control, and improvement. These three universal management processes, often called The Juran Trilogy, are the first building block of TQM. Juran and Godfrey (1990a) provide a summary of contributions from the work force and self-directing work teams in the United States.

### Research Challenges

This is an area in which there has been much progress in the past few years, but there is little documentation and very little solid research. There is an immediate need for well-researched and well-written case studies. Some companies, such as Eastman Chemical, have had startling results but have not had the time to capture on paper what has been done and how it has achieved such results.

Many quality professionals believe that there is a critical sequence of events and learning that must take place before one can implement self-directing work teams. The basic quality control and quality improvement are essential. There must be ample opportunity to participate on teams and gain teamwork and facilitation skills. There must also be an open environment of sharing of the company's vision, mission, objectives, financial results, and other important information.

What are the necessary skills? What tasks are appropriate for self-directing work teams? What tasks are not appropriate? Is there a best order in which to implement the different parts of self-directing work teams?

## Partnering

One of the most exciting trends in TQM is partnering. Many companies are including key suppliers and customers in quality improvement, planning, and control activities. The ISO 9000 series of standards has become the internationally accepted definition of a quality assurance system. These standards provide a good starting point for contractual relationships by defining a solid quality management structure.

But many companies are going far beyond contractual relationships. Many customer-supplier relationships in the United States are evolving quickly to resemble those pioneered by Toyota and other leading Japanese automotive companies.

Quality improvement teams across companies were first introduced by an Alcoa-Kodak team several years ago. This presentation was a striking event at the time. Now it is common practice: A chemical company producing plastic films recently described how it works with a converter and a food-producing company that uses the plastic packages. Only a few years ago, personnel from the different companies were not even allowed inside each other's plants because of supposed proprietary processes. Now team members even have ID cards for all three companies so they can walk in on weekends and evenings if they need to make a process change.

Walton (Walton and Huey 1992) clearly described his policy for success in his book "Sam Walton: Made in America." One of the top-ten rules is controlling expenses better than anyone else, and one of Wal-mart's key ways of doing this is partnering with its suppliers. Walton describes how Wal-Mart changed its relationship with one of its most important suppliers, Procter & Gamble.

> But it really wasn't until 1987 that we began to turn a basically adversarial vendor/ retailer relationship into one that we like to think is the wave of the future: a win-win partnership between two big companies both trying to serve the same customer. (186)

Lou Pritchett of Procter & Gamble described the same situation (Walton and Huey 1992).

> We both decided that the entire relationship between vendor and retailer was at issue. Both focused on the end user—the customer—but each did it independently

of the other; no sharing of information, no planning together, no systems coordination. We were simply two giant entities going our separate ways, oblivious to the excess costs created by this obsolete system. (186)

Wal-Mart used the changes it made with Procter & Gamble as a model for many other vendor relationships.

In our situation today, we are obsessed with quality as well as price, and, as big as we are, the only way we can possibly get that combination is to sit down with our vendors and work out the costs and margins and plan everything together. By doing that, we give the manufacturer the advantage of knowing what our needs are going to be a year out, or six months out, or even two years out. Then, as long as they are honest with us and try to lower their costs as much as they can and keep turning out a product that the customers want, we can stay with them. We both win, and most important, the customer wins, too. The added efficiency of the whole process enables the manufacturer to reduce its costs, which allows us to lower our prices. (187)

Working together across the many functional departments such as engineering, design, manufacturing, and marketing is challenging enough, but when the team includes suppliers, the challenges multiply. Motorola's development of the MicroTac Lite cellular phone is a good example. During the first customer focus-group studies at the beginning of design in 1986, Motorola's team was horrified at how often customers dropped the phone. Although the team members agreed quickly on the design standard that the phone must withstand a four-foot fall, they disagreed greatly on how to meet this requirement (Nussbaum 1993). The normal way would be to build thicker, stronger walls, but this would greatly add to the phone's weight and size. Working closely with plastics suppliers such as GE, the design team was able to push plastics technologies to the point where walls $1/_{32}$-inch thick were sufficient. These cross-functional and cross-company teams worked so well that Motorola had a full year's head start over its Japanese rivals when the phone hit the market.

*Research Challenges*

This is another area in which the research opportunities are wide open. The possibilities are just now being explored. Godfrey (1993a) used a chamber of commerce broadcast and panel discussion to summarize the current state of the art and explore how Toyota (thought by many to be the world leader in this area) is building close relationships with its U.S. suppliers. Womack, Jones, and Roos (1990) give one of the best discussions of this concept in print anywhere.

There is a need for case studies in partnering. Far too little has been written. Too much that has been written is still too sketchy, too anecdotal, and too results oriented without giving the details of how the relationships were developed and what the key management questions were. For instance, what quality information should be shared? What market and sales information should be shared? How should cross-company quality teams be managed? What are the risks? What are the possible gains? Are there fundamental differences between multiple-company partnering activities and two-company partnering? What are the different kinds of partnering relationships? What are the advantages and disadvantages of these different relationships ?

## Self-Assessment and Benchmarking

Benchmarking and self-assessment may be two of the most useful trends to develop in the past twelve years. Companies in the United States, Mexico, Australia, South America, Europe, Africa, Southeast Asia, and even Japan are using the criteria of the MBNQA to assess their current performance against a reasonable set of guidelines for TQM. By far, the greatest impact that the MBNQA has had is its use as a self-assessment tool by thousands of companies and organizations throughout the United States.

Many other companies are using the ISO 9000 series of standards both for self-assessment and third-party assessment. In Europe, companies are also beginning to use the new criteria of the European Quality Award to measure their performance against a stringent set of requirements.

The area of self-assessment, especially using the MBNQA or the European Quality Award, is also quite new. Some recent studies are beginning to show the power of these assessments (Godfrey, 1993b and 1993c).

The Xerox Business Products and Systems division went through an intensive review process of its own in 1989. It claims to have found 513 warts—its internal name for what the MBNQA examiners would call areas for improvement. The division used these warts to create action plans to prepare for the examiners' site visit and for a five-year strategic planning process. Senior managers took responsibility and accountability for these action plans.

Ronald D. Schmidt, chairman, president, and CEO of Zytec Corporation, described in testimony before the Technology and Competitive Subcommittee of the U.S. House of Representatives Committee on Science Space, and Technology how self-assessment had helped his company (U.S. Congress 1992).

> Our sixth strategy...was to use the Malcolm Baldrige National Quality Award criteria to further improve our company. We used the knowledge gained from [our first application] to make some process improvements and reapplied in 1991, and as they say, "the rest is history."

Fred Smith (1990), CEO of Federal Express, echoes Schmidt's remarks, "Applying for the MBNQA is a major undertaking, but it is an incredibly valuable experience."

These internal company assessments are becoming widespread in the United States. Placek (1992) reports a number of examples. Convex Computer Corporation makes the award a visible goal, sending a clear message to everyone that quality is the company's top priority.

AT&T has established the Chairman's Quality Awards as a process to encourage the company's business units and divisions to meet the MBNQA criteria. The Chairman's Quality Awards process is structured to encourage cooperation among AT&T's various businesses and to encourage winning in the marketplace.

AT&T's first winners of the Chairman's Quality Award in 1991 included its Universal Card Services, Information Management Services, Switching Systems, and Transmissions Systems. In 1992, two of these divisions, AT&T Universal Card Services and AT&T Transmissions Systems, won the MBNQA.

These assessments can provide senior managers with a clear baseline of current quality performance levels. When these managers are willing to take the time to understand the criteria, understand what their own assessment scores mean, and understand what is necessary to improve these scores, they can process to develop meaningful and realistic action plans for improving their organizations.

A very important first step in this process is understanding the performance level of one's own organization and comparing it to that of another organization. This benchmarking, both on a personal and an organizational level, is one of the most important trends in modern quality management. When asked by a reporter if there was a single most important thing a company could do to change the company culture and achieve remarkable results, Donald Peterson (1992), former chairman of Ford Motor Company, answered: "There sure is. Each company must find out which other companies in the world are best in that industry. Then, each company must benchmark operations against the most efficient—and most profitable—foreign and domestic businesses.... Those that do—such as Xerox—have had incredible results."

Peterson went on to explain that Ford began by comparing its manufacturing processes, design, marketing, financial management, and quality with the best of the Japanese operations. According to Peterson (1992),

comparisons should be based on speed, capital investment, wasted effort, number of employees, and any other yardstick with which the company can measure both its own and others' operations.... The next step is to get managers in the key departments to acknowledge that another business is doing all or part of their job better. That becomes easier when the CEO says that he looks on the benchmarking as an opportunity, not as criticism. Good managers are energized by that challenge.... Next, send groups of managers to visit the companies with the superior operations.

Companies in the United States have been refreshingly open about sharing their quality management strategies, concepts, methods, and tools with each other. Perhaps it is because everyone realizes how much there is to learn and that there is no way that any one company can possibly invent all of this itself. Everyone must learn from one another.

Ford included union representatives on the visiting teams. Later it assembled teams from key people in the affected departments to discuss the ideas they had encountered. Ford then decided which of those ideas it would implement and how it would do so.

This type of benchmarking, first popularized by the open discussions, articles, and books by people from Xerox, is now opening managers' eyes to new possibilities. It gives them new ways of thinking about managing their companies, and often provides them with entirely new visions of how far it is possible to go.

*Research Challenges*

This entire area is exceedingly new in the United States. The articles written, some of them excellent (Camp 1990), have focused primarily on how to do benchmarking. There have been few thorough studies on the results of benchmarking, how often findings are actually applied, and what results have been attained. There is a strong suspicion that much of what passes for benchmarking is no more than industrial tourism.

There has also been little published research in self-assessment. There is no doubt that it is becoming a widely used tool in the United States by senior managers of leading companies. But what do these assessments consist of? How closely do they follow the MBNQA or other criteria? What modifications do companies make when training their own examiners? Should examiners be from within the business unit or from outside it? What is the role of external examiners? What added value do they bring that is not available within the company?

## Customer Focus

Today, companies are focusing on customers beyond what was ever believed reasonable or even possible. The importance of going beyond the goal of satisfied customers to loyal or delighted customers was recently demonstrated by Banc One. As is well known, banking is not a thriving business in the United States, but somehow Banc One has been doing well. In fact, Banc One is the second most profitable bank in the world. There are important lessons to be learned in its approach to customers.

Banc One has developed several statistical models to understand customer behavior as a function of customer satisfaction. It has found that delighted customers, those who are much more than merely satisfied, are five times as likely to buy other financial products from the bank as customers who are just satisfied. Moreover, these delighted customers are also four times less likely to leave the bank than those who are just satisfied.

In fact, Banc One was surprised to discover that there is very little difference between customers who are satisfied and those who are neutral or even dissatisfied. These customers are continuously shopping around. On the other hand, the very satisfied, or delighted, customers are the real revenue providers, the loyal ones, the ones who come to a company first when they need a product that the company might have. Even if the company doesn't yet have the product, the delighted customers will be the ones to give new ideas and help the company design new products. In short, loyal customers work with an organization.

This kind of relentless focus on the customer is one of the hallmarks of Wal-Mart's spectacular success. Robert C. Goizueta, chairman and CEO of the Coca-Cola Company, explains his view of Wal-Mart's focus on the customer (Walton and Huey 1992).

> Sam Walton understands better than anyone else that no business can exist without customers. He lives by his credo, which is to make the customer the centerpiece of all his efforts. And in the process of serving Wal-Mart's customers to perfection (not quite perfection, he would say), he also serves Wal-Mart's associates, its share owners, its communities, and the rest of its stakeholders in an extraordinary fashion—almost without parallel in American business. (173)

When the Apple product development team started working on the PowerBook® in 1990, it carefully studied other laptops and notebooks already in use. The team saw only small desktop personal computers. It decided to study how real people were using these things. "They discovered people didn't really want 'small' computers per se, they wanted mobile computers" (Nussbaum 1993). People were using these laptops on planes, in cars, at home, and even in bed. They were often struggling to find a place to put their hands and a surface for the mouse. This led to two distinct features of the PowerBook—the trackball pointer and the palm rest in the front of the keyboard. These and other features have propelled Apple from nowhere to marketplace leader in notebook computers. As Bob Brunner, manager of Apple's design department states: "The user focus permeates everything we do now. There's no more of: 'Here's a great technology, let's go sell it someplace.'" (Nussbaum 1993).

This focus on customers is driving companies to extraordinary lengths. Since Sony introduced the first Walkman in 1979, it has marketed 227 different models. On average, that means a new model every three weeks!

Akio Morita (Morita, Reingold, and Shimomura 1986), chairman and CEO of Sony, explains this passion for the customers in his book, *Made in Japan*. He uses Honda as an example.

> A few years ago Yamaha decided the time was right to challenge Honda for a bigger share of the Japanese market in motorcycles and motorscooters. Honda had a clear lead then, but was investing heavily in a new automobile assembly plant in the United States, and so Yamaha put out a line of new models and began a lively

advertising campaign. The Honda management responded instantly, despite its heavy financial burden. It struck back with a new model introduction every single week for over a year! (206)

From banking to retailing to the automobile industry, the companies that are achieving the greatest successes share the same obsession: making the customer the center of everything they do. It's not enough anymore to merely satisfy the customer; customers must be delighted—surprised by having their needs not just met, but exceeded.

*Research Challenges*

Companies are trying many new means to incorporate customer focus in every activity. One technique is the coupling of industrial design with strong, modern project management methodologies. Industrial design is using ethnographic tools, such as videotaping human behavior and observing actual work environments, to connect companies directly to their customers. As General Electric's Seth Banks states, "Industrial design understands the needs of the customer and knits the customer into the fabric of our product development (Nussbaum 1993).

These tools are just beginning to be explored. How to couple the real needs of users with the designers and then with the advanced technology known only by the engineers and the product developers depends on far more skills and organization than just the familiar tools of quality function deployment. Charles L. Jones, head of industrial design and human interface strategy at Xerox, believes that industrial design can help link the needs of users to advanced technologies and that this is the key to their growth and survival (Nussbaum 1993). One of the main challenges is linking the various parts of the decentralized company and even affiliated companies into a design team with a strong focus on the customer. Cross-functional teams of industrial designers, engineers, manufacturers, and distributors are common in leading companies. Yet little research has been done on these organizational forms, information needs, shared analyses, and other means used to manage these teams smoothly and efficiently.

IBM has virtually built a product development team by electronically linking fifteen of the company's design studios around the world. The hardware and software are available, but are the design methodologies? One of IBM's first designs from this new team, the Think Pad, is a smashing success. Is it known how to do design reviews in this type of environment? What changes are needed in reliability prediction and estimation or design-for-manufacturability methods when products are simultaneously designed for manufacture in multiple locations with multiple-source parts?

There are many research opportunities even in the most mundane customer-focus areas. Focus groups are still, for most companies, amateur operations.

Little thought goes into the design of the groups, the questions or exercises used, the data collection techniques, the analysis methods, or the presentation and uses of the findings. Many companies are overwhelming themselves and their customers with multiple, overlapping focus groups often addressing the same or similar areas of interest.

Even the modest customer satisfaction survey is a good target for solid research. So many surveys appear to be just random data gathering of customer perceptions and opinions with little effort for intelligent follow-up and meaningful investigations. The more important questions of customer retention and customer loyalty have barely been touched. Even a research survey paper in this area would have wide readership and interest. Recent work in this area highlights some of the issues (Godfrey 1993e; Fay, n.d.).

## Strategic Quality Management

It is much easier to discuss all of these wonderful ideas— customer focus, process design, benchmarking—than to put them into practice. Peter Behrendt, now president and CEO of Exabyte, put this in perspective years ago when he was a senior manager at IBM. "I was told to focus on costs, revenues, inventory, and quality," he recalls. "I felt like a kamikaze pilot with a quota of four ships."

In the past few years, there has been an increasing emphasis on strategic quality management. Indeed, in many competitive markets, quality has become the single most important factor for success. In testimony to the U.S. Congress (1992) Curt Reimann, director for quality programs at the National Institute of Standards and Technology, stated this clearly, "There is now far clearer perception that quality is central to company competitiveness and to national competitiveness."

The elements of strategic quality management are not too difficult to understand. At the thirtieth Anniversary Congress of the Asian Productivity Organization in 1992, Hideo Sugiura, former chairman of the Honda Motor Company, explained the roles of senior management and strategic quality planning better than anyone. He described four "sacred obligations" of management.

1. A clear vision of where the company is going—this must be clearly stated and communicated to every member of the organization in language he or she understands.
2. Clear definitions of the small number of key objectives that must be achieved if the company is to realize its vision.
3. Translation of these key objectives throughout the entire organization so that each person knows how performing his or her job helps the company achieve the objectives.
4. A fair and honest appraisal so that each and every employee knows how his or her performance has contributed to the organization's efforts to achieve the key objectives, accompanied by guidance as to how the individual can improve this performance.

In the United States, this process of defining the vision, stating the objectives, and translating them throughout the organization has come to be known in most companies as strategic quality planning. In some companies it is sometimes called *hoshin kanri*, policy deployment, or even hoshin planning. For some organizations it has become the single most important tool, allowing the organization to set clear priorities, establish clear target areas for improvement activities, and allocate resources to the most important things that must be done. For other organizations, it has become a bureaucratic nightmare, one more excuse to resume paralysis by analysis and allow endless meetings and planning to take the place of real action or accomplishment.

To be effective, strategic quality planning must be used as a tool—a means to an end—and not as the goal itself. It must be an endeavor that involves people throughout the organization. It must capture existing activities, not just add more activities to already overflowing plates. Finally, it must help senior managers face difficult decisions, set priorities, and eliminate many current activities—not just start new ones.

Companies that have carefully implemented strategic quality planning and iterated plans throughout the organization in true catchball fashion are reporting many breakthroughs. (*Catchball* is a Japanese term describing a two-way communication between the executive leadership and top managers, in which managers are asked to analyze goals and, in turn, ask their subordinates a similar question, and so on. The responses are summarized and passed back up through the organization.) For many companies, it is the first time in the history of the organization that everyone has had a clear picture of where the organization is going, why it is going there, and what activities are necessary to get there. For others, it is the first time people have felt that their views were important and seen evidence of the incorporation of their ideas into the organization's priorities.

Many organizations report that it is the first time they have systematically reviewed each planned project. That is better known, in the language of quality management, as a problem scheduled for solution, or a new opportunity to be seized. Companies have forced themselves to determine whether they have provided adequate resources, training, and skills for the people doing the job and whether they have active supervision and management support in place.

These organizations have rediscovered the true value of strategic quality planning. It is not another job; it is a tool for improving the way they do the jobs they must do. It is a tool for ensuring that they are focusing on the right things and providing the leadership and support to do those things right.

Recently this author participated in a remarkable workshop. A leading U.S. company had decided to get its entire board of directors involved in TQM. It asked the board to participate in setting the quality goals, to help create the new measurements for quality management and customer satisfaction, and to help identify opportunities for improvement.

The board response was incredible. Board members were eager to participate in benchmarking, to spend entire days at board meetings on quality objectives, to personally become more knowledgeable about TQM, and to make quality the first agenda item at every board meeting.

Strategic quality management isn't a project that an organization undertakes, like benchmarking, process design, or even customer focus. For those companies that have truly learned and adopted the theory and practice of strategic quality management, it is the way to do whatever the organization does.

*Research Challenges*

Recent surveys—such as the ones by Delta Consulting (1993), Ernst and Young and the American Quality Foundation (1992), and Development Dimensions International and the Quality and Productivity Management of leading American companies are placing on integrating quality management into the business and strategic planning process. Yet these surveys barely scratch the surface. They stress the need and demonstrate how little has been done, but do little to enlighten others on what has been done or how it has been done.

Many companies have made considerable progress in this area. Few have had the time to carefully document or share with others their means or results. Case studies are badly needed. A few are emerging and provide a good starting place. Colicchio (1988) describes some of Hewlett-Packard's early efforts, and Kane (1990) gives an overview of several companies' efforts, as do Huizenga and Dmytrow (1992).

Aubrey (1993) explores the area of board involvement in TQM and his findings are disturbing. Not only do boards play minor roles in TQM, the overwhelming majority also feel that quality is a management matter. The prognosis for the future is equally grim. Only a small number of senior executives and board members think that the board will play a greater role in the future. Experts in governance, such as Carver (1990), author of *Boards that Make a Difference*, feel differently. Carver states: "Boards should certainly deal more proactively with quality." What is the proper role of the board? What are the boards of leading companies doing now? This is another wide-open area for quality management research.

This whole area should become one of the emerging hot topics in sociotechnological engineering, organization design, and related academic departments and disciplines. The management aspects are daunting, the communication needs staggering, and the power stunning. Yet, in one recent study (Ernst & Young 1993), only one percent of hospital CEOs stated that the organization's vision, mission, and key objectives were understood by everyone in the organization.

## Summary

It doesn't take looking into a crystal ball to recognize the importance of the ten trends discussed. The benefits of focusing on the customer, of partnering, benchmarking, business process quality management, and above all strategic quality planning, are self-evident. The need for intense education and training is a fact of life that will be with companies for years. Revolutionary rates of improvement are becoming a way of life. Quality management has expanded to all industries and all functions. Information systems and information technology are becoming key success factors for all areas of the organization, especially quality management. Self-directing work teams are already making a major impact in many companies and will be used by more companies every year.

The results are plain to see, in organizations ranging from Banc One to Wal-Mart to Honda. It's a safe forecast to say that these trends will define the direction of quality management for the next ten years. It's just as safe a forecast to say that the business climate will be far from sunny and mild. Across the country, and indeed worldwide, it will be the companies on the leading edge of these trends that will weather the coming decade best.

## Acknowledgments

IMPRO and The Juran Trilogy are registered trademarks of Juran Institute, Inc. Think Pad is a registered trademark and TrackPoint is a trademark of International Business Machines Corporation. Northstar is a registered trademark of General Motors Corporation. MicroTac Lite is a registered trademark of Motorola, Inc. PowerBook is a registered trademark of Apple Computer, Inc.

## References

Akao, Y., "History of Quality Function Deployment in Japan," in *The Best on Quality: Targets, Improvement, Systems,* vol. 3, ed. H. J. Zeller (Munich: Hanser Publishers, 1990), 183–94.

AT&T Quality Technology Center, *Analyzing Business Process Data: The Looking Glass* (Indianapolis, Ind.: AT&T Customer Information Center, 1990a).

———, *PQMI: Tips, Experiences, and Lessons Learned* (Indianapolis. Ind.: AT&T Customer Information Center, 1990b).

Aubrey, C. A., II, "Should the Board of Directors Be Involved in TQM?" *National Productivity Review* (1993), 37–323.

———, *Quality Management in Financial Services* (Wheaton, Ill.: Hitchcock Publishing, 1988).

———, "Market Damage Survey" (Wilton, Conn.: Juran Institute and Banc One. Photocopy).

Aubrey, C. A., II, and P. K. Felkins, *Teamwork: Involving People in Quality and Productivity Improvement* (Milwaukee: ASQC Quality Press, 1988).

Babich, P., "Customer Satisfaction: How Good Is Good Enough?" *Quality Progress,* 25(12) (1992): 65–67.

Berry, T. H., *Managing the Total Quality Transformation* (New York: McGraw-Hill, 1991).

Berwick, D. M., Godfrey, A. B., and Roessner, J., *Curing Health Care: New Strategies for Quality Improvement* (San Francisco: Jossey-Bass, 1990).

Box, G. E. P., "Signal-to-Noise Ratios, Performance Criteria, and Transformations," *Technometrics* 30 (1988): 1-40.

———, "Studies in Quality Improvement: Signal-to-Noise Ratios, Performance Criteria, and Statistical Analysis," part I, report no. 4 (University of Wisconsin: Center for Quality and Productivity Improvement, 1986a).

———, "Studies in Quality Improvement: Signal-to-Noise Ratios, Performance Criteria, and Statistical Analysis," part II, report no. 4 (University of Wisconsin: Center for Quality and Productivity Improvement, 1986b).

Box, G. E. P., Hunter, J. S., and Hunter, W. G., *Statistics for Experimenters* (New York: John Wiley & Sons, 1978).

Boyett, J. H., and Conn, H. P., *Workplace 2000—The Revolution Reshaping American Business* (New York: E. P. Dutton, 1991).

Camp, R. C., "Competitive Benchmarking: Xerox's Powerful Quality Tool," in *Making Total Quality Happen,* research report 937, ed. The Conference Board (New York: The Conference Board, 1990), 35-42).

Carver, J., *Boards That Make a Difference: A New Design for Leadership in Non-Profit and Public Organizations* (San Francisco: Jossey-Bass, 1990).

Clark, K. B., and T. Fujimoto, "The Power of Product Integrity," *Harvard Business Review* (1990), 107-18.

Colicchio, D. F., "Quality Methods in Business Planning," in *Total Quality Performance,* research report 909, ed. The Conference Board (New York: The Conference Board, 1988), 50-52.

Conti, T. A., "Critical Review of the Current Approach to Quality Awards," *Proceedings of the European Organization for Quality Congress,* (Brussels: European Organization for Quality, 1992), 130-39.

Daigle, D. H., "Baldrige: A Framework for Quality in Engineering and Research," *Proceedings of 1992 Symposium on Management for Quality Research and Development* (Wilton, Conn.: Juran Institute, 1992).

Development Dimensions International, and the Quality and Productivity Management Association, "A Business Strategy Comes of Age," *Industry Week* (1993): 40-44.

Early, J. F., "Strategies for Measurement of Service Quality," in *1989 ASQC Quality Congress Transactions—Toronto* (Milwaukee: ASQC, 1989a)s.

———, "Improving Consumer Price Indexes," *Journal of Official Statistics* (Statistics Sweden), 6(2) (1989b).

Early, J. F., and Dmytrow, E. D., "Managing Information Quality in the CPI," in *1986 ASQC Quality Congress Transaction—Anaheim* (Milwaukee: ASQC, 1986).

Ernst & Young, and the American Quality Foundation, *International Quality Study: Health Care Industry Report* (Cleveland, Ohio: Ernst & Young, 1993).

Fay, C., "Customer Loyalty: The Ultimate Measure of TQM" (Wilton, Conn.: Juran Institute. Photocopy.)

Galvin, R. W., "The University TQM Challenge Grant." Paper presented at IMPRO92, Chicago, 1992.

———, "Role of the Chief Executive in Quality Management." Paper presented at IMPRO89, Atlanta, 1989.

Garvin, D. A., " How the Baldrige Award Really Works," *Harvard Business Review* (1991), 80-93.

Gilder, G., *Microcosm: The Quantum Revolution in Economics and Technology* (New York: Simon and Schuster, 1989).

Godfrey, A. B., " The Malcolm Baldrige National Quality Award: Five Years of Progress, Five Thousand Lessons Learned," in *The Best on Quality,* vol. 5, ed. J. D. Hromi (Milwaukee: ASQC Quality Press, in press).

———, "Information Quality—An Important Challenge for Modern Quality Management," in *Proceedings of the European Organization for Quality Congress* (Helsinki: European Organization for Quality, 1993a).

———, "A Review of the Malcolm Baldrige National Quality Award and How Companies Are Using the Award for Self-Assessment" (Wilton, Conn.: Juran Institute, 1993b).

———, "Total Quality Management: Critical Issues on Planning, Measurement, and Implementation." Paper presented at Total Quality Management Satellite Broadcast Series, George Washington University Continuing Engineering Education Program (Washington, D.C., 1993c).

———, "The Cutting Edge of Quality," in *Quality Learning Series,* ed. U.S. Chamber of Commerce (Washington, D.C.: U.S. Chamber of Commerce, 1993d).

———, "Customer Satisfaction, Customer Retention, or Customer Loyalty?" *Proceedings of the 1993 Trustee Series,* ed. The Conference Board (New York: The Conference Board, 1993e).

———, "Quality and the Workforce in the United States," in *Better Quality of Work Life Through Productivity* (Tokyo: Asian Productivity Organization, 1992a).

———, "The Road to TQM: Basic Concepts," in *Top Management and Quality,* ed. H. D. Seghezzi (Munich: Hanser Publishers, 1992b), 46–67.

———, "Robust Design—A New Tool for Health Care Quality," *Quality Management in Health Care* (1992c).

———, "Road Map to Total Quality Management—A Review of Recent Activities Around the World," *Proceedings from the Global Quality Congress on Quality— The Strategy for the 90s* (Singapore: 1992d).

———, "Information Quality—A Key Challenge for the 1990s," in *The Best on Quality: Targets, Improvement, Systems,* vol. 4, ed. H. J. Zeller (Munich: Hanser Publishers, 1991a), 31–48.

———, "Lessons Learned—Quality in the Service Industries," *Proceedings of the Joint Statistical Meetings* (Atlanta, 1991b).

———, "Total Quality Theory and Practice," *Proceedings of the Meeting the Challenge Conference* (Moscow, 1991c).

———, "Training and Education for Companywide Quality Management in the United States," in *Transactions of 6th EOQC European Seminar of the Education and Training Committee* (Paris: European Organization for Quality, 1988).

———, "Training and Education of Engineers for Quality, Productivity, and Reliability. *Proceedings of the International Communications Conference 85* (1985).

Godfrey, A. B., Berwick, D. I., and Roessner, J., "Can Quality Management Really Work in Health Care?" *Quality Progress* (1992), 23–27.

Godfrey, A. B., and Kammerer, E. C., "Service Quality Versus Manufacturing Quality—Five Myths Exploded," in *The International Service Quality Handbook,* ed. AMACOM (New York: AMACOM, in press).

Godfrey, A. B., Phadke, M. S., and Shoemaker, A. S., "The Development and Application of Robust Design Methods—Taguchi's Impact in the United States (in Japanese)," *The Journal of the Japanese Society for Quality, 16*(2) (1986), 33–41.

Holmes J. D., and McClaskey, D. J., "Improving Research Using Total Quality Management," *Proceedings of 1992 Symposium on Management for Quality in Research and Development* (Wilton, Conn.: Juran Institute, 1992).

Holub, A., "The Added Value or the Customer-Provider Partnership," in *Making Total Quality Happen,* research report 937, ed. The Conference Board (New York: The Conference Board, 1990), 60–66.

Hooper, J., "Quality Improvement in Research and Development," *Proceedings of 1990 Symposium on Management for Quality in Research and Development* (Wilton, Conn.: Juran Institute, 1990).

Hudiburg, J. J., *Winning With Quality: The FPL Story* (White Plains, N.Y.: Quality Resources, 1991).

Huh, Y. U., Pautke, R. W., and Redman, T. C., "Data Quality Control," *Proceedings of the International Software Quality Exchange*, 7A-1-7A-27 (Wilton, Conn.: Juran Institute, 1992).

Huh, Y. U., Keller, F. R., Redman, T. C., and Watkins, A. R., "Data Quality," *Information and Software Technology*.

Huizenga, T. P., and Dmytrow, E. D., "Total Quality Management," in *Maynard's Industrial Engineering Handbook*, 4th ed., ed. W. K. Hodson (New York: McGraw-Hill, 1992).

Iau, R., "Information Technology and Information Society: A Misplaced Synergism," in *Better Quality of Work Life Through Productivity* (Tokyo: Asian Productivity Organization, 1992).

Juran, J. I., *Juran on Quality by Design* (New York: Free Press, 1992).

———, "A Look Back—Ten Years of IMPRO," *Proceedings of IMPRO92* (Wilton, Conn.: Juran Institute, 1992).

Juran, J. M., and Godfrey, A. B., "Worker Participation—Developments in the USA," *Proceedings of the International Congress of Quality Control Circles* (Tokyo: 1990a).

———, "Total Quality Management (TQM)—Status in the U.S.," *Proceedings of the Senior Management Conference on TQC* (Tokyo: Japanese Union of Scientists and Engineers, 1990b).

Juran, J. I., and Gryna, F. M., *Quality Planning and Analysis*, 3rd ed. (New York: McGraw-Hill, 1993).

Kacker, R. N., "Taguchi Methods," in *Handbook of Statistical Methods for Engineers and Scientists*, ed. H. M. Wadsworth (New York: McGraw-Hill, 1990).

Kacker, R. N., and Shoemaker, A. C., "Robust Design: A Cost-Effective Method for Improving Manufacturing Processes," *AT&T Technical Journal* 65(2) (1986), 39–50.

Kacker, R. N., and Tsui, K. L., "Interaction Graphs: Graphic Aids for Planning Experiments," *Journal of Quality Technology*, 22 (1990), 1–14.

Kaihatsu, H., "TQC in Japan," in *Making Total Quality Happen*, research report 937, ed. The Conference Board, (New York: The Conference Board, 1990), 7–10.

Kane, E. J., "Linking Quality to the Business Strategy," in *Making Total Quality Happen*, research report 937, ed. The Conference Board (New York: The Conference Board, 1990), 21–29.

Kane, V. E., *Defect Prevention: Use of Simple Statistical Tools* (New York: Marcel Dekker, 1989).

Kano, N., and Koura, K., "Development of Quality Control Seen Through Companies Awarded the Deming Prize," *Reports of Statistical Application Research*, 37(1–2) (Tokyo: Japanese Union of Scientists and Engineers, 1990), 79–105.

Kerwin, K., and Woodruff, D., "Caddy's 295-HP Smoothie," *Business Week* (1993), 69.

Kester, A. Y., ed., *Behind the Numbers—U.S. Trade in the World Economy* (Washington, D.C.: Committee on National Statistics, National Research Council, and National Academy Press, 1992).

Kondo, Y., "The Development of Quality in Japan," in *The Best on Quality: Targets, Improvement, Systems*, vol. 3, ed. H. J. Zeler (Munich: Hanser Publishers, 1990), 41–87.

Leon, R. V., Shoemaker, A. C., and Kacker, R. N., "Performance Measures Independent of Adjustment: An Explanation and Extension of Taguchi's Signal-to-Noise Ratios," *Technometrics* 29 (1987), 253—65.

Massing, W., "Some Aspects of Human Influence on Quality," in *The Best on Quality, Targets, Improvement Systems*, vol. 3, ed. H. J. Zeller (Munich: Hanser Publishers, 1990), 7–16.

McClaskey, D. J., "Using the Baldrige Criteria to Improve Research," *Proceedings of 1992 Symposium on Management for Quality Development* (Wilton, Conn.: Juran Institute, 1992).

Morita, A., Reingold, E. M., and Shimomura, M. S., *Made in Japan* (New York: E. P. Dutton, 1986).

Nussbaum, B., "Hot Products: Smart Design is the Common Thread," *Business Week* (1993), 57.

Pall, G. A., *Quality Process Management* (Englewood Cliffs, N.J.: Prentice Hall, 1987).

Papay, L. J., "Process Quality is *The* Driver of Corporate Competitiveness," in *Making Total Quality Happen*, research report 937, ed. The Conference Board, (New York: The Conference Board, 1990), 30–34.

Peterson, D., "How Donald Peterson Turned Ford Around," interview in *Boardroom Reports* (1992).

Phadke, M. S., *Quality Engineering Using Robust Design* (Englewood Cliffs, N.J.: Prentice Hall, 1989).

———, "Design Optimization Case Studies," *AT&T Technical Journal*, 65 (2) (1986), 51–68.

Phadke, M. S., Kackers, R. N., Speeney, D. V., and Grieco, M. J., "Off-Line Quality Control in Integrated Circuit Fabrication Using Experimental Design," *The Bell System Technical Journal*, 62 (5) (1983), 1273–1309.

Placek, C., "Baldrige Award as Quality Model," *Quality* (1992), 17–20.

Poppa, R. R., "Excellence Through Quality—The Bottom-Line Results of a Quality Program," *Proceedings of IMPRO92* (Wilton, Conn.: Juran Institute, 1992).

Rayner, B., "Trial-by-Fire Transformation: An Interview with Globe Metallurgical's Arden C. Sims," *Harvard Business Review* (1992), 117–29.

Redman, T. C., *Data Quality: Management and Technology* (New York: Bantam Books, 1992).

Reichheld, F. F., and Sasser, W. E., Jr., "Zero Defections: Quality Comes to Services," *Harvard Business Review* (1990), 105–11.

Reimann, C. W., "The First Five Years of the Malcolm Baldrige National Quality Award," *Proceedings of IMPRO92* (Wilton, Conn.: Juran Institute, 1992).

Robson, D., "Total Quality Management in a Research Organization: A Self-Assessment," *Proceedings of 1992 Symposium on Management for Quality in Research and Development* (Wilton, Conn.: Juran Institute, 1992).

Rummler, G. A., and Brache, A. P., *Improving Performance: How to Manage the White Space on the Organization Chart* (San Francisco: Jossey-Bass, 1990).

Schlange, T. G., "Quality Information Systems," *Proceedings of IMPRO91* (Wilton, Conn.: Juran Institute, 1991).

Seitschek, V., "Computer-Aided Quality Information Systems," in *The Best on Quality: Targets, Improvement, Systems*, vol. 4, ed. H. J. Zeller (Munich: Hanser Publishers, 1991), 59–66.

Senge, P. M., *The Fifth Discipline* (New York: Doubleday Currency, 1990).

Shoemaker, A. C., and Kacker, R. N., "A Methodology for Planning Experiments in Robust Product and Process Design," *Quality and Reliability Engineering International*, 4 (2) (1988), 95–103.

Smith, F., "Our License to Practice." Reprint. *Federal Express Corporation Information Book* (Memphis, Tenn.: Federal Express, 1990).

Snee, R. D., "Creating Robust Work Processes," *Quality Progress* 26 (2) (1993), 37–41.

Sprague, P. J., "Information, the Future Engine of Productivity," *Better Quality of Work Life Through Productivity* (Tokyo: Asian Productivity Organization, 1992).

Stalk, G., Jr. and Hout, T. M., *Competing Against Time* (New York: Free Press, 1990).

Starr, M. K., ed., *Global Competitiveness—Getting the U.S. Back on Track* (New York: W. W. Norton & Company, 1988).

Stoner, J. A. F., Werner, F. M., and the Corporate Finance-IBM Study Group, *Remaking Corporate Finance: The New Corporate Finance Emerging in High-Quality Companies*, ed. F. D. Baldwin (New York: Fordham University, Graduate School of Business Administration, 1991).

Sugiura, H., "Productivity in the Work Place: The Honda Story," *International Productivity Congress* (Tokyo: Asian Productivity Organization, 1992).

Taguchi, G., "Quality Engineering in Japan," *Communications in Statistics: Theory and Methods*, 14 (11) (1985), 2785-801.

"Ten Years After: Learning About Total Quality Management—A Study of CEOs and Corporate Quality Officers of the Business Roundtable," (New York: Delta Consulting Group, 1993).

Thurow, L., *Head-to-Head, the Coming Economic Battle Among Japan, Europe, and America* (New York: William Morrow and Company, 1992).

U.S. Congress House Subcommittee on Technology and Competitiveness of the Committee on Science, Space, and Technology, *Hearing on the Malcolm Baldrige National Quality Award*, 102nd. Cong., 2nd sess., 5 February 1992 Hearing, 103-09.

Wachniak, R., "Only the 'Best of the Best' Win U.S. National Quality Award," in *The Best on Quality: Targets, Improvement, Systems*, vol. 3, ed. H. J. Zeller (Munich: Hanser Publishers, 1990), 199-213.

Walton, S., and Huey, J., *Sam Walton: Made in America, My Story* (New York: Doubleday, 1992).

Wedderburn, H., "Product and Process Improvement Using the Taguchi Method of Experimental Design," *Proceedings of the International Conference on Quality Control* (Tokyo: Japanese Union of Scientists and Engineers, 1987).

Wheelwright, S. C., and Clark, K. B., *Revolutionizing Product Development: Quantum Leaps in Speed, Efficiency, and Quality* (New York: Free Press, 1992).

Womack, J. P., Jones, D. T., and Roos, D., *The Machine That Changed The World* (New York: Rawson Associates, 1990).

Zeller, H. J., "Knowledge-Based System for Computer-Aided Quality," in *The Best on Quality: Targets, Improvement, Systems*, vol. 4, ed. H. J. Zeller (Munich: Hanser Publishers, 1991), 49-58.

# 21

# Selected Readings and Resources in Quality

*Jennifer Lehr*

## Associations and Organizations

American Association for Higher Education
One Dupont Circle
Suite 360
Washington, DC 20036-1110
202-293-6440
FAX: 202-293-0073

American Council on Education
1 Dupont Circle
Suite 800
Washington, DC 20036
202-939-9300

American Society for Quality Control (ASQC)
611 E. Wisconsin Avenue
PO Box 3005
Milwaukee, WI 53207-3005
414-272-8575
FAX: 414-272-1734

American Society for Training and Development
PO Box 1443
1640 King Street
Alexandria, VA 22313
703-683-8100
FAX: 703-683-1523

Association for Quality and Participation
801 W 8th Street
Cincinnati, OH 45203-9946
(513)381-1959
FAX: 513-381-0070

Association of American Colleges and Universities
1818 R Street N.W.
Washington, D.C. 20009
202-387-3760
FAX: 202-265-9532

Association for Supervision and Curriculum Development
1250 N. Pitt Street
Alexandria, PA 22314
703-549-9110
FAX: 703-836-7921

National Education Association
1201 16th Street N.W.
Washington, DC 20036
202-833-4000

National Institute of Standards and Technology
US Department of Commerce
Gaithersburg, MD 20899-0001

The Center for Schools of Quality
PO Box 810
Columbia, MD 21044
410-997-7555
FAX: 410-997-2345

## Educational Resources and Consultants

Chart House International
Learning Corporation
221 River Ridge Circle
Burnsville, MN 55337
800-328-3789

Coopers & Lybrand Corp.
2400 Eleven Penn Center
Philadelphia, PA 19103
215-963-8000
FAX: 215-963-8700

Goal/QPC Headquarters
13 Branch Street
Methuen, MA 01844-1953
508-685-3900
FAX: 508-685-6151

Joiner Associates
3800 Regent Street
PO Box 5445
Madison, Wl 53705-0445
800-669-8326

Juran Institute, Inc.
11 River Road
PO Box 811
Wilton, CT 06897-0811
203-834-1700

Noel Levitz Centers, Inc.
Noel Levitz Office Park
2101 ACT Circle
Iowa City, IA 52245
319-337-4700
FAX: 319-337-5274

ODI
25 Mall Road
Burlington, MA 01803
1-800-ODI-INFO
FAX: 617-273-2558

Stat-a-Matrix Institute
2124 Oak Tree Road
Edison, NJ 08820-1059
908-548-0600
FAX: 908-548-0409

Zenger-Miller
1735 Technology Drive
6th Floor
San Jose, CA 95110
408-452-1244
FAX: 408-452-1155

## Periodicals

*The Journal of Quality Technology*
Published by ASQC

*The Journal for Quality and Participation*
Published by Joiner Associates

*Quality Digest*
Published by QCI International

*Quality Engineering*
Co-Published by ASQC and Marcel Dekker, Inc.

*Quality Management Journal*
Published by ASQC

*Quality Progress*
Published by ASQC

*Technometrics*
Co-Published by ASQC and the American Statistical Association

*TQM in Higher Education*
A monthly newsletter published by Magna Publications

## Baldrige and Baldrige-Based Assessments for Higher Education

Malcolm Baldrige National Quality Award
United States Department of Commerce Technology Administration
National Institute of Standards and Technology
Route 270 and Quince Orchard Road
Administration Building, Room A537
Gaithersburg, MD 20899-0001

Tradition of Excellence Higher Education Quality Self-Assessment Program
University Program for Quality and Communication Improvement
Rutgers-The State University of New Jersey
4 Huntington Street
New Brunswick, NJ 08903

## Internet Sources

| DEMING-L | The W. Edward Deming Forum |
| Address: | listserv@uhccvm.uhcc.hawaii.edu |

| QUALITY | TQM in Manufacturing and Service Industries |
| Address: | listserv@pucc.princeton.edu |

| TQM-L | Total Quality Management in Higher Education |
| Address: | listserv@ukanvm.cc.ukans.edu |

| TQMEDU-L | Total Quality Management in Education |
| Address: | listserv@admin.humberc.on.ca |

| TQMLIB | Total Quality Management for Libraries |
| Address: | listserv@cms.cc.wayne.edu |

| CQI-L | Continuous Quality |
| Address: | listserv@mr.net |

| BPR | Business Process Reengineering |
| Address: | mailbase@mailbase.ac.uk |

| GSCQHE | Graduate Student Coalition for Quality in Higher Education |
| Address: | gscqhe@ctrvax.vanderbilt.edu |

## Books

*The Quality Approach*

Barker, J. A. *Future Edge: Discovering the New Paradigms of Success.* New York: William Morrow & Company, 1992.

Ciampa, D. *Total Quality: A User's Guide for Implementation*. Reading, Mass.: Addison-Wesley, 1992.

Costin, H. I., ed. *Readings in Total Quality Management*. Fort Worth, Tex.: Harcourt Brace, 1994.

Crosby, P. B. *Quality is Free*. New York: McGraw-Hill, 1979.

_____. *Quality Without Tears: The Art of Hassle-Free Management*. New York: McGraw-Hill, 1984.

_____. *Running Things*. New York: McGraw-Hill, 1986.

_____. *Let's Talk Quality: 96 Questions You Always Wanted to Ask Phil Crosby*. New York: McGraw-Hill, 1990.

Deming, W. E. *Quality, Productivity, and Competitive Position*. Cambridge, Mass.: MIT Center for Advanced Engineering Study, 1982.

_____. *Out of the Crisis*. Cambridge, Mass.: MIT Center for Advanced Engineering Study, 1988.

Dobyns, L., and Crawford-Mason, C. *Thinking About Quality: Progress, Wisdom, and the Deming Philosophy*. New York: Time Books, 1994.

Drummond, H. *The Quality Movement: What Total Quality Management is Really all About!* East Brunswick, N.J.: Nichols Publishing, 1992.

Feigenbaum, A. V. *Total Quality Control*. New York: McGraw-Hill, 1983.

Gabor, A. *The Man Who Discovered Quality*. New York: Random House, 1990.

Gitlow, H. S., and Gitlow, S. J. *The Deming Guide to Productivity and Competitive Position*. Englewood Cliffs, N.J.: Prentice Hall, 1987.

Goetsch, D., and Davis, S. *Introduction to Total Quality*. New York: Macmillan, 1994.

Hosotani, K. *Japanese Quality Concepts: An Overview*. White Plains, N.Y.: Quality Resources, 1992.

Imai, M. *Kaizen: The Key to Japan's Competitive Success*. Cambridge, Mass.: Productivity Press, 1986.

Jablonski, J. R. *Implementing Total Quality Management: An Overview*. San Diego, Calif.: Pfeiffer and Company, 1991.

Juran, J. M. *Quality Planning and Analysis*. New York: McGraw-Hill, 1980.

_____. *Juran on Planning for Quality*. Cambridge, Mass.: Productivity Press, 1988a.

_____. *Quality Control Handbook* (4th ed.). New York: McGraw-Hill, 1988b.

_____. *Juran on Leadership for Quality: An Executive Handbook*. New York: The Free Press, 1989.

Main, J. *Quality Wars*. New York: The Free Press, 1994.

McClosky, L., and Collett, D. *TQM: A Basic Text*. Methen, Mass.: GOAL/QPC, 1993.

Peck, S. M. *A World Waiting to be Born: Civility Rediscovered*. New York: Bantam Books, 1993.

Riley, P. *The Winner Within: A Life Plan for Team Players*. New York: G. P. Putnam's Sons, 1993.

Roberts, H. V., and Sergesketter, B. F. *Quality is Personal: A Foundation for Total Quality Management*. New York: The Free Press, 1993.

Ross, J. E. *Total Quality Management: Text, Cases, and Readings*. Delray Beach, Fla.: St. Lucie Press, 1993.

Senge, P. M. *The Fifth Discipline: The Art and Practice of the Learning Organization*. New York: Doubleday Currency, 1990.

Shiba, S., Graham, A., and Walden, D. *A New American TQM: Four Practical Revolutions in Management*. Cambridge, Mass.: Productivity Press, 1993.

Walton, M. *The Deming Management Method*. New York: Putnam, 1986.

*The Quality Approach in Business, Health Care, and Government*

Albrecht, K. *At America's Service: How Corporations can Revolutionize the way They Treat Their Customers.* Homewood, Ill.: Dow Jones-Irwin, 1988.

Albrecht, K., and Zemke, R. *Service America! Doing Business in the New Economy.* Homewood, Ill: Dow Jones-Irwin, 1985.

Arnold, W. W., and Plas, J. M. *The Human Touch: Today's Most Unusual Program for Productivity and Profit.* New York: John Wiley & Sons, Inc., 1993

Berry, L. L., and Parasurman, A. *Marketing Services: Competing Through Quality.* New York: The Free Press, 1991.

Berry, T. H. *Managing the Total Quality Transformation.* New York: McGraw-Hill, 1991.

Berwick, D. M., Godfrey, A. B., and Roessner, J. *Curing Health Care: New Strategies for Quality Improvement.* San Francisco: Jossey-Bass, 1990.

Blanchard, K., and Bowles, S. *Raving Fans: A Revolutionary Approach to Customer Service.* New York: William Morrow and Company, Inc., 1993.

Block, P. *Stewardship: Choosing Service over Self-Interest.* New York: William Morrow & Company, 1992.

Camp, R. C. *Benchmarking: The Search for Industry Best Practices that Lead to Superior Performance.* Milwaukee, Wis.: ASQC Quality Press, 1989.

Carr, D. K., and Littman, I. D. *Excellence in Government: Total Quality Management in the 1990s.* Arlington, Va.: Coopers & Lybrand, 1990.

Carr, D. K., Dougherty, K. S., Johansson, H. J., King, R. A., and Moran, D. M. *Break Point: Business Process Redesign.* Arlington, Va.: Coopers & Lybrand, 1992.

Chang, Y. S., Labovitz, G., and Rosansky, V. *Making Quality Work: A Leadership Guide for the Results-Driven Manager.* New York: Harper Business, 1993.

Clancy, K. J., and Shulman, R. S. *The Marketing Revolution: A Radical Manifesto for Dominating the Marketplace.* New York: Harper Business, 1991.

Connellan, T. K., and Zemke, R. *Sustaining Knock Your Socks off Service.* New York: American Management Association, 1993.

Davenport, T. H. *Process Innovation: Reengineering Work Through Information Technology.* Boston: Harvard Business School Press, 1993.

Garvin, D. A. *Managing Quality: The Strategic and Competitive Advantage.* New York: The Free Press, 1988.

Gerteis, M., Edgman-Levitan, S., Daley, J., and Delbanco, T. L. *Through the Patient's Eyes: Understanding and Promoting Patient-Centered Care.* San Francisco: Jossey-Bass, 1993.

Guinta, L. R., and Praizler, N. C. *The QFD Book: The Team Approach to Solving Problems and Satisfying Customers through Quality Function Deployment.* Portland, Oreg.: Productivity Press, 1993.

Hammer, M., and Champy, J. *Reengineering the Corporation: A Manifesto for Business Revolution.* New York: Harper Business, 1993.

Harrington, H. J. *Business Process Improvement: The Breakthrough Strategy for Total Quality, Productivity, and Competitiveness.* New York: McGraw-Hill Inc., 1991.

Hiam, A. *Closing the Quality Gap: Lessons from America's Leading Companies.* Englewood Cliffs: Prentice-Hall, 1992.

Hunt, V. D. *Quality Management for Government.* Milwaukee, Wis.: ASQC, Quality Press, 1993.

Johnson, R. S. *TQM: Management Processes for Quality Operations.* Milwaukee, Wis.: ASQC Quality Press, 1993.

Lathrop, J. P. *Restructuring Health Care: The Patient Focused Paradigm.* San Francisco: Jossey-Bass, 1993.

Lawler, E. E. I., Mohrman, S. A., and Ledford, G. E. J. *Employee Involvement and Total Quality Management: Practices and Results in Fortune 1000 Companies.* San Francisco: Jossey-Bass, 1992.

Lovelock, C. H. *Services Marketing: Text, Cases, and Readings.* Englewood Cliffs, N.J.: Prentice-Hall, 1984.

Marszalek-Gaucher, E., and Coffey, R. J. *Transforming Healthcare Organizations: How to Achieve and Sustain Organizational Excellence.* San Francisco: Jossey-Bass, 1990.

Miller, L. M. *Design for Total Quality: A Workbook for Socio-Technical Design.* Atlanta, Ga.: The Miller Consulting Group, Inc., 1991.

Nadler, D. A., Gerstein, M. S., Shaw, R. B., and Associates. *Organizational Architecture: Designs for Changing Organizations.* San Francisco: Jossey-Bass, 1992.

Nadler, G., and Hibino, S. *Breakthrough Thinking: Why We Must Change the Way We Solve Problems, and the Seven Principles to Achieve This.* Rocklin, Calif.: Prima Publishing, 1990.

Persico, J., Jr. *The TQM Transformation: A Model for Organizational Change.* White Plains, N.Y.: Quality Resources, 1992.

Peters, T., and Austin, N. *A Passion for Excellence: The Leadership Difference* (2nd ed.). New York: Warner Books, 1985.

Phillips, D. T. *Lincoln on Leadership: Executive Strategies for Tough Times.* New York: Warner Books, 1992.

Rummler, G. A., and Brache, A. P. *Improving Performance: How to Manage the White Space on the Organization Chart.* San Francisco: Jossey-Bass, 1990.

Russell, J. P. *The Quality Master Plan: A Quality Strategy for Business Leadership.* Milwaukee, Wis.: ASQC Quality Press, 1990.

Ryan, K. D., and Oeetreich, D. K. *Driving Fear out of the Workplace: How to Overcome the Invisible Barriers to Quality, Productivity, and Innovation.* San Francisco: Jossey-Bass, 1991.

Sashkin, M., and Kiser, K. J. *Putting Total Quality Management to Work: What TQM Means, How to Use It, and How to Sustain It over the Long Run.* San Francisco: Berrett-Koehler Publishers, 1993.

Scholtes, P. R. *The Team Handbook: How to use Teams to Improve Quality.* Madison, Wis.: Joiner Associates Inc., 1988.

Spechler, J. W. *Managing Quality in America's Most Admired Companies.* San Francisco: Berrett-Koehler Publishers, 1993.

Tomasko, R. M. *Rethinking the Corporation: The Architecture of Change.* New York: American Management Association, 1993.

Whitely, R. C. *The Customer Driven Company: Moving from Talk to Action.* New York: Addison-Wesley Publishing Company, 1991.

Zeithaml, V. A., Parasurman, A., and Berry, L. L. *Delivering Quality Service: Balancing Customer Perceptions and Expectations.* New York: The Free Press, 1990.

Zuckerman, M. R., and Hatala, L. J. *Incredibly American.* Milwaukee, Wis.: ASQC Quality Press, 1992.

## The Quality Approach in Education

Anderson, M. *Impostors in the Temple: American Intellectuals are Destroying our Universities and Cheating our Students of their Future.* New York: Simon & Schuster, 1992.

Angelo, T. A., and Cross, K. P. *Classroom Assessment Techniques* (2nd ed.). San Francisco: Jossey-Bass, 1993.

Astin, A. W. *Assessment for Excellence: The Philosophy and Practice of Assessment and Evaluation in Higher Education.* New York: Macmillan, 1991.

Astin, A. W. *What Matters in College?: Four Critical Years Revisited.* San Francisco: Jossey-Bass, 1993.

Banta, T. W., and Associates. *Making a Difference: Outcomes of a Decade of Assessment in Higher Education.* San Francisco: Jossey-Bass, 1993.

Barnett, R. *Improving Higher Education: Total Quality Care.* Bristol, Conn.: Open University Press, 1993.

Cornesky, R. *Using Deming to Improve Quality in Colleges and Universities.* Madison, Wis.: Magna, 1990.

_____. *The Quality Professor: Implementing TQM in the Classroom.* Madison, Wis.: Magna, 1993.

Cornesky, R., and McCool, S. *Total Quality Improvement Guide for Institutions of Higher Education.* Madison, Wis.: Magna, 1992.

Costin, H. I., ed. *Readings in Total Quality Management.* Fort Worth, Tex.: Harcourt Brace, 1994.

Fields, J. C. *Total Quality for Schools.* Milwaukee, Wis.: ASQC Quality Press, 1993.

Gourman, J. *The Gourman Report: A Rating of Graduate and Professional Programs in America and International Universities.* Los Angeles: National Educational Standards, 1987a.

_____. *The Gourman Report: A Rating of Undergraduate Programs in American and International Universities.* Los Angeles: National Educational Standards, 1987b.

Harris, J., and Baggett, M., eds. *Quality Quest in the Academic Process.* Methuen, Mass.: GOAL/QPC., 1992

Jordan, T. E. *Measurement and Evaluation in Higher Education: Issues and Illustrations.* London: Falmer Press, 1989.

Kerr, C., Gade, M. L., and Kawaoka, M. *Troubled Times for American Higher Education: The 1990s and Beyond.* Albany, N.Y.: SUNY Press, 1993.

Lewis, R. G., and Smith, D. H. *Total Quality in Higher Education.* Delray Beach, Fla.: St. Lucie Press, 1994.

Mayhew, L. B., Ford, P. J., and Hubbard, D. L. *The Quest for Quality.* San Francisco: Jossey Bass Publishers, 1990.

McCormick, B. L. *Quality and Education: Critical Linkages.* Eye on Education, Inc., 1993.

Meister, J. C. *Corporate Quality Universities: Lessons in Building a World-Class Work Force.* New York: Irwin Professional Publishing, 1994.

Miller, R. I. *Applying the Deming Method to Higher Education.* Washington, D.C.: College and University Personnel Association, 1991.

Rinehart, G. *Quality Education.* Milwaukee, Wis.: ASQC Quality Press, 1993.

Seymour, D. T. *On Q: Causing Quality in Higher Education.* Phoenix, Ariz.: Oryx Press, 1992.

_____. *Total Quality Management in Higher Education: Clearing the Hurdles.* Methuen, Mass.: GOAL/QPC, 1993.

Sherr, L. A., and Teeter, D. J. *Total Quality Management in Higher Education.* San Francisco: Jossey-Bass, 1991.

Teeter, D., and Lozier, G. G. *Pursuit of Quality in Higher Education: Case Studies in Total Quality Management.* San Francisco: Jossey-Bass, 1993.

Tuckman, B. W., and Johnson, F. C. *Effective College Management: The Outcome Approach.* New York: Praeger, 1989.

Weinstein, L. A. *Moving a Battleship with Your Bare Hands: Governing a University System.* Madison, Wis.: Magna Publications, 1993.

Wilshire, B. *The Moral Collapse of the University: Professionalism, Purity, and Alienation.* Albany: State University of New York Press, 1990.

Wingspread Group on Higher Education. *An American Imperative: Higher Expectations for Higher Education*. Racine, Wis.: The Johnson Foundation, 1993.

## *Quality Strategies and Tools for Assessment and Planning*

Angelo, T. A., and Cross, K. P. *Classroom Assessment Techniques* (2nd ed.). San Francisco: Jossey-Bass, 1993.

Astin, A. W. *Assessment for Excellence: The Philosophy and Practice of Assessment and Evaluation in Higher Education*. New York: Macmillan, 1991.

Banta, T. W., and Associates. *Making a Difference: Outcomes of a Decade of Assessment in Higher Education*. San Francisco: Jossey-Bass, 1993.

Bogan, C. E., and English, M. J. *Benchmarking for Best Practices: Winning through Innovative Adaptation*. New York: McGraw Hill, 1994.

Brown, M. G. *Baldrige Award Winning Quality: How to Interpret the Malcolm Baldrige Award Criteria* (3rd ed.). White Plains, N.Y.: Quality Resources, 1993.

Camp, R. C. *Benchmarking: The Search for Industry best Practices that Lead to Superior Performance*. Milwaukee, Wis.: ASQC Quality Press, 1989.

George, S. *The Baldrige Quality System: The Do-it-Yourself way to Transform your Business*. New York: John Wiley & Sons, Inc., 1992.

Gitlow, H., Gitlow, S., Oppenheim, A., and Oppenheim, R. *Tools and Methods for the Improvement of Quality*. Boston: Irwin, 1989.

Johansson, H. J., McHugh, P., and Pendlebury, A. J., Wheeler III, W. *Business Process Reengineering: Breakpoint Strategies for Market Dominance*. West Sussex: John Wiley & Sons, 1993.

Jordan, T. E. *Measurement and Evaluation in Higher Education: Issues and Illustrations*. London: Falmer Press, 1989.

King, B. *Hoshin Planning: The Developmental Approach*. Methuen, Mass.: GOAL/QPC, 1989.

Lynch, R. L., and Cross, K. F. *Measure Up! Yardstocks for Continuous Improvement*. Cambridge: Blackwell Publishers, 1991.

Mahoney, F. X., and Thor, C. G. *TQM Trilogy: Using ISO9000, the Deming Prize, and the Baldrige Award to Establish a System for Total Quality Management*. New York: AMA, 1994.

Marconi, J. *The Malcolm Baldrige National Quality Award Self-Assessment Workbook*. Methuen, Mass.: GOAL/QPC, 1993.

Miller, L. M. *Design for Total Quality: A Workbook for Socio-Technical Design*. Atlanta: The Miller Consulting Group, Inc., 1991.

Mintzberg, H. *Structure in Fives: Designing Effective Organizations*. Englewood Cliffs, N.J.: Prentice-Hall, 1983.

Nadler, D. A., Gerstein, M. S., Shaw, R. B., and Associates. *Organizational Architecture: Designs for Changing Organizations*. San Francisco: Jossey-Bass, 1992.

Ruben, B. D. *Tradition of Excellence: Higher Education Quality Self-Assessment Program*. New Brunswick, N.J.: Rutgers University Program for Quality and Communication Improvement, 1995.

## Book Chapters, Articles, Papers, and Reports

### *The Quality Approach*

Boje, D. M., & Winsor, R. D. "The Resurrection of Taylorism: Total Quality Management's Hidden Agenda." *Journal of Organizational Change Management* 4 (1993): 58–71.

Deming, W. E. "The Need for Change." *Journal for Quality and Participation* (March 1988):48-49.

Dusharme, D. "W. Edwards Deming Remembered." *Quality Digest* 14(1) (1994): 7.

Fairhurst, G. T. "Echoes of the Vision: When the Rest of the Organizational Talks Total Quality." *Management Communication Quarterly* (1993): 331-71.

Fairhurst, G. T. & Wendt, R. F. "The Gap in Total Quality: A Commentary." *Management Communication Quarterly* (1993): 441-51.

Fuchs, E. "Total Quality Management from the Future: Practices and Paradigms." *Quality Management Journal* 1(1) (1993): 26-34.

Garvin, D. "How the Baldrige Award Really Works." *Harvard Business Review* 69(6) (1991): 80-95.

Godfrey, A. B. "Ten Areas for Future Research in Total Quality Management." *Quality Management Journal* 1(1) (1993): 47-70.

Hiam, A. "Does Quality Work? A Review of Relevant Studies (No. 1043)." The Conference Board (1993).

Jones, D. "Concentration on Quality Spreading Wide." *USA Today* (1993).

Juran, J. M. "Strategies for World Class Quality." *Quality Progress* 24 (March 1991): 81-85.

_____. "World War II and the Quality Movement." *Quality Progress* 24(12) (1991): 19-24.

Lamoglia, J. "Top Ten Lessons of Quality Improvement." *Human Resources News* (1992): A16.

Parasuraman, A., Zeithamel, V. A., & Berry, L. L. "A Conceptual Model of Service Quality and its Implications for Future Research (Report No. 84-106)." Marketing Science Institute (1984).

Petelin, G. "Quality: A Higher Level of Mediocrity?" *Australian Journal of Communication* 19(2) (1992): 140-52.

Pettegrew, L. S. "The Dark Side of Quality: A Critique of the Quality Movement in America." Paper presented to the Business faculty, Queensland University of Technology, Brisbane (September 1992).

Rogers, C. C., & Roethlisberger, F. J. "Barriers and Gateways to Communication." *Harvard Business Review* (1991): 106-11.

Steingard, D. S. & Fitzgibbons, D. E. "A Postmodern Deconstruction of Total Quality Management (TQM)." *Journal of Organizational Change Management* 6(4) (1993): 72-87.

Steingraber, F. G. "Total Quality Management: A New Look at a Basic Issue." Delivered to the Institutional Investor CEO Roundtable, Naples, Fla. (1990).

Zemke, R. "TQM: Fatally Flawed or Simply Unfocused?" *Training* (1992): 8.

_____. "A Bluffer's Guide to TQM." *Training* (1993): 48-55.

## The Quality Approach in Business, Health Care, and Government

Adams, J. N. "Quality Improvement Through Teamwork in Colorado." *Public Productivity & Management Review* 15(2) (1991): 237-40.

Barrier, M. "Small Firms Put Quality First." *Nation's Business* (May 1992): 22-32.

Barron, C. A. "Getting Serious About Service." *The New York Times Magazine* (11 June 1989): 23, 50, 52.

Beck, M. W. "The Samurai or the Cowboy?" *NACUBO Business Officer* (1994): 27-35.

Bell, H. W., & Hanseman, N. J. "Alphabet Soup of Management Tools: Cincinnati's ASEP Process Resembles TQM, CQI, and QPS." *NACUBO Business Officer* 27(7) (1994): 36-39.

Bleakley, F. R. "The Best Laid Plans: Many Companies Try Management Fads, Only to See Them Flop." *The Wall Street Journal* (6 July 1993): A1, A6.

Brown, M. B. "Defining Quality in Service Businesses." *Quality Digest* (April 1988): 8-14.

Byrne, J. A. "Do Quality Gurus Live up to Their Name? Well, Yes and No." *Business Week* (1991): 52-57.

_____. "Management's New Gurus." *Business Week* (31 August 1992): 44-52.

_____. "The Horizontal Corporation." *Business Week* (20 December 1993): 76-81.

Carey, J., Neff, R., & Therrien, L. "The Prize and the Passion." *Business Week* (1991): 58-59.

DeCarlo, N. J., & Sterett, W. K. "History of the Malcolm Baldrige National Quality Award." *Quality Progress* 23(3) (1990): 21-27.

Drucker, P. F. "The Emerging Theory of Manufacturing." *Harvard Business Review* 68 (1990): 40-48.

_____. "The New Productivity Challenge." *Harvard Business Review* 69 (1991): 69-79.

_____. "A Turnaround Primer." *The Wall Street Journal* (2 February 1993).

Ettore, B. "Benchmarking: The Next Generation." *Management Review* 82(6) (1993): 10-16.

Fisk, R. P., Brown, S. W., & Bitner, M. J. "Tracking the Evolution of the Services Marketing Literature." *Journal of Retailing* 69(1) (1993): 61-103.

Fuchsberg, G. "Management: Quality Programs Show Shoddy Results." *The Wall Street Journal* (14 May 1992).

_____. "'Total Quality' is Termed Only a Partial Success." *The Wall Street Journal* (1 October 1992): B1, B7.

_____. "Baldrige Awards May be Losing Some Luster." *Wall Street Journal* (1993): B1 and B5.

Garvin, D. A. "Quality on the Line." *Harvard Business Review* 61(5) (1983): 65-75.

_____. "Quality Problems, Policies, and Attitudes in the United States and Japan: An Exploratory Study." *Academy of Management Journal* 29 (1986): 653-73.

_____. "Competing on the Eight Dimensions of Quality." *Harvard Business Review* 65 (1987): 101-09.

_____. "How the Baldrige Award Really Works." *Harvard Business Review* 69(6) (1991): 80-95.

Gulden, G. K., & Reck, R. H. "Combining Quality and Reengineering for Operational Superiority." *Perspectives on the Management of Information Technology* 8(1) (1991): 1-12.

Hall, G., Rosenthal, J., & Wade, J. "How to Make Reengineering Really Work." *Harvard Business Review* 71 (1993): 119-31.

Hammer, M. "Reengineering Work: Don't Automate, Obliterate." *Harvard Business Review* (1990): 68(4), 104-12.

Hammonds, K. H. "Where Did They go Wrong? Why Some Quality Programs Never get off the Ground." *Business Week* (1991): 34-38.

Harari, O. "Ten Reasons Why TQM Can't Work." *Management Review* 82(1) (1993a): 33-38.

_____. "The Lab Test: A Tale of Quality." *Management Review* 82(2) (1993b): 55-58.

_____. "Think Strategy when you Think Quality." *Management Review* 82(3) (1993c); 58-60.

_____. "Three Very Difficult Steps to Total Quality." *Management Review* 82(4) (1993d): 39-43.

_____. "The Eleventh Reason Why TQM Doesn't Work." *Management Review* 82(5) (1993e): 31-36.

Healy, J. R. "Winner: It's All in the Chemistry." *USA Today* (2 April 1993).

Jacob, R. "TQM: More than a Dying Fad? *Fortune* (18 October 1993): 66-72.

Kordupleski, R. E., Rust, R. T., & Zahorik, A. J. "Why Improving Quality Doesn't Improve Quality (or Whatever Happened to Marketing?)." *California Management Review* (1993).

Krantz, K. T. "How Velcro got Hooked on Quality." *Harvard Business Review* 67 (1989): 60-64.

Leonard, F. S., & Sasser, W. E. "The Incline of Quality." *Harvard Business Review* 60(5) (1982): 163-71.

Ludeman, K. "Using Employee Surveys to Revitalize TQM." *Training* (1992): 51.

Mathews, J., & Katel, P. "The Cost of Quality." *Newsweek* (7 September 1992): 48-49.

McKenna, J. F. "TQ Government." *Industry Week* (4 November 1991): 13-19.

Niven, D. "When Times get Tough, What Happens to TQM?" *Harvard Business Review* 71 (1993): 2-11.

O'Neil, R. M., Harwood, R. L., & Osif, B. A. "A Total Look at Total Quality Management: A TQM Perspective from the Literature of Business, Industry, Education, and Librarianship." *Library Administration & Management* 7(4) (1993): 244-54.

Peters, T. J. "Common Courtesy: The Ultimate Barrier to Entry (Part I)." *Hospital Forum*, 10-16.

————. "Common Courtesy: The Ultimate Barrier to Entry (Part I)." *Hospital Forum*, 51-56.

"The Promise of Reengineering." *Fortune* (3 May 1993): 94-97.

Rayner, B. "Trial-by-Fire Transformation: An Interview with Globe Metallurgical's Arden C. Sims." *Harvard Business Review* 70 (1992): 13-25.

Saracevic, T. "Quality in Information Banks." *Quality in the Services Provided by the Intermediary Specialist.* Guadalajara, 1993.

Schroeder, D. M. & Robinson, A. G. "America's Most Successful Export to Japan: Continuous Improvement Programs." *Sloan Management Review* 32(3) (1991): 67-79.

Sensenbrenner, J. "Quality Comes to City Hall." *Harvard Business Review* 69 (March/April 1991): 64-75.

Shapiro, B. P., Rangan, V. K., & Sviokla, J. J. "Staple Yourself to an Order." *Harvard Business Review* 70 (1992): 113-22.

Sinioris, M. E. "TQM: The New Frontier for Quality and Productivity Improvement in Health Care." *Journal of Quality Assurance* (September/October 1990): 14-17.

Sisco, R. "What to Teach Team Leaders." *Training* (1993): 62-67.

Stewart, T. A. "Reengineering: The Hot New Managing Tool." *Fortune* (23 August 1993): 41-48.

Taguchi, G., & Clausing, D. "Robust Quality." *Harvard Business Review* 68 (1990): 49-59.

Taylor, P. W. "Working with Quality at the New York State Department of Transportation." *Public Productivity & Management Review* 15(2) (1991): 205-12.

Total Quality Forum V. "A Report of Proceedings of the Total Quality Forum V: Rise to the Challenge: Best Practices and Leadership." Schaumberg, Ill.: Motorola University, 1993.

Troy, K. L. "Quality Training: What Top Companies Have Learned (No. 959)." *The Conference Board,* 1991.

Zeithamel, V., A., Berry, L. L., & Parasuraman, A. "Communication and Control Processes in the Delivery of Service Quality." *Journal of Marketing* 52 (1988): 35-48.

## The Quality Approach in Education

Assar, K. E. "Case Study Number Two: Phoenix: Quantum Quality at Maricopa." *Change* 25(3) (1993): 32-35.

Axland, S. "Looking for a Quality Education?" *Quality Progress* 24(10) (1991): 61-72.

Banta, T. W., Phillipi, R. H., Pike, G. R., & Stuhl, J. H. "Applying Deming's Quality Improvement Strategies to Assessment in Higher Education." Final Report. Knoxville: University of Tennessee, Knoxville, Center for Assessment Research Development, 1992.

Bernowski, K. "Restoring the Pillars of Higher Education." *Quality Progress* (1991): 37-42.

Blumenstyk, G. "Colleges Look to 'Benchmarking' to Measure How Efficient and Productive They Are." *The Chronicle of Higher Education* 14 (1993): A41-A42.

Boyer, E. L. "Creating the New American College." *The Chronicle of Higher Education* 15(27) (1994): A48.

Brigham, S. E. "TQM: Lessons We Can Learn from Industry." *Change* 25(3) (1993): 42-48.

Carothers, R. L. "Trippingly on the Tongue: Translating Quality for the Academy." *AAHE Bulletin* 45(3) (1992): 6-10.

Chaffee, E. E., & Seymour, D. "Quality Improvement with Trustee Commitment." *AGB Reports* (1991): 14-18.

Chickering, A. W., & Potter, D. "TQM and Quality Education: Fast Food or Fitness Center?" *Educational Record* (1993): 36-36.

Coate, L. E. "TQM on Campus: Implementing Total Quality Management in a University Setting." *NACUBO Business Officer* (1990): 26-35.

Concord, C. S. "Why Total Quality Management (TQM) has Already 'Failed' in American Higher Education." Paper Presented at the Society for College and University Planning 28th Annual Meeting, Boston, Mass., 1993.

Cotter, M., & Seymour, D. "Kidgets." *Quality Digest* 27 (September 1993).

Crump, W. D. "About Those Quality Control Programs." *Planning for Higher Education* 22(1) (1993): 36-39.

Cyert, R. M. "Universities and U.S. Competitiveness." In *Proceedings from the Second Annual Symposium on the Role of Academia in National Competitiveness and Total Quality Management,* edited by William J. Petak, pp. 13-16. Los Angeles: University of Southern California.

_____. "Universities Competitiveness, and TQM: A Plan of Action for the Year 2000." *Public Administration Quarterly* 17(1) (1993): 10-18.

Deutsch, C. H. "Corporate Lessons in Campus Quality." *New York Times* (4 August 1991).

Dixon, T. C., & Gardiner, R. B. "Quality Management in Higher Education." *Australian Journal of Communication* 19(1) (1992): 107-29.

Elliot, R. "Employers Demand Improved Quality in Education for Business." In *Proceedings from the Second Annual Symposium on the Role of Academia in National Competitiveness and Total Quality Management,* edited by William J. Petak, pp. (133-37). Los Angeles: University of Southern California.

Entin, D. H. "Case Study Number One: Boston: Less than Meets the Eye." *Change* 25(3) (1993): 28-31.

Ewell, P. T. "Total Quality & Academic Practice: The Idea We've Been Waiting For?" *Change* 25(3) (1993): 49-55.

Fisher, J. L. "TQM: A Warning for Higher Education." *Educational Record* 74(2) (1993): 15-19.

Froiland, P. "TQM Invades Business Schools." *Training* 30(7) (1993): 52-56.

Fuchsberg, G. "Baldrige Awards to Add Schools and Hospitals." *The Wall Street Journal* (24 November 1993).

Gales, R. "Can Colleges be Reengineered?" *Across the Board* (1994): 16-22.

Gartner, W. "Dr. Deming Comes to Class." *Journal of Management Education* 17(2) (1993): 143-58.

Giametti, A. B. "Leadership and Standards in American Universities." *Society* 27(6) (1990): 41-44.

Godbey, G. "Beyond TQM: Competition and Cooperation Create the Agile Institution." *Educational Record* (1993): 37-42.

Hansen, W. L. "Bringing Total Quality Improvement into the College Classroom (No. 97)." University of Wisconsin, 1993.

Hemingson, D., & Behrens, K. "How to Reengineer the Administrative Process." *Management Issues* (1993): 1,7,12.

Henderson, R. L. "An Analysis of the State of TQM in Academia." *Report No. ADA,* Monterey, Calif.: Naval Postgraduate School (1991): 246-966.

Higgins, R. C., Jenkins, D. L., & Lewis, R. P. "Total Quality Management in the Classroom: Listen to Your Customers." *Engineering Education* (1991): 12-14.

Horine, J. E., Hailey, W. A., & Rubach, L. "Shaping America's Future: Total Quality Management in Higher Education." *Quality Progress* 26(10) (1993): 41-62.

Ivancevich, R. L., & Ivancevich, S. H. "TQM in the Classroom." *Management Accounting* 74(4) (1992): 14-15.

Keller, G. "Increasing Quality on Campus." *Change* (1992): 48-51.

"The Lattice and the Ratchet." *Policy Perspectives* 2(4) (1990). A publication of the Pew Higher Education Roundtable, University of Pennsylvania, Philadelphia, Pa.

Mangan, K. S. "TQM: Colleges Embrace the Concept of 'Total Quality Management.'" *Chronicle of Higher Education* 13 (1992): A25-A26.

Marchese, T. "TQM Reaches the Academy." *MHE Bulletin* 44(3) (1991): 3-9.

_____. "TQM at Penn: A Report on First Experiences." *AAHE Bulletin* 45(3) (1992): 3-5.

_____. "TQM: A Time for Ideas." *Change* 25(3) (1993): 10-13.

Masters, R. J., & Leiker, L. "Total Quality Management in Higher Education: Applying Deming's Fourteen Points." *CUPA Journal* (1992): 27-31.

Melan, E. H. "Quality Improvement in Higher Education: TQM in Administrative Functions." *CUPA Journal* (1993): 7-18.

Melissaratos, A., & Arendt, C. "TQM Can Address Higher Ed's Ills." *NACUBO Business Officer* (1992): 32-35.

Milbank, D. "Academe Gets Lessons from Big Business." *The Wall Street Journal* (15 December 1992).

Mingle, J. R. "The Political Meaning of Quality." *AAHE Bulletin* 42 (May 1989): 8-11.

Mullin, R., Wilson, G., & Grelle, M. "TQM: Revolution or Just Another Fad?" In *Commissioned Paper for American Association for Higher Education "Double Feature Conference,"* Chicago, Ill., 1993.

Nagy, J., Cotter, M., Erdman, P., Koch, B., Ramer, S., Roberts, N., & Wiley, J. "Case Study Number Three: Madison: How TQM Helped Change an Admission Process." *Change* 25(3) (1993): 36-40.

Neel, C. W., & Snyder, W. T. "Building Responsive Universities: Some Challenges to Academic Leadership." In *Competing Globally Through Customer Value,* edited by M. J. Stahl & G. M. Bounds, pp. 67-72. Conn.: Quorum, 1991.

Olian, J. D. "Everybody's Enamored with Total Quality: Will Academia be Smitten?" *Synthesis: Law and Policy in Higher Education* 3(3) (1991): 184-89.

O'Neil, R. M., Harwood, R. L., & Osif, B. A. "A Total Look at Total Quality Management: A TQM Perspective from the Literature of Business, Industry, Education, and Librarianship." *Library Administration & Management* 7(4) (1993): 244-54.

Oppenheim, R. "Quality in the Classroom, Part 1: Quality and the Extended Process." *TA News* 1(1) (1992a): 1-2.

_____. "Quality in the Classroom, Part II: Who Owns the Problem." *TA News* 1(2) (1992b): 1-2.

Paton, S. M. "TQM Thrives at Babson College." *Quality Digest* 13(9) (1993): 32–43.

Peterson, M. W., & Cameron, K. S. "Total Quality Management in Higher Education: From Assessment to Improvement." Unpublished bibliography, 1993.

Reese, L. D., & Parmenter, V. F. "Improving Quality and Efficiency: A Case Study from the University of Florida." *NACUBO Business Officer* 27(7) (1994): 41–44.

Robinson, J. D. I., Akers, J. F., Atrzt, E. L., Poling, H. A., Galvin, R. W., & Allaire, P. A. "An Open Letter: TQM on the Campus." *Harvard Business Review* 69(6) (1991): 94–95.

Ross, J., & Ross, J. "Into Africa." *TQM Magazine* 3(4) (1993): 49–53.

Rubach, L., & Stratton, B. "Teaming up to Improve U.S. Education." *Quality Progress* (1994): 65–68.

Ruben, B. D. "What Undergraduate Students Remember: Thoughts on Teaching, Learning and Interpersonal Communication." *T & L Newsletter* (Spring 1993): 1.

Rush, S. C. "Productivity or Quality: In Search of Higher Education's Yellow Brick Road." *NACUBO Business Officer* (1992): 36–42.

Schargel, F. P. "Promoting Quality in Education." *Vocational Education Journal* (1991): 34–35.

––––––. "Total Quality Education in Brooklyn." *Quality Digest* 13(9) (1993): 48–53.

Seymour, D. T. "TQM on Campus: What the Pioneers are Finding." *AAHE Bulletin* 44 (November 1991): 10–18.

––––––. "TQM: Focus on Performance, Not Resources." *Educational Record* (1993a): 6–14.

––––––. "Quality on Campus: Three Institutions, Three Beginnings." *Change* 25(3) (1993b): 14–27.

––––––. & Collett, C. "Total Quality Management in Higher Education: A Critical Assessment." (Appl. Rep. No. 91-01) Methuen, Mass., GOAUQPC, 1991.

Shafer, B., S, & Coate, L. E. "Benchmarking in Higher Education: A Tool for Improving Quality and Reducing Cost." *NACUBO Business Officer* (1992): 28–35.

Total Quality Forum V. "A Report of Proceedings of the Total Quality Forum V: Rise to the Challenge: Best Practices and Leadership." Schaumberg, Ill.: Motorola University, 1993.

Wendt, R. "Learning to 'Walk the Talk': A Critical Tale of the Micropolitics at a Total Quality University." *Management Communication Quarterly* 8(1) (1994): 1–45.

*Quality Strategies and Tools for Assessment and Planning*

"A Framework for Action: How Four Organizations use the Baldrige Criteria to Drive their Total Quality Process." *ODI Newsbrief* 8(1): 8–11.

Astin, A. W. "Why Not Try Some New Ways of Measuring Quality?" *Educational Record* 63(2) (1982): 10–15.

Bell, H. W., & Hanseman, N. J. "Alphabet Soup of Management Tools: Cincinnati's ASEP Process Resembles TQM, CQI, and QPS." *NACUBO Business Officer* 27(7) (1994): 36–39.

Benson, P.G., Saraph, J.V., & Schroeder, R.G. "The Effects of the Organizational Context on Quality Management: An Empirical Investigation." *Management Science* 37 (1991): 1107–124.

Broadhead, J. L. "The Post-Deming Diet: Dismantling a Quality Bureaucracy." *Training* (February 1991): 41–43.

DeCarlo, N. J., & Sterett, W. K. "History of the Malcolm Baldrige National Quality Award." *Quality Progress* 23(3) (1990): 21–27.

Ettore, B. "Benchmarking: The Next Generation." *Management Review* 82(6) (1993): 10–16.

Ewell, P. "Assessment: What's it all About?" *Change* (November/December 1985): 32–36.

_____. "Assessment: Where are We?" *Change* (January/February 1987): 23–28.

_____. "Assessment and TQM: In Search of Convergence." In *Total Quality Management in Higher Education,* edited by L. A. Sherr & D. J. Teeter, pp. 39–52. New Directions for Institutional Research No. 71. San Francisco: Jossey-Bass, 1991.

Gulden, G. K., & Reck, R. H. "Combining Quality and Reengineering for Operational Superiority." *Perspectives on the Management of Information Technology* 8(1) (1991): 1–12.

Hall, G., Rosenthal, J., & Wade, J. "How to Make Reengineering Really Work." *Harvard Business Review* 71 (1993): 119–31.

Hammer, M. "Reengineering Work: Don't Automate, Obliterate." *Harvard Business Review* 68(4) (1990): 104–12.

Hemingson, D., & Behrens, K. "How to Reengineer the Administrative Process." *Management Issues* (1993): 1,7,12.

Kaplan, R. S., & Norton, D. P. "Putting the Balanced Scorecard to Work." *Harvard Business Review* 71 (1993): 134–47.

Kathawala, Y., Elmuti, D., & Toepp, L. "An Overview of the Baldrige Award: America's Tool for Global Competitiveness." *Industrial Management* 33(2) (1991): 27–29.

Keehley, P., & Medlin, S. "Productivity Enhancements through Quality Innovations." *Public Productivity & Management Review* 15(2) (1991): 217–28.

Kinni, T. B. "A Reengineering Primer." *Quality Digest* 14(1) (1994): 26–30.

"The Promise of Reengineering." *Fortune* (3 May 1993): 94–97.

Reimann, C. W. "The Baldrige Criteria Speak for Themselves." *Quality Progress* (May 1991): 43–44.

Reimann, C. W., & Hertz, H. S. "The Malcolm Baldrige National Quality Award and ISO 9000 Registration: Understanding Their Many Differences." *ASTM Standardization News* (1993): 42–53.

Scheuing, E. E. "Baldrige Criteria Become National Quality Standard." *Planning Review* 18(5) (1990): 44–45.

Shafer, B. S., & Coate, L. E. "Benchmarking in Higher Education: A Tool for Improving Quality and Reducing Cost." *NACUBO Business Officer* (1992): 28–35.

Slater, R. H. "Integrated Process Management: A Quality Model." *Quality Progress* (1991): 75–80.

Soter, T. "A Business Plan for Education." *Management Review* 82(6) (1993): 10–16.

Stewart, T. A. "Reengineering: The Hot New Managing Tool." *Fortune* (23 August 1993): 41–48.

# Contributors

KEN ALBRECHT is a management consultant, speaker, and prolific writer. He consults and lectures internationally and has assisted with the development of service management programs for a number of major corporations. He is the co-author of the best seller *Service America!* (Dow Jones-lrwin) and author of nine other books, as well as numerous articles on various aspects of management effectiveness and organizational performance. His consulting firm, Karl Albrecht & Associates, specializes in service management, corporate strategy, and organization development.

TRUDY W. BANTA is vice-chancellor for planning and institutional improvement and professor of higher education at Indiana University-Purdue University, Indianapolis. Prior to assuming her current position in August, 1992, she was the director of the Center for Assessment Research and Development and a professor of education at the University of Tennessee, Knoxville. Since 1983 she has edited two published volumes on assessment, written over sixty articles and reports, and contributed twelve chapters to other published works. A third edited work, *Making a Difference: Outcomes of a Decade of Assessment in Higher Education,* was published by Jossey-Bass in 1993.

ROBERT L. CAROTHERS is the president of the University of Rhode Island, where he has served since 1991. Prior to his appointment at Rhode Island, he was the chancellor of the Minnesota State University System and, before that, president of Southwest State University. He also served as professor of English, dean of arts and humanities, and vice-president for administration and student services at Edinboro University of Pennsylvania. A graduate of Edinboro University in England, Carothers received his M.A. and Ph.D. from Kent State University and his Juris Doctor from the University of Akron. He has been active in leadership development for two decades and recently has worked with and written about quality management in higher education.

L. EDWIN COATE is vice-chancellor for business and administrative services at the University of California at Santa Cruz. Previously, he was vice-president of finance and administration at Oregon State University, where he did extensive pioneering work with Total Quality Management and Business Process Reengineering. Prior to joining OSU, Dr. Coate was visiting scholar/practitioner at the University of Washington, where he taught in the Graduate School of Public Administration and in the civil engineering department. Dr. Coate has twenty-five years of finance and administrative experience in universities, federal and state governments, and private practice. He received a bachelor's degree in engineering from OSU and a master's degree in public administration from San Diego University, and was awarded a doctorate in human behavior from the United States International University.

NEIL J. DeCARLO is a communications specialist in the quality improvement department at Florida Power & Light Company, Juno Beach, Florida. He holds a B.A. in psychology from Harding University in Searcy, Arkansas. He is pursuing an M.A. in communications from Florida Atlantic University in Boca Raton, Florida.

RICHARD CYERT is president emeritus and professor of economics and management of Carnegie Mellon University, and is internationally recognized for his work in economics, behavioral science, and management. He became Carnegie Mellon's sixth president on 1 July 1972, and was officially installed on 9 March 1973. Dr. Cyert retired from the presidency of the university on 30 June 1990. He headed the Carnegie Bosch Institute, endowed by Germany's Bosch Corporation, to study and improve international management from 1990 to 1992. Dr. Cyert has authored or co-authored twelve books and has written more than 100 articles for professional journals in the fields of economics, behavioral science, and management. Dr. Cyert holds a Ph.D. from Columbia University and a B.S. from the University of Minnesota.

PETER F. DRUCKER is a writer and consultant and since 1971, has been the Clarke Professor of Social Science & Management at the Claremont Graduate School in Claremont School, which named its Graduate Management Center after him in 1987. Dr. Drucker has published 28 books which have been translated into more than twenty languages and is a consultant specializing in strategy and policy for both business and non profit, and in the work organization of top management. He has worked with many of the world's largest corporations and with small and entrepreneurial companies; with non profits such as universities, hospitals and community services; and with agencies of the U.S. Government as well as the Free-world governments and those of Canada and Japan. Dr. Drucker holds a doctorate in Public and International Law from Frankfurt University (Germany) and has received honorary doctorates from American, Belgian, English, Japanese, Spanish, and Swiss universities. He is Honorary Cahirman of the Peter F. Drucker Foundation for Non-Profit Management.

BLANTON A. GODFREY is chairman and Chief Executive Officer of Juran Institute, Inc. Under Dr. Godfrey's leadership, Juran Institute has expanded its worldwide activities to include a premier consulting practice, and development and distribution of resources and support materials in managing for quality. Prior to joining Juran Institute in August, 1987, Dr. Godfrey was with AT&T Bell Laboratories in Holmdel, New Jersey. He headed the Quality Theory and Technology Department, which is responsible for applied research in the areas of quality, reliability, and productivity. Dr. Godfrey holds an M.S. and Ph.D. in Statistics from Florida State University and a B.S. in Physics from Virginia Tech. He is an Adjunct Associate Professor at Columbia University where he teaches a graduate course in quality management and control in the School of Engineering and Applied Science.

LEWIS J. HATALA is chairman and CEO of the Partners in Discovery Group, a consulting firm based in Atlanta aiding clients in their implementation of quality and productivity improvement initiatives. During his twenty-eight-year career with AT&T he succeeded in integrating the human side of quality into the day-to-day business of AT&T's manufacturing operations. He is a recognized authority on the American Quality Archetype, a cultural study of unique American performance characteristics. An author, speaker, and consultant in the field of quality, productivity, and breakthrough performance, Mr. Hatala was featured in the recent PBS documentary "Quality—Or Else." His best-selling book, *Incredibly American: Releasing the Heart of Quality,* co-authored with Marilyn Zuckerman, defines the human side of quality in America.

JOSEPH M. JURAN, Chairman Emeritus, Juran Institute, has since 1924 pursued a varied career in management as engineer, industrial executive, government administrator, university professor, impartial labor arbitrator, corporate director, and management consultant. This career has been marked by a search for the underlying principles that are common to all managerial activity. Applied to the specialty of management for quality, this search has produced the leading international reference literature and the leading international training courses, training books, and videocassettes. A holder of degrees in engineering and law, Dr. Juran maintains an active schedule as author and international lecturer while serving various industrial companies, governmental agencies, and other institutions as a consultant.

FRANCIS L. LAWRENCE is president of Rutgers, The State University of New Jersey, where he has served since 1990. Under his leadership, the university has restored the balance between teaching and research, while renewing its commitment to service to the state. In a climate of fiscal stringency, he has been successful in reducing administrative costs and improving performance through rigorous self-studies of processes and productivity. His Quality and Communication Improvement program is now engaged in the application of Malcolm Baldrige standards to the improvement of both academic and administrative aspects of higher education in Rutgers' Cook College. In 1994, Governor Christie Whitman freed New Jersey's colleges and universities from the bureaucratic oversight of a state agency and placed the coordination of higher education under a Presidents' Council and a lay Commission. Dr. Lawrence chairs the Council and sits on the Commission, which work with the boards of trustees of public and independent institutions to improve the quality of New Jersey higher education.

JENNIFER K. LEHR is a doctoral student in the School of Communication, Information, and Library Studies at Rutgers University, where she is also a graduate assistant to the Rutgers University Program for Quality and Communication Improvement. Lehr also has the honor of being the first Rutgers University/ Johnson & Johnson Organizational Communication and Quality Fellow for the 1994-95 academic year. Lehr received both her M.A. and B.A. degrees in communication from William Paterson College in Wayne, New Jersey.

TED MARCHESE was born and raised in New Jersey and holds a bachelor's degree from Rutgers University (in English literature), a law degree from Georgetown University, and a Ph.D. in higher education from the University of Michigan. At the American Association for Higher Education since 1982, Marchese's responsibilities have been in the area of publications and conference management. He edits the *AAHE Bulletin* and other Association periodicals; in 1987, with Exxon support, he wrote AAHE's best selling "The Search Committee Handbook." Since 1984, he has been executive editor of *Change* magazine, the second most widely read publication in higher education. Since 1989, Marchese has led AAHE efforts to bring concepts of Total Quality Management (TQM) into university life.

EUGENE H. MELAN is a professor of business at Marist College where he teaches courses in management of operations and serves as teacher, adviser, and consultant in the implementation of TQM and process quality. Prior to this, he had an extensive and varied career in both technical and management positions at the IBM Corporation. As an IBM program manager for quality improvement, he was involved in developing, teaching, and implementing quality improvement methods and was a founding member of the Quality Institute. He has served as a consultant to major organizations such as Bell Laboratories, DuPont, MCI, and the University of Pennsylvania. The author of numerous professional papers, articles, and a book on process management, Mr. Melan is a Fellow of the American Society for Quality Control and is a member of the Board of Examiners of the New York State Excelsior Award for Quality.

WARREN NEEL is dean of the College of Business Administration at the University of Tennessee in Knoxville. The College of Business is the largest professional unit on campus, with nine departments and a worldwide executive education program. Dr. Neel served in the governor's cabinet, having been appointed by Governor Lamar Alexander in November 1985. In that capacity he helped develop the plan for Tennessee to take maximum advantage of the SATURN decision to locate its $3.5 billion construction project in Spring Hill, Tennessee. Dr. Neel received his Ph.D. from the University of Alabama. He taught in the graduate school of the University of Southern California, as well as at the University of Tennessee, Knoxville.

JUDY D. OLIAN is professor of Management and Organization at the Maryland Business School, University of Maryland. She specializes in research and practices linking organizational objectives with human resource strategies. She has written and consulted extensively in this area. A recent focus of her writing and consulting has been in the area of TQM in higher education. In her role as American Council of Education Fellow, and later Assistant to the President, she assisted the President in designing and initiating implementation of the University of Maryland's continuous improvement effort. In addition to her faculty role, she is director of the IBM-TQ Project at the University of Maryland.

BRENT D. RUBEN is a distinguished professor of communication and executive director of Rutgers QCI—the University Program for Quality and Communication Improvement at Rutgers—The State University of New Jersey. Dr. Ruben is author or editor of more than twenty-five books and fifty articles and book chapters on communication processes and functions in interpersonal, educational, health, and organizational settings, and serves as a consultant in organizational quality assessment and improvement for business, education, and government in these areas. He is a Malcolm Baldrige examiner, a member of the NIST National Education and Health Care Sector Pilot Advisory Group, and developer of the Baldrige-based Tradition of Excellence Higher Education Quality Self-Assessment Program.

SEAN C. RUSH is Chairman of Coopers and Lybrand's Higher Education/Not-for-Profit practice. He has more than seventeen years of administrative, consulting, and policy-level experience with colleges and universities, state government, health care institutions, and service sector companies. Mr. Rush's experience encompasses financial planning, operations management, and improvement utilizing Total Quality Management, mergers, organizational analysis, management auditing, institutional strategy, and business planning. His work has ranged from large, multi-institutional studies to individual department analyses. His clients have included Harvard University, The Pennsylvania State University, Rutgers University, Boston University, Texas Select Committee on Higher Education, University of South Carolina, Swarthmore College, Texas A&M University, and many others.

DANIEL SEYMOUR is the president of Q-systems, a quality management consulting firm, and he is a visiting scholar at the Claremont Graduate School. Since receiving his B.A. from Gettysburg College, and M.B.A. and Ph.D. degrees from the University of Oregon, Seymour has worked in industry, and as a professor and administrator at the College of William and Mary, the University of Rhode Island, and UCLA. He is a Fulbright scholar and the author of ten books in business and higher education, including his recent best-selling book for the American Council on Education and Oryx Press entitled *On Q: Causing Quality in Higher Education* (1992). The book is in its third printing.

WILLIAM T. SNYDER is chancellor and professor of engineering science and mechanics at the University of Tennessee, Knoxville. He received the B.S. degree in mechanical engineering from the University of Tennessee, Knoxville, and the M.S. and Ph.D. degrees in mechanical engineering from Northwestern University. Dr. Snyder joined the UT Space Institute faculty in 1964 as associate professor of aerospace engineering. He earned the rank of professor at UTSI and came to UT, Knoxville as professor and head of the Department of Engineering Science and Mechanics in 1970. Dr. Snyder was named dean of engineering in 1983 and served in that position until he as named Chancellor on 20 July 1992. Prior to joining UT, he was on the faculties of the State University if New York at Stony Brook and North Carolina State University.

W. KENT STERETT is assistant vice-president of quality at Union Pacific Railroad in Omaha, Nebraska. Sterett joined Union Pacific after eighteen years of management experience at Florida Power & Light, where he was responsible for the creation of FPL's quality initiative, which was awarded Japan's Deming Prize. He has been active in the development of the Malcolm Baldrige National Quality Award and has served as a judge since its inception.

RON ZEMKE is a management consultant, journalist, and behavioral scientist and has become one of the best-known and most widely quoted authorities on the United States' continuing service revolution. As senior editor of *TRAINING Magazine* and *The Service Edge* newsletter, he has covered the emergence and development of the global service economy. In 1972, he founded Performance Research Associates, a Minneapolis-based consulting group that specializes in needs analysis, service-quality audits, and service-management programs for business and industry. He has authored or co-authored eleven books, including *Delivering Knock-Your-Socks-Off Service* (AMACOM), *Managing Knock-Your-Socks-Off Service* (AMACOM), *The Service Edge: 101 Companies That Profit From Customer Care*, and *Service America! Doing Business in the New Economy.*

MARILYN R. ZUCKERMAN is Director, Quality Planning for the AT&T Corporate Quality Office. Her organization provides the AT&T company with the short- and long-range direction for AT&T's Total Quality Approach. Her major focus is the human side of quality. Prior to her current position, Ms. Zuckerman managed the Quality Planning organization of AT&T Network Systems. Formerly, she held management position in AT&T's Data Systems, Human Resources and Services organizations. Ms. Zuckerman is a frequent speaker at management seminars and conferences. She develops and conducts workshops in the areas of improving organizational effectiveness and human performance. Her studies on the cultural aspects of quality in America have been published in several journals. Her first book, *Incredibly American: Releasing the Heart of Quality*, was co-authored by Lewis J. Hatala and was featured in the recent three-part Public Broadcast System TV program, "Quality—Or Else."